Screwed By The Aliens

Screwed By The Aliens

By Timothy Green Beckley and Sean Casteel
With Contributions By: Tim Swartz, William Kern,
Brad Steiger, John Keel, Scott Corrales,
Michael Grosso, Nomar Slevik, Allen Greenfield,
Richard Shaver, Nigel Watson, Hercules Invictus,
Paul Dale Roberts, Greg Little, Aileen Garoutte,
Raven De La Croix, Eve Lorgen

Copyright 2018 by Timothy Green Beckley
dba Global Communications/Conspiracy Journal

All rights reserved. No part of these manuscripts may be copied or reproduced by any mechanical or digital methods and no exerpts or quotes may be used in any other book or manuscript without permission in writing by the Publisher, Global Communications/Conspiracy Journal, except by a reviewer who may quote brief passages in a review.

Published in the United States of America By
Global Communications/Conspiracy Journal
Box 753 · New Brunswick, NJ 08903

Staff Members
Timothy G. Beckley, Publisher
Carol Ann Rodriguez, Assistant to the Publisher
Sean Casteel, General Associate Editor
Tim R. Swartz, Graphics and Editorial Consultant
William Kern, Editorial and Art Consultant

Sign Up On The Web For Our Free Weekly Newsletter
and Mail Order Version of Conspiracy Journal
and Bizarre Bazaar
www.ConspiracyJournal.com

**Order Hot Line: 1-732-602-3407
PayPal: MrUFO8@hotmail.com**

CONTENTS

INTRODUCTION - Tim Beckley iv
SECTION ONE - SETTING THE STAGE FOR THE MADDENLY ILLOGICAL 1
Chapter One: Proof You Could Be An Exophiliac - Tim Beckley 2
Chapter Two: Shock And Awe - Caveat Emptor To One And All - Tim Beckley 6
Chapter Three: Sex and Drugs And UFOs - Adam Gorightly 20
SECTION TWO - LOVE AND RAPTURE AMONG THE ANCIENT ONES 30
Chapter Four: Sexual Abduction As Old As Humanity - Allen Greenfield 31
Chapter Five: Some Call Them Nocturnal Demons - Tim Beckley 38
Chapter Six: God Of My Fathers - Hercules Invictus 47
Chapter Seven: Sexual Abductions Through The Ages - Greg Little 53
SECTION THREE - THOSE AMAZING SEXY FLYING SAUCER PEOPLE 68
Chapter Eight: Sex and Saucers - Nigel Watson 69
Chapter Nine: Intergalactic Sex - Brad Steiger 81
Chapter Ten: Bedroom Invaders - John Keel 91
Chapter Eleven: The ET Guide to Picking Up Earth People - Tim Swartz 101
SECTION FOUR - CLOSE ENCOUNTERS OF THE PERSONAL AND PRIVATE KIND - 113
Chapter Twelve: David Huggins and Crescent Soul Mate From The Stars 114
Chapter Thirteen: Abduction Seduction - Raven de la Croix 122
Chapter Fourteen: An Aerial Molester - Paul Dale Roberts 126
SECTION FIVE - ALIENS IN THE CINEMA 130
Sinema - Alien Sex Cinema - Creative Couplings - Tim Beckley 131
SECTION SIX - AN INVESTIGATION INTO THE RIDDLE OF THE LOVE BITE 143
Chapter Fifteen: The Anomalous Work of Eve Lorgen 144
SECTION SEVEN - THE REAL INVADERS ARE FROM MARS 162
Chapter Sixteen: The Bad Guys Are From Uranus - Sean Casteel 163
Chapter Seventeen: Sex, Shaver, the Dero and The Cavern World - Tim Beckley ... 175
Chapter Eighteen: Karla Turner's The Morally Outrageous - Sean Casteel 185
Chapter Ninteen: The Sexual Misadventures of Ted Rice 191
Chapter Twenty: Rape of Aussie Researcher - John Stuart 199
SECTION EIGHT - ONLY IN SOUTH AMERICA 212
Chapter Twenty-One: Antonio Villas-Boas: An Alien Heat - Scott Corralles 213
Chapter Twenty-Two: Brazilian Abduction - Dr. Walter Buhler 224
SECTION NINE - THE HYBRIDS AND THE PREGNANCIES 231
Chapter Twenty-Three: Mysteries and Unexplained Pregnancies - Brad Steiger 232
Chapter Twenty-Four: The Christa Tilton Story - Tim Beckley 243
SECTION TEN - IT'S ALL IN THE DNA 255
Chapter Twenty-Five: Hair of the Alien - Tim Swartz 256
Chapter Twenty-Six: Screen Memories - William Kern 263
SECTION ELEVEN - EXAMINING THE PATTERNS AND SYMBOLS 277
Chapter Twenty-Seven: Planet Earth Space Lab - Aileen Garoutte 278
Chapter Twenty-Eight: The Symbolism of Alien Sex - Michael Grosso, Ph. D. 284
CONCLUDING WORDS BY BARBARA BARTHOLIC 292
THOSE SALACIOUS ALIENS PULP MAGAZINE COVERS - Nomar Slevik 295

THEY SAW THAT THEIR DAUGHTERS WERE FAIR AND TOOK THEM AS WIVES

"And it came to pass, when men began to multiply on the face of the earth, and daughters were born unto them, that the sons of God saw the daughters of men that they were fair; and they took them wives of all which they chose...There were giants in the earth in those days; and also after that, when the sons of God came in unto the daughters of men, and they bore children to them."

—Genesis 6:1-2, 4

THEY TAUGHT THEM SORCERY, INCANTATIONS AND THE DIVIDING OF ROOTS AND TREES

"It happened after the sons of men had multiplied in those days, that daughters were born to them, elegant and beautiful. And when the angels, the sons of heaven, beheld them, they became enamored of them, saying to each other, 'Come, let us select for ourselves wives from the progeny of men, and let us beget children' ... Then they took wives, each choosing for himself; whom they began to approach, and with whom they cohabited; teaching them sorcery, incantations, and the dividing of roots and trees."

—Enoch 7:1-2, 10

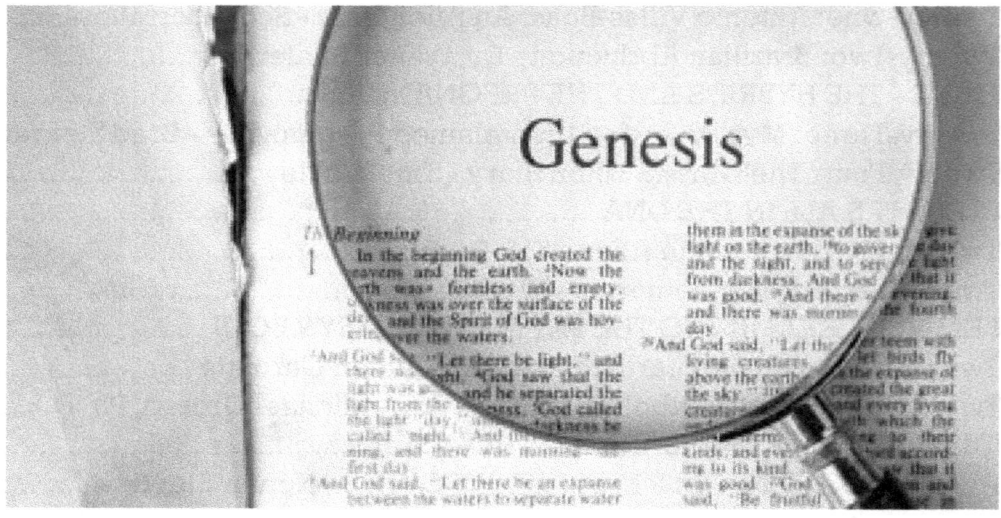

THE MEANING OF IT ALL
HAVE WE ALL BEEN SCREWED BY THE ALIENS?
By Timothy Green Beckley

"The experience of a close encounter with a UFO is a shattering physical and mental ordeal. The trauma has effects that go far beyond what the witness recalls consciously. New types of behavior are conditioned, and new types of beliefs are promoted. The social, political and religious consequences of the experience are enormous...."

—Astrophysicist Dr. Jacques Vallee - *"Messengers of Deception"*

This book's title has a double meaning.

As you turn the pages herein you will see that we have approached the sexual nature of UFOs, their alien occupants, and the reproduction process of the Ultra-terrestrials with an open mind. It's easy to laugh and guffaw upon reading reports of anal probes and those who claim that they have fathered a rather large family of star children, or who have sex with reptilians just about every Saturday night. We admit to a bit of chuckling from time to time ourselves, but this is potentially a very important aspect of UFO research that for the most part has been neglected because of what some see as its offensive nature.

But just because something is offensive or not to your liking doesn't mean that you should ignore it altogether. The phenomenon is not going to go away. So let's study it and let the chips fall where they may (a very trite statement, but one that immediately comes to mind).

The second meaning, for me at least, is the fact that I sometimes feel I have been "screwed by the aliens." Though I have had three UFO sightings, written and published a gazillion books and magazines, I am still at a loss as to what precisely the UFO enigma consists of. We have close encounters, bedroom invaders, abductions, government cover-ups, a cry for disclosure and everything to the far left and the far right.

I could have gone out and gotten a regular job, but, no, "they" led me to follow them, to chat them up and to devote my life to understanding their purpose. So, in a sense, yes, I have been "screwed by the aliens." But, like with sex, it has been a pleasurable experience (for the most part).

If I have learned one thing over the years, don't get wrapped up with one thing in life. Don't let the aliens screw you.

Bless you and keep well – and out of their reach.

Tim Beckley

Visit our YouTube Channel – Mr. UFO's Secret Files

Our Blog -spectralvision.wordpress.com

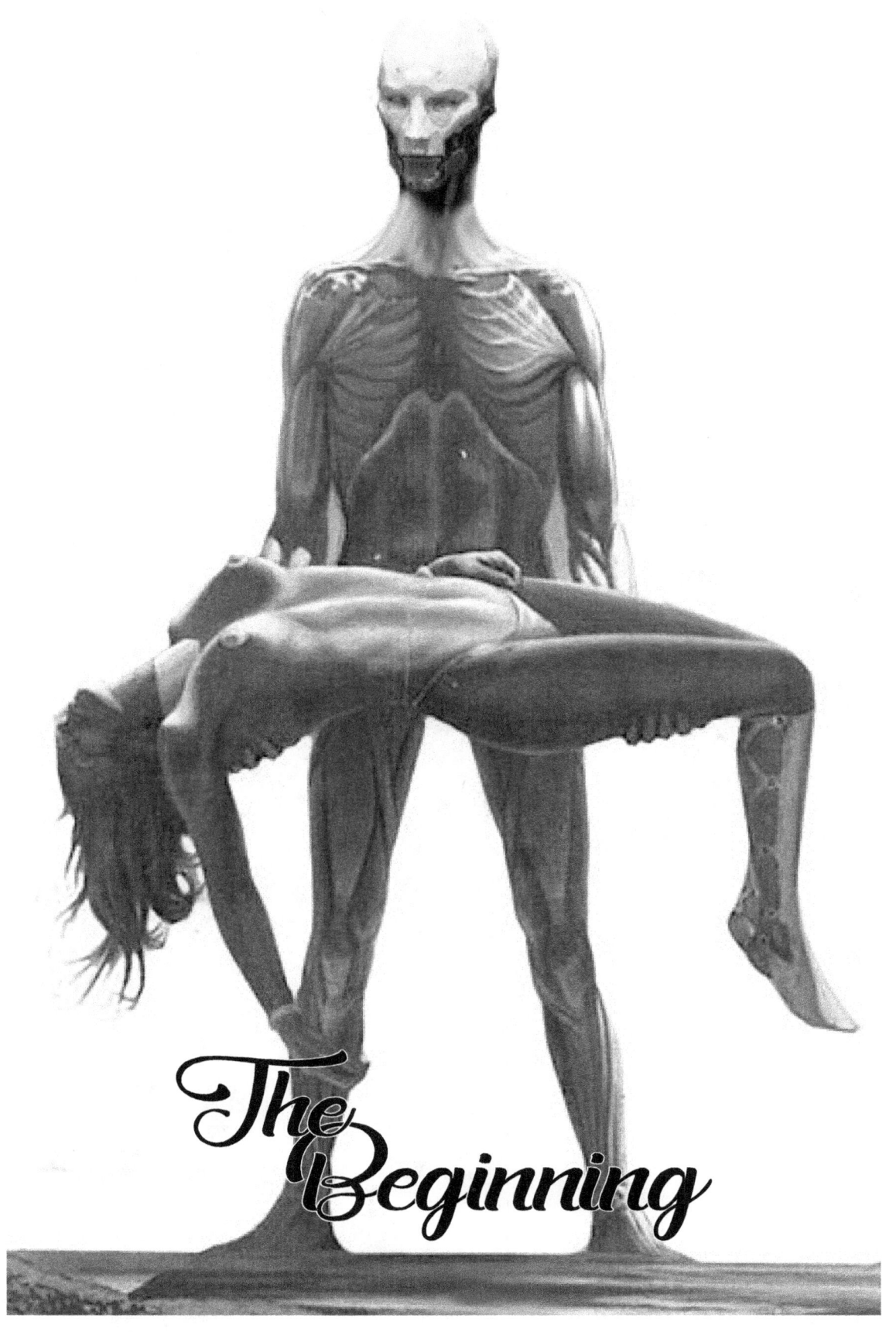

SCREWED BY THE ALIENS

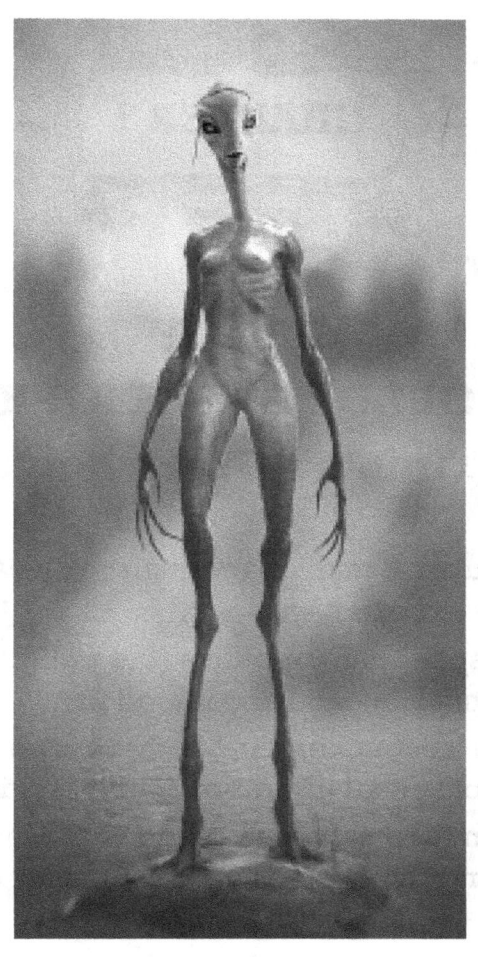

SECTION ONE – SETTING THE STAGE FOR THE MADDENINGLY ILLOGICAL

Chapter One: Proof You Could Be An Exophiliac
By Tim Beckley

Chapter Two: Shock and Awe Caveat Emptor To One And All
By Tim Beckley

Chapter Three: Sex and Drugs and UFOs
By Adam Gorightly

SCREWED BY THE ALIENS

CHAPTER 1

PROOF
YOU COULD BE AN EXOPHILIAC!
By Timothy Green Beckley

It doesn't matter if you are a man or a woman – you can have sex with an alien. Or at least that's what the experts say.

It's an entirely new aspect of Exopolitics (the political implications of the Extraterrestrial Presence) that has to be accounted for.

Personally, I would not recommend it, but there is no accounting for individual tastes in this "New Age" of sexual liberation and individuality.

Some guys, who liken themselves to being real players, groove on the idea that they might be pimping themselves out to some far off – and far out – lady of the night.

While gals tell me that they definitely get their best groove on when it comes to feeling the scales of their reptilian mates . . . now that's a real ribbed condom if you ask me.

From what I have been told you can be either part of the population that would like to caress an ET all evening long and perhaps even bat a home run with "him." Or you can dislike the little bugger immensely and try to shove 'em away if "he" comes a-calling in the middle of the night.

Your reaction even has a name – oh, yes, it does!

If you crave alien sex you definitely are an "Exophiliac."

On the other hand, if you shy away from those greys and want them to keep their six-fingered mitts to themselves, you are a bit harder to classify. Astrophobia is a fear of outer space and everything in it, so that would include ETs. Xenophobia is a fear of anyone from another place. Perhaps we can create our own verbiage to describe this fear – something like Exophobic perhaps? As I see it, if it's good for you, it works for me.

Hey, there's always one extreme fetishist in every neighborhood. This time it

SCREWED BY THE ALIENS

just happens to be the guy with the big UFO collection, that's all.

By the way, if you fear the unknown in general (like your mother hates your interest in Bigfoot or Dogman, let's say) she would have neilasparophobia. In which case you better hide your copy of the "Fortean Times" underneath your mattress next to that soiled copy of "Penthouse" tucked away there from when you were a teenager. .

All this according to a Dr. Anil Aggrawal, who teaches Forensic Medicine at the Maulana Azad Medical College, India, and edits a peer-reviewed Internet journal on Paraphilias. Sexual crimes and their medicolegal aspects has been his special area of research for the last 25 years. He lives in New Delhi with his wife and a personal library of over 20,000 books.

YOU CAN STIMULATE YOUR SEX LIFE WITH UFOs!

And if your prefer to be an armchair UFOlogist, you can still participate in the world of alien sexual dynamics simply by reading ample amounts of literature on the subject, or you can join a UFO group and become part of the ever growing number of UFO sky-watchers worldwide. Is there an explanation for this connection between UFOs and a healthy libido? Of course, says Nigel Watson, our crony from the UK and contributor to this work of fine paranormal literature and author of such volumes as "The UFO Investigators Manual" and "UFOs of the First World War."

"Perhaps the anxiety and wonder of seeing something exceptional in the sky arouses the witness," he explains. "Or some might claim that randy aliens are deliberately sending out beams that will stimulate witnesses so that they can have their wicked way with them."

Of course, Nigel, why hadn't we thought of that?

Watson was quoted in an article in the British "Daily Mirror" as part of an effort to prove the hypothesis that a visit to a UFO hot spot might facilitate a scandalously robust night of alien rubbernecking.

"Panamanians claim they are enjoying close encounters of the stirred kind whenever they see an unidentified flying object," maintains the widely read, blue-collar tabloid, "with more than a third (37%) admitting to having an immediate desire for sex straight afterwards."

The "Daily Mirror" points out that, "The Central American country is awash with alien sightings – with an incredible 1 in 16 of the population claiming to have seen a UFO in their lifetimes. A survey by the Cid Gallup company – which appeared in the El Siglo newspaper – said more than a third reported having intense 'sexual desire' after the experience."

The survey was conducted in Panama with a sample of 1,200 respondents between June 7th and June 20th, 2012, with a 2.8% margin of error. Nigel Watson reminds us that the concept of mating with Ultra-terrestrials is nothing new, going

SCREWED BY THE ALIENS

back centuries, though the breeding process seems to have been revved up at times.

"By the 1980s, alien abduction researchers in the USA accepted that women are routinely abducted, impregnated and then re-abducted a few weeks later for the extraction of the hybrid fetus."

The British journalist will have an opportunity to prove his accusations as we turn the pages of this extensive volume, further contending that, "These activities explained the short-lived pregnancies experienced by female abductees. As for male abductees, they either claimed to have had intercourse with an alien woman or their sperm was extracted by mechanical means by the aliens."

Theorizing further for the "Daily Mirror," Nigel was quoted as saying: "There have been various claims over the years that aliens are visiting Planet Earth to copulate or probe human beings in a sexual context. In his book 'Communion,' Whitley Strieber famously described being abducted by aliens who inserted a one-foot long anal probe inside him. It seemed to be a living entity, so when it was taken out he was surprised to see it was a mechanical device. The case of Antonio Villas Boas is also outstanding. He claimed in 1957 that he was dragged inside a flying saucer and forced to have sexual intercourse with a beautiful alien woman. When he left, she pointed at her stomach, at him and then at the sky, implying she would have his child somewhere in outer space."

We will be hearing much more about the very famous Antonio Boas incident throughout our visit to the alien's boudoir.

Nigel dismisses the notion that these claims are "the product of sleep paralysis, where people are unable to discern the difference between fantasy and reality during the period between sleeping and waking."

It's a notion we dismiss as well, as the evidence to be presented so rightly points out!

REMEMBERING THE PAST

Those who don't remember the past are doomed to repeat the class of UFOs 101, because being literally "screwed by an alien" is nothing new. If you track the many similar types of cases found in occult literature down through history and substitute "aliens" for succubus, incubus, gnomes or any other residents of the twilight kingdom, you will come up with pretty much the same scenario. Only its terminology has changed. These said changes vary according to the time period you happen to reside in or are doing research on. It's really a mixed bag of nuts (pardon the expression) but we don't plan on softening our language, assuming we are dealing with, and catering to, an audience of mature adults.

No, this isn't porno, but it might as well be to some individuals, as many of the cases described are about as salacious as they come . . . The only difference between what I wrote about for the "Forum" magazines and this material – is that this

SCREWED BY THE ALIENS

material is said to be true and not fluffed up by some hotshot Park Avenue editor (oh pardon, that would have been me) for purposes of arousing titillation.

SUGGESTED READING

FORENSIC AND MEDICO-LEGAL ASPECTS OF SEXUAL CRIMES AND UNUSUAL SEXUAL PRACTICES, by Dr. Anil Aggrawal.

WANTED: The Reptilians should be placed on an intergalactic FBI most wanted list for their formidable deeds against humans.

After reading this book it will become clear why we should call off such festivals honoring ETs.

Dr. Anil Aggrawal, Forensic Medicine.

Nigel Watson believes that a good UFO sighting could improve your sex life. Think of what a UFO flap could do!

SCREWED BY THE ALIENS

CHAPTER 2

SHOCK AND AWE
CAVEAT EMPTOR TO ONE AND ALL
By Timothy Green Beckley

Trust me, you can't believe everything you read.

Especially not in this arena of endeavor where one story sounds more extreme than the next.

Indeed, Caveat Emptor: Let the reader beware.

When someone says they have had sex with an alien, what evidence could you possibly ask for?

Many individuals who have been raped do not want to tell what happened to them and so they don't even report their victimization even to the authorities. If you do not testify in court, the person who did the molestation will not receive justice under any circumstances.

Hypnosis is a fairly decent follow-up in some cases, but you know experiencers can be "led" in no uncertain terms by the individuals who are hypnotically regressing them to disclose the parts of their encounters they do not consciously recall. And then you have the just plain old falsehoods (i.e. liars) or the misrepresented. The press – the tabloids – are always looking to sensationalize such an encounter to make it as juicy as possible, adding their own details. It is bad enough that the person involved has had to undergo an outrageous debasement, but now they also have to put up with a disinformation campaign on the part of the media.

Such is the case of Niara Terela Isley, a former military tracking officer, who was quoted widely as having been kidnapped and taken to the far side of the moon. She was repeatedly raped there by reptilians, but says it never happened the way it was laid out in the press. Instead, the author of the self-published "Facing The Shadow, Embracing The Light" insists that she has had to deal for the most part with malicious military types who are part of MILAB, a black ops program

SCREWED BY THE ALIENS

where SS-like thugs masquerade as aliens that go about raping and pillaging as part of a "false flag" or mind control program.

"I am a highly sensitive person and an introvert. I NEVER express myself in such dramatic terms. What happened to me in the military was horrific, but, to my knowledge, was primarily perpetrated by renegade 'super soldiers' and not reptilians. Did I see reptilians as part of my experience? Yes, a couple of times, as recalled in the pages of my book. But not in the manner alluded to by these articles with their ugly and sensationalized headlines. And misquoting me to boot. No one should have to live with the kinds of e experiences that will haunt me for the rest of my life. But I do. I do it as successfully as I can, with lots of time in the healthy beauty of nature, with a morning spiritual practice that includes meditation and contemplation, with as little drama as possible. Because, you see, when the experiences are as bad as the ones I live with, they don't need extra drama or embellishment. At least among average folks who are not drama kings or queens, who have some personal compassion, sensitivity and empathy."

Despite, or because of, this "disclaimer," there are many who might like to seek out her website:

facingtheshadowembracingthelight.com

There are, as the reader will find out, a multitude of disturbing and perplexing problems and situations that deal us a harmful hand as we probe the subject matter presented from a variety of dedicated, hard-working researchers.

The entire matter is stressful and causes anxiety.

ALIEN ABDUCTION WITNESS AND VICTIM ACCOUNTS

A breakdown of the various phenomena that confront us is presented by ClassifiedUFO.com

"There are mixed and varied alien abduction reports from violent to Angelic, and they have to be screened and studied with a skeptical mind before taken seriously, as some witnesses are obviously just suffering delusions or wanting public notice. Over the decades after WWII many animals were discovered dead from bizarre medical operations and when Army personnel began giving statements of witnessing UFOs and abduction cases, the phenomenon started to be taken seriously in the press. The cases varied from wild accounts of female abductees remembering only being 'psychically' manipulated by an alien to perform oral sex on an unknown unconscious male aboard a UFO ("They took control of my head, neck and mouth to perform oral sex and collected the semen"), to also that of a male who stated he only remembered being abducted and forced naked on top of an unknown woman, observed by several aliens as he had sex with her. She was restrained and unconscious; he had sex with her under observation, being instructed only at the moment of orgasm to ejaculate into a tubed suction device. Other accounts simply tell of visitations of angelic aliens who en-

SCREWED BY THE ALIENS

ter a bedroom in bright light and stare into the eyes of suburban housewives with an aura of heightened sexual stimulation that causes immediate multiple orgasms. These few famous abduction cases below are from authentic witnesses who passed lie detectors, tried to get therapy for their experiences and appear very genuine."

WHAT IS MILAB?

While not the focus of our work, you will come across mention of this outrageous MILAB program from time to time.

There is an old chestnut in the field floating around which says that a "secret space program" exists and that this black ops underground society has signed some sort of pact with a group of reptilians who have established bases on Earth. Together the scaly ones and this offshoot branch of the military are violating women in the most vile of ways. In a number of cases this military group pretend to be aliens themselves and seem to have an underhanded, concealed project of their own which is difficult to understand, but which "The Love Bite" author and contributor to this volume lays out accordingly:

"To say Milabs is a Pandora's Box is an understatement. The Milab experience itself is diverse. It can include the classic alien abduction types of experiences, but also occult ritual and cult abuse elements, dissociation, post-traumatic stress disorder, multiple personality disorder, military abductions, political manipulation, medical experimentation, interrogations, black operations, time travel, bilocation to alternate locations such as underground military installations or off planet bases on the moon or Mars.

"More anomalous reports of being 'pulled into alternate timelines, dimensions and realities occur,' where the line between real, imagined, physical, astral or virtual reality is blurred. Shared group dreaming occurs as well, while some Milabs have clear awareness of astral operations, remote viewing, telepathy, astral tagging and programming dynamics. Astral and energetic tantric sexual interactions (some being astral rituals) are commonplace for some Milabs, who have expanded awareness on subtle levels of reality. And it is these types of subtle programming that we need to take heed of, because programming can happen on very subliminal, astral and refined energetic levels as well. Well, that is, if we want to regain our own sovereignty, we must work to expand awareness, clear traumas, integrate and heal. Then extend what we do know to others with integrity."

LIKE A VIRGIN

I confess I am not sure when I began to take reports of sexual coupling between humans and aliens seriously. For a long time, I had thought such accounts must be meritless because, certainly, there is no way, come hell or high water, that a species from space would want – or literally, physically COULD have – sex with an earth woman. After all, who says that aliens even have the same type

SCREWED BY THE ALIENS

of sex organs or express love or sexual feelings in the same way that we do?

I guess I was like a virgin. Because such case histories do exist, and, as this book demonstrates, there is a virtual proliferation of them that is hard to ignore.

Take, for example, the case of "Pamela," as told by William Hamilton, who held a position in the mid-1960s in the USAF Security Service, and who later went on to write the book "Cosmic Top Secret."

"Sometimes she would go to bed with night clothing on and wake up without clothing. One time she found grass in the bed and on the floor. Sometimes she would go to bed in her room, then find herself in another part of the house, usually the family room, and find she had dirty feet even though she bathed the previous night. On occasion she would hear her name called from outside, then wake up on the sidewalk outside blocks from her home.

"She would have vivid and lucid dreams from the age of 16. She would find herself inside a craft and receiving instructions on how to fly the craft. She remembers seeing symbols on panels. She saw a huge crystal in the center of the craft. When she first got married at age 17, she still went on having the dreams. Her first husband was a skeptic and thought the dreams were just dreams.

"In 1982, Pamela had married Al and Al brought her to his hand built home at the foothills of the Tehachapis in California. The incidents started to step up as soon as she moved into Al's five-sided house on two-and-one-half acres of desert property.

"One of Pamela's new visitors was a reptilian humanoid (reptoid) that stood at least seven feet tall. I remember when my friend TAL told me about his initial experience of seeing a reptoid in his house in Santa Fe, New Mexico, in 1979. TAL had a map placed on the hallway wall showing sites of UFO landings, underground caverns and animal mutilations. One night, he saw a seven-foot-tall reptoid staring intently at his map. The reptoid looked solid, but also translucent, in that he could also see through him. At the moment of confrontation, the reptoid turned to look at TAL, and TAL hurled a stuffed animal at him from the bed. The stuffed animal went sailing through the reptoid, who looked a little astonished at the foolish human act, then hit the wall behind the creature. The reptoid's eyes seem to reveal a great deal of intelligence. The reptoid proceeded to touch a point on his belt and disappeared.

"Pamela's reptoid had luminous, amber-colored eyes like a cat's and skin that was charcoal, green and grey in color. His massive chest sported a breast plate, much like that worn by Roman soldiers. He had sharp claws on his four fingers. When he would appear in the room, the air would thicken, Pamela would hear a high-pitched sound in her ears as as well as buzzing and clicking. In seconds, she found it difficult to breath. Her chest would feel as if it were crushed. She was paralyzed and immobilized and the reptoid would literally flip her on her stom-

SCREWED BY THE ALIENS

ach. Then he would proceed with a type of tantric sexual intercourse that would leave her absolutely exhausted. She never feared him. She sensed he was extremely powerful and very aggressive, as if a member of a warrior caste. She even felt protected by him. She could not smell the reptoid. Greys were different. She could smell them. They had the smell of decaying bodies, putrid.

"Pamela often awoke with scoop marks on her legs or holes in her hips, or triangular marks on her back as well as bruises and scratches and puncture marks. These began appearing in childhood. One time she had five distinct scratches across her left upper arm. We believe that the reptoid left his claw marks on her in this one particular incident. The scars from these scratches are still visible to this day."

This detailed account contains some elements of mind control on the part of the aliens, who seem to possess the ability to insert a degree of "pleasure" into the minds (and bodies) of their human subjects, so as not to scar the person for life. But nothing can erase the true nature of the aliens' crimes against humanity.

Obviously, we seem to be dealing with an interdimensional group similar to Nazi war criminals – the reptilians being the SS of the evil alien forces.

Colleen Johnson of the group "Malevolent Alien Abduction Research" (MAAR) says many women have had to struggle subconsciously with the excruciating drama that has unfolded before their eyes, but which has been pushed out of their conscious recollection. MAAR's representative outlines this nasty program of deception in complete detail, including all its sinister elements:

"Out of those who claim abduction, a majority of abductees do not remember what's happened to them. It's only a small percentage (estimating 3 to 4 percent) who claim that they have had partial to total recall of their experiences. Out of this group, another majority are experiencing massive trauma in conjunction with their abductions – anything from being mind-controlled with disaster images that are being forced into their minds by artificial means, seeing loved ones tortured if they do not cooperate, seeing what appears to be clones of themselves, forced to hold alien/hybrid children, themselves forced into submitting to painful experimentations, even being given a deadly disease for non-cooperation. Many female abductees are reporting autoimmune disorders like Fibromyalgia or Chronic Fatigue Syndrome as well as a sudden onset of female urinary tract infections and a host of female problems which eventually lead in some cases to hysterectomy."

Johnson's sentiments on the subject seem to parallel to a large extent the findings of the late Dr. Karla Turner, whose research we will tap into further on.

MAAR elaborates: "If the creatures creating this type of misery for their captives were here on a peaceful mission to help humanity, why does this sort of abusive treatment happen with the same style of administration reminiscent of the Nazi German concentration camp doctors? I have come to believe something is

SCREWED BY THE ALIENS

more than amiss; something sinister is happening to the abduction populace without regard for the abductee. 'Why us and why now?' someone might ask. What is it we possess that is unique from other species? My thought is survival – theirs verses ours."

Here are a few thoughts which might hold clues to some of the answers we should be seeking. Other researchers have suggested some of the following ideas and concepts courtesy /www.maar.us/alien_agenda.html

1. Population control and population culling or hybridization of our species – We pose some type of threat to their survival; the ability to overcome and adapt to infectious disease; we have a superior physical adaptation or strength, hardiness of stock; even a potentially longer lifespan than most species.

2. Genetic interbreeding program – We may be physically compatible with their species and they have an absolute need for survival to the degree that they are interbreeding with our species or experimenting with DNA. Some noted researches have suggested changing DNA to be genetically compatible with theirs so they can co-inhabit our planet. Others have suggested they couldn't survive within our environment without this type of hybridization.

3. They are of an alien/demonic origin and are changing the DNA codes in an attempt to destroy our species or soul essence – We may possess the ability to literally live beyond the physical shell of our bodies and become a detriment to their survival because we have a soul essence which could be unique to our species.

4. Some abductees possess the ability to telepathically communicate, transcend dimensional walls and could become a threat to them.

5. Humans are nothing more than a food supply and livestock food producers – They don't eat us physically, but instead feed off our emotions – trauma, pain, sadness, sexual arousal. In essence we are nothing more than livestock, milk cows, hens of sorts, They feed from our energy like we use proteins such as milk, butter, and eggs to sustain our energy.

As you can tell the entire situation is a fluid, sordid mess.

A FILE CABINET FULL OF REPORTS

There is no end to the number of cases of sexual molestation and pregnancies, fetus removals, as well as a few welcome instances of unearthly copulation.

We pulled out cases contributed by credible investigators, others submitted directly by the individuals involved, and additional reports obtained from independent research of our own.

SUZANNE BROWN FROM CHESHIRE

In 1965, Suzanne Brown claims she was visited numerous times in Chester, Cheshire, England, by a five-foot-tall Nordic alien with shoulder length blond hair

SCREWED BY THE ALIENS

who wore a skintight membrane suit. Originally the visits, which began when she was just twelve, were relaxed and even "loving," but, by the time they ended, she says she was terrified. According to Suzanne, the creature communicated via telepathy; he called himself Myriko. At one point, she was taken onboard a spaceship where she met other humans. A few months later, and while home alone, she began experiencing terrible pain from pressure in her lower abdomen. The pressure was crushing and becoming very painful. She then opened her eyes and Myriko confronted her. Telepathically, he told her not to worry, that his people were merely taking what was theirs. She passed out and, after waking up, realized that her clothes were soaked with blood and it looked like she had suffered a miscarriage. Her pregnancy appeared to have been terminated. Finally Myriko took her onboard a craft and showed her what seemed to be a nursery. There was an infant entity lying in a nearby cot, gray skinned and frail. It was apparently her child. Somehow she knew it was her child. Her final visitation was when she was 39-years old. – Classifiedufo.com

EROTIC FEELINGS – FROM THE FILES OF ALBERT ROSALES

A 46-year old beautician, Antonia Fischer, had felt for years as if someone or something had been trying to make contact. One night she experienced what appeared to have been a very lucid dream (or at least she thought so). She suddenly found herself in a small, strange room, a sort of cabin, with just a bed. Everything appeared to be made out of chrome or a similar material. There was a light source, but she couldn't tell where it came from. Suddenly a door opened and a woman came in; she could not remember many of the details but thought the woman was human. The woman "spoke" to Antonia without moving her mouth, and seemed rather upset or angry.

The strange woman hurled a suit at Antonia, which was made of a strange material, feather-light, yet robust. Antonia was then instructed to remove her clothing and put the strange suit on, which clung to her body like a "second skin." The strange woman then said somewhat cynically, "Let's see how you survive the flight through the rings."

Antonia was unsure what the woman meant and felt terribly confused. The woman then left and the door closed behind her. At this point, Antonia suffers a blackout. She then came to, and was seized by a rather unpleasant vibration that gradually became stronger. However, the strong vibrations suddenly stopped and shortly thereafter the strange woman returned to the room. The stranger then scrutinized Antonia carefully, from top to bottom. Then, as if she was pleased with Antonia's condition for some reason, she suddenly seemed to have gained "respect" for Antonia. "Lovingly," she commanded Antonia to follow her. They both then entered a long corridor that seemed to go in circles and deep below them. Then, in front of them, a door, where none had been visible, appeared. The woman

SCREWED BY THE ALIENS

placed the palm of her hand on the door and it opened quietly. They both entered, and before Antonia stood a tall, human-looking man, which seemed to be a bit "spurious" in nature (semi-solid?). The man was about 2.30 m tall, had olive-green skin and normal-looking eyes. But the eyes had a strange hypnotic effect on Antonia and seemed to be the only "real" element of the tall being, Antonia thought.

As Antonia stared at the being, without moving his lips he said, "I have imagined you, Earth child, quite differently." He said "child" even though Antonia was a full-grown adult. Antonia began to think, rather amused, how different the man looked. He began to smile as he apparently had read Antonia's thoughts. The tall man-like figure then led Antonia into a lab-like room. There was a big glass tub about four to five meters long and two to three meters wide that resembled an aquarium. At this point Antonia suffers a slight lapse of memory and finds herself naked inside the glass tub. The tub is filled with a dark, mossy-green, gelatinous substance. This gel adapts to her body without sticking and is pleasantly warm. Antonia also saw the tall man sitting inside the tub. He was about 1-meter away from her, without touching her. The gelatinous mass covers her just above her breasts, and the man a little less, corresponding to his size. He looks at Antonia intensively. His eyes seem to attract Antonia and suddenly energy starts to flow through her body. She had no chance to react, but neither did she really want to. Never before had she had such an intense erotic feeling; it went way beyond, human sensations.

Anyway, Antonia knew that she was being "used," but did not feel unimportant about it. At no time did the man touch her, but everything seemed to run mentally from his will. Then he pointed with his right hand to the wall parallel to them. The wall then glided silently to the side and a screen or monitor covering the whole wall became visible. On this monitor Antonia sees a sort of biological fusion and process. She saw six oocytes (from her womb) and six sperm threads rubbing against them and fertilizing the oocytes. This process was as impersonal as anything she had experienced. She looked at the man inquiringly, but now he seemed, after this visibly successful fertilization, rather cool and authoritarian, but not rude. Then again, there was another memory gap. When Antonia became aware again, she was shown six infants. They looked human but have the olive skin of their "father." They explained to Antonia that the children had to stay, and she would be able to see them again in a few years. This she would understand in the coming years, she was told. The scene was confusing for Antonia because the children seemed to have been presented shortly after fertilization, which is biologically impossible (at least for humans). After another memory gap, Antonia was back in her bed. HC addendum Source: Johannes Fiebag "Sternen Tore" Sie sind Hier ("Star gates" They are here) Type: G Comments: Bizarre account to be sure, perhaps Antonia was shown images of "her" children in a future sense?

SCREWED BY THE ALIENS

Translated by Albert S Rosales

MILITARY REPORT

Carl Moore was an Airman Second Class in the Air Force and he had top secret clearance. September 7, 1965, at Pease Air Force Base. While on duties outside the base, a craft appeared that was off in the distance and he tried to copy what he saw by drawing it on a small sheet of paper. Before he could finish it, the craft was directly above his head. It was close enough that he couldn't see the sky because it took up the whole of his view. The craft landed and spoke to him with his own words. The aliens exited the craft and tapped a "wand" on his head and all went black.

This was the first time he was taken aboard and his "visit" was comprised almost totally of genital medical examinations. These were the typical "grays," which were actually broken down into two types, one a "worker class" and the other the "bosses." The larger "bosses" were smarter. Both types, he said, have eyes like us, only their pupils were so large that you couldn't see the whites. He described their forehead as being like a melon. A small hole for ears and a walnut shaped feature immediately behind the hole. He was gone for two days and repeat visits happened. The visitations happened with enough regularity that he was eventually left lucid during them. He later described a third type – a Nordic leader – and a fourth type of being that was a female with green skin. Her eyes were different in shape than the "grays," having a more almond shape compared to the "grays'" teardrop shape. He describes her having bright red, straight pubic hairs. Gathered around her were young ones that looked nothing like her, though she claimed them as her own. After a time of more "medical" experiments, they finally stopped the visitations. — Classifiedufo.com

PORNO IMAGES

JOHN SMITH, during the 1980s, had an alien abduction from his car. A bright light appeared and he went drowsy and saw fleeting images. They were a sort of pale gray color, naked, with no hair, and no visible sexual organs of any sort. Although humanoid in appearance, they were clearly alien. Their arms, legs and torsos were spindly, and their heads were shaped like an inverted drop of water; a little bit like an egg maybe, but slightly more exaggerated. The nose was tiny, and the mouth was just a slit, but it was the huge eyes that commanded his attention.

The eyes dominated the entire face, and indeed were the most noticeable feature that the beings possessed. They were almond-shaped and slanted upward. They were jet black, although they reflected the lights from the craft. He felt compelled to look into the eyes of one being. He felt himself mesmerized, and unable to look away. He was being told – somehow – to follow the creature. This offended his dignity, and he fought the compulsion. At this, the being produced (he didn't

SCREWED BY THE ALIENS

see from where) a short, black rod, which was about a foot in length, with a bright blue/white light at the end. The being pointed this at him, and it fired a beam of blue light into his body.

He remembers being led into a UFO and taken into a room, removing his clothes and laying on an examination table. A probe was inserted into his nose. Following this rather unpleasant operation, his body was then bathed in a warm light, which seemed to pass up and down his torso, penetrating to his very bones. Suddenly, he was aware that he was feeling sexually aroused, which made him feel first amused, and then embarrassed. He was aware of some pressure around his genitals, followed by a feeling that something was being attached to his penis, which was, by now, erect. Sexual imagery seemed to flash in front of him somehow, as if erotic pictures were being fed directly into his mind. He seemed to have no control over this, and felt it was something that was being induced in him. He ejaculated, and then felt a momentary pain as the device was removed from his genitals. An alien female appeared and calmed him. He was taken from the UFO and woke up in his car. Classifiedufo.com

STEPHANY COHEN, of Lancaster Close, Bromley, UK, 2013 – The eccentric psychic claims she is visited by various aliens for sexual encounters which can lead her to heightened state of sexual arousal and hour-long orgasms beyond anything a human partner can deliver. "I call them Team Spirit, and we have a UFO, a flying saucer, we go off to planets within our own solar system but also to way out in the solar system ... It happens in my mind as it happens when my physical body is asleep. My spirit will then leave ... A dream is a friendly way of letting you know what you've been doing without scaring you ... That's what dreams really are. People would actually be afraid if they were face-to-face with an alien." Cohen says she has also had inter-alien sex with an Alien Cat people, an Alien Reptile people, an Alien Octopus people, as well as the Alien Grays, who give raptures like strong orgasms and you don't know where it comes from. Grays, Cohen says, have been coming to Earth for thousands of years and some so-called humans are the sons and daughters of these aliens.

Classifiedufo.com

A LETTER TO "UFO UNIVERSE"
ALIEN MATES: CHOSEN TO BE AN ALIEN'S HUSBAND

I had found your magazine, "UFO Universe," the first issue, very interesting, so I bought two copies.

The article by Brad Steiger really triggered my memory.

At the age of 12, a strange thing happened to me. One night in May of 1967 – it was near 11:30 P.M. – when I was aroused by a blinding white light. I had thought at first that it was heat lightning, but the light seemed to fill my whole room.

I thought at first I should be afraid, but I wasn't. I felt very relaxed and at peace.

SCREWED BY THE ALIENS

A strange feeling came over me. I was no longer alone in my room. I could feel the presence of something or someone moving around in the room. That was all I really remember from my encounter.

That very same night I had a very detailed dream. I dreamed I was out walking somewhere and I found on the ground a 1906 Indian head penny.

When I awoke the next morning, I could remember my dream in great detail. In the progression of that very same day, while on my paper route, I had sat down my heavy bag of papers on the first step at one of the houses I delivered to.

Well, when I reached down to pull out a paper from my bag, I saw something flat and round in a freshly tilled flower bed. After I had picked it up and wiped off the dirt, there was a 1906 Indian head penny I had only dreamed of the night before. To this very day I can still remember the exact spot it was found.

Ever since that night of the blinding light I have had those kinds of dreams. I don't have them all the time, just once in a while. I now dream of a full day's events, and in the same week I will find myself repeating that day in detail at work.

It is a very weird feeling to know what is going to happen before it does. I know now that the aliens that visited me did something to my mind. I have heard voices at times when there was nobody around. I have also acquired a type of cluster headaches that is very painful at times.

I had had EKG's and KAT scans and doctors have found nothing to cause them. From voices I have heard lately, I am to search for others like myself who have had encounters with aliens. I am to communicate with these people and record their names for future space colonies.

Those visitors that communicate with me have told me, we (meaning earthlings) are to be prepared for future evacuation of earth.

Another encounter occurred at the age of 14. A strange man walked up to me and sat down beside me at a lunch counter in a ten cent store.

The person started talking to me about UFOs: He told me that he knew that I had seen aliens in the past and that I would see more in the future. The person was holding tightly in his right hand an old, badly beaten paperback book called "Flying Saucers and the Bible." He handed the book to me and told me to read it carefully and that its contents would open my eyes to a reality that others could not fathom.

The person patted my hand, holding the tattered book, and told me to hold on tightly to this book, it will help guide you toward a journey in the future.

I looked down at the book in my hand with amazing wonder, then looked up to speak to him and he was gone.

After I had read through the book, I placed it among my other books, and when I went back to get it to show to a friend, it was gone. It was nowhere to be

SCREWED BY THE ALIENS

found. To this day I still search through my things, hoping it will turn up.

I am hoping I might find another copy of that book through others that have had a similar encounter.

Recently, on Friday the 1st of July of 1988, I received a telepathic message from my visitors, whom I had not heard from for many years.

The symbols I will write in this letter, is the message given me. The message came to me while I was at work between the time of 2:30 P.M. and 4:00 P.M. The message came with sharp pains deep within my head.

I can only speculate an interpretation, but I feel my speculation will not be far wrong. Many aliens from other worlds have made a stop on Earth to choose a human mate or companion that will soon accompany them on a journey. The journey is to that alien's planet to mate with and begin a new race of beings to inhabit newly found planets in distant galaxies able to sustain a type of human life, because soon earth, as we know it, will be no more.

Soon a great number of spacecraft will be coming to claim their new eternal companions.

Before the year 2000, two hundred thousand humans will be removed from the earth.

I myself have been chosen as a companion to an alien female. A'yora is the name of the female; her facial features remind me more so of an insect by the shape of her eyes and head. Even though her head may be different, the body is almost identical to a human, though they have longer toes and fingers and also they have a small five to six inch tail at the base of their spine.

My companion has only shown herself to me once. My feelings toward this female were at first questionable. But now I find myself feeling compassion for this being. Her speech is foreign to my ear, but yet it translates in my mind as if it were spoken in the King's English.

I now find myself feeling alien to my own world.

My wife has noticed changes in me, such that she questions whether or not I am the same person she had married. The alien female is becoming more and more attractive to me, and my human wife less and less.

It doesn't seem long till my life here on Earth will be wiped clean from my mind and a new life elsewhere will replace it. I am now looking forward to my new life with my new companion.

Ashland, Ohio

A SEXUAL "COMING OF AGE" – WITH ALIEN INTERVENTION

You wanted sex stories?

I was twelve. Up to that age, I slept in pajamas but that one night something in my head told me to sleep naked (something I have done since), so I did. During

SCREWED BY THE ALIENS

the night I was woken violently to see a hooded figure step back as if startled and vanish. Thinking it was a dream I went back to sleep. About two weeks later I felt myself sit up and talk to this figure. I went back to sleep. This happened numerous times but the irritating thing was I never remember what we said. I knew I was awake somehow but not fully.

So I eventually turn thirteen. The figure wakes me one night and takes me to a room with white walls, a bed and a TV. I was told to lie on the bed and shown some footage of London during WWII. The figure told me I was "nearly ready."

Nothing happens for ages. I turn fifteen. I awake to find the figure (who I think is male) stroking my body – I relax and let it. I awake the next morning feeling refreshed. A few night later I awake and the figure has somehow got me lying on top of my bed – this is kinda tough to say – and it was touching me in a sexual way. Bluntly, it was masturbating me. I seemed to let it for a while then freaked. I screamed and my mom came racing in. She woke me and I was under the duvet. I didn't tell her and said it was a bad dream. I got up in the morning and noticed on my arm a perfect triangle of three dots about four centimeters apart. I had them for weeks.

During that time I had a sexual "dream." It was with a deformed woman. I was convinced it was the hooded figure trying to be in the form of a woman. The figure – whose face I never saw – goes away.

Fast forward to a new girlfriend and new job. 2008. A girl starts at my work. She claims to be psychic and tells me I have a dark figure who follows me around. She tells me she seems to remember me from a white room with a TV, and I was naked. She tells me to stop letting this figure suck my "happiness" out of me. I still do "crash down" from being so fed up for no reason sometimes. The girl leaves. A new girl replaces her and we become really good friends. We hug and have a friendly peck on the cheek every day. One day she hugged me and then that night she texted me. She tells me that when she hugged me that day she jumped out-of-body and saw us and a figure in black whispering in my ear. This brings you up to date. I don't know if this is the kind of thing you wanted. I don't mind you using my name. I tell you this because you asked and because the night I was touched sexually still bothers me.

Thanks, Rev. Dave Moore.

SCREWED BY THE ALIENS

James Bartley describes his military MILAB abduction experiences on YouTube

The organization MAAR speculates openly about the agenda of the aliens . . . and their agenda appears dark and sinister.

Despite false claims in the press regarding sex with reptilians, Niara Terela Isley says she was involved in a series of horrendous MILAB experiences on the far side of the moon.

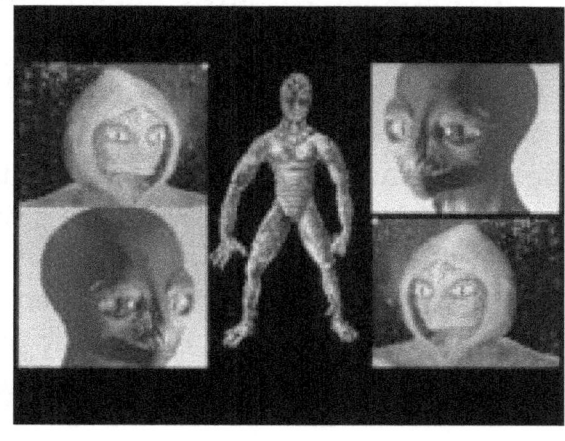

The Reptoids seem to be among the most sinister beings, subjecting humans to all manner of physical torture and mental torment.

SCREWED BY THE ALIENS

SEX, DRUGS AND UFOS
By Adam Gorightly

EDITOR'S NOTE: When it comes to the arrival of the Sexterrestrial and the appearance of their craft or vehicles of descent, the trio of words in the title take on appropriate meaning, as they are all interrelated. Shamans along the Amazon, after digesting Ayahuasca, often report encounters with UFOs and aliens that appear remarkably like encounters from other parts of the world where witnesses are not under any drug influence. This article is excerpted from Darklore Volume 3, which is available from Amazon US and Amazon UK.

ABOUT ADAM GORIGHTLY

Adam Gorightly has been chronicling fringe culture and conspiracy politics in an illuminating manner for more than two decades. He has authored a number of books, including "Historia Discordia: The Origins of the Discordian Society," "The Shadow Over Santa Susana: Black Magic, Mind Control and the Manson Family Mythos," and "Happy Trails to High Weirdness: A Conspiracy Theorist's Tour Guide." His most recent book is "Caught In The Crossfire: Kerry Thornley, Oswald and the Garrison Investigation." You can visit his website at: www.adamgorightly.com.

Stories of alien entities engaged in sexual soirées with human abductees and consorts have been recounted from the beginning of the UFO phenomenon, and perhaps since time immemorial. This theme of alien-human sexual high jinx has been a mainstay in sci-fi literature going back to Edgar Rice Burroughs' John Carter of Mars, who – after reigning victorious over the red planet's many strange creatures – won the affections of Martian princess, Deja Thoris. Illustrations of scantily clad earth gals being abducted by bug-eyed aliens were featured time and again in the pulps of the 40s and 50s, further imprinting this titillating theme of sex and

SCREWED BY THE ALIENS

saucers on the mind at large.

Drugs, as well, have played an integral role in the experience – in particular psychedelics, which induce a frame of mind more attuned to witnessing the UFO phenomenon and its associated critters, who not only take the form of alien greys, but reptoids, humanoids, and even Bigfoot. What I'm postulating is a vast spectrum of experiences which could be categorized as "UFO sightings."

In the 1970s, a 19-year-old girl attributed the birth of her bluish-skinned, web-footed baby to being sexually accosted on a California beach by a contingent of (you guessed it!) blue-skinned, web-footed aliens. This is but one example of the many purported UFO encounters featuring sexual intercourse or rape. To this end, let us trace the phenomenon back through time and draw parallels between recent UFO/alien encounters, and those of a similar variety that have occurred throughout recorded history.

BIBLICAL RAPE AND ALIEN VIOLATIONS

In the early 20th century, Aleister Crowley used hallucinogenic drugs in combination with sex magick and "Enochian calls" to invoke otherworldly entities. These Enochian calls were presumably derived from the Book of Enoch, which relates the story of wicked angels who abducted and mated with human women. The Old Testament says, "The sons of God came in unto the daughters of man." This intercourse and interaction resulted in a hybrid race, the Nephilim. These biblical tales could also possibly be (and have been) interpreted as an alien invasion that came to earth to practice genetic manipulation.

The offspring of this mating, as noted, was the Nephilim – who, in turn, went on to further commingle with the earth gals, and as recorded in Genesis, taught their earthling lovers, "sorcery, incantation, and the dividing of roots and trees." UFO researcher Guy Malone equates the "dividing of roots" to the use of shamanic drugs.

Parallels can be drawn between the Nephilim and the changelings of fairy lore. As Jacques Vallee noted in "Passport to Magonia," these sexually charged stories were sanitized in later fairy tales. Such un-sanitized tales are, however, prevalent in Scottish lore, which speaks of beautiful creatures of an aerial order, who frequently took the form of succubi, seducing young men. This is what Vallee suggests may be going on in the case of many current day abductees: that it is a continuation of a tradition of encounters with incubi and succubi that in modern times has taken the form of ET encounters. Modern day encounters often feature aliens abducting men and women from their beds – often during sleep, or semi-sleep states or trances – and taking them aboard futuristic craft where they are probed and violated, semen samples taken and ova extracted. And, of course, the ever-present anal probe...

SCREWED BY THE ALIENS
SLEEPING WITH THE ALIEN

One of the early contactees who had dalliances with the fairer alien sex (allegedly) was Howard Menger. Menger, as the story goes, enjoyed regular meetings with Marla – a buxom blonde bombshell from outer space who claimed to be five hundred years old, but didn't look a day over twenty-one…which is the legal age for alien women to have sex with earthmen, I guess. Menger was so smitten with this unearthly gal with otherworldly curves that he divorced his then-wife to marry Marla – who nowadays goes by the name of Constance, or Connie Menger, and appears as human as you or I. Go figure…

In 1952, Truman Bethurum claimed meetings with a gone space gal named Aura Rhanes from the Planet Clarion, the captain of a flying saucer who was "tops in shapeliness and beauty." Over a three month period, Aura visited Truman a total of ten times, sometimes even materializing in his bedroom, much to the chagrin of his wife. In fact, Bethurum's wife cited Rhanes in her divorce petition. So early on we can see how these alien babes were already causing problems between us earth guys and our women folk – like there weren't already enough problems going on between the sexes. Thanks, Venus! This is not to say that the earth gals haven't had their fair share of dalliances with interplanetary studs.

In 1956, Elizabeth Klarer allegedly fell head over heels for a humanoid-alien named Akon, who took her to his home planet Meton where he seduced her, saying: "Only a few are chosen for breeding purposes from beyond this solar system to infuse new blood into our ancient race." Sounds like a line Akon probably used more than once. While shacking up with Akon on Meton, Klarer got knocked up and gave birth to a son courtesy of her intergalactic suitor. Klarer finally had to leave Meton because she was having trouble breathing in the planet's atmosphere. Klarer's last meeting with Akon was in 1963, when she was apparently visited, at her South African home, by Akon and her son.

"UFO Warning," written by New Zealander John Stuart, recounted his experiences in the early 50s with a group called "Flying Saucer Investigators." The back cover of "UFO Warning" reads, "FORCED INTO SEX ABOARD A FLYING SAUCER." However, this provocative title wasn't exactly accurate, as the story's comely heroine, Barbara Turner – who worked with Stuart in his UFO investigations – was actually forced into sex while alone in her bedroom one night, when thirteen invisible creatures allegedly raped her.

At a later date, Stuart and Turner saw what they described as a "loathsome, hideous, evil, disgusting, horrifying" creature standing eight feet tall with fur and webbed feet. Apparently Turner seemed ready to succumb to the sexual advances of this otherworldly pervert, but for some reason said furry monster abruptly departed.

SCREWED BY THE ALIENS
PUTTING THE 'CONTACT' INTO 'CONTACTEE'

In 1952, George Adamski – in the company of six other people – purportedly witnessed a flying saucer land in the Mojave Desert carrying a long, blonde-haired Venusian named Orthon. According to Adamski, he was then taken aboard Orthon's ship and flown around the Universe. Little did Adamski know at the time that he had befriended an alien sex fiend!

Adamski's secretary, Laura Mundo, claimed that in the early 60s "sexual developments" transpired between Adamski's female followers and certain spacemen hanging out at Adamski's Mt. Palomar pad, one of whom was Orthon. During this period, a promiscuous young woman named Sonja claimed to have met Orthon there and engaged with him – and a number of other space brothers – in an orgy which swingin' Sonja described as "out of this world."

Although Adamski is generally identified as the original contactee of the modern UFO era, a fellow named Samuel Eaton Thompson – in Washington State in 1950 – experienced a saucer landing and contact with its inhabitants, who welcomed him aboard their ship. Like Orthon, the saucer people were Venusians with long blonde hair and perfect features. But unlike Orthon, they were naked as jaybirds.

There have been many reports of nude aliens. In the late 1960s, Woodrow Derenberger was picked up by apparent alien beings and transported to their home planet, Lanulos. There he was surprised to discover that most Lanulosians strutted their stuff in the buff, on a sort of outer space nudist colony.

Another kinky episode in UFO lore was the 1957 Antonio Villas-Boas case. Villas-Boas, a 23-year-old Brazilian farmer, was allegedly taken aboard a UFO, then slipped an aphrodisiac mickey and "forced" to have hardcore sex with an attractive red-haired, pointy-breasted femanoid who made odd animal-like grunting noises during their "close encounter."

Apparently, Brazilians have had a number of sexual encounters with alien sex fiends. In 1979, 25-year-old Antonio Ferreira witnessed a saucer land, followed by the appearance of some robots who abducted Ferreira and took him aboard their craft. There Ferreira encountered a repulsive female alien with bad breath and icy-cold skin, as well as red pubic hair (a feature noted in the Villas-Boas case). Wanting nothing to do with this skuzzy alien broad, Ferreira resisted. In response, the robots tore Ferreira's clothes off and gave him an injection, causing him to succumb. Then the rascally robots covered Ferreira in an amber-colored oil (emotion lotion, perhaps?) followed by the alien dame jumping his Brazilian bones.

Perhaps the most well-known abductee is Whitley Strieber. Many aspects of Strieber's recounted experiences appear clearly sexual in nature, one of which featured a wrinkled old alien grey gal who instructed him to make it "harder."

SCREWED BY THE ALIENS

When Strieber realized it was his you-know-what she was encouraging him to harden, he became understandably horrified, although upon later reflection the incident left Strieber somewhat confused and, admittedly, aroused. Another common feature of the alien abduction experience is the probing of earthling rectums with electronic probes, which Strieber described in Communion:

...The next thing I knew I was being shown an enormous and extremely ugly object, gray and scaly, with a sort of network of wires on the end. It was at least a foot long, narrow, and triangular in structure. They inserted this thing into my rectum. It seemed to swarm into me as if it had a life of its own. Apparently its purpose was to take samples, possibly of fecal matter, but at the time I had the impression that I was being raped, and for the first time I felt anger...

Later in the saga, Strieber recounted having semen drawn from his 'johnson' with some sort of vacuum device – alluding once again to the sexual nature of his "communion."

Anal probes, insemination, pokes and scratches, and other intrusive behavior are commonly attributed to these otherworldly visitors. Some have even suggested, like Strieber, they are a form of rape. Or, conversely, it could be conjectured that anal probes are intergalactic sex toys. Whatever the case, the aliens seem to have a fond fascination with penises, rectums, and other assorted human protuberances and orifices. But of course this should come as no surprise, as we humans also have a fond fascination with same. Perhaps it's the alien in us all!

REAL LOVE AND THE MANCHURIAN CANDIDATE

In 1973, Claude Vorilhon – while exploring an extinct volcano in the French countryside – experienced an encounter with a small, bald, green-skinned fellow with a goatee on his chin and halo over his head, who arrived in the requisite spacecraft. This fellow introduced himself as Yahweh, and informed Claude that he had come to earth to visit him specifically, and that Claude was the chosen one to spread the message of the Elohim, an alien race of ascended masters.

Yahweh cranked up his spaceship and took Claude – at seven times the speed of light – to the Elohim's home planet, where he met up with Jesus, Moses and Buddha. At some point in this adventure, Claude was given a scented bath by six perfectly formed biological robot babes, who subsequently treated him to some steamy robot sex.

During his sexual initiation, Claude was appointed the Elohim's ambassador to Earth. Upon his earthly return, Claude adopted the name Rael and soon after began proselytizing as "the last prophet." This, of course, led to what some would term a free-love saucer cult – the Raelian Movement. Rael, bless his depraved little heart, has encouraged sexual promiscuity among his frolicking followers all in search of an Elohim-blessed "cosmic orgasm." Talk about a big bang!

A more recent alleged human/alien sexual encounter began at a logging camp

SCREWED BY THE ALIENS

in the Manchurian province, when a Chinese man named Meng witnessed an alien craft crash. Meng started off toward said craft, and was gazing at it across a valley, when something hit him in the head and knocked him silly. Following Mr. Meng's UFO related head smacking, he found himself levitating above his bed one night. While his wife and daughter slept soundly below, a three-foot-tall, six-fingered alien dame with braided fur on her legs proceeded to straddle Meng's waist and start in on him, alien sex style. After forty torrid minutes of levitational copulation, this braided-fur alien babe then departed, vanishing through a wall, as aliens are apt to do. A month later, Meng claimed, he was transported up into a spaceship. When Meng asked to see the woman he'd had sex with, his abductors said that this was impossible, but that in 60 years, "on a distant planet the son of a Chinese peasant will be born."

According to the International UFO Reporter, a young Australian, Peter Khoury, was in bed early one morning in 1992 when two "unusual looking naked women" appeared from out of nowhere. One – a tall blond – tried to force Khoury to put his face on her breast, but he resisted and decided to bite off a piece of her nipple, although this strange woman apparently felt no pain. Shortly afterward, both women vanished. Afterwards, Khoury discovered two humanoid-looking hairs wrapped painfully around his purple penis. He saved one of these hairs in an envelope, and years later gave it to a group of Australian scientists to analyze. The result, apparently, indicated that these women were hybrids of some sort, with DNA close to that of humans.

Probably the one person on this planet most responsible for the advance of alien-human sexual relations is Pamela Stonebrooke, a talented jazz singer also known as "The Intergalactic Diva." Stonebrooke has claimed numerous sexual bump and grinds with a group of fun-loving alien reptilians, who she believes are preparing her for an apocalyptic planetary upheaval. I bet they tell that to all the earth gals.

STRANGE ATTRACTOR

So what's attracting these apparent otherworldly beings? One theory suggests that women's menstrual cycles are at the root of many of these strange encounters. Fortean researchers have long noted that Bigfoot, various monsters, apparitions, ghosts and UFO sightings often happen near lover's lanes, or during women's menstrual periods. Some ancient cultures suspected that women's menstrual cycles open a gateway into the void, through which certain 'forces' can be invoked – a theory Carlos Castaneda entertained in The Second Ring of Power. It has been noted by certain researchers that – in addition to the uncanny ability to locate women experiencing their menstrual periods – Bigfoot and other reported Fortean beasts tend to appear when the moon is full. Of course, menstruation itself is believed to have a basic concurrence with moon cycles. According to occultist Ken-

SCREWED BY THE ALIENS

neth Grant, the human menstrual flow is the vehicle of the lunar vibration. Grant seems convinced that this peculiar force gives rise to an entity known to the ancient Egyptians as the Ape of Thoth, a beast which loomed large in Aleister Crowley's magical practices. Maybe Bigfoot and the Ape of Thoth are more closely related than has been previously suspected. Also, some of the stranger Bigfoot sightings have coincided with the appearance of UFOs. This lends credence to the theory that Bigfoot is more paranormal in nature, rather than an actual flesh-and-bones beastie.

Dr. Wilhelm Reich theorized that a mysterious life force, Orgone – closely connected with human sexuality – could be gathered in containers which he invented called Orgone Accumulators, devices that are used to promote optimal health and wellbeing. In "The Rebirth of Pan," author Jim Brandon speculated that the energy collected in Orgone Accumulators was akin to automobiles containing erotically-inclined couples parked in lover's lanes engaged in carnal couplings. What this suggested to Brandon is that the power behind these manifestations – UFOs and other paranormal materializations – may not be entirely under control, but are acting chaotically, like a moth to light, in response to whatever is gathered in metal boxes, such as sexual energy. In essence, aliens – or whatever "they" are – feed off this sexual human energy like psychic vampires.

The Cloudbuster – another Reich invention which resembled a large Gatling gun-like contraption – could theoretically pull rain out of the clouds. Additionally, Reich discovered that his Cloudbuster could drain energy from lights in the sky, dimming them from view. In essence, the Cloudbuster was also an Orgone Accumulator of sorts, sucking Orgone from the atmosphere. While experimenting with the Cloudbuster, Reich encountered what he perceived as UFOs, and came to believe that they were coming to Earth to suck up Orgone and exhaust a waste product he dubbed Deadly Orgone Energy (DOR). DOR, Reich contended, was causing adverse environmental effects on the planet. At some point, Reich decided to aim the Cloudbuster on a contingent of UFOs he observed over his Rangeley research facility, which caused said UFOs to turn tail and retreat. This led Reich to triumphantly proclaim that "tonight, for the first time in the history of man, the war waged for ages by living beings from outer space upon this Earth…was reciprocated."

THE DRUGS DO WORK

Sex, as I've exhaustively documented, is a common theme in UFO lore, as much as some ufologists might prefer to keep it hidden in the closet, like J. Edgar Hoover in drag. But talk of drugs and their relation to UFOs seems even more verboten, as it's perceived by many that making these connections only further marginalizes and confuses the UFO research field. And so, for the "serious" researcher, if it's established that witnesses were under the influence of mind-altering substances

SCREWED BY THE ALIENS

during their encounters, then the experience is immediately relegated to the ufological round file.

However, I consider this approach a bit hasty, because the types of states accessed by psychedelic drugs might be at the core of what the UFO experience is really about. Which is not to say that UFO encounters are hallucinations – quite the contrary. What plant entheogens do is enable us to see a broader spectrum of what is actually around us, and to access states we aren't normally able to perceive, much in the same manner that shamans of ancient traditions – through the use of magic ritual – are able to "see" on a higher level, tune into the cosmos, help people overcome sicknesses and to discover truths about themselves. The shamanic drug ayahausca has been used for hundreds of years in this manner, its usage often taking the form of vision quests.

One of the most recent luminaries to address this subject is Graham Hancock in his book "Supernatural: Meetings with the Ancient Teachers of Mankind." The book documents Hancock's shamanistic ayahausca voyages and the grey-skinned entities he's encountered, whom he regards as his teachers or guardian angels.

A chemical compound found in ayahausca is dimethyltryptamine (DMT), which – it should be noted – is also created naturally in the human brain. In this regard, there may be a relationship between the release of DMT into the pineal gland and mystical experiences. The pineal gland, some claim, is where our third eye resides, and when we are able to open our third eye, this leads to an acceleration of our spiritual evolution and eventual illumination.

What Terence McKenna discovered under DMT's influence was a world inhabited by creatures he described as "self-transforming machine elves." Interestingly enough, others conducting DMT experimentation have encountered these same entities on a consistent basis, and often in strikingly similar detail to what McKenna observed. This illustrates the possibility of a multiverse, or multiple dimensions, that are accessed – in certain cases – through ritualized drug use, in the same way that the aethers are opened up by the practice of ritual magic.

Another pioneer of the 1960s psychedelic revolution was Dr. John Lilly, known for his groundbreaking work with dolphins, as well as the invention of the isolation tank. In the early 1970s, Lilly began experiencing a series of supposed interstellar communications with a network of alien entities known as ECCO – an acronym for "Earth Coincidence Control Office." These communications were achieved through the use of the drug Ketamine.

Many people have encountered UFOs on magic mushrooms, including Terence McKenna. One such magic mushroom contactee was the late comedian Bill Hicks, who – during a late 80s psilocybin trip – was taken aboard what he perceived to be an alien ship. Hicks often talked about this experience during stand-up routines; although most people had no idea whether to take him seriously when he

SCREWED BY THE ALIENS

referred to the seven balls of light that transported him aboard an alien ship, that he described as...

...all white light inside, like a conch shell, and it seemed like there were thousands of other people on the same channel, communicating at this high speed...There was nothing scary or evil about it. It was just really positive and happy, a really good vibration all around.

On August 19, 2000, actress Ann Heche was found wandering outside a rural ranch field near Fresno, California, dressed in a sports bra and shorts and babbling about a spaceship. In 1995, Ms. Heche began hearing disembodied voices instructing her that she was "Celestia from the Fourth Dimension." At a mountain lodge in the Sierras, an ethereal voice instructed Heche to swallow a hit of Ecstasy and then report to Fresno for a space-brother rendezvous. After leaving said lodge, Heche drove five hours, which was unusual since Fresno was only eighty miles away. At some point, the aforementioned ethereal voice told Heche to pull over and walk into a field where a spaceship was scheduled to land. When friends came to see her the next morning at a local hospital, Heche said she had suddenly snapped out of her Celestia head trip and was "sane" for the first time in thirteen years.

All of this comes back full circle to my own psychedelic UFO experience, the connection in this case being Fresno, which on the surface appears to be nothing more than your average Central California cookie-cutter town. However, behind the façade of strip malls, Walmarts and fast food outlets, Fresno seems to be a magnet for high weirdness, such as my own UFO freak out, recounted in Darklore Volume 1.

SCREWED BY THE ALIENS

Adam Gorightly is the author of various books and peer papers on the paranormal.

Under the influence of mind altering drugs, the shamans along the Amazon and in other areas of the world, including Peru, are able to draw both aliens as well as the craft. There is a remarkable resemblance when these drawings are compared to descriptions of legitimately "real" UFOs and their occupants.

SCREWED BY THE ALIENS

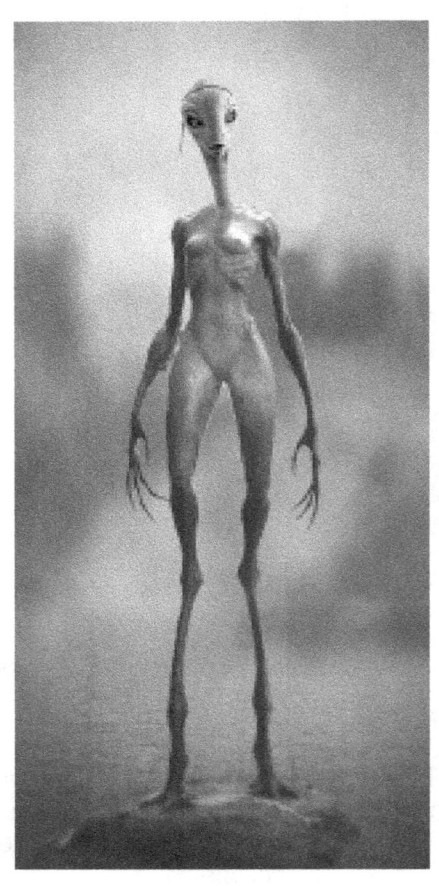

SECTION TWO – LOVE AND RAPTURE AMONG THE ANCIENT ONES

Chapter Four: Sexual Abduction As Old As Humanity
By Allen Greenfield

Chapter Five: Some Call Them Nocturnal Demons
By Tim Beckley

Chapter Six: God of Our Fathers Our Divine Sexual Heritage
By Hercules Invictus

Chapter Seven: Sexual Abductions Through The Ages
By Greg Little

SCREWED BY THE ALIENS

CHAPTER 4

SEXUAL ABDUCTION IS AS OLD AS HUMANITY
By Allen Greenfield

EDITOR'S NOTE: I feel I have known Allen Greenfield almost as long as we have both been on the Earth. We started out corresponding, chatting on the telephone and exchanging newsletters when we were both teens. And we even appeared together on the James Randi talk show when he replaced the emperor of the all night talk show hosts, Long John Nebel, who moved from WOR to WNBC. Allen and I spent a few New Year's Eves together and over the years have continued our mutual exchange of information.

Allen is a past member of the Society for Psychical Research and has twice been the recipient of the "UFOlogist of the Year Award," given by the National UFO Conference (aka Congress of Scientific UFOlogy). His book "Secret Ciphers of the UFOnauts" discusses UFOs in terms derived from Carl Jung. His "The Story of the Hermetic Brotherhood of Light" includes discussion of the Hermetic of Light vs. Helena Blavatsky. He has photographed a "ghost" at Christ Church in Georgia and spent some time in both Brown Mountain, NC, looking for the spook lights there, as well as talking with the late Brooksville, Florida, resident John Reeve about his face-to-face encounter with a mysterious "alien" gentleman who gave him a parchment with strange writing on it.

****

"We are dealing with a yet unrecognized level of consciousness, independent of man but closely linked to the earth.... I do not believe anymore that UFOs are simply the spacecraft of some race of extraterrestrial visitors. This notion is too simplistic to explain their appearance, the frequency of their manifestations through recorded history, and the structure of the information exchanged with them during contact.

"[An] impressive parallel [can] be made between UFO occupants and the popular conceptions of demons. [UFOs can] project images or fabricated scenes designed to change our belief systems." "...human belief... is being controlled

SCREWED BY THE ALIENS

and conditioned," "man's concepts are being rearranged," and we may be headed toward "a massive change of human attitudes toward paranormal abilities and extraterrestrial life.

"The 'medical examination' to which abductees are said to be subjected, often accompanied by sadistic sexual manipulation, is reminiscent of the medieval tales of encounters with demons. It makes no sense in a sophisticated or technical or biological framework: any intelligent being equipped with the scientific marvels that UFOs possess would be in a position to achieve any of these alleged scientific objectives in a shorter time and with fewer risks.

"...the symbolic display seen by the abductees is identical to the type of initiations ritual or astral voyage that is imbedded in the [occult] traditions of every culture." Thus, "the structure of abduction stories is identical to that of occult initiation rituals." - Dr. Jacques Vallee

AN ABDUCTION/RAPE CASE AMONG THE "ANCIENT GODS"

Diodorus Siculus, Library of History 5. 2. 3 - 5. 5. 1 (trans. Oldfather) (Greek historian C1st B.C.):

"The Sikeliotai (Sicilians) who dwell in the island [Sicily] have received the tradition from their ancestors, the report having ever been handed down successively from earliest time by one generation to the next, that the island is sacred to Demeter and Kore (Core) [Persephone]; although there are certain poets who recount the myth that at the marriage of Plouton (Pluto) [Haides] and Persephone, Zeus gave this island as a wedding present to the bride...The fact that the Rape of Kore [Persephone] took place in Sikelia (Sicily) is, men say, proof most evident that the goddesses made this island their favorite retreat because it was cherished by them before all others. And the Rape of Kore, the myth relates, took place in the meadows of the territory of Enna. The spot lies near the city, a place of striking beauty for its violets and every other kind of flower and worthy of the goddess. And the story is told that, because of the sweet odor of the flowers growing there, trained hunting dogs are unable to hold the trail, because their natural sense of smell is balked.

"And the meadow we have mentioned is level in the center and well-watered throughout, but on its periphery it rises high and falls off with precipitous cliffs on every side. And it is conceived of as lying in the very center of the island, which is the reason why certain writers call it the navel of Sikelia. Near to it also are sacred groves, surrounded by marshy flats, and a huge grotto which contains a chasm which leads down into the earth and opens to the north, and through it, the myth relates, Plouton, coming out with his chariot, effected the Rape of Kore. And the violets, we are told, and the rest of the flowers which supply the sweet odor continue to bloom, to one's amazement, throughout the entire year, and so the whole aspect of the place is one of flowers and delight.

SCREWED BY THE ALIENS

"Both Athene and Artemis, the myth goes on to say, who had made the same choice of maidenhood as had Kore and were reared together with her, joined with her in gathering the flowers, and all of them together wove the robe for their father Zeus. And because of the time they had spent together and their intimacy, they all loved this island above any other, and each one of them received for her portion a territory, Athene receiving hers in the region of Himera . . . Artemis received from the gods the island of Syrakouse (Syracuse) . . . Like the two goddesses whom we have mentioned, Kore, we are told, received as her portion the meadows round about Enna; but a great fountain was made sacred to her in the territory of Syrakousa and given the name Kyane or 'Azure Font.'

"For the myth relates that it was near Syrakousa that Plouton effected the Rape of Kore and took her away in his chariot, and that after cleaving the earth asunder he himself descended into Haides, taking along with him the bride whom he had seized, and that he caused the fountain named Kyane (Cyane) to gush forth, near which the Syrakousans each year hold a notable festive gathering; and private individuals offer the lesser victims, but when the ceremony is on behalf of the community, bulls are plunged in the pool, this manner of sacrifice having been commanded by Herakles on the occasion when he made the circuit of all Sikelia, while driving off the cattle of Geryones.

"After the Rape of Kore, the myth goes on to recount, Demeter, being unable to find her daughter, kindled torches in the craters of Mount Aitna (Etna) and visited many parts of the inhabited world . . . The inhabitants of Sikelia (Sicily), since by reason of the intimate relationship with Demeter and Kore with them they were the first to share in the corn after its discovery, instituted to each on the goddesses' sacrifices and festive gatherings . . .

"That the Rape of Kore took place in the manner we have described is attested by many ancient historians and poets. Karkinos (Carcinus) the tragic poet, for instance, who often visited Syrakousa and witnessed the zeal which the inhabitants displayed in the sacrifices and festive gatherings for both Demeter and Kore, has the following verses in his writings:

"'Demeter's daughter, her whom none may name, by secret schemings Plouton [Haides], men say, stole, and then he dropped into earth's depths, whose light is darkness. Longing for the vanished girl her mother searched and visited all lands in turn. And Sikelia's land by Aitna's crags was filled with streams of fire which no man could approach, and groaned throughout its length; in grief over the maiden now the folk, beloved of Zeus, was perishing without the corn. Hence honour they these goddesses even now.'"

FAIRY LORE AND FAIRY ABDUCTIONS

The term 'fairy' originates with the Middle English word faerie, as well as fairie, fayerye and feirie, which were borrowed directly from the Old French faerie. In

SCREWED BY THE ALIENS

Middle English the word meant either enchantment, the land of enchantment, or the collective noun for those who dwelt in fairyland. In etymological terms 'fairy' is rooted in the word fay or fae from faery or faerie meaning 'realm of the fays.' The appellation erie eventually came to define a trade, craft, or place such as midwifery, fishery, cookery, thievery, and nunnery, and thence to wizardry, witchery, roguery and knavery.

Fairies have occupations and amusements, they have offspring and have fights (MacCulloch, 1912), and in folklore and fairy tales they share many commonalities in their relations to mortals, which fall into six categories. Firstly: (1) fairies help human beings; (2) fairies can also harm humans; (3) humans can be abducted by fairies for their own purposes; (4) fairies can exchange their own offspring for human babies and thus the belief in the 'changeling'; (5) humans can be induced to visit fairyland and; (6) mortals can for a while have a fairy lover or mistress. Indeed, there is much in folklore that is concerned with protection against fairy malevolence, crediting these creatures with powers beyond that of mere mortals, and that resemble witchcraft, wizardry and practices of medicine men (MacCulloch, 1912). All occupations found in primitive communities were followed by fairies that included hunting, dancing, herding and farming, as well as being skilled smiths, shoemakers, weavers and spinners (Briggs, 1957).

One fear of fairy retribution is the abduction of women and children. This reflects a dependency on humans whereby young women and expectant mothers are stolen in order to nurse fairy offspring, and the fairy compulsion for human women to assist as midwives and suckling nurses (Rhys, 1901), or seduce mortal men and women. A stolen baby is replaced with a misshapen fairy baby, known in Ireland as the changeling. The changeling was a replacement for an abducted human baby. Old human females were also kidnapped and made to live as slaves in fairyland. The same could happen with the abduction of human midwives.

The popular conception of a fairy is that of a very small diminutive, sometimes tiny, creature resembling a pygmy. They are often shown as angelic, young or childlike, who are sometimes winged human-like winged sylphs. However, they can also be depicted as short, wizened troll-like gnomic figures with red or green eyes, or as tall handsome beings. Fairies have therefore a variable size, which they can change or appear as birds and animals (Sayce, 1934). In appearance some accounts describe the fairy as having the stature of a year-old child who nonetheless resembles a bearded old man, which is rooted in beliefs in ancestral spirits. In appearance and disposition sometimes they are beautiful, sometimes they are hideous.

In folklore fairies are described as humanoid with magical powers and the ability to shape-shift, with a propensity for malice and mischief whose origins are even demonic. It is also believed that fairies cannot tell lies. It is among the fairy

SCREWED BY THE ALIENS

lore of the Celtic peoples there occurs the widespread theme of a race of 'little people' who were driven underground by invading tribes.

Fairies are attributed with ability to become invisible at their own choosing, and affected by donning a magic cap, cloak or using certain herbs, and thus they can "...disappear, change their shape, and appear as human beings..." (Sayce, 1934). This fairy characteristic is bestowed by their power of glamour, shape-shifting and casting illusions." (Briggs, 1957). The word 'glamour' was a Scottish term introduced into English literature that means magical, fantastic with the ability to juggle with the sight (Edwards, 1974). In other words, glamour is a magical charm cast by devils, wizards, a coup d'oiel in order to deceive the eye of the perceiver. Indeed, humans have to be especially careful in their dealings with the fairies.

AMOROUS FAIRY LOVERS

These diminutive beings are also deemed extremely long-lived if not immortal, as well as being "...dangerously amorous and have a tricksy love of practical jokes." (Briggs, 1957). Their domain is regarded as being underground, a subterranean abode in tumuli, barrows, under hills or even beneath rocks and stones, and as ghosts "...haunt waste places, caves, rocks, ruins, and waterfalls, to have homes beneath lakes and to be associated with uncanny objects such as snakes, will-o-the-wisps, megalithic monuments..." (Sayce, 1934).

Fairies, however, rarely harm mortal humans, which includes those they abduct or lure to fairyland. Nonetheless a mistreated fairy is not incapable of retaliation by spoiling crops and setting fire to a household. The relationships between faerie and mortals can be further appreciated by the stories about fairy and mistress lovers which in literary terms often possess a drama and poetry. Such fairy stories have an established pattern of four main strands of: (1) a human loves a supernatural; (2) the spirit or fairy consents to the human dependent upon certain conditions and provisos; (3) the human eventually breaks the agreed taboo and loses his fairy lover, finally; (4) the lover attempts to retrieve or recapture the loved one, sometimes being successful. A similar set of conditions apply to fairy tales about fairy mistresses.

All fairies are ascribed as being intensely enamored of dancing, music, singing, feasting and revelry that may persist as "...actual rites of orgiastic character..." (MacCulloch, 1912), and so have their origin in rustic festivals and agricultural magical practices.

There are many tales of the abduction of human beings by fairies, often of women to act as mortal midwives at the birth of fairy children. There are numerous analogous stories of an accidental visit, or by invitation, to fairyland. Abductees, especially children, are either lured, enchanted or seduced, in order to convey them to the realm of the fairies. Many stories relate of fairies searching for mortal women to nurse fairy children.

SCREWED BY THE ALIENS

Lactating human mothers, who are always rewarded, or those with children, are taken because human milk is prized highly by fairies. The newborn human is especially at risk of fairy abduction. Fairy babies are substituted as a replacement which is then branded as a "changeling." This belief in England appears to be a combination of Celtic ideas of the "people of the hills" with the Germanic elf-dwarf concepts. Explanations vary but usually the fairy child returns to its own domain.

SUGGESTED READING

SILVER BRIDGE, by Gray Barker. Introduction by Allen Greenfield.

ANGEL SPELLS

SAUCERS AND SAUCERIANS PANP PRESS 1975

THE COMPLETE SECRET CIPHER OF THE UFONAUTS

THE BOOK OF LIES, edited by Richard Metzger

VICTORIAN FIRE: SECRETS OF SEXUAL MAGICK

Allen Greenfield

SCREWED BY THE ALIENS

• All manner of "alien" and "spirit" seduction have become woven into pop culture such as the book "Fairy Prince's Concubine" by Ophelia Upmoore.

• Fairies ride a moonbeam looking for enchanting love with an earth mate.

• While Persephone screams out her rape.

———————————————

• The 2009 calendar below showcases the covers of Fantastic Adventures, Startling Stories and other famous pulp magazines of the 1930s and 40s. Anyone with an interest in the bizarre or in American pop culture will find Alien Abduction irresistible.

• Aliens and earth babes seem to go together - so much so from this cover of one of Ray Palmer's magazines. Ray knew how to sell magazines!

• Some of the covers got a bit rough even getting into some fairly heavy SM scenes like this space "maiden" being strangled..

SCREWED BY THE ALIENS

CHAPTER 5

SOME CALL THEM NOCTURNAL DEMONS OTHERS NASTY BEDROOM INVADERS
By Timothy Green Beckley

Though encounters with "aliens" may be relatively new in the overall scheme of UFOs and the paranormal, a jaunt down history's occult memory lane will quickly show that sex and the supernatural are one big bundle of "joy," depending upon your disposition and what side of the veil you find yourself on.

As noted throughout this – with few exceptions – NONFICTION work, you might be called upon – chosen! – without warning – to mate and perhaps assist in a procreation ritual (i.e. "genetic experiment" in the case of a UFO seduction) that could be something right out of "Rosemary's Baby."

As our associates Dr. Gregory Little and Adam Gorightly endeavor to demonstrate within these pages, we have been made to copulate with "the Other," the term the late Brad Steiger used for these life forms that have been present with us since time began. Some participants see this form of sexual intercourse as kind of a "sweet surrender," while others who have been poked and probed in all their orifices claim they had no choice in the matter and were, simply put, raped – in some cases nearly clawed to death – by beings whose odious forms cause some of us to shudder when going to bed at night.

As strange as it may seem, such dreaded incidents are being taken more seriously by psychiatrists and psychologists According to a report published in the peer-reviewed publication "Frontiers of Psychiatry," a team of researchers looked at 12 studies of the incubus phenomenon that included nearly 1800 cases as pulled from a cross section of reports from the United States, Canada, China, Japan, Italy and Mexico.

According to independent researcher Tereza Pultarova, with a Masters from the University of Prague, reporting for "Live Science": "The researchers found that over 1 in 10 people, or 11 percent of the general population, will experience the incubus phenomenon in their lifetimes. That means that there is an 11 percent

SCREWED BY THE ALIENS

chance for any given individual to experience this [the incubus phenomenon] at least once during their lives," a Dr. Bloom stated.

"But in certain groups, the odds of 'encountering' an incubus are higher. Among people with psychiatric disorders, as well as among refugees and – somewhat surprisingly – students, the odds of experiencing the incubus phenomenon are as high as 41 percent," Bloom said.

"The analysis also found that people sleeping on their backs are more likely to experience the phenomenon. Alcohol consumption and irregular sleeping patterns also make an incubus visit more probable," Bloom added.

Though the frightening experience gets frequently dismissed as "just a bad dream," Bloom noted that the incubus phenomenon can lead to additional problems, including anxiety, difficulty sleeping due to fear and even delusional disorder, a mental illness akin to schizophrenia.

In the paper, the researchers speculated about a possible link between the incubus phenomenon and sudden unexpected death syndrome, a situation in which a healthy person inexplicably dies in his or her sleep.

"People who have experienced the incubus phenomenon often report a level of anxiety that is 'off the scale,'" Bloom said. "Many of them have the feeling that they will actually die during an attack. Whether that ever happens is unknown, even though for a person experiencing it, it is not hard to imagine this [happening]."

The analysis also found that the form of the incubus figure and how people react to it can vary based on the person's cultural background.

For example, "Patients with a Muslim background often tell me that they see the incubus phenomenon as a proof that they are being haunted by a jinn, an invisible spirit created by Allah out of smokeless fire," Bloom said.

Sometimes, however, the incubus may take on a much more friendly and entertaining form. "I recently spoke to a healthy 15-year-old girl who had experienced the incubus phenomenon," Bloom said. "She found four miniature penguins dining at a table on her chest, and had been thrilled and amused rather than scared."

All agree that the incubus is demon in male form who attacks and lays upon sleepers in order to have intercourse with them. The female counterpart is the succubus, an entity who will give the male a case of "blue balls" like you would never believe.

Traditionally, the incubus most often pursues sexual relations with a woman in order to father a child, as in the legend of Merlin. Tradition holds that repeated intercourse with such entities may result in the deterioration of one's health or even death.

One of the earliest mentions of an incubus comes from Mesopotamia circa

SCREWED BY THE ALIENS

2400 BC where Gilgamesh's father is said to have been Lugalbanda, who appeared to his mother in a dream and had sexual relations with her, thus making Gilgamesh the first hybrid offspring to be born into our world. There are other instances of nightly demonic possession which produced, if not earthbound children, some form of ghostly offspring which could haunt a palace or humble home without fear of being vanquished back to where they came.

St. Augustine touched on the topic in De Civitate Dei ("The City of God"); there were too many alleged attacks by incubi to deny them. He stated, "There is also a very general rumor. Many have verified it by their own experience and trustworthy persons have corroborated the experience others told, that sylvans and fauns, commonly called incubi, have often made wicked assaults upon women."

One might be able to substitute this bold statement with a similar one made in modern times by the late Budd Hopkins, as well as researcher David Jacobs, who have chronicled "sexscapes" with purported aliens from greys to Nordic types.

The controversial pros and cons of this overall perverse phenomena raged for centuries among those of Christian disciplines. Thomas Aquinas insisted that demons were sterile; therefore the only way the incubus could impregnate a woman was by receiving the semen from a succubus who had received it from a man. Also, aiding in this theory was the idea that demons were able to change their sex at will. Aquinas further asserted that a demon could use semen lost during a wet dream so a man could be "at one and the same time a virgin and a father." A similar view was noted when King James refuted the idea that angelic entities can reproduce and instead offered a suggestion that a devil would carry out two methods of impregnating women: the first, to steal the sperm out of a dead man and deliver it into a woman. If a demon could extract the semen quickly, the transportation of the substance could be instantly transported to a female host, before it became "stale and cold."

Centuries before our current thoughts of multiple sexual disciplines and transgenderism, there were a few bold philosophers of the abnormally abnormal who believed that these nighttime visitors could shape-shift from male to female at will, depending upon their sexual preferences on any given evening while considering all the possibilities they might be confronted with. To them, a juicy piece of flesh was a juicy piece of flesh, though there were some of lesser mind who steadfastly believed incubi were totally disdainful of homosexuality, were strictly heterosexual and found copulating with a male either unpleasant or detrimental. This would seem to indicate that there were no bisexual bedroom invaders floating around.

In some of the Asian communities, just to make sure that they were not targeted, men who were having problems with crawling and creeping entities on a regular basis would go to bed making their wives wear lipstick and stockings and

SCREWED BY THE ALIENS

would hang phallic objects over the other side of the bed so as to let the demon know there was a female present and they should go unharmed under all circumstances. Thank you very much. Very chivalrous of you, kind sir!

As I've come to understand the principles of the phenomena at hand, calling upon an exorcist would offer no assistance. And, try as they might, it is unclear how many men or women were saved by saying their prayers before going to bed, this at least according to Franciscan friar Ludovico Maria. Others, bent on driving out their demandingly, devilish aggravators, would sleep next to Christian relics obtain through the local parish (for a hefty price no doubt), or would have a kneeling surrogate repeatedly make the sign of the cross through the darkness till the first light of dawn. In the case of President Donald Trump this would be known as "a fixer"!

DWARVES AND GNOMES

There are, it should be noted, a variety of names given to these creepy, crawly, nocturnal parasites. Those living in the regions of the Alps mostly dreaded the transgressions of hairy dwarfs, gnomes and a variety of "little people."

Do we hesitate to say that such minions have been observed trying to kidnap and harass UFO witnesses, mostly women? Just ask Rosa from a rural city in Tuscany who received unwanted attention in 1954 from both the press and from her would-be alien interlopers who tried to steal both her stockings (a normal enough fetish for some earthlings, but apparently also a cosmic fetish), as well as a bouquet of flowers from her steady beau, no doubt more of a handsome hunk than the creatures who took it upon themselves to try and have their way with this very frightened lady.

THE POPOBAWA

According to "X Magazine" blogger David Russell, if you reside in Zanzibar you had better watch out for the Popobawa, an incubus who will make matters worse by returning if he isn't allowed to have his way with you on demand.

"The infamous Popobawa has struck again, causing panic in the Zanzibar islands off the coast of Tanzania in Africa. The 'creature,' described as a cyclops dwarf with bat-like wings and ears, and sharp talons, is feared for its nasty habit of sodomizing men while they sleep in their beds. The presence of the often invisible Popobawa can be detected by an acrid smell or a puff of smoke. Sometimes, the Popobawa is visible to everyone except the terrified victim. It is believed to take human form by day, but with pointed fingers. After doing its vile deed, the Popobawa instructs its victims to spread the word about their ordeal or it would be back."

Certainly this unwelcome invader cannot be placed in the category of being welcomed by most, though we have heard rumors that a few have not shunned him as most straight men certainly would.

SCREWED BY THE ALIENS

THE TIN TIN "MAN"

Listen, I never put anyone down because of their looks, but the Tin Tin is in his own league when it comes to personal hygiene and appearance. This guy has a snout that could do great damage, regardless of his sexual preference in humans, and we can only imagine what that would entail. But if you are a woman and shave you will apparently not be sought out by the Jimmy Durante of the paranormal. Hirsute is the key word in what he likes. Hey, everyone has their own calling.

THE IGNIS FATUOUS

OK, stand back. Being of Hungarian heritage I should have no problem taking care of the Ignis Fatuous, who is said to transform itself into a demonic figure akin to a featherless chicken from a mere will o' the wisp (known to UFO skeptics as marsh gas). It haunts the woods for the most part, but it can follow you home, especially if you live in a ginger bread house way back in the forest and are looking to make a feast out of Hansel and Gretel. Then you get what you deserve, in which case Mr. Ignis could be a friend as long as he keeps his hands to himself while visiting my pad in the wee hours.

THE YACUMANA AND THE CHULLACHAQUI

Stay away from the Ayahusca if you don't want to "hallucinate" or become possessed by the Yacumana and Chullachaqui, who are the best known of numerous demons that you might conjure up as you travel and get high with the locals along the Amazon River. Yacumana is a demon of the water (boa man); Chullachaqui can transform itself to mimic any person, which we assume could be a highly attractive jungle nymph, one moment to your liking and the next having you scared out of your wits as you try to make it back to civilization without being molested or preyed upon. The male of the duo will make you believe he is a charmingly handsome, well-endowed lover, only to have him draw you into the river and attempt to drown you while he attempts to have sex with you, whether you welcome such a watery aggression or not.

HAUNTED BY SEX DEMONS

Nandor Fodor, in "The Haunted Mind" (New York: New American Library, 1968), states on page 180: "Many people today are skeptical of the very idea of the incubus/succubus under the assumption that spirits cannot assume tangible form. But the history of the occult shows this to be false. In addition, there are many incubus/succubus experiences associated with poltergeist phenomena. Robert Curran's book 'The Haunted: One Family's Nightmare' recounts a contemporary example of an incident with a succubus (a devil that rapes a man).

"In this case, Jack Smurl of West Pittston, Pennsylvania, who had moved with his family into a house inhabited by a poltergeist, was attacked by a succubus. Smurl described the succubus as a woman 'around 65 or 70' with 'serpentine-snake-

SCREWED BY THE ALIENS

like scales' who paralyzed him in some way, had sexual intercourse with him, and left him covered with a pungent, sticky fluid. The demonic nature of the poltergeist was seen not only in its stench, but also in its destructive ability, its desire to harm people, its aversion to Christian items, and also in its sexual activity."

Note that this quote comes from a period before the "reptilian alien factor" can be taken into consideration in describing such events, thus leading us to believe that there must be some connection between the occult and UFO phenomena to be found throughout the prevailing literature of the last hundred or more years. Researchers should do a search for more cases of this nature to compare them to what is happening in the field of UFOlogy.

NO ESCAPE FROM THE FAIRY-WOMAN

Jacques Vallee, without a doubt one of the most recognizable figures in the UFO field, for years has made a study of phenomena that could be said to be "outside the box." He has long advocated a more earthbound or parallel universe theory for the origin of the UFO phenomena as opposed to the ETH theory.

Says Vallee in his book "Confrontations": "The medical examination to which abductees are said to be subjected, often accompanied by sadistic sexual examination, is reminiscent of the medieval tales of encounters with demons. It makes no sense, in a sophisticated or technical framework, that any intelligent being equipped with scientific marvels that UFOs possess would not be in a position to achieve any of these alleged scientific objects in a shorter time and with fewer risks."

Vallee draws upon the following case study in his early work, "Passport to Magonia," to illustrate a comparison between the UFO episodes today and those involving occult phenomena from bygone periods:

"There is no gap between the fairy-faith and ufology regarding the sexual question. This is apparent from the study made by Wentz, who records, for example, the following story:

'My grandmother Catherine MacInnis used to tell about a man named Laughlin, whom she knew, being in love with a fairy-woman. The fairy-woman made it a point to see Laughlin every night, and he, being worn out with her, began to fear her. Things got so bad at last that he decided to go to America to escape the fairy-woman.

'As soon as the plan was fixed and he was about to emigrate, women who were milking at sunset out in the meadows heard very audibly the fairy-woman singing this song:

"What will the brown-haired woman do, When Laughlin is on the billows?"

'Laughlin emigrated to Cape Breton, landing at Pictu, Nova Scotia; and in his first letter home to his friends be stated that the same fairy-woman was haunting him there in America.'

SCREWED BY THE ALIENS

"The comments by Wentz on this case are extremely important: 'To discover a tale so rare and curious as this ...is certainly of all our evidence highly interesting. And aside from its high literary value, it proves conclusively that the fairy-women who entice mortals to their love in modern times are much the same, if not the same, as the succubi of Middle Ages mystics."

****

We could probably go on to describe even more obscure entities who want to have sex with you. Unless you come across a true Aryan or Nordic Space Brother, I would recommend that you hold off on having sex with a being who could be out of your league. It might have been beholding in Genesis, but this is the Twenty First Century and most of us probably consider ourselves part of, or sympathetic to, the overall women's movement, and that includes putting sexual predators behind bars where they belong.

Or, in the case of some Ultra-terrestrial hell bent on having its way, I say send them back to hell – if that's where they came from – or off to some other universe that is not parallel to ours.

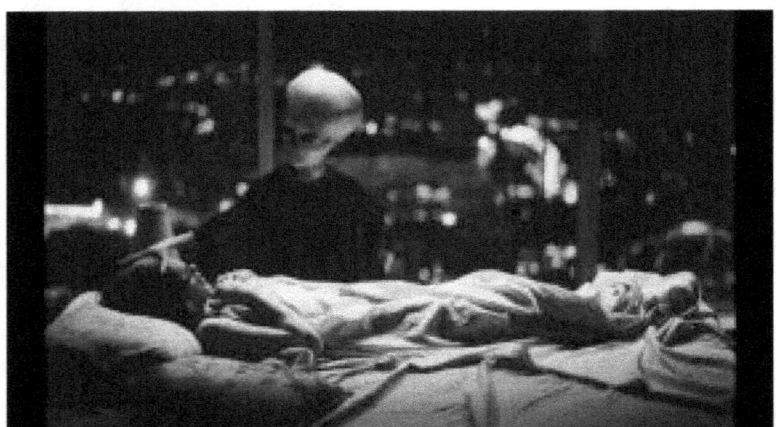

It often begins in the bedroom and ends on an examination table, somewhere that no one will see what is to be done to the unsuspecting.

They come in the dead of night, first to give you pleasure, some say, then to take your soul back with them.

The Sexterrestestrials have fostered an entirely new genre of popular culture, from books to comics to records.

SCREWED BY THE ALIENS

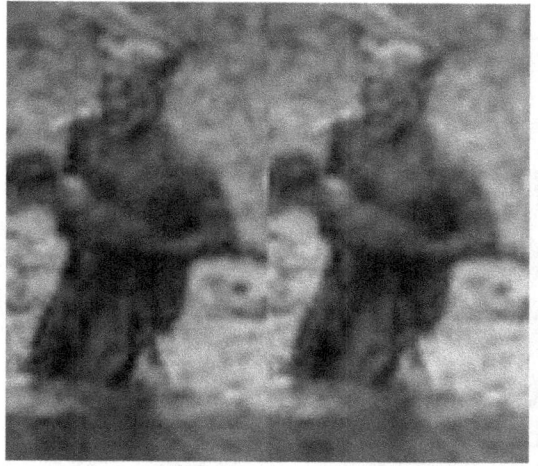

Is this an actual photograph of what could be a "water Incubus" encountered along the Amazon River?

A bedroom invader: "alien" to some – a sexually demented demon to others!

The Tin Tin has a snout that can only be painful no matter how he may wish to use it.

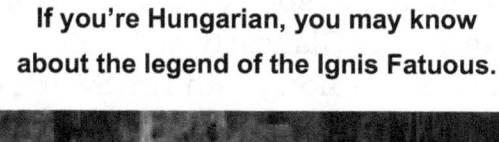

If you're Hungarian, you may know about the legend of the Ignis Fatuous.

SCREWED BY THE ALIENS

Timothy Green Beckley is a UFO and paranormal pioneer. Over the years he has written over 25 books on everything from rock music to the secret MJ12 papers. He has been a stringer for the national tabloids such as the Enquirer and editor of over 30 different magazines. His longest running effort was the newsstand publication UFO UNIVERSE which went for 11 years.

Today he is the president of Inner Light/Global Communications and editor of the Conspiracy Journal and Bizarre Bazaar. He is one of the few Americans ever to be invited to speak before closed door meetings on UFOs presided over by the late Earl of Clancarty at the House of Lords in England. He is co host of Exploring the Bizarre along with Tim Swartz over KCORradio.com and archived on YouTube under "Mr UFOs Secret Files."

SCREWED BY THE ALIENS

CHAPTER 6

GOD OF MY FATHERS: OUR DIVINE SEXUAL HERITAGE
By Hercules Invictus

Many people believe that humanity was created by celestial forces (either singular or plural, perhaps self-directed or maybe even mechanical) at some point in cosmic time. Others believe that our natural evolution was interrupted and that we were modified by advanced intelligences for reasons of their own. We may have been created to serve them, or to assist them in some inscrutable way with their own evolution.

Theories abound and, as Socrates would assert, not one of us truly knows. But we can speculate and delight in sharing (or debating/defending the merits of) our speculations.

As an Olympian, I personally believe that we (perhaps some of us, perhaps all of us) are direct descendants of Zeus, and that Zeus is quite literally our primordial Father. The ancient lore of my people informs me that this is so and I have no reason to doubt it. Though I always strive to maintain an open mind and remain receptive to new ideas, I remain a hard-core traditionalist in many ways.

In the second century CE, Justin Martyr suggested that the children of Zeus (whom the Romans knew as Jupiter) were seeded without sexual union (as was his Savior Jesus Christ). Justin's view was widely supported by pagan mystics and philosophers who insisted that the divine sexual dalliances described in Greek Mythology were purely symbolic. Their opinions remain attractive to many moderns who wish to defend (or revive) the ancient faiths. Although their beliefs are sincere, they are contradicted by the mountains of material preserved through Greco-Roman folklore, literature and art. The Olympians were (and still are) depicted as actively romancing and oftentimes mating with mortal beings. These unions are often fruitful and humanity is periodically blessed with infusions of divine blood.

Zeus is especially renowned for joyously spreading his seed far and wide,

SCREWED BY THE ALIENS

impregnating Titanesses, fellow Olympians, Star Maidens (Pleiads), Nymphs, Muses, Humans and even Mother Earth herself.

OUR HEAVENLY FATHER

The thundering Zeus, Lord of Dark Clouds, was most widely honored throughout the Mediterranean world during the ascendancy of Greece and Rome. The youngest son of the Titans Kronos and Rhea, who ruled Olympus before him, he was raised secretly on the isle of Crete by Amalthea the She-Goat (whose pelt is the mighty Aegis and whose horn is the Cornucopeia) and protected by the fierce and heavily armed Idean Daktyls. As a youth he infiltrated the Titan court and served his parents as Royal Cup Bearer. He then succeeded in freeing his captive siblings, as well as the One-eyed and Hundred-handed children of Earth imprisoned by Kronos. With these, and some help from a handful of disgruntled Titans, Zeus led a rebellion that toppled his father's regime and established his own High Seat on Greece's most holy mountain.

He then divided the governance of our world by drawing lots with his brothers. Zeus won the Heavens, Poseidon won the Waters and Hades won the Underworld. The Earth remained a neutral ground for all.

HOLY FAMILY SECRETS

Zeus and his fellow Olympians are Celestial intelligences, beings of light who can assume various forms to facilitate interacting with us. They are highly evolved Sylphs who dwell in the Aether with other Aerial beings.

The Ruling Council during Greco-Roman times, enshrined in Greek Mythology, was (in alphabetical order) Aphrodite, Apollo, Ares, Artemis, Athena, Demeter, Hephaestus, Hera, Hermes, Hestia, Poseidon, and of course Zeus. Collectively they were known as the Dodekatheon (Twelve Gods). In truth there are numerous Olympians and the Seat-Holders on the Council have varied, even during historical times.

The Olympians have always been associated with the planets and stars. Some of them are still honored through the names of the days of the week and the Seven Heavenly Bodies: the Sun (Apollo and others), Moon (Artemis and others), Mars (Ares), Mercury (Hermes), Jupiter (Zeus), Venus (Aphrodite) and Saturn (Kronos) known to Classical Antiquity. They are often called Planetary Deities in occult literature. Because of this, the case has been made that they are actually alien beings originating beyond our Earth. As they are Celestials this idea has some merit and is well worth exploring. In Astro-Mythology Zeus/Jupiter is honored on Thursdays and is called the Major Benefic as he is beneficial and generous in most of his interactions with humanity. The connection between Olympus and Outer Space has largely entered the popular imagination through speculative multimedia about Ancient Astronauts/Aliens and television shows such as Star Trek and Stargate SG-1.

SCREWED BY THE ALIENS

These Celestials claim to have created us and maintain that they still guide our evolution. They appear to be intimately involved in the everyday affairs of mortals and especially with certain individuals destined to play special roles on the world stage. They also, as noted, intermix with and sometimes incarnate through us.

Like all his kin, Zeus can choose to remain invisible, put on a psychedelic light show or appear in human, animal or hybrid form. In the lore the Thunderer is said to have assumed many such guises whilst wooing his lady loves including bulls, showers of golden rain, snakes and swans.

CELESTIAL SEX, GREEK STYLE

Zeus' unions with mortals are either physical or vividly mimic physicality. Indeed, they are described as intense sexual encounters (sometimes enhanced by special effects). And hands-on selective breeding seems to be the preferred technique for this Olympian's divinization of humanity rather than in vitro fertilization and/or cloning.

Several types of entities, including Space Aliens and the Fae, seem fixated on the human reproductive system and need us, anecdotally, to periodically infuse their dying race with our primitive vitality. Sexual activity of some sort is often described in the literature as well as in modern personal accounts. The offspring of these unions are usually wan or sickly and are sometimes stolen or secreted away by the Others. Olympians, in contrast, seem to embody and express extreme vitality and enjoy sensual pleasure for its own sake. They are not vampire-like beings stealthily stealing energy but instead bestow boons. The Children of Olympus are demigods, future heroes, leaders, visionaries and other extraordinary individuals.

Other Aerial beings who perform experiments, including sexual experiments, on humanity sometimes insist that we are mere vessels or containers and that they have a right to interfere with our lives. A few even maintain that we volunteered for these unpleasant experiences (or gave them our permission) before birth. I have argued, in my article Games of the Gods, published in Timothy Green Beckley's anthology "The MATRIX Control System of Philip K. Dick," that we (or some of us) are but vehicles or projections of the Olympians in the here-and-now. This is reinforced by the ancient belief that our existence is an illusion and that we serve as a form of entertainment or instruction for the Celestials. The Simulation Hypothesis suggests much the same and may shed some light on what these Aliens are attempting to communicate.

THE CHILDREN OF JUPITER

To win over Hera, Zeus appeared to her as a cuckoo bird in distress. This is symbolically significant as the cuckoo deposits its eggs (individually) in the nests of other birds, often replacing a pre-existent egg laid by the host. Once hatched,

SCREWED BY THE ALIENS

the changeling is unwittingly raised by its adopted parent(s) until it can leave to pursue its own destiny.

Many of the god-born are said to be twins, only one of them fully gifted with divine attributes by the Celestials. Perhaps this is an important key (factual or symbolic) to understanding the dynamics of divine souls seeded in human forms and in human environments.

It must be noted that not all of Zeus' divine offspring are immortal. The Celestial and Elemental Children of Zeus sometimes served as Kings and Queens in and beyond the borders of Greece. Many dynasties in Europe, Asia and Africa proudly claimed descent from the Lord of Dark Clouds.

Many of the Children of Jupiter who lived among us subsequently ascended to Olympus and/or were immortalized in the Heavens as constellations.

To list all of Zeus' children begotten by mortal mothers is beyond the scope of this humble chapter. Below is a brief description of the six most famous Demigods fathered by the Olympian Thunderer, individuals who are still spoken of today:

Alexander the Great: In historical times Zeus appeared as a large amorous snake to Queen Olympia of Macedonia and sired Alexandros, who conquered and Hellenized the known world during his brief sojourn of thirty three years on the mortal sphere.

Castor and Pollux: (aka the Dioskouroi) These powerful twins were inseparable in life. Alas, Pollux was immortal and Castor was not. Together they joined the Argonauts and quested after the Golden Fleece, instructing heroes in the manly arts and having many other adventures. Zeus seduced their mother Leda in the form of a Swan. Their sister was Helen of Sparta/Troy. Reluctant to have death divide them, Father Zeus immortalized the brothers as the constellation Gemini.

Dionysus: Semele was a Priestess of Zeus. He spied her bathing in a river while soaring overhead in Eagle form and subsequently courted her. Together they produced Dionysus, who ultimately joined his father on Olympus (displacing Hestia) where he became the god of Wine and Revelry. Dionysus lived a very difficult life. He survived the death of his mother while still in her womb, was torn apart by Titans while still a youth, and was driven mad by Hera and descended into the Underworld while he was still alive. Aside from his revelries, he found comfort in the arms of Ariadne, daughter of Minos.

Hercules: Grandson of Perseus and rightful heir to the throne of the Perseids. The mightiest man who ever lived. Zeus assumed the semblance of Alcmene's husband Amphitryon to seduce her. Their lovemaking spanned three days, Hercules performed Twelve Labors which correspond with the Zodiac, sailed with the Argonauts and defended both Olympus and Hellas during the Gigantomache. Became an Olympian, a driver of the Sun Chariot and was further immortalized as a constellation. Was the first and greatest Pan-Hellenic Hero. Was honored as both

SCREWED BY THE ALIENS

an Ascended Human Hero and a full Olympian God.

Minos: The son of Europa, who was wooed by Zeus in the form of a far-ranging Bull. They had six children together, but only Minos is still widely remembered. Best known for being the King of Crete, breaking his promise to Poseidon and having the Labyrinth built to hide his subsequent shame (in the form of the Minotaur). Now one of three judges in Hades' Underworld.

Perseus: Zeus loved and impregnated Danae, Perseus' mother, in the guise of golden rain that entered through the gated windows of the tower in which her father King Acrisus, fearing the fulfillment of a dire prophecy, had imprisoned her. Perseus slew the gorgon Medusa, rescued the Princess Andromeda, slew two evil kings and became the King of Argos.

Later he, and several of those he knew, made it all the way to the night sky.

Thank you Father Zeus for the Gift of Life

Thank you Mother Hera for the Many Blessings I enjoy

I ask the Lords and Ladies of Mount Olympus for their Wise Counsel

And Loving Guidance with Transforming This World into an Elysium for All!

Onwards!

© Hercules Invictus

About Hercules Invictus

Hercules Invictus is a Lemnian Greek, a proud descendant of Argonauts and Amazons. He is openly Olympian in his spirituality and worldview, dedicated to living the Mythic Life and has been exploring the fringes of our reality throughout his entire earthly sojourn. For over four decades he has been sharing his Olympian Odyssey with others.

Having relocated the heart of his Temenos to Northeastern New Jersey and the Greater New York Metropolitan Area, he is now establishing his unique niche locally and contributing to his community's overall quality of life. Hercules is also recruiting Argonauts to help him usher in a new Age of Heroes.

Hercules currently hosts The Elysium Project, Pride of Olympus and Voice of Olympus e-radio shows on the Spiritual Unity Radio Network. He currently writes for The Magic Happens and Paranoia Magazine, has published two e-books on Kindle, Olympian Ice and The Antediluvial Scrolls, and has been contributing to Timothy Beckley's awesome anthologies.Hercules founded or co-founded Mount Olympus LLP, Olympian Heroic Path, Olympian Shamanic Path, Cosmic Olympianism, Mythic Atlantis, Living Theurgy, the Regional Folklore Society of Northeastern PA and the Center for the Study of Living Myth here in NJ. He also spearheaded many of the real-world Age of Heroes initiatives and the fictive Mythic Adventure tales.For more information please Friend him on Facebook or visit his website: http://www.herculesinvictus.net

SCREWED BY THE ALIENS

Author and researcher, Hercules Invictus

Right: Castor and Pollux

Below: The Children of Jupiter.

Below Left: The Gods of Olympus.

Fae have become a part of our popular culture.

Minos (above) and Zeus (right). Were they ETs?

SCREWED BY THE ALIENS

SEXUAL ABDUCTIONS THROUGHOUT THE AGES
By Dr. Gregory Little

EDITOR'S NOTE: As the saying goes, there is nothing new under the sun. And the same can be said for today's sexual encounters with beings who we suspect are extraterrestrials, but for which we have no real proof. Some researchers have pegged the Ultra-terrestrials as demonic in nature, and point their finger toward Hell and its diabolical ruler, Satan. We won't debate the fact that Satan is a Christian creation and our concept of what goes on in the fiery furnace below needs to be updated (see our chapter on the Shaver Mystery). Dr. Gregory Little has been championing the belief that history is merely repeating itself when it comes to sexual encounters with UFOs and their occupants. The more recent stories are similar to tales from previous eras in which the protagonists (i.e. molesters, rapists, anal probers and impregnators) were thought of in more "mundane" terms: as earthbound spirits, members of the elemental kingdom and interdimensional beings here to satisfy their own warped pleasures not available, perhaps, in their non-physical form.

* * * * * * * * * *

Excerpt from: Grand Illusions: The Spectral Reality Underlying Sexual UFO Abductions, Crashed Saucers, Afterlife Experiences, Sacred Ancient Sites, and Other Enigmas-1994 by Dr. Gregory L. Little

The abduction stories form a continuum with old legends and beliefs ...They do contain a message ...given to us by the hidden parts of our being.— John Rimmer - (The Evidence for Alien Abductions - 1984)

Once upon a midnight dreary, while I pondered, weak and weary, Over many a quaint and curious volume of forgotten lore - While I nodded, nearly napping, suddenly there came a tapping, As of someone gently rapping, rapping at my chamber door.— Edgar Allan Poe - (The Raven)

"We stepped into the fringe of reality," Karla Turner replied to a questioner – after relating her incredible story to an immense group at the 1992 Ozark UFO

SCREWED BY THE ALIENS

Conference. "Our book comes from my journal that I kept (about these events)."

Karla [now deceased; a victim of the insidious cancer many "abductees" mysteriously succumb to – B. B.], who holds a Ph.D. in English, hypnotized her husband Casey in the mid-1980s to attempt to find the source of Casey's anxiety and tension.

Casey, a computer software consultant, had been seeing a therapist at the time and was suffering with a variety of nervous problems. What they found in the hypnosis was not what they expected. Casey had numerous memories of alien contact – sexual contact. One of his earliest memories was a white-haired old woman appearing in his bedroom when he was 13 years old. She had a deeply wrinkled face and deep, piercing eyes. Unable to resist, he had sexual intercourse with her. Casey also recalled other times that creatures entered his bedroom and forced him to have sex.

One such experience left him with claw marks on his back, while another incident in 1987 resulted in a painful scar on the back of his leg. Interaction with the abductors wasn't limited to Casey. Karla told of walking into her home at night when a being grabbed hold of her arm. The creature told her it was her mother, but Karla stated that it looked like a giant grasshopper.

Another time, Karla was coming home through her backyard when she felt like she "had hit an electric fence. I wasn't feeling right...wasn't moving right ...there was a glow everywhere ...I stopped...and saw four gray beings standing side by side in my backyard." "I assumed I was having a hallucination (but) I'm awake - why? I felt I could see through them and they talked to me telepathically. "'Greetings, we are your ancestors,' they said. 'We are a part of you, but we are real.' "I couldn't move as I normally do," Karla continued. "Then two females behind me came up close - they started buzzing. They are giving you some instructions, they told me."

Karla and Casey have become involved with a variety of MUFON investigators since the uncovering of their memories, as well as conducting a variety of their own investigations.

They have somewhat specialized in sexual abductions and been influenced by the popular books "Intruders," "Missing Time," and others. Karla told a story about a grandmother with her young grandson. The grandmother had been a widow for several years when she was forced to drink a liquid handed to her by an alien who appeared in her bedroom late one night. After she drank the thick fluid, she became young again. A reptilian-like alien then attempted to have intercourse with her, but she resisted. Then the alien brought in her dead husband, who began making sexual advances to her. The grandmother had intercourse with the creature that appeared as her husband, but eventually saw that it was a reptilian. After finishing with the grandmother, the reptilians had anal and oral

SCREWED BY THE ALIENS

intercourse with her young grandson.

LINDA MOULTON HOWE'S SEXUAL ENCOUNTER STORIES

At the 1992 Ozark UFO Convention, cattle mutilation expert Linda Moulton Howe also focused on sexual abduction stories.

She told a story about one man who had become so plagued by a particular female alien coming to him each night that he repeatedly masturbated before sleeping so that he would have trouble getting an erection when the aliens appeared.

Howe stated that the aliens are probably collecting genetic material from cattle and humans. In discussing how the beings appear, Howe said that "the air itself is like a curtain they can go behind." They come out of "tears in the air." The "modern" aliens associated with sexual abductions now appear to fall into three broad categories. The traditional grays are nearly always present. Male grays seldom engage in intercourse, but some female grays do. The grays often connect bizarre devices to the sex organs of abductees and insert needles in an apparent attempt to collect sperm and ovum samples. Then there are the more sinister creatures described as reptilian, grasshopper-like, or mantis-like. These creatures, whose sexual organs are described as ice cold, often have intercourse with humans.

Finally, there are creatures that, except for their dress, would be indistinguishable from humans. They are sometimes described as Nordic in appearance – tall blondes with blue eyes.

These abductors have, at times, had intercourse with abductees. All of the appearances taken on by the abductors appear to be fluid and plastic; that is, they can easily change their shape to whatever they wish. Aileen Garoutte, director of the abductee support organization UFOCCI, has interviewed and used regression hypnosis on numerous abductees who have claimed sexual contact with the aliens. One couple was abducted during a drive between Princeton and Penticton in British Columbia, Canada. Two hours of missing time occurred during their trip that was later "remembered" as a "classic" abduction.

Both were given a special drink, medical exams, and had sexual encounters with the aliens. The woman became pregnant as a result of the abduction, though she had been using two different types of birth control. After their abduction she had spots on her body, including over her ovaries, and her husband had a ring of spots across his groin.

Literally dozens of similar stories have been uncovered by UFOCCI) SEXUAL ABDUCTION EXPERIENCES AREN'T NEW

Given the current intense interest in alien sexual encounters, many people seem to feel that such reports are relatively recent.

They aren't. Sexual encounters with alien abductors are not new to ufology.

SCREWED BY THE ALIENS

On October 15, 1957, 23-year old farmer Antonio Boas was plowing a field at his farm near Minas Gerais in Brazil. It was night as Boas was trying to catch up on the plowing. Looking up into the sky, Boas saw a brightly lit red object descending from the sky. It was his third UFO sighting that week.

This time, however, the object landed in his field. Out of the egg-shaped object came four aliens outfitted in metallic space suits with helmets. As the creatures glided toward him, Boas tried to escape on the tractor, but it stalled. Boas jumped off and started running. A few moments later he was captured and dragged into the spaceship.

There he was taken into a circular room where he was restrained while one of the creatures took a blood and skin sample from his chin. Then he was stripped and moved to another room where only a white plastic couch sat in the center of the room. His body was sponged with a clear, oily liquid, and then the four creatures left. A few moments later, clouds of gray smoke filled the room, causing Boas to vomit. Then a hidden slit opened in the wall, through which a beautiful, naked, alien woman walked. She had blond-white hair parted in the middle, large blue eyes, thin lips, high, prominent cheekbones, and a pointed chin. She was under five feet tall. Boas clearly remembered her blood-red pubic hair and her well-separated, pointy breasts. The female began rubbing her body against Boas and he quickly embraced her. According to Boas, they had intercourse two times, during which the alien barked and growled like an animal. After the second time, she got off the couch and walked to the hidden door. She pointed to her stomach and then to the sky. Then she walked out. Moments later, two of the space-suited aliens returned with his clothes. He dressed and was given a tour of the ship, after which he was released. In the month that followed his encounter, Boas became ill with symptoms similar to radiation sickness. In addition, small purplish wounds developed on his hands. In his book "The Ufonauts," Hans Holzer related the May 2, 1968, abduction of teenager Shane Kurz. Under regression hypnosis, Ms. Kurz told of being abducted while walking through a field and being levitated into a saucer. Inside the saucer several gray aliens placed her on a table, stripped her, and rubbed a thick liquid on her. She was told that the liquid was a stimulant and that she was being tested for pregnancy with a device that was lowered onto her.

Then the leader told her that they wanted to make a "half" with her. One of the beings quickly sexually penetrated her. He made animal sounds and a humming noise during the act. Kurz was then released.

Shortly after this incident (which she did not remember at the time) her menstrual period stopped for a year. She had a sudden, unexplained weight loss exactly nine months after her abduction. It was the weight loss that led her to a doctor and eventually to uncovering the memory of the abduction. Budd Hopkins' "Intruders" (1987) and "Missing Time" (1981) are filled with distinctively sexual

SCREWED BY THE ALIENS

abductions. And if you don't look at the long-term perspective of the phenomenon, it is easy to be misled into thinking the sexual abductions are a recent happening: "Intruders" makes what appears to be happening in UFO abductions more clear. Genetic experimentation is being conducted on unwilling human subjects by an extraterrestrial civilization far different from our own... Through the process of interbreeding, the technology involved in producing test tube babies, and cloning, they are producing a hybrid race.

But appearances can be deceiving.

ABDUCTIONS THROUGH THE AGES

UFO-like abductions and alien sexual encounters are nothing new.

Witches supposedly were taken into the air for meetings with the devil. People who had been abducted by fairies were left with distinctive body scars similar to those in UFO abductees.

And the incubus and succubus of medieval times did the exact same things to their human subjects as today's sexually-inclined aliens do to their abductees.

According to fairy lore, fairies create a circular cluster of small bruises as their mark. The phenomenon is known as "fairy bruising" and is a sign of either favor or disfavor. The ring of bruises is often found around the genitals.

They did this, according to various 17th century accounts, by pinching their victims:

If lustie Doll, maide of the Dairie, Chance to be blew-nipt by the fairie. Marston's Mountebanks Masque

"An Encyclopedia of Fairies" (Briggs, 1976) gives numerous ancient examples of fairy abductions.

Almost always a special drink was given to the abductee. This drink, usually described as a thick liquid, was an essential part of the fairy abduction. Women are abducted much more often than men, and some fairies take special delight in repeatedly capturing women for amorous motives. In short, some fairies simply liked having sexual relations with mortals. Fairies abduct their victims through paralysis; then they simply carry (levitate and fly) the abductee away into "fairyland."

Fairyland is always nearby; under normal conditions we can't see or perceive it. The paralysis induced on the victim is how fairies get their abductee to enter fairyland. The modem word "stroke" (meaning paralysis) is derived from the ancient terms "elf-stroke" and "fairy-stroke." Fairies travel in circular globes of light, sometimes called a "will-o-the-wisp." There are so many different types of fairies that going through them would be tedious. Some of them, however, are virtually indistinguishable from what have been described as demons. One particular type, the "bogie," looks a lot like the traditional Bigfoot. Virtually every society has some lore of these "little people" and myths of them forcing their sexual atten-

SCREWED BY THE ALIENS

tions on human victims. Fairy lore has a tradition of thousands of years. Fairies have been said to be abducting humans, human babies, flying in lighted globes, striking paralysis and amnesia on their victims, forcing strange drink on their victims, and having sexual relations with humans for all time.

If we could remove the mythological aspect from fairy abductions and dress them a little differently, the folklore reports of a thousand years ago would be virtually indistinguishable from present UFO abduction reports.

The same thing could be said for the reports of demons. As my eyes fell on the demon drawings in "Plancy's Dictionaire Infernal" (1863), I was struck by their similarity to the famous 1955 Kelly-Hopkinsville UFO case. Imagine the demons as gray in color, and they would also fit the description of the ubiquitous grays in recent abductions. There are many in the UFO field (as well as various religious leaders) who believe that the creatures associated with UFOs are demons. The similarity of some demons to the grays of UFO reports are probably no coincidence. The resemblance between modern UFO abduction reports and ancient accounts of demonic visitations are striking, indeed. Ulrich Molitor's "De Laniis et phitonicis mulieribus" (1489) shows the first known engravings of demons who abduct and then have sexual relations with humans.

Olaus Magnus' "Historia de gentibus septentrionalibus" (1555) contained engravings of the devil and demons carrying women (witches) away for sex.

The early accounts of these are similar to UFO abductions; however, in that era it was not seen as a good thing to happen to you (as contrasted to many UFO abductees who view it as a positive and special experience). In the early days of the church, people who told of having visitations by "demons" were tolerated. Somewhat later, they were fined or removed from the church. It was in the 15th century that the church was no longer content to simply throw the "witches" and "sorcerers" out of the church. From that point onward they sought to wring confessions out of suspected witches and then burn or hang the accused.

To have sex with a demon meant you were a witch or a sorcerer.

Witches almost always had sexual relations with the demons or Satan himself and they were said to have some power over elemental demons. It is the lower orders of the demons that supposedly take on the appearance of UFO-like beings and fairies. In fact, in many of the witch trials in the 15th and 16th centuries, the "lower orders" of demons were described as leprechauns, gnomes, and other fairies. According to this ancient witch lore, Satan and demons had their favorite humans for sex. Both women and men were abducted for sex, but women were favored. Most victims were unwillingly abducted in their bedrooms at night. Many victims described several demons (of different types) being present at the time of their abduction. Some of the demons "stood by," just watching, during the act. The first written mention of Satan himself forcing sex on a victim was probably at the

SCREWED BY THE ALIENS

trials of Artois.

The writer Vignate (1468) chronicled the trial. Here too, was the first mention of Satan's sexual organ as being cold as ice. This statement is similar to what some UFO abductees have said about their abductors who forced sex on them – particularly the insects or grasshopper-like creatures.

Far more frequent was mention of sexual intercourse forced on victims by demons known as incubus or succubus.

"Essentially, the incubus is a lewd demon or goblin which seeks sexual intercourse with women... the corresponding devil which appears to a man is the succubus."

(Dictionary of Witchcraft and Demonology)

Guazzo's (1608) "Compendium Maleficarum" stated:

"(The demon) can assume either a male or female shape; sometimes he appears as a full-grown man, sometimes as a satyr."

St. Augustine firmly believed that demons abducted people and forced sexual relations on them:

"(Demons) have often injured women, desiring and acting carnally with them."

Virtually no one disputed the existence of these sex-seeking demons.

Martin Del Rio (1599) wrote of the reality of the incubus in the "Disquisitionum Magicarum,"

"...to disagree (with their existence) is only obstinacy and foolhardiness; for it is the universal opinion of the fathers, theologians, and writers on philosophy, the truth of which is generally acknowledged by all ages and peoples."

Peter Binsfeld's "De Confessione Maleficarum" (1589) stated, "(The incubus) is an indisputable truth which is not only proved most certain by experience, but also is confirmed by history."

ANCIENT CROSSBREEDING AND GENETIC EXPERIMENTATION

Just like modern UFO abductors do, demons have long been collecting sperm samples from male victims.

According to the ancient reports, the succubus gathers semen from the male victims so that the demon can fully perform the sex act and sometimes impregnate its female victim when acting as an incubus.

In Thomas Aquinas' 13th century book "Summa Theologica," he wrote: "...if sometimes children are born from intercourse with demons, this is not because of the semen emitted by them, or from the bodies they have assumed, but through the semen taken from some man for this purpose, seeing that the same demon who acts as a succubus for a man becomes an incubus for a woman."

It was believed even then that a crossbreeding of sorts was occurring between the demons (fairies) and humans.

SCREWED BY THE ALIENS

Tradition has it that the magician Merlin was the result of crossbreeding between Satan and a human female. And most readers are familiar with the many matings of the Greek and Roman "gods" with humans. Their offspring spurred many of the great legends and myths of old.

For several thousand years there have been reports of alien abduction for sexual purposes. Because of the number of reports coming from early church members, much attention was given the phenomenon during the 1200s and 1300s.

Here are a few summaries by the church from this time period:

De Trinitate: "Devils do indeed collect human semen...therefore devils can transfer the semen which they have collected and inject it into the bodies of others."

Bonaventura wrote: "Devils in the form of women yield to males and receive their semen; by cunning skill, the demons preserve its potency, and afterwards,... they become incubi and pour it into female repositories."

Just as in modern UFO reports, the incubus desiring to have sex with a human will adjust its shape to one that lowers the resistance of its victim.

In 1698, Johann Klein reported on a court case where a woman claimed to have been impregnated by her long-gone husband. A creature taking his form appeared to her at night in her bedroom where she simply couldn't resist. Many other victims of an incubus claimed that the incubus appeared to them as a person (deceased) they knew and loved. Some of the most interesting reports about the incubus come from nuns. During the mid-1400s, many nuns in certain sites were victims of incubus attacks, with the nuns often displaying amnesia over the event. The copious amounts of semen present left no doubt that something physical actually happened. Other accounts of incubus attacks leave one with the definite impression that something physical was happening rather than the experience being a purely psychological event. One impressive account had numerous witnesses. The writer Sinistrari wrote of a nun that was locked into a small, nearly barren cell after dinner.

She was alone when they closed the door; shortly thereafter, however, sounds of passion (between two people) came from the cell. When the cell was immediately opened for inspection, no one but the nun was in it.

Another nun then bored a small hole through the wall and was astonished to see a youth "appear" on the bed with the nun. Quietly, the nun gathered other sisters to view the scene in the cell between the locked-up nun and the "youth."

When they went back into the cell, the youth again disappeared. However, the nun confessed that she had been intimate with an incubus for some time and that he appeared as the youth that they had seen. None of the nuns recognized the youth, nor was he seen again. In addition, that report indicated that there was no way that anyone could escape the cell holding the nun. He simply appeared and

SCREWED BY THE ALIENS

then vanished. Another interesting feature of medieval witch reports that parallels modern UFO reports is the so-called Devil's Mark. This is not the same thing as a witch's mark, but is rather a mark conferred upon victims by the Devil himself. According to ancient beliefs, the Devil marks his victims for identification. The mark is scratched on the victim with a talon.

The marks are usually a straight scar in an odd spot, typically not seen without some difficulty, or some sort of a tattoo. Daneau (1564) stated in "Les Sorciers" that,

"(Not a witch exists) upon whom (the Devil or a demon) doth not set some note or token of his power and prerogative over them."

Sinistrari's "De Demonialitate" stated that the mark of the Devil "is imprinted on the most secret parts of the body."

Were we not in "modern" times, the marks seen on many UFO abductees would be seen as the marks of the Devil.

Cuts on the back of the leg, purplish circular spots, bruises, circles of warts and spots surrounding the abdomen and genitals, facial holes and nasal cavity holes all would have qualified. These were the exact same marks and areas of the body used for the Devil's mark.

These are also similar to the "fairy bruises."

MUSINGS ON ABDUCTIONS

For a number of reasons, most people studying UFO abductions are deeply disturbed by the parallels between ancient and modern UFO abduction reports.

They are so disturbed that they refuse to even see that any relationships exist. I am astonished at how many contemporary investigators – professionals who should know better – simply refuse to see the historical perspective of this phenomenon.

It is easy to be smug and say, "This is different, we aren't superstitious anymore, these are modern times." But in 500 years a lot of what we deeply believe will be laughed at and ridiculed.

Many, many people want to believe that UFOs are crafts from other worlds carrying advanced extraterrestrial beings. Many want to believe that the sexual abductions represent genetic experimentation and crossbreeding by extraterrestrials. The simple fact is that believing that is far more comforting than accepting the possible reality of what has been described in the prior few pages.

Most of us don't want to really believe that there are actual beings that exist that have been called "demons" or "fairies" or a "devil." Contemplation of such possibilities is deeply disturbing. It touches the darkest and most remote areas of our psyche. It energizes the most fearsome and powerful psychological processes of our minds. "Nuts-and-bolts" ufologists avoid studying or even acknowledging

SCREWED BY THE ALIENS

abductions by stating that these aren't "true" UFO reports.

I have heard numerous ufologists state over and over, "We know these (UFOs) are physical craft, they are spaceships. The psychic and parapsychological stuff doesn't have anything to do with these craft. Anything but what I'm studying is 'New Age' bunk."

It's as if they stick their noses down and look at the little piece of the gigantic puzzle before them, refusing to open their eyes to the fact that they are ignoring the big picture. It is important to understand that I am not saying that UFOs are piloted by demons. I am not saying that fairies and demons are the rapists who force themselves on their abducted victims. There is a real problem with terminology here – most of us have a preconceived idea of what a fairy or a demon is, and I really don't want to conjure up that image. What I am saying is that there is a process that has been ongoing – probably for all of humanity's history – that manifests itself through the appearance of archetypal creatures and beings. John Keel was one of the first to recognize this. Others, including Vallee, Clark, and many British ufologists have long pointed out the resemblance between modern UFO reports and the ancient traditions.

It doesn't really matter what we call the process underlying UFOs, abductions, and all of the related phenomena, but it is important to see that they all tie together.

Even the dreaded and paranoia-producing "government" has long-recognized this connection in their earliest reports (although changes in policy precluded too much future mention of it). John Keel's "UFOs: Operation Trojan Horse" cites the preface from a 1960s publication by the U.S. Air Force Office of Scientific Research called "UFOs and Related Subjects: An Annotated Bibliography."

In that report it was stated: A large part of the available UFO literature is closely linked with mysticism and the metaphysical. It deals with subjects like mental telepathy, automatic writing, and invisible entities, as well as phenomena like poltergeist manifestations and possession...

Many of the UFO reports now being published in the popular press recount alleged incidents that are strikingly similar to demonic possession and psychic phenomena which have long been known to theologians and parapsychologists.

ABDUCTIONS AND THE PARANORMAL

In July 1990, ufologist Brent Raynes published the results of a statistical survey he conducted on 46 people who reported contact with or sightings of UFOs in the publication "UFO Perceptions." A little over a quarter of them were abductees, with the rest having some close contact with UFOs.

Raynes' survey clearly showed that people who have any sort of UFO experiences also have a variety of other "paranormal" experiences.

SCREWED BY THE ALIENS

Here are some of the results:
- 87% had repeating psychic experiences
- 72% had telepathic experiences
- 70% had more than one UFO experience
- 70% reported some precognitive experiences
- 63% reported "out-of-body" experiences
- 59% reported experiences with poltergeists

In addition, Raynes conducted a survey of his UFO percipients' medical and psychological histories.

Most of his medical findings were within normal expectations of a sample of adults randomly drawn from the population. However, the psychological findings appear to strongly suggest a Post-Traumatic Stress Disorder (PTSD) cluster of findings.

Here are a few findings from Raynes' extensive statistical list:
- 4% admitted to drug abuse
- 7% had been institutionalized at some point for mental problems
- 9% admitted to alcohol abuse
- 17% had asthma
- 20% admitted to suicidal impulses
- 22% were sleepwalkers
- 26% engaged in compulsive behaviors
- 28% experienced amnesia
- 28% experienced severe depression
- 35% had insomnia
- 37% had anxiety attacks

In recent years, PTSD has become one of the favorite diagnoses of recovery-oriented mental health professionals.

When the symptoms are seen, childhood abuse (sexual, physical, and emotional) are often immediately suspected. Many professionals (myself included) view this quick diagnosis tendency as a temporary fad; however, there is no denying the trauma that childhood abuse inflicts upon its many victims. Rick Rotter, a former MUFON Section Director, suggested to me that all UFO abductees are reliving a form of post-traumatic stress syndrome. This is not really a new idea. But what was rather unique about Rick's idea was that he felt abductees were experiencing the abduction because of long-standing trauma due to childhood sexual abuse. That is, the memory of a UFO abduction (and the sex that occurs during the abduction) represents a reliving of a childhood memory of an adult human who perpetrated sex abuse on the young child.

SCREWED BY THE ALIENS

Because the memory of the person perpetrating the abuse (usually the child's father, mother, grandparents, or other relative) is so traumatic, their memory is twisted and adjusted so that a "monster" or otherworldly creature is believed to have performed the act on them. "Inner Child Theory" and other pop psychology beliefs relate to this idea. A review of classic abduction cases can certainly lend some support to this view. Just reading the sexual abductions in the beginning of this chapter can support this belief.

The problem is that perhaps somewhere between 10% to 25% of the entire population has had some form of childhood sexual abuse. (There is great disagreement as to the reliability of childhood sex abuse statistics – virtually all should be seen as unreliable guesstimates.)

Thus, statistically speaking, 10% to 25% of abductees should show childhood sexual abuse. Most abductees are screened for childhood sexual abuse and the results seem to show that between 10% to 25% were victims – not the much higher numbers expected with the sexual abuse trauma hypothesis. I have more than a passing interest in childhood sexual abuse. I co-authored a chapter in a medical text, "Sexology" (Bianco & Serrano, 1990), on treating sexual abuse disorders and co-authored another paper in a hypnosis journal on it. Alcoholism, drug abuse, and various relationship and personal problems are quite frequently seen in victims of childhood sexual abuse – therein lies my professional interest in the issue.

But are UFO abductions related to it? Not in my experience or my colleagues' experience. Because childhood sexual abuse is a hot topic right now in recovery circles, it is invoked for virtually every single problem seen in adults.

Victims' groups (sometimes called survivors' groups) believe that almost every physical and medical problem, relationship difficulty, psychological problem, and career problem is caused by childhood sexual abuse. When someone is seen with any kind of problem, they say that it must be as a result of childhood sexual abuse.

What this boils down to is this: Ufologists investigating abductees should almost always see the symptoms of PTSD if the abduction was experienced as traumatic by the abductee. But PTSD symptoms only indicate that some sort of trauma occurred – not what the trauma was.

Because an undetermined percentage of people (probably between 10% to 25%) were victims of childhood sexual abuse, that same percentage should show up in people who claim UFO abductions. Today, most ufologists investigating abductees screen out the abductees who have experienced childhood sexual abuse. Most professionals who have investigated ufology to any depth agree that the childhood sexual abuse problem has next to nothing to do with UFO abductions. I agree with most professionals on this. Rotter's Sexual Trauma Hypothesis bears a striking resemblance to another abduction explanation. In the

SCREWED BY THE ALIENS

early 1980s, an English professor, Dr. Alvin Lawson, suggested that abductees are reliving the trauma of birth. Here, "the fetus is unwillingly taken from a place of security (the womb) to an uncontrollably unknown world (the outside)." (Little, 1984)

Lawson explains the humanoid abductor's appearance as symbolically representing a fetus. Of course, when you are born you can't see your appearance (as a fetus). And all of us were born – so we might expect many more people to have abduction experiences.

Few people today take Lawson's hypothesis seriously.

ABDUCTIONS – SEPARATING WHEAT FROM CHAFF

There is no doubt that a lot of abductions have occurred.

The 1992 Roper Survey suggested that at least 2% of the population has been abducted. Thus, over 5 million Americans alone may have had the experience. Are there really that many visitors from other worlds here? If 2% of the world's population has been abducted over the last 40 years (as has been suggested by ufologists), then at least 90 million people have been abducted in the world.

This means the clever aliens are grabbing 2.25 million of us each year (assuming we each get to have only one abduction).

Over 6,000 abductions are then occurring each day with about 257 abductions occurring each and every hour.

· Are all of these abductions caused by extraterrestrial beings flying around in craft? Or do they represent something else?

· Are modern UFO abductions just a modern version of a phenomenon that has occurred and been documented over thousands of years?

I am certain this is what they are.

Before the modern era of UFOs, those who claimed contact with non-human entities were placed in occult, spiritualistic, apparitional, hallucinatory, psychotic, or pixilated categories. Some ufologists – again, those who adhere to the extraterrestrial hypothesis – argue that abductions aren't part of the UFO phenomenon. They are wrong. For abductions are an integral part of the UFO myth.

Abductions are almost always cited as evidence of alien contact, and ufologists will use cases that fit their theory while discarding the rest as unrelated, purely psychological, or hoaxes.

This is another example of selective perception and confirmation bias – attending to only those facts or tidbits of information that already confirm your beliefs. It's time that we began fitting all of the pieces of the gigantic ufology puzzle together.

It's time we recognize that we are interacting with something that is very real, but it's not alien extraterrestrials.

SCREWED BY THE ALIENS

SUGGESTED READING

PEOPLE OF THE WEB: WHAT INDIAN MOUNDS, ANCIENT RITUALS AND STONE CIRCLES TELL US ABOUT MODERN UFO ABDUCTIONS, APPARITIONS AND THE NEAR DEATH EXPERIENCE

THE ARCHETYPE EXPERIENCE: RESOLVING THE UFO MYSTERY AND THE RIDDLE OF BIBLICAL PROPHECY USING C.G. JUNG'S CONCEPT OF SYNCHRONICITY

PATH OF THE SOUL

LIGHT QUEST

ABOUT DR. GREG LITTLE:

Dr. Greg Little has a master's degree in psychology and a doctorate in counseling & educational psychology from Memphis State University (now the University of Memphis). He is a Nationally Certified Psychologist specializing in criminal treatment since 1975. His treatment programs for criminal personality, substance abuse, trauma, and veterans are in use in all 50 states and in 8 countries. He is author or coauthor of 64 books and has been featured in 14 documentaries on History, History2, Discovery, National Geographic, SyFy, MSNBC, and the Weather Channel. His 3 books on UFOs (1984; 1990; 1994) are considered to be

classics in the field and incorporate plasma physics and concepts from Carl Jung into his ideas. Since 1982 he has been active in writing about Native American mounds and spiritual practices and spent over 10 years investigating underwater sites in the Bahamas and ancient sites in Central America. He is the author of the authoritative Illustrated Encyclopedia of Native American Indian Mounds & Earthworks (2009, 2nd edition 2016) and Path of Souls (2014), which reveals the meaning of mysterious symbols found on ancient mound culture artifacts and how a death ritual that sent souls to the stars was performed.

SCREWED BY THE ALIENS

A sex-crazed Incubus attacks an unwilling partner.

Men were often teased by a Succubus taking human form to lure them into intercourse.

In historical accounts, women found themselves at the mercy of slimy creatures instead of greys and reptilians.

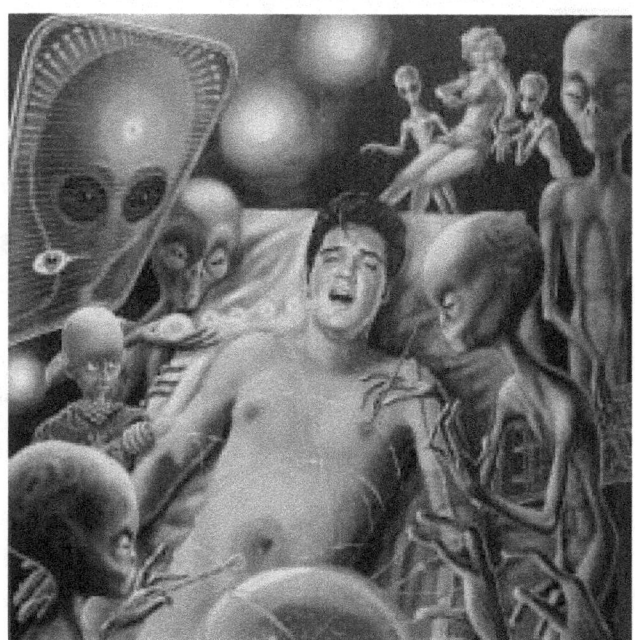

Today's "aliens" are more forthright with their demands.

SCREWED BY THE ALIENS

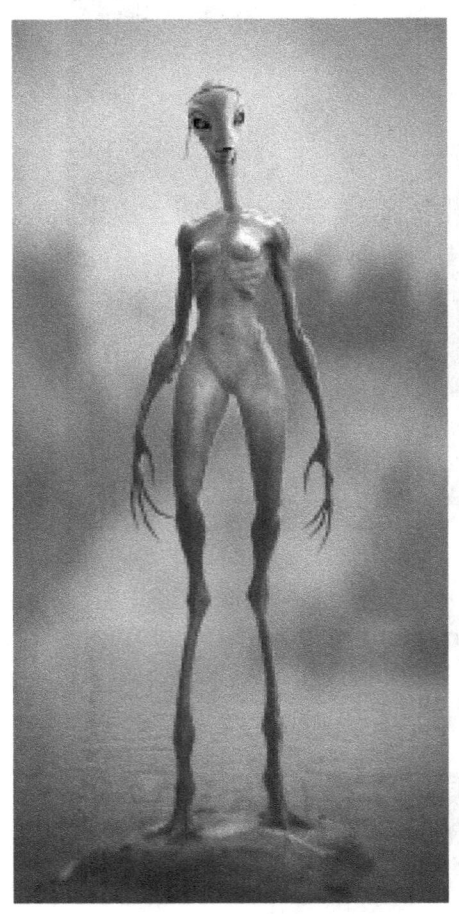

SECTION THREE
THOSE AMAZINGLY SEXY FLYING SAUCER PEOPLE

Chapter Eight: Sex and Saucers
By Nigel Watson

Chapter Nine: Intergalactic Sex
By Brad Steiger

Chapter Ten: Bedroom Invaders
By John Keel

Chapter Eleven: A Flying Saucer Love Story
By Tim Swartz

SCREWED BY THE ALIENS

SEX AND SAUCERS
By Nigel Watson

EDITOR'S NOTE: An easy, breezy step into sex and flying saucers, Lab 101. Watson is a topnotch – and perhaps sometimes over the top – British researcher, a modern day Charles Fort. Nigel Watson has researched and investigated historical and contemporary reports of UFO sightings since the 1970s. He is the author of such books as "Portraits of Alien Encounters" (VALIS, 1990), "Phantom Aerial Flaps and Waves" (VALIS, 1990), "Supernatural Spielberg" (with Darren Slade, VALIS, 1992), editor/writer of "The Scareship Mystery: A Survey of Phantom Airship Scares, 1909-1918" (DOMRA, 2000) "The UFO Investigations Manual" (Haynes, 2013), and "UFOs of the First World War" (The History Press, 2015). He has also written for numerous books, publications and websites, including Magonia, Paranormal Magazine, Fortean Times, Wired, Flipside, How It Works, All About Space, Fate, Strange Magazine, Beyond, History Today, Aquila, Alien Worlds, UniLad, The Unexplained, Flying Saucer Review, UFO Magazine India and UFO Magazine (USA).

****

Villas Boas's famous story of encountering a lady in a flying saucer – actually, it was egg-shaped, which emphasizes its relationship with creation and birth – is not the only one concerning sexual intercourse with aliens in South America.

One night in 1976, cowman Liberato Anibal Quintero had an inexplicable impulse to go outside his home near El Banco, Colombia. He was rewarded by the vision of a beam of light in the sky. Then he saw a large, luminous, egg-shaped craft land nearby. Several small beings came out of this object and captured Quintero. As he struggled to escape, he suddenly became unconscious.

The next thing he knew he was naked and being massaged by three naked women inside the UFO. He made love to one of the women, whom he described as insatiable. The woman was short, with well-formed small breasts, soft skin, but no visible navel, and was very hairy. All-in-all, Quintero found her attractive. She

SCREWED BY THE ALIENS

barked like a dog during intercourse, and these barks were answered by barks from elsewhere on the ship. He was given a yellow-color drink that gave him the stamina to make love to the other two women. After this, he was knocked unconscious by an injection in his back. On regaining consciousness, he found himself lying on the grass outside his home. Though it does include doorway amnesia, it sounds suspiciously like a copycat of Villas Boas's story except that Quintero had three barking women instead of one. (1)

BLUE BEAM FROM THE SKY

In the town of Pelotas, Brazil, Jose Inacio Alvaro was studying at home in the early hours of 3 March 1978, when he saw a thin blue beam of light in the sky. The next thing he knew, it was 4 am, and he was in a street a long way from his home. He had no knowledge of what had happened for the past two hours.

Confirming the UFO connection, there were reports of a disk shaped UFO in the area that night, and one person said they saw Jose Inacio laid out in the street that morning. He offered to help him but he just got up and walked off like an automaton.

He recollected under hypnotic regression that in this "missing" period he was in a bare, circular room where he found himself naked with a tall, dark-haired and equally naked woman. She touched his forehead and said that he was safe. He quickly responded to her caresses and they had sexual intercourse on a net-like structure. His description of their sexual act was so graphic that the researchers erased the tape of the hypnosis session. (2)

The next incident occurred in the town of Botucatú. Juan Valerio da Silva went outside to get some water, and the next thing he knew it was a few hours later and he was naked and covered in oil. To find out what happened to him on the evening of 30 November 1982, he was hypnotically regressed. He recalled being stripped and being forced to have sexual intercourse with a dark-skinned woman, who had long black hair. In what he called "this strange place" tattoos were etched into his skin. After this incident he had several other encounters with these aliens and he obtained telekinetic powers. In addition, he was told that his eldest son was the product of alien genetic experimentation.

MECHANICAL MEN

Another sexual encounter occurred on 28 June 1979, at 3 am, when Antonio Carlos Ferreira was working as watchman at a furniture factory. His experience in the city of Mirassol, Sao Paulo, Brazil, was recalled under hypnotic regression conducted by Walter K. Buhler, who was involved in the investigation of Villas Boas's encounter.

The encounter began when Ferreira saw three small beings come towards him just moments after a strange light had landed nearby. They wore helmets, tight-fitting suits and what looked like breathing equipment. They paralyzed him

SCREWED BY THE ALIENS

with a red beam of light and carried him to a disk-shaped craft, which was parked where the light had landed. This craft took him into space where he was transferred to a larger ship. His captors seemed to be "mechanical men," who left him with two humanoid beings.

One of these beings had dark skin and red hair; the other had lighter skin with black hair. They did not have eyelashes or eyebrows, and both had wide, thick lips, large slanted eyes, and sharply defined chins.

These beings put him on a couch in a small room and told him by telepathic means that he would not be harmed. Just as he felt calmer, a naked woman appeared. Unlike Villas Boas's attractive space woman, Ferreira's had bad breath, small breasts, a cold body, dark skin and a large chin. He found her ugly and repulsive.

As the aliens tried taking off his clothes Ferreira fought back, and they had to resort to subduing him with an injection. They coated him with amber oil, and then put the woman on top of him. After the sex act, he was again coated with this oil.

The use of oil compares with the Villas Boas and Juan Valerio da Silva stories. Like Villas Boas's space woman, Ferreira's also had red pubic hair. At one time during his capture he had difficulty breathing and he was given a drink that helped him breath normally. The aliens said they were from another planet and that they would return to show him his hybrid child at some future date. He had further abductions in 1983, but he has no memory of what they did to him on those occasions.

GENETIC SAMPLES

Eelias Seixas said he was abducted with two other men on 25 September 1980, in Goias State, Brazil. The main part of his encounter could only be recalled under hypnosis. This revealed that two 6-foot-tall Asiatic-looking entities took hair samples and inserted needles with wires attached to them into his fingers. This sounds very much like the examination process the abductees Betty and Barney Hill went through.

Then the naked abductee was put on a table, where he was sexually aroused by images put into his mind. His semen was collected by a tube placed over his penis (this is also something that is alleged to have been done to Barney Hill).

During the abduction, the aliens told him he was required for genetic purposes and that they would implant something in his head to keep track of him. The painful and disturbing procedure put Seixas off sex for the next few months, and sometimes he heard things in his head at night.

Timothy Good and Dr. Richard Haines interviewed Sexias in 1988 and found him to be an impressive witness and thought he told the truth. (3)

It is interesting to note that all these sexual encounter reports emerged after

SCREWED BY THE ALIENS

the Villas Boas story was published and discussed by ufologists in the mid-1960s. Ufologists, as well as UFO percipients, were now prepared to talk and write about such experiences.

UFO researchers Brad Steiger and Joan Whritenour related an account of an unnamed Californian woman who said she was raped by a UFO occupant in the 1960s. As a result of this encounter, she gave birth to a stillborn baby. Her doctor confirmed that this was true and that the baby seemed to be the product of dubious breeding. Unfortunately, this is all we know about this incident, but it does anticipate the type of case that became the focus for Budd Hopkins' and David Jacobs' abduction research (4)

HYBRID BABIES

Jean Sheldon, a Michigan girl, said that in the summer of 1966, she was seduced by some spacemen. A 50-foot diameter, silvery disk landed next to her parked car, and a levitation beam drew her into the craft. Inside she was confronted by three 5-foot-tall, male humanoids who were stark naked. As she noticed that they had green eyes, she heard these telepathic words echo in her mind, "My dear earth woman...we wish to mate with you. It will be easier on your personality if you do this willingly..."

Joan was stunned by the boldness of this request, and before she could react they led her to a bed-like machine. They eagerly stripped her and for an hour she had sexual intercourse with all three humanoids, more than once.

Although she confessed that she had been very excited sexually by her unusual encounter, she admitted that on reflection, the experience brought about "spasms of unnatural delight mixed with shame and revulsion."

These aliens informed Jean that their two races were compatible, and that their mating had been in the interests of scientific experimentation. (5)

That same year, Miss Marlene of Melbourne, Australia, said: "Believe it or not, I was held captive in a flying saucer, raped and made pregnant by a man from outer space." This chain of events began on the night of 11 August, when she walked alone to a small country store for some cigarettes. A strange humming sound preceded the appearance of a "weird" light in the sky. Then she saw a silvery disk, 50 feet wide by 10 feet high, land about 30 feet in front of her. She said: "A sliding door opened and a man – a tall, handsome man wearing a sort of loose-fitting metallic green tunic – stepped out. He stared at me with eyes that seemed to give off light rays. I wanted to scream – but I was petrified."

During a telepathic conversation which followed, the spaceman told how she had been selected to become the first woman on earth to have a child by a man from his planet. They then went inside the man's craft, where they had sexual intercourse.

When leaving the craft, she fell over a switch and became unconscious. On

SCREWED BY THE ALIENS

recovering, she found herself alone in the field with a burnt ankle. Returning to her friends, Marlene was surprised to learn that she had been missing for seven hours. In support of her story, a large indentation was found in the field where the craft had landed.

A local doctor said that her burn was not something you would get in a field but did not shed any more light on the matter. We are informed that she did become pregnant, presumably as a result of this extraterrestrial union, but nothing more is known about her child. (6)

PHANTOM GASSER

1966 was a busy year for such incidents. John Keel reported that a space man, wearing a long white robe, grabbed a schoolteacher and took her away in a black Cadillac. She was rendered unconscious by a spray of gas, and then she found herself inside a flying saucer. It was here that a well-endowed space man raped her. (7)

From 1966 to 1967, Keel kept getting all sorts of cryptic messages and predictions from a network of silent contactees. One of his contactees, called Jane, was informed that women were being artificially inseminated to produce special children for the aliens. After that he came across a number of pregnant women, but he discovered that they all suffered from phantom pregnancies. He thought that the aliens or the phenomenon that controlled them was playing tricks with him, yet abductees suffering phantom pregnancies have continued to the present day. (8)

PULSATING BLUE LIGHT

Dr. Johannes Fiebag, a German abduction research specialist, has investigated abduction reports in Austria, Switzerland and Germany. One of his abduction cases involved a twenty-one-year-old man who lived in Switzerland. On the night of 10 May 1994, he woke to see a pulsating blue light in his bedroom. He felt like he was floating, but he could not remember anything else about this incident.

Under hypnotic regression, he recalled being on a table when a dark-eyed, slim, white skinned, bald woman climbed on top of him. Despite feeling sick, he became aroused and had sex with her. He also had sex with a second woman and then a third one who looked more human. The experience left him feeling traumatized. The man had a history of encounters since childhood. (9)

PHANTOM PREGNANCIES

In the 1980s, I met and interviewed Martin Bolton (pseudonym), who had visions of, and telepathic communications with, three young space women. On their behalf he window-shopped for female attire and watched pornographic films.

These ladies were the good aliens; the bad aliens beamed pain to his brain and for a three-year period stretched his penis during the night. On several occasions they afflicted him with phantom pregnancies. It seems like he was being

SCREWED BY THE ALIENS

punished for lusting after the alluring space women, whom he could never attain. (10)

Bolton's case is not exceptional. According to John Keel, a rumor claiming contactee Woodrow Derenberger was pregnant spread around the Ohio Valley. After encountering an alien called Ingrid Cold, from the planet Lanulos. Derenberger received regular telepathic messages and visits from Cold and other aliens, His encounter took place on Interstate 77 near Parkersburg in November 1966.

In 1967, he was taken by Cold's spaceship on a return flight to Brazil. Later he got to visit their home planet. Lanulos was a pleasant place occupied by semi-nude people. In this context, the reports that he was going to give birth to a half-human, half-alien child, who would become a great leader, was not too unusual. Needless to say, this did not happen. (11)

Phantom pregnancies in female abductees are quite common in the literature. Many female abductees do not even realize that aliens have made them pregnant until they are hypnotically regressed, or some event triggers their memory.

PAMELA STONEBROOKE

One such case involves Pamela Stonebrooke. In 1998, she made the shocking announcement that she had had sexual intercourse with a reptilian alien. Her first encounter was in 1993, when she woke up one night and found herself in an odd-shaped, metal-walled, room, surrounded by stereotypical gray aliens with large, black eyes. A woman told her not to be frightened and took her into another room where four girls, who looked like a combination of alien and human, grabbed at her arms and called her Mommy.

Stonebrooke admitted that she had an interest in the paranormal and had taken astral trips to other planets, but when she woke up the next morning, the memory of the alien encounter was much more vivid. Bruises on her arms proved to her that this had really happened and had not been a dream or psychic projection.

This event made her recall other encounters that involved medical procedures conducted in a detached and cold fashion by aliens. She also began to realize that they were responsible for four false pregnancies she had in the past. For the next year and a half, she felt traumatized by these memories, but after that she saw these events as a chance to consider her beliefs and put them into a larger context. After coming to terms with these experiences, she awoke one night to find a handsome, blond man making love to her.

Telepathically the man told her that she was safe, and that he was no stranger to her. He then shape-shifted into a snake-skinned, reptilian alien. The act of sex with him was the best she had ever had, as it combined emotional, spiritual and physical feelings.

Since then, the same reptilian has re-visited her but has not bothered "dis-

SCREWED BY THE ALIENS

guising" himself as a handsome man anymore. Stonebrooke, who was a Los Angeles, California-based jazz singer, said that, partly under hypnotic regression, the aliens had shown her an apocalyptic vision that might happen in the future. She did not regard these encounters as dreams or anything of that nature, though it is significant that she regarded her reptilian alien as familiar and "part" of herself.

The reptilian alien was so familiar because he was a projection of her own psyche and part of her own unconscious mind. This would indicate that these experiences were lucid dreams that fitted in with her interest in New Age topics. (12).

ANOTHER REPTILIAN ENCOUNTER

Juan Rivera Feliberti of Puerto Rico recounted another sexual encounter that has some reptilian elements to it. Back in 1934, he was flying a kite one day when he found himself floated up to a UFO. Inside this craft, he saw a blonde-haired girl who was about six years old. She gave him a small box that he was allowed to take home with him. This device released ape-like entities that he had trouble controlling.

Several years later, he was fishing on a beach when he met her again. She was a young woman now and it was not long before they had sex. Altogether they had sex about four times He noted that her skin was soft but scaly, her breasts were lower than a human female's and she had no pubic hair. (13)

The small box could have proved the validity of his claims, but there is no mention of this being checked or seen by any independent parties.

RAPED BY REPTOIDS

Tara Green reported on her website that she has been raped by reptoid aliens since childhood. Looking back, she thought that injuries she sustained as a child were caused by reptoids who had a large penis. In contrast, human hybrid aliens have a straw-like penis that comes out of a sheath. The hybrids carry out sexual intercourse by pulling the victim's legs apart and inserting their penis. They stare into the eyes of the victim, but they do not make any movements. The victim just feels something instinctively repulsive moving inside her, and then it is all over after about a minute.

Finding these experiences understandably terrifying and traumatic, Green decided to use her website to help women to identify and cope with "Signs of Alien Hybrid Rape." (14)

Prior to this, she created a "Knight's Project" in June 2000 to help women ward off alien rape through the use of magic. They wrote to more than 30 ufologists for their support, but the best response they got was the view that "you can't resist abduction, sorry." With the demise of the Knight's Project, her new website began on 8 August, 2001, where her nineteen point list of indicators of alien abuse

SCREWED BY THE ALIENS

was chilling to behold: This ranged from rips and holes in your underwear, inner thigh bruises, odd pimples, rape fantasies, panic attacks, to fear of sex.

Green admitted that she had two episodes of non-alien sexual abuse at a very young age, so it could be that she had shaped her ongoing fears in terms of alien abuse as a method of coming to terms with these traumatic events. We might also consider Green's website to be a hoax. If so, it did skillfully draw upon the fears of abduction "victims" that have been voiced elsewhere. We should also note that the name Green Tara in Buddhist tradition is the female embodiment of Buddha, who helps to overcome obstacles, saves us from danger and brings fertility.

"A SECRET TO BE MAINTAINED FOREVER"

The harrowing case of a thirty-one-year-old woman only known as Mrs. X occurred near Taunton, Somerset, England. She was driving along a country lane (the B3187) at 11.30 pm on 16 October 1973, when her Mini saloon car's engine and lights failed. As she looked at the engine, she heard a humming sound all around her.

A tall robot placed his hand on her shoulder and she understandably lost consciousness. Briefly she recalled seeing a landed flying saucer in a field, and then she woke to find herself strapped to a table inside a circular room. Three humanoid men who were dressed like surgeons examined her naked body and took blood and nail samples. They left her alone for a few minutes then one of these men returned. He stared at her lower regions for a long time before attaching a pin to her thigh. As the pin had a numbing effect on her body, the male alien had sexual intercourse with her.

Shortly afterwards she found herself standing, fully dressed, beside her car. She got home at 2.30 am. None of the aliens showed any emotion throughout her encounter, nor did they blink or breathe. Her greatest fear was that she had been made pregnant, so she was relieved when she got a negative result from a pregnancy test.

Two months later, two men, who seemed to know all about her encounter, visited her home. They warned her not to speak about this event, and the same message that this was, "A secret to be maintained forever" was given to her in the following three years by telephone, letters and further visits.

These threats ended after a furniture van had tried running Mrs. X off the A38 road between Taunton and Exmouth. Mrs. X finally felt able to tell her story six years later in 1979. (15)

The doorway amnesia, robot, medical examination, paralysis, emotionless aliens and the sinister MIB visitations all sound very familiar. This would be a classic case, except that I have it on very good authority that the whole story is either a bizarre hallucination or an out-and-out hoax.

SCREWED BY THE ALIENS
BREEDING PROGRAM

In David Jacobs' book, "Secret Life," he relates that abductees have been forced to have sex with fellow abductees whilst the aliens watched like voyeurs at a peep show. John Mack's book, "Abduction," reports the recollection of an abductee, who, whilst onboard a flying saucer, transmuted into an alien and then had sex with a female, human abductee.

Several of these cases refer to the aliens carrying out some kind of breeding program. Jean Sheldon and Miss Marlene Travers both claimed they were made pregnant by aliens in 1966. Sometime in the 1970s, an unnamed nineteen-year-old woman in California gave birth to a blue skinned baby with webbed feet. She said it was the product of intercourse with six humanoid beings that came out of a flying saucer whilst she was walking along a beach. Like her baby, they had blue skin and webbed feet.

THE APPLETON AFFAIR

The encounters with aliens experienced by Mrs. Cynthia Appleton of Fenham Street, Birmingham, crosses the contactee and abduction categories, although her Nordic-type visitors remind us of George Adamski's alien visitor Orthon and MIB.

She was given cosmic warnings and told that she was special, but, unlike most contactees, she was not given a mission or a philosophy to promote, and the encounters seemed to be involuntary.

It all started when Mrs. Appleton had a blackout in her sitting room on 16 November 1957. Three days later, an image of a man slowly appeared in front of her.

This apparition scared her, but through telepathy, he told her not to be afraid. He explained that he was from the planet Gharnasvarn (Venus as we know it) and that he was able to communicate with her because she had a unique brain that tuned to his "frequency."

The man was tall with long blond hair. Mrs. Appleton thought he looked like a Greek athlete, presumably because he wore a covered helmet, although his suit of silver foil resembling cellophane must have detracted from this image. He warned her about our use of atomic weapons and our war-like behavior. (16)

In January she got another visit from this man and a shorter man who had curlier hair. They told her they were projections, though on six further occasions they visited her in a large black car with tinted glass (unusual for a car of that period) and knocked on her front door.

On these visits, they ditched their garish silver suits for sober business suits and hats. They provided her with scientific information that included a description of a laser device, before it was invented by human scientists, and a means to cure cancer. She told them this information was too complex for her to understand, but they carried on, giving it to her anyway.

On the last visit, which took place on 18 August, 1958, the tallest alien told her

SCREWED BY THE ALIENS

that she would have a baby weighing 7 pounds, 3 ounces (3.3kg), with fair hair, in May 1959. He said that her husband was the father but the baby was "of the race of Gharnasvarn" and should be called Matthew (meaning "gift from God").

Mrs. Appleton was surprised by this information, yet her doctor confirmed her pregnancy. Virtually on the predicted day (1 June, 1959) she gave birth to a fair-haired boy who weighed only one ounce off the predicted weight. There were no more alien visitations after that and nothing more is known of what happened to the Appleton family. (17)

The original appearances of the beings from Gharnasvarn are more suggestive of ghosts or hallucinations, yet how do we square them with their seemingly physical visitations and their correct prediction of her pregnancy? Now well into adulthood, what has become of Matthew of the race of Gharnasvarn?

On the whole these sexual encounters contain a high level of fear and fantasy. Whether they are factual or not is another matter.

REFERENCES:

1. Gordon Creighton, "UFO, Occupants and Sex in Columbia," Flying Saucer Review, Vol. 23, No. 1, June 1977, 14-18.

2. Scott Corrales, "An Alien Heat: Chronicles of Sex and Saucery," www.geocities.com/INEXPLICATA2000/issue6/2.htm

3. Timothy Good, Alien Liaison: The Ultimate Secret, (London: Arrow, 1992), 79.

4. Brad Steiger and Joan Whritenour, Flying Saucers Are Hostile (New York: Tandem, 1967).

5. Otto O. Binder, Flying Saucers Are Watching Us (New York: Belmont, 1968).

6. Ibid.

7. John Keel, Our Haunted Planet (London: Futura, 1975), 139.

8. John Keel, Visitors from Space (St. Albans: Panther, 1976), 197.

9. K. Wilson, "UFO Abductions In Germany, Austria and Switzerland. A Lecture by Johannes Fiebag, Ph.D," www.alienjigsaw.com/yk2/ufo-abdu.html

10. Nigel Watson, Portraits of Alien Encounters, (London, VALIST, 1990) 165-180.

11. Keel, Visitors from Space,139.

12. Michael Lindemann, "Jazz Singer Tells of Sex With 'Reptilian' Alien," www.cfree.org/Contact/Abduction/Cases/Case007.html

13. Corrales, ibid.

14. Her original website is no longer available, there is a note about her project at: "The Knight's of the Round Table Project Source: Tara Green," www.caus.org/pers_contact/pc101600.shtml

SCREWED BY THE ALIENS

15. Barry King, "The Strange Case of Mrs X. Part 1,"Strange Phenomena, Vol. 1, No. 1, 1979, 13-17.

Barry King, "The Strange Case of Mrs X. Part 2," Strange Phenomena, Vol. 1, No. 2, 1979, 24-28.

Express & Echo (Exeter, England), "Close encounter of an intimate kind," August 23, 1979.

16. Timothy Good, Alien Base: The Evidence for Extraterrestrial Colonization of Earth (New York: Avon, 1998), 194 and 207.

Martin Kottmeyer, "Titium and Aston's CE3K," Magonia Supplement, No. 20, October 1999, 1-2.

17. Jenny Randles, Men In Black: Investigating the Truth Behind the Phenomenon (London, Piatkus, 1997), 59-66.

Andy Roberts, "The Space Baby," Fortean Times, No. 191, Special Issue 2004, 32-38.

British UFO and Fortean researcher Nigel Watson takes us inside the sexy saucer lab 101.

A memorable story and an amazing vocalist: please check out Pamela Stonebrooke on YouTube (Alien Version)
https://www.youtube.com/watch?v=rqF_ED7Oopl

SCREWED BY THE ALIENS

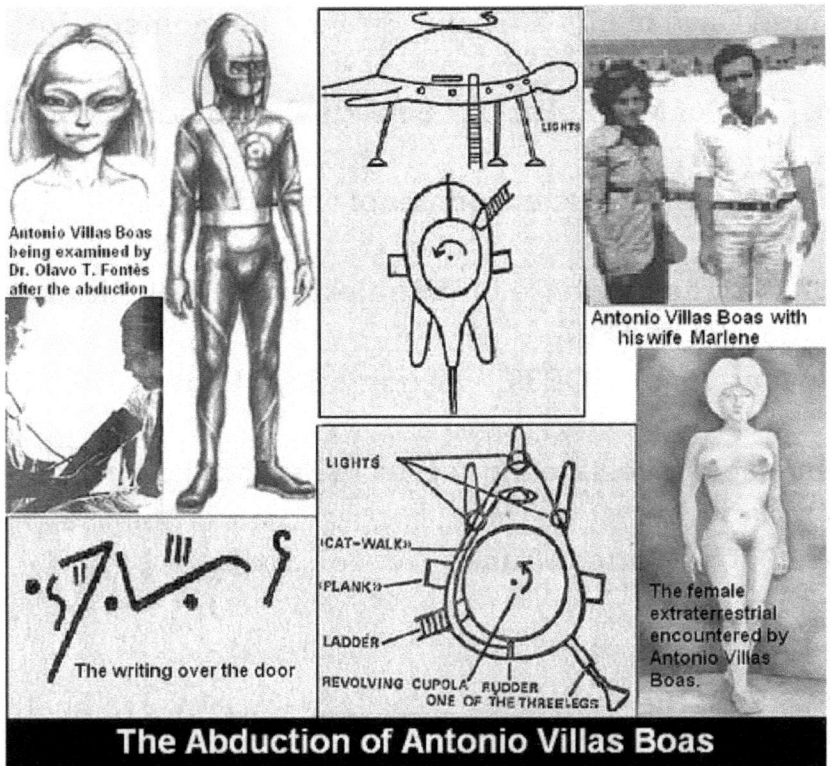

The Abduction of Antonio Villas Boas

Mr. Boas's "incident" with a space woman who wanted sex with him has been translated into just about every language all over the world.

Here is the "proof" that Cynthia Appleton's story is legitimate — a clipping from a British broadsheet (more reliable than a tabloid in the UK).

Jose Inacio Alvaro as a grown man with his own child. He is said to have had more repeated contact with space beings than anyone else in Brazil. Many of them were sexual in nature.

SCREWED BY THE ALIENS

INTERGALACTIC SEX
By Brad Steiger

EDITOR'S NOTE: A dear friend, the late researcher Brad Steiger details the strange forces behind the UFO mystery that have shown a longstanding interest in women – evidenced by bizarre physical examinations, "possessions," and sexual assaults. Why do aliens seem so enamored with our women? Don't they have the ability to "rejoice" in their own kind? There is all sorts of intermingling between the species. Some have a gentle touch, but most are as harsh and dominating as an outlaw biker.

****

The buildings loomed ghostly in the darkness as Maria Moreira and Maria Gracas, both 17 and friends of longstanding, hurried home from evening Mass. Suddenly a dark form leaped out of nowhere and flashed a light at the girls.

Maria Moreira gasped as the light burst in her face like a flashbulb. At the same instant her companion tried to cover her eyes, making a spasmodic sign of the cross.

As quickly as he had arrived, the dark man was gone. But it will be a long time before the citizens of Itabara, Brazil, forget his brief visit. Since the April night when the bizarre encounter took place, the two Marias have become the subjects of scientific and ecclesiastical investigations, have been considered for the rite of exorcism, and have convinced the town that they are possessed by devils.

A few days after being accosted the two girls began to fall into trances – both together and separately. While so entranced, the girls spoke in French, Greek, and other languages no more native to them than Sanskrit. Neither Maria has any formal education and neither has ever spoken any language except their native Portuguese. It is easy, then, to imagine the astonishment of their families, friends, and neighbors when the two began to quote long, philosophical passages from St. Thomas Aquinas and St. Augustine – and in formal, scholarly Latin.

It is likely that some of the Itabara's people wished that all the utterances of

SCREWED BY THE ALIENS

the young unwilling girls were in obscure tongues.

Among persons who flocked to the girls' homes to witness the trance scenes were some whose love lives could not stand the light cast by the dark stranger's victims. Others, whose fingers had played fast and loose with their neighbor's property, also wished that the Marias would recite in a language less commonly understood. Known very well, however, to local priests, who were called in to "drive out the devils," were the obscene Latin epithets bestowed upon them for their pains.

Three months after that fateful April night, on July 17th, Maria Gracas fell into a trance right after the noon meal. By this time her mother's fright had somewhat given way to curiosity. When she heard her daughter mumbling in the bedroom, she put down the bowl she was washing and went to her side. "What is it, child?"

Maria lay prostrate on the bed. Her unblinking eyes were fixed on the ceiling and her mouth quivered. The eyes of the girl's mother darted to the crucifix on the wall. With trembling fingers she crossed herself. "mmm... Uncle Manuel! Look out! Look ... oh!"

Half an hour later Maria Gracas's Uncle Manuel was injured when his vintage auto collided with another car, exactly as Maria had described it to her mother while entranced.

The two unwilling girls baffled both the Church and science. Father Francisco Trombert, a Roman Catholic authority on evil spirits, who investigated the twin phenomena on the orders of his bishop, remarked, "I have been unable to find a satisfactory parapsychological explanation for what has been happening." Father Trombert offered as a possible explanation the theory that the girls might have suffered a traumatic experience while taking part in a séance.

"This case," said Father Trombert, "is unique to me. I have catalogued most of the main phenomena to be found in cases of so-called demon spirits – but this one puzzles me most."

Prof. Raul Marinuzzi, a teacher of parapsychology at the Franciscan Institute of Culture in Belo Horizonte, Brazil, said little more.

Professor Marinuzzi theorized that the strange happenings might be due to "an exceptionally well-developed capacity on the part of the girls for mentally storing things subconsciously."

Perhaps the professor is right. But how would Maria Gracas "store" a future event – like her Uncle Manuel's accident – in her subconscious? Is it significant that neither the religious authorities nor the scientists commented on "the dark man" who apparently precipitated the chain of events surrounding the strange case of the unhappy teenagers? Can he be explained in strictly Freudian terms, a symbol of sex and evil hallucinated by two teenage girls about to cross the boundary of womanhood? Or could the mysterious stranger have been a mani-

SCREWED BY THE ALIENS

festation of UFO intelligence somehow testing, programming, or evaluating the young women?

The flash of light is, I believe, most significant. One thinks of the revelatory experience which is so often prefaced by a "blinding light." In the vernacular we speak of someone having "seen the light." We know that certain split second flashes can place men and women into a mental state similar to trance or hypnotic sleep. A great deal of information can be transferred when one has direct access to the unconscious. And we are learning that knowledge is more readily transferred when accompanied by physical trauma.

Whatever that dark entity did when he flashed the light in the eyes of the two Marias, the one certain thing in a vast catalogue of speculations is that their lives will never be the same again.

Although it seems to be a subject that hardly anyone wants to discuss, the lives of a good many women around the world have been changed because of their sudden interaction with UFO intelligences. Regardless of the investigators who would rather ignore this entire area of research, it would appear that the Great Aerial Mystery has a keen interest in our women.

The reaction of most people to the suggestion that there is often evidence of sexual examination or molestation in connection with certain UFO sightings is a torrent of abuse directed toward the researcher who has dared to utter such "sensationalistic claptrap." In spite of accusations of prurient interest as our sole motivation, such researchers as John A. Keel, Jerome Clark, and I have entered such a highly-charged emotional area as far as our respective reputations will permit. I must mention, however, that the case studies which I shall share in this article are a result of my own research and I hereby absolve my above mentioned colleagues from all responsibility.

In the spring of 1970, a coed in Wisconsin witnessed a low overflight of a UFO while she was parked with her boyfriend in a local lover's lane. The sighting startled them at the time and put a damper on their amorous activities, but by the time they pulled up in front of her dorm, she had calmed down and neither of them mentioned the experience for several minutes before she went to her room.

An hour or so later, she was lying in her bed, drifting off to sleep. With some irritation, she became aware that something was pulling at her bedclothes, then tugging at her leg. She opened her eyes to see a hideous, hairy creature grinning lustfully at her and pulling her slowly across the bed.

"I was paralyzed," she told one of my correspondents. "I could neither move nor cry out. There was no mistaking what plans the grotesque male creature had in mind for me. Then I thought very intensely, 'God save me!' There was a very brilliant flash of light at the ceiling, and the creature disappeared. I wore a cross for a long time after that."

SCREWED BY THE ALIENS

A young career woman from San Diego wrote that she had witnessed what she thought was a UFO. That night, immediately after she had turned off her bed lamp, she heard a buzzing sound around her head. Readers familiar with literature in the UFO and psychic fields will note that many witnesses of both UFO and paranormal phenomena have reported such a buzzing or rasping sound prior to the appearance of either kind of manifestation.

"It moved in circles, and I can only describe it as a bee buzzing. Then it seemed to have a man's voice, and it kept buzzing over and over, 'I love you! I love you!' Whenever I turned the light on, it would go away. The second I snapped the lamp off, it would be back buzzing around my head.

"A few nights later, I had the sensation of someone getting into bed with me, and I heard the sound of breathing beside me. It smelled like rotten seaweed, and I was so frightened that I couldn't move. The next day the bed was wet on that side."

An extremely lengthy letter from a young female chemist told of her sexual liaison with an invisible ufonaut after she had a close sighting of an unidentified flying object.

"I lay on my bed one night, just dozing off. Then I heard the steady tread of footsteps coming up the stairs. I knew the doors' were locked and that I was alone. I lay there in fear, as the footsteps came closer and closer. At last they stopped beside my bed, and as the bedclothes were torn off my body, I wanted to scream, but could not. I lay unable to move as the thing lifted my nightgown and mounted me. I knew as only a woman can know that the thing was male."

Are the above accounts, regardless of how sincerely they may have been expressed, really examples of sexual psychopathology? Sexual repression, frustration, loneliness, and confusion may breed a whole stable of psychological demons to delude men and women who may have become mentally disoriented due to shock, sorrow, or sexual deprivation.

"The next thing happened just before my daughter-in-law was killed in a car wreck. I had been nervous for weeks. It's usually in the summertime, June, July, and August, that these things happen to me the most. This one hot night I was lying on a couch downstairs when all of a sudden I jumped up and ran to the door, as if I was waiting for something to happen.

"I had stood there for only a short time when I had a vision of a police car driving up to our house with its flashing red light shining in my eyes. The light hurt my eyes, and I heard a man's voice shouting something about death.

"I got so upset that I went to Dr. Mason. I told him about the phantom police car and the red light. He could see the red marks around my eyes; but, of course, he wouldn't believe my story.

He sent me to the hospital for five shock treatments. [UFO eyewitnesses

SCREWED BY THE ALIENS

are often victims of conjunctivitis and other types of eye inflammation – author.]

The witness was asked, "You mean the red marks around your eyes that I can still see first appeared after the visitation of that phantom patrol car?"

Mrs. Adams: "Yes, that was in 1965. Right away my eyes started itching and bothering me, and then these red ridges appeared. They've been there ever since. [That is, for five years – author.]

But, anyway, the hospital didn't help me, because I continued seeing the red lights flashing, even while I was under treatment.

"Then I found out that my daughter-in-law was driving my son to work in the mornings, and I knew that she was going to be the member of the family who was going to be killed. I told Dr.

Mason this and he wanted to put me back in the hospital. But on August 31st that year she was killed instantly as she was returning home after taking my son to work."

The witness was asked, "How did your family react to the memory of your premonition after it had been fulfilled?"

Mrs. Adams: "They didn't want to talk about it."

"What about this walking sound that you hear?"

Mrs. Adams: "It sounds like it starts back at the front end of the hall and comes to the top of the stairs. I think the footsteps sound like a male."

"Any cold drafts or cold areas that you have noticed?"

Mrs. Adams: "Oh, yes. And once I saw what appeared to be a man in a heavy sweat shirt walking up the stairs. I thought at first it was my husband, but then I heard him coughing in the downstairs bathroom."

"Have you ever seen any lights?"

Mrs. Adams: "Yes, I have awakened sometimes and I've seen lights. That happened last night."

(Worley, the researcher asking the foregoing questions, accompanied Mrs. Adams down to the basement workshop where he and his research assistant were able to speak to Mr. Adams. Worley comments: "One gained the impression that the man of the house could tell us a great deal more, but he preferred to keep busy at his work in the basement and ignore things he couldn't understand." Worley gained admissions from Mr. Adams that he had heard screams on two occasions, walking sounds quite often, and the noises of the stairs squeaking and various doors slamming.)

Mrs. Adams: "Every Christmas we've been in this house something strange has happened. It seemed like there was some kind of presence here last Christmas. After everybody left and went home that night, my husband and I sat alone in the living room. It was real cold that night, and, of course, the doors were closed

SCREWED BY THE ALIENS

tight.

"All at once something that howled like the wind came in through the front door. My husband looked around at the front door, but I knew it wasn't open. It howled through the house and went out the back. It was just like some wind blew through the house. For some reason I started crying, and I cried for three days. It was just like some kind of presence had come in."

Worley telephoned Mrs. Adams again on June 4, 1970. He was told that there had been no developments since December 1969, with the exception of an animal-like scratching that had been heard several times near an upstairs door. Mrs. Adams told Worley that she was staying "close to God" by reading her Bible and by an association with a fundamentalist religious group that was sending members to call on her.

On Sept. 8, 1970, Worley telephoned again. He learned that things had been relatively peaceful in the Adams house with the exception of several nights in July. Mrs. Adams had prayed and the disturbances had ceased.

Worley's last report was filed on June 13, 1971: "All is peaceful at subject's home. However, I thought I detected a note of tiredness or sadness. Subject prays and reads Bible. She will call me if she gets into difficulty. I hope and pray her tormenter of so many years is gone for good."

In 1969 and 1970 I began to receive a number of letters from several sections of the U.S. and Canada that detailed a certain kind of report with a monotonous sameness. The letters were from young college women who claimed to have been sexually molested after a close sighting of a UFO. The young women seemed quite sincere. The majority of them were majoring in the physical sciences, were proud of high marks in their subjects, and invited me to check them out with the administrators at their respective colleges.

"Dear Mr. Steiger," a typical letter began, "I am not a nut; I am on the dean's list at M College, majoring in physics. Last summer I saw a flying saucer at close range. It hovered over my car for several miles as I drove to my parents' farm home. It was definitely a metallic object. Shortly after that sighting, I was aware of something in my bedroom as I was preparing for bed. I could see nothing, but I could not shake a feeling of uneasiness ... I was not yet asleep when I felt a pressure on the bed beside me. When I sat up, I felt something fondling my breasts. I wanted to scream, to get out of bed, but I was unable to move ... I remember nothing more until I awakened the next morning, but I have reason to believe that something made love to me while I slept. I believe this incident was associated in some way with my sighting the UFO."

Are some of our finest and brightest young women actually consorting with beings from other worlds, or have the incubi modernized their approach in order to seduce the more sophisticated of our technologically advanced women?

SCREWED BY THE ALIENS

Except for the sighting of the UFO prior to the visit of the bedroom invader, the letters which I received from serious and sincere young college and professional women might just as well have been accounts of our lusty, sexually aggressive incubus.

As I related in my book, "Mysteries of Time and Space," I considered it all a bizarre kind of put on ("Let's give Brad Steiger something really weird to write about, girls!") but each letter was supported by too many details and invited too many avenues of verification. And then I began to notice a pattern that may have meant nothing – and may mean everything. A couple of the girls had sent along their birth data. On a hunch, and because I did not have too many other good ideas, I asked a number of my correspondents for their birthdates. Interestingly enough, the young women were all born in March, April, and May of 1948.

The first major UFO "flap" of modern times began in June 1947, and continued rather briskly throughout the summer. My young women correspondents were born nine months later.

Now, 22 years later, UFOs had become a part of their lives – coupled with what may have been a kind of sexual examination or liaison (none of them claimed to be pregnant). I cannot help wondering how many of their mothers and their grandmothers and their great-grandmothers had had similar experiences; and I wonder if these young women will one day give birth to very "special" babies.

If the ufonauts are a cousin species from some other reality, there is no more effective way of gaining a world than by seeding a crossbred race to operate from within Man's own species.

The members of this hybrid tribe may not even be consciously aware that they are a bit more than human. They may possess some inbred knowledge of a signal for which they are quietly waiting. They may be special, yet unsuspecting people, who are being shepherded by their cosmic Big Brothers. On an unconscious level, perhaps in what may seem only to be strange dreams, this new race is being tutored and developed in a program that may involve several generations of mental and physical progression.

If, as I have theorized in the past, the UFO itself is an illuminated, rather amorphous, glob of intelligent energy, then its three-dimensional projections of examining doctors and naked, pliant females are but psychically constructed ploys to extract the semen from human males in one instance and to deposit the fertile seed into human females in another instance. An entity, then, does not have to have a physical body to impregnate a female Homo sapiens. As long as it can project vivid three-dimensional images to a witness, it can manipulate a male into having relations with such an illusion and a female into receiving that male's seed through the agency of a hallucination of a husband or a lover.

SCREWED BY THE ALIENS

Even that peripheral UFO phenomenon, known as the Men-in-Black, has moved steadily into the arena of sexual molestation. Not long ago I wrote the following letter to a young couple who were under siege by the phenomenon:

"It is incredible how the phenomenon travels about like some cosmic repertory theater, changing its character actors, but retaining its basic multi-level plot structure. I say this not to minimize the morass in which you and Mary find yourselves, but, hopefully, to enable you to maintain always your perspective. Your erstwhile tutors have now moved the action into the personal arena. The penny-dreadful terrors have been abandoned, and the much juicier area of interpersonal relationships is being mined. Don't play the game! As John Keel has always emphasized, belief is the enemy. The phenomenon conforms to your belief structure.

"Traditionally, the phenomenon has been particularly interested in lovers and the male-female relationship. Fairies had an obsessional interest in bringing some couples together – and in breaking up the romances of other couples. In all cultures, girls approaching puberty or women experiencing menstruation have found themselves the seat of paranormal manifestations. The phenomenon has . . . moved into the personal arena as a part of [its] compulsive interest in male-female activities. The entities sometimes act like the dirty old men with raincoats on their laps who attend porno movies.

"Don't provide them with such entertainment. Don't play their game! I suppose it is only natural for male members of Homo sapiens to be protective toward their women. The compulsion to guard one's women against alien molestation is certainly as old as our earliest cultures. Men may sit in darkened theaters and glory vicariously in lusty Vikings snatching squealing Villasssge maidens and racing off with the struggling women thrown over their shoulders. But after the lights have come on and the fantasy is ended, those same male theater patrons are left with the uneasy thought that the whole scene would not be so entertaining if it were their women some brutish louts were making off with.

"Although the UFO intelligences do seem to have a more than casual interest in our women, their ultimate purpose may not be all that sinister. If one can steel his mind to the thought, it may be that whatever is going on is really for the general good and enrichment of Homo sapiens. Jerome Clark has a case in his files that may serve to reassure all of us.

"Martha Anderson was a 21-year-old contactee in Minnesota who had been undergoing the usual array of eerie phenomena which UFO researchers have come to expect – unexplained footsteps; knocking sounds; and fainting spells that baffled the staff of a local hospital.

"'I like to return to one part of Martha Anderson's story when I feel myself getting too pessimistic about the nature of the intelligences behind the great

SCREWED BY THE ALIENS

enigma we are trying so desperately to solve,'" Clark said. "'We picture the ufonauts as somber, humorless creatures bent on the harmful manipulation of Mankind, and we never suspect that they may be as weak as we are, victims of the same silly foibles and country bumpkin mannerisms common to all of us who dwell on this celestial rock we call Earth.'

"One night Martha had awakened, shivering from a cold draft that had passed through her room. She sensed that she was not alone, and she lay on her stomach. Her face pointed in the direction opposite to where she imagined the intruder stood. She had started to doze, when the sense of uneasiness returned. She felt someone lying next to her. She could not move, and she lay paralyzed with fright, waiting for something to happen.

"'And then,'" Clark said, "'quite without explanation, her brassiere unsnapped. And a moment later she knew that whoever or whatever had been there was gone. Perhaps alien beings capable of so preposterous, so pointless, so childish a gesture, need not be feared all that much.'"

SUGGESTED READING

Brad Steiger's final book with Sherry Hansen Steiger: HAUNTED — MALEVOLENT GHOSTS, NIGHT TERRORS AND THREATENING PHANTOMS

REAL GHOSTS

REAL VAMPIRES

REAL ALIENS

On "Mr. UFO's Secret Files" our YouTube channel, check out "Brad Steiger's Final Interview" and "Brad Steiger Tribute – 50 Years of PSI Memories"

SCREWED BY THE ALIENS

"Cosmic Love": A sexy SctFi podcast page.

< A tender moment between Earth woman and alien.

"Visitors of the Night" 1995 made-for-TV movie featuring Candace Cameron, who is repeatedly abducted and probed by space aliens and is desperate for help.

SCREWED BY THE ALIENS

CHAPTER 10

THE MYSTERY OF THE BEDROOM INVADERS
By John Keel

EDITOR'S NOTE: The late John A. Keel was one of the best philosophers and "free thinkers" when it came to the nature of the UFO phenomenon. I knew John quite well and it's easy for me to say that he was NOT a wide eyed believer in extra-terrestrialism, more content to place their original closer to home. He was the author of such works as "Trojan Horse," "The Eighty Tower," and "The Mothman Prophecies," from which a movie was made starring Richard Gere. Keel coined the term "Ultra-terrestrials," which I try to also use in describing the entities we are referring to; though the "Saucerians" sometimes will do, and if I don't want to sit and explain myself we can go back to using the term "alien" and you can do the changing of the word in your own mind.

Back when Keel originally submitted this material for use in my "UFO Universe" magazine, I did not know quite what to make of it. What exactly were "Bedroom Invaders"? And why can't I keep them out by locking my doors? Well, the reason is that they can pop right through the walls and take you up and out of your bed to another place and time for a variety of experiments – lots of them related to un-cozy sex. Keel was not much into using profanity, and I think our talk on sex was somewhat limited, and so I call this article – and now a chapter in this book – more worldly (or otherworldly, I suppose you can say) a "soft beginning" to what was to be expanded upon in the years to come as an intriguing and often titillating topic for discussion and debate. Today's researchers are perhaps not as squeamish as JAK was, but he was able to dangle a branch of UFOlogy that had been hiding (here we go again), you could say, under the covers!

By the way, there is now a musical group called "The Bedroom Invaders," most likely because of John Keel.

****

Have you ever awakened suddenly in the middle of the night with the feeling that someone or something was standing near your bed watching you? Many

SCREWED BY THE ALIENS

people have had this experience, and those mysterious intruders have proven to be not burglars but bizarre entities who can appear and vanish like "ghosts."

They are, in fact, the basis for many chilling ghost stories. But there is now mounting evidence that strongly suggests the entities are in some way related to the flying saucer enigma.

Strange, unusual and unidentified persons of unusual stature and appearance have been popping up all over America – and the world – in recent years. Police have pursued them without success. Many of the witnesses have been reluctant to discuss their encounters, fearful of ridicule from friends, co-workers and neighbors.

In many cases, the "mystery men" have been described as wearing capes and hoods; something like a monk's cowl. They are nearly always of unusual size, both height and girth. At first, ufologists were inclined to dismiss such episodes as the work of pranksters and hoaxers, but now identical reports have come from nearly every state and from several foreign countries. The "prowlers" show a tendency to appear in UFO flap areas, while test studies in non-flap areas have failed to turn up similar reports.

Large, broad-shouldered men wearing capes and hoods have been seen all over the world, usually walking along desolate roads in thinly populated areas. In October, 1967, three men were driving along Route 2 in West Virginia when they saw a big, caped man walking beside the road, a most unusual sight in that area. They stopped the car and looked back, but he was gone. There were open fields on both sides of the road and no place for him to hide.

A group of eight men wearing thick black cowls startled motorists near Caterham, England, on July 28, 1963, according to newspaper reports collected by the British journal, "Flying Saucer Review." Witnesses said that the mystery men departed by running and leaping across the road. Their actions were silent and quite odd. More than a century earlier, there were repeated appearances of a strange caped man in England. He appeared during the 1830s and was able to run with amazing swiftness and leap great distances with ease. He became known as "Springheel Jack," and extensive searches failed to ever locate him.

Caped and hooded men have occasionally been reported as the pilots of flying saucers and other unidentified flying objects. Some of the cases go far back in history, long before the first flying saucer reports beginning in 1947. One such reports was from the crew of a Norwegian freighter in 1934. Norway, Sweden and Finland had a massive wave of sightings of "ghost airplanes" and strange flying lights beginning in December 1933 and continuing through the spring of 1934. The Air Forces of all three countries tried in vain to track down and capture the "ghost fliers," and the witnesses numbered in the thousands.

Late in January, 1934, the freighter "Tordenskiold" was on a routine run along

SCREWED BY THE ALIENS

the Norwegian coast between Tromso and Kabelvag when a "great grayish machine" suddenly appeared in the sky and swooped down over the ship. As it passed low over the ship, a brilliant beam of light shot down from the object and lit up the deck "like daylight." Such searchlights are commonly reported from all over the world. Captain Sigvard Olsen and his crew reported that the mysterious craft was so close that the pilot was clearly visible in the cabin. They described the pilot as being dressed in some kind of cloak or cape with a hood covering his head. He also wore some sort of heavy glasses or goggles. These types of pilots are reported frequently.

Mr. Jerome Clark, a leading American ufologist, sent me the following report in March, 1967: I have been told of two similar cases in Minnesota. The first incident occurred last April. According to the witness, he and a friend had been driving along the highway about 11:30 PM. They were several miles from the nearest town and they could not see any other cars on the road and because the terrain in that area is very flat, their visibility was unlimited. So they were shocked and surprised when in their headlights they saw three large men walking abreast and toward them from the other lane of the highway. The men were dressed in black cowls that covered the upper half of their faces; there were slits for their eyes. The strangers, whoever or whatever they were, paid no attention to the car and continued on as if it had never passed.

The second incident occurred in Minnesota several years ago. An acquaintance was taking a shortcut home through an alley. He was not paying attention to the direction he was going and almost walked into another person. The stranger seemed quite startled and turned to stare in surprise. The man was very tall and massive, and was dressed in a black cape that covered the top half of his face, and he appeared to carrying something that resembled a large black bag.

From Cape Cod to the lower tip of Florida, we have heard of unidentified prowlers roaming the countryside at night. During the UFO flap around Point Pleasant, West Virginia, in 1966-67, several witnesses told me that giant leering faces had peered into the windows of their homes. Upon inspection, some of the windows were too high for ordinary men to reach. They described the men's faces as being "evil," with silver-gray hair. In the winter of 1966-67, an unusually tall prowler (about 6' 6") in coveralls with silver-gray hair caused a turmoil among the residents of Provincetown, Massachusetts. There had been numerous sightings by fishermen in the area. More recently, isolated farmers in Delaware County in upper New York have been chasing a mysterious intruder who has appeared around their homes at night, peering into windows and grinning idiotically. Witnesses say that he has silver-gray hair and is dressed in some kind of coverall garment.

As in so many other cases, the New York prowler has eluded pursuers by easily leaping over high obstacles and running faster than any of the rugged farmers.

SCREWED BY THE ALIENS

There is no known human in the area who fits the description of the prowler.

The caped giant has also been reported in New Jersey. A family in Cape May who had reported a number of UFO sightings over the Coast Guard radio installation near their home, told me that a tall man in a white cape had appeared around their home in January, 1967. The following day they found human-like footprints in the snow. The footprints led to a huge wall that would have been difficult to climb, let alone leap over. The footprints continued on the other side of the wall as if the entity had passed through the wall, and to a nearby shed where they abruptly stopped.

In the spring of 1966, an Air Force WAF returned to her ground floor apartment on the edge of closely guarded McGuire AFB in New Jersey one evening and heard a sound in her bedroom. She investigated and found the window open and a pair of pale hands with extraordinarily long fingers resting on the sill as if preparing to climb in. She screamed and the hands withdrew. She found the AP who searched the area, admitting they had pursued a very tall entity with his "sweater" pulled over his head. Even in that uncomfortable state, the entity was able to run swiftly and to leap over obstacles with ease.

The WAF, a Master Sergeant, whom I have known for fifteen years, was puzzled by my interest in the "sweater" detail and in the long fingers. My technique is to tell witnesses as little as possible about previous sightings in order to avoid influencing their responses. In the many reports now being analyzed, witnesses have frequently described long fingers. It is now such a common description that it is accepted as a normal feature of at least one type of alien being. There is rarely any mention of the long-fingered aliens in print, so there is little chance that witnesses might have heard of that feature from previous encounters.

I asked if she had any previous experiences and she recounted one incident she had nearly forgotten.

Several years previously, she had been staying in a motel in Mexico when she awoke to find a giant cowled figure standing over her bed. It extended one arm above her and she reached out to touch it. As soon as her fingers contacted the air, the entity crumbled and vanished.

"It felt powdery, like ashes," she explained.

So, what do powdery ghosts have to do with flying saucers?

Such stories are not unusual; they are simply not widely known, not even by the fans of UFO magazines which are generally more interested in little grays rather than creepy giants and vanishing prowlers. In a few cases, the objects have crumbled into a powdery metal when touched or struck by another object.

One New Jersey investigator reported a case involving a disintegrating substance. On August 18, 1966, a disk-shaped object discharged some shares of flaming metal directly above some telephone poles near Lions Lake, New Jersey. The

SCREWED BY THE ALIENS

witnesses retrieved some samples which proved to be honey-combed, aluminum-like castings smelling sharply of sulfur. Although it was placed into a box, it rapidly melted down to the size of a pea. Since chemical analysis can cost thousands of dollars, the sample has never been tested.

New Jersey has been a hotbed of UFO reports and strange incidents in years past. Sergeant Ben Thompson, Patrolman Ed Wester, and several others saw a blazing white object "as big as a car" moving slowly at low altitude over Pompton Lakes and the Wanaque Reservoir about 9:45 PM on October 10, 1966. There have been many sightings in that area. Forty miles south of Wanaque, in Elizabeth, New Jersey, two 16-year-old boys had a frightening experience that same night, and about the same time. They encountered one of the giant grinning men.

The boys, James Yanchitis and Martin Munov, were walking home along 4th Street and New Jersey Street in Elizabeth, when they reached a corner parallel to the New Jersey Turnpike. The Turnpike is elevated here and there is a very steep incline dipping down from the busy highway to 4th Street. A very high wire fence runs along the street, making it impossible for anyone to scramble up the incline to the Turnpike. There are bright streetlights on that corner and it was there that the boys encountered "the strangest guy we've ever seen."

Yanchitis spotted him first. "He was standing behind that fence," the youth told me later. "I don't know how he got there. He was the biggest man I ever saw."

"Jimmy nudged me," Martin reported, "and said, 'Who is that guy standing behind you?' I looked around and there he was, behind that fence. Just standing there. He pivoted around and looked right at us, and then he grinned a big old grin."

Three days later I visited Elizabeth with Jim Moseley, then publisher of Saucer News, and Chuck McCann, an old friend. We interviewed the boys separately at length in the home of Mr. George Smith and they each told the same story. The man was well over six feet tall and was dressed in a "sparkling green" coverall garment that seemed to shimmer in the streetlights. He wore a broad black belt around his waist.

McCann, who is a TV star and a movie actor (the deaf idiot in "The Heart Is A Lonely Hunter"), is a big man, about 6' 2" tall, but both boys said the entity they saw was taller than Chuck and much broader. He had a dark complexion and small round eyes, beady, set far apart. They could not remember any hair, ears or nose, nor did they notice his hands. He was standing in the underbrush behind the fence and his feet were not visible.

There had been some violent incidents in the neighborhood and the boys were reluctant to tarry to study the strange character. They hurried home. Later there were reports that a tall green man had chased a resident down the same street that night, but we were unable to track down those reports.

SCREWED BY THE ALIENS

The big mystery seemed to be: How did this being get behind the fence and what was he doing there? We thought perhaps his car had become disabled on the Turnpike and he came down the steep incline to seek help. But he just stood there and never asked the boys to call someone or ask for help. He seemed to be watching someone in a house across the street.

A giant grinning man behind a fence in Elizabeth on a night of UFO sightings proves nothing, of course, although I have heard of the giant grinning man many times during my travels.

Less than a month after that incident, a sewing machine salesman from Mineral Wells, West Virginia – Woodrow Derenberger – was driving home from Marietta, Ohio, on a rainy night in November, 1966, when an object, shaped like the chimney of a kerosene lamp dropped out of the sky and landed on the highway directly in front of his truck. He slammed on the brakes and stared in astonishment as a man clambered out of the object and strolled towards him, his lips fixed in a broad, reassuring grin. Derenberger described him as being a little less than six feet tall, with a dark complexion and slightly elongated eyes. He wore a dark coat and blue trousers which were quite shiny and had a "glistening" effect.

As the man neared the door of the truck, Derenberger heard a voice which asked him to roll down the window. The man stepped up to the door with his arms crossed over his chest and his hands under his armpits – perhaps to conceal his long fingers. He continued to grin and, although his lips never moved, Derenberger swears he distinctly heard a voice and somehow communicated with the being via telepathy. The discussion was brief and pointless, which is common during initial contacts. The being said his name was "Cold" and that his country was less powerful than America. He asked Derenberger who he was, where he was going, and a few other simple questions. He then said he would be back, turned and walked to the object and flew away.

Woodrow Derenberger, who had never read any UFO literature prior to this incident, thus entered into the stultifying world of the "contact."

Sixty miles south of Mineral Wells, hundreds of people were fearfully living in another part of the Twilight Zone around the little town of Point Pleasant. One family, Mr. and Mrs. James Lilly and their children, have had the full range of unexplained UFO activities around their home on the Camp Coneley Toad. Brilliant flying lights appeared at tree-top level in the area almost nightly in March and April, 1967, and hundreds viewed the objects from the Lilly's front yard. Their television sets would malfunction every time one of the things flew over and their telephone would be unusable. Automobiles in the vicinity began to stall without cause.

Their daughter-in-law, Doris Lilly, who lived in the south end of Point Pleasant,

SCREWED BY THE ALIENS

began to receive annoying phone calls early in March 1967. Each evening, around 5 P.M., her phone would ring and when she answered she heard only a bizarre metallic voice speaking in an incomprehensible language, guttural and rapid. The calls came only when she was alone.

"It was as if they knew when I came home," she noted.

This kind of mysterious hoaxing has been reported by witnesses in many other areas.

Part of my somewhat unorthodox investigation routine includes a discussion of the witnesses' dreams during a UFO flap. One of my carefully worded key questions is: "Did you ever dream there was a stranger in your house in the middle of the night?" When I directed the question to Mrs. Lilly, she urged her 16-year-old daughter, Linda, to tell me about the "nightmare" she'd had that March. Linda was reluctant to discuss it but, with a little coaching, she told how she awoke one night and saw a large figure hovering over her bed.

"It was a man. Very broad. I couldn't see his face very well but I could see that he was grinning at me. Jim was working on the river; he's a riverboat captain on the Ohio."

"She woke me up with a terrible scream," Mrs. Lilly added. "She cried out that there was a man in her room. I told her she was dreaming but she screamed again."

"He walked around the bed and stopped right over me," Linda said. "I screamed again and hid under the covers. When I looked again, he was gone."

"She came running into my room," Mrs. Lilly said. "'There is a man in my room, she said. There is!' She has refused to sleep alone ever since."

When I asked for a full description, Linda said she thought he had been wearing a "checkered shirt." It was a detail I wasn't anxious to hear. I tried to maintain my professional pose. "The man in the checkered shirt" again. I'd heard a lot about him in recent months.

He (or "it") turns up everywhere. A young lady in Florida wrote to me to relate a very strange story about an ex-boyfriend. She said he had confided that he was a UFO "contactee." Her well-written letter reflected a fine, sensitive mind and good education. I answered her in my usual cautious manner and asked her a couple of unexpected questions.

Had she ever awakened in the middle of the night to find a "stranger" in her room?

She replied: "Did I ever!" Then she explained how she was awakened one night a few weeks after breaking up with her boyfriend and found a very large man standing beside her bed...a man wearing a checkered shirt! She cried out and he backed away and disappeared into the hallway. She and others searched the premises, but nothing had been stolen or disturbed.

SCREWED BY THE ALIENS

Occult literature is replete with references to "ghosts" wearing checkered shirts but occultists tend to ignore this seemingly irrelevant detail.

Completely unknown to my female correspondent, the "man in the checkered shirt" had frequently appeared in the home of Mr. and Mrs. George Glines of Pensacola, Florida, beginning in 1963. During a hurricane that year, Mr. Glines said, "I was lying on the couch in the living room and looked up to see that someone wearing a plaid sport shirt was in the room. I got up and took a couple of steps toward him. As I did, he backed away and vanished. I turned on the light but he was gone. I checked the doors, and they were all locked. I didn't mention it until my son-in-law saw it, too, because I didn't want to upset my wife."

In the ensuing months, all members of the household observed the elusive entity. Poltergeist activity occurred, and other witnesses and friends heard rapping on the walls and footsteps when there was no one present. In May 1964, the home burned to the ground.

Burning houses and mysterious fires go hand in hand with UFO activity. The sudden destruction of UFO witnesses' homes is so frequently reported that mere coincidence must be ruled out. In March 1966, a family on Long Island reported a UFO landing near their home. All kinds of strange phenomena broke loose around them and serious UFO researchers dismissed them as publicity-seeking nuts. A few months later, their home burned to the ground, but fire investigators were unable to determine the cause of the blaze.

The home of a contactee in New Mexico, Paul Villasss, was burned to the ground after he released photos of UFOs hovering low over his property.

In West Virginia, an abandoned building a mile or so from the Lilly home burned to the ground during a pouring rain, much to the bewilderment of local firefighters.

Grass fires often erupt in fields and meadows hours or days after UFOs are seen in the area.

Several barns and abandoned buildings have been destroyed by fires in New York's Delaware County since the "prowler" first made his appearance there.

This, of course, does not mean that everyone who observes a UFO or the man in the checkered shirt is going to suffer a mysterious fire, but there are many uneasy correlations in the data now being presented.

Several well investigated cases in South America reveal that mysterious intruders have been discovered in homes. Many have been described as "little men about three feet tall." So we wonder if the planet has been divided up into zones with "little men" in one section and "giants in checkered shirts" in another.

These reports have generated a lot of mail. On May 25, 1968, a young man reported that he was awakened in his girlfriend's bedroom in Superior, Wisconsin, to see a huge shape hovering over the bed. It appeared to be at least 6' 6" tall

SCREWED BY THE ALIENS

with a massive head and broad shoulders. It moved from one side of the bed to the other, then vanished.

Other reliable, non-demented people in New England and in the Midwest have experienced similar night visitations. It is remarkable how the children of many UFO witnesses suddenly become obsessed with the notion that someone is lurking in their bedrooms late at night. Perhaps all of the UFO talk in the household produces a hysterical reaction. But these mundane explanations are difficult to apply in many cases. UFO witnesses rarely relate the appearance of "prowlers" with UFO incidents. And students of supernormal phenomena have always tended to separate and isolate the various fields of interest in the occult and widely divergent manifestations.

Professional psychiatrists and psychologists have been hearing these "bogeyman" stories for years and simply pigeonhole them as symptoms of hysteria and schizophrenia because neither of those disciplines have any valid ideas to explain the similarities and correlations in these accounts. The usual explanation for schizophrenia, which is really a little-understood mental disorder, is that the subconscious moves in and takes control of the conscious mind. However, as we explore further into the UFO mystery, we must ask if it is not somehow possible for outside influences to do the same thing.

Acute alcoholics sometimes suffer from "Korsafoff's psychosis," a disorientation of time and space, and the hallucinations of delirium tremens are well-known. Usually in these cases, the patient thinks he sees small animals, bats and grotesque insects. Other kinds of hallucinations among the seriously disturbed might produce sexual symbols, but not giant silver-haired creatures in checkered shirts.

The mystery of unidentified flying objects has been one of the most discussed and least adequately investigated phenomenon of modern times. There are hundreds of little-known and rarely reported aspects to the overall situation which demand closer scrutiny not only by astronomers and physicists, but by psychiatrists, psychologists and students of the occult. Perhaps the mysterious entities in black capes and hoods or checkered shirts are the same kind of entities who have historically been mistaken for ghosts, and the nocturnal intruders may be part of the same bewildering package of surprises.

Instead of leading us to the discovery of an extraterrestrial intelligence with an advanced technology, the study of UFOs and the manifestations which accompany them may carry us forward into the unexpected: into a parallel world which has always coexisted with us but is separated from us by unknown laws of time and space.

We may simply be experiencing random glimpses of that parallel world and are merely struggling to fit it into the framework of our own environment.

In short, the hooded men walking along the barrens in Minnesota and those

SCREWED BY THE ALIENS

grinning fellows standing behind fences in New Jersey may simply be passing through from their world to ours and back again. Like tourists at a zoo, they may occasionally step into a bedroom to get a closer look at us odd humans in our natural habitats.

SUGGESTED READING
OPERATION TROJAN HORSE
THE MOTHMAN PROPHECIES
DISNEYLAND OF THE GODS
THE EIGHTY TOWER
STRANGE MUTANTS

Below: Chatting, two very astute men of the paranormal and Fortean phenomena, Jacques Vallee and John A. Keel

The late researcher John Keel takes on the appearance of a Man in Black.

A musical group "The Bedroom Invaders" now exists. This is the cover of one of their albums.

SCREWED BY THE ALIENS

A FLYING SAUCER LOVE STORY
THE ET GUIDE TO PICKING UP EARTH PEOPLE
By Tim R. Swartz

The headlines were as astonishing as they were lurid...

"Women had sex with aliens and gave birth to hybrid babies," "The beautiful women who claim ET's got them pregnant," "Mothers to Alien Hybrids?" The stories could easily appear in grocery store tabloids, yet many people have come forward with incredibly similar stories and admitted that they have had sexual encounters with "extraterrestrials."

UFOs and sex is a topic that many UFO researchers are loathe to investigate. The subject of UFOs by itself faces enormous credibility problems. Now, if you throw into the mix reports of humanoid creatures abducting and sexually molesting their captives, it is enough for most researchers to give it all up entirely and take up beekeeping.

Another problem that faces those who want to do a proper investigation is the puritan attitude towards sex that still prevails in Western culture. Sexuality is something that normal, decent people do not discuss, study or write about. Stories about sex between humans and the "flying saucer" people are guaranteed to deliver swift and blinding condemnation from the morality police and make beekeeping look even more attractive.

NOTHING NEW UNDER THE SUN

It is not as if stories of non-human seduction are all that new. Ancient mythologies are full to overflowing with tales of gods, goddesses, angels, demons and everything else in between going out of their way to find humans with the purpose of a little ethereal hanky-panky. In Greek mythology, Zeus had his way with a human woman, Alcmene, with Heracles being the result of their celestial tryst.

In the Middle Ages there were numerous accounts of demonic possession and

SCREWED BY THE ALIENS

sexual exploits with male and female demons (incubi and succubi). People would claim that they had been seduced by succubi and incubi respectively, awakening only after the demons were finished and gone. Nocturnal ejaculations were seen as physical evidence that the demons were collecting sperm for interbreeding purposes. Church records in Europe cited numerous accounts of nuns stating that they had been raped in the night by incubi and injected with sperm collected by the demons.

An intense interest in human sexuality is also a common theme in Faerie mythology. Modern representations of the wee folk show them as innocent, magical little creatures who flit about the tall grass and sleep within the sweet recesses of flowers. However, in places where people believed in the existence of fairies and elves, it was thought that they were lustful, nasty and cruel creatures. They would be just as happy killing someone or snatching them away for sordid sexual purposes.

This belief persists today, especially in Iceland, where many locals are very cautious in their daily activities so as not to disturb the invisible elves that inhabit certain areas of the country. One woman, Hallgerur Hallgrímsdóttir, has even written a book describing her sexual encounters with Icelandic "huldufólk" (hidden people).

"I was wandering around alone in Icelandic nature, and he just came to me and whispered things into my ear, you know, dirty talk," she explains.

Hallgerur, in her book, "Please YoursELF - Sex with the Icelandic Invisibles," writes that, compared to elves, sex with humans is boring.

"Elf sex is possibly the safest and best sex on earth. They don't carry sexually transmitted diseases and you can't get pregnant or make an Elverine pregnant unless you both want to, which is not unheard of. And YES there are female elves, elverines. And they're HOT HOT HOT, even to girls. That reminds me: All elves are bisexual, but guys and girls not ready for some same sex action don't worry, no elf will do anything you don't want to. They can sense your longings and not-longings."

Let's compare what Hallgerur stated about elf sex with what the woman mentioned at the start of this article said about sex with extraterrestrials.

Bridget Nielson, from Sedona, Arizona, recalled a sexual encounter with an alien on board a spaceship: "It was great. It was an incredible super raw, super primal sexual experience. There was a real freedom and we were really going for it. It was the best sex I ever had."

THE BEST SEX EVER

The key word with these paranormal encounters is "best." In comparison, the other-worldly lovers definitely appear to have an edge over more mundane human suitors. The late Playboy model and actress, Anna Nicole Smith, told FHM

SCREWED BY THE ALIENS

magazine that when she was still living in Texas a ghost would get under the covers with her while she was trying to sleep.

"The ghost would crawl up my leg and have sex with me. I used to think it was my boyfriend, and one day I woke up and it wasn't...it was, like, a spirit. I was freaked out about it, but it never hurt me and it gave me some amazing sex so I had no problem."

This is a subject that can easily turn into a great big dirty joke, and who can blame some writers for treating it as such? Nevertheless, history shows that people do experience all sorts of paranormal sexual phenomenon, so it would be remiss not to take a closer look at these stories and give them the proper study that they deserve.

Taking into consideration the multitudes of anecdotes involving sex with deities, demons, elves, ghosts, etc. should we regard the reports of perverse UFO occupants as part of the same paranormal phenomenon, or something completely different? Those who believe that UFOs are strictly physical spacecraft from other planets see no similarities. They argue that the early mythologies of paranormal sexual encounters are coincidental when compared to the modern UFO cases.

One of the earliest known cases of UFO abduction turning into a sexual encounter involved the Brazilian farmer Antônio Vilas-Boas. This 1957 incident has been sufficiently covered numerous times, so there is no need to go into the details for this article. Vilas-Boas's story is important for two reasons: 1. Like the old stories of succubi taking sperm from the men they seduced, Vilas-Boas's "alien" lover also took a sample of his sperm. 2. The Vilas-Boas case appears to provide the framework that other, future, UFO-sex incidents will emulate.

A FLYING SAUCER LOVE STORY

Elizabeth Klarer from South Africa claimed that she had a series of "Space Brothers"-type of UFO contacts between 1954 and 1963. What made Klarer's contactee events so different from the others at that time was her claim that she was swept off her feet by a romantic extraterrestrial. This torrid love affair would eventually lead to her becoming pregnant with an otherworldly child. Considering society's oppressive atmosphere about sex, this was pretty hot stuff for the time...especially the mind-blowing idea that women could also actively seek out and enjoy a romp in the sack, be it with a human or something else.

Klarer was not shy about relating her experiences and her photographs of the Meton spaceships were widely published. However, the juicy details of her extraterrestrial fling were often omitted in books and articles about her. It wasn't until 1980, when she published her book "Beyond the Light Barrier," that all the details about her cosmic romance were revealed.

Klarer writes that she was told by Akon, her alien lover, "We rarely mate with Earth women. When we do, we keep the offspring to strengthen our race and

SCREWED BY THE ALIENS

infuse new blood."

Klarer's description of their otherworldly love making reads more like a Harlequin Romance than a typical contactee book.

"Picking me up in his arms, he carried me to the silken platform by the curved wall. Its firm softness supported our bodies with luxurious comfort, as I gave myself to the man from outer space. I surrendered in ecstasy to the magic of his lovemaking. Our bodies merged in magnetic union as the divine essence of our spirits became one, and in doing so I became whole."

The result of their pairing, according to Klarer, was a son who they named Ayling. In accordance with Akon's wishes, Klarer returned to Earth while their hybrid son remained on his father's planet, perhaps to be taught in the ways of picking up gullible Earth women.

Klarer's book reads like romantic fantasy fulfillment, however, some cases are practically pornographic in detail. In the book "The Abduction Enigma" by Kevin D. Randle, Russ Estes and William P. Cone, one woman told the authors that during an abduction experience a 5-ft alien climbed on top of her, looked deep into her eyes and said, "What you need is a good fuck!" The alien then proceeded to give her "the most profound orgasm of my life."

CAN YOU BELIEVE IT?

There are a couple of accounts that have been retold time and again, but I have not been able to find any substantial evidence that the stories are true, or even that the victims even existed. A California woman named Claudette Cranshaw supposedly witnessed in 1967 a glowing, round UFO land near her when she was out for a stroll on the beach near Blanca, California. She said that six blue-skinned web-footed humanoids jumped out of the landed craft and proceeded to chase her down and gang rape her. Later, Cranshaw gave birth to a stillborn blue-skinned, web-footed baby which she said was proof of her extraordinary tale.

Another report that has been a favorite in a number of UFO books involves a woman named Jean Sheldon. Sheldon said that she was driving in Michigan on April 2, 1967, when she saw a 50ft. disc with a glowing red dome fly down and land near her car. A door under the craft opened and she was pulled inside by some sort of force beyond her control. Inside, she was confronted by three naked male humanoids with green eyes. Through telepathy, the men said to Sheldon "My dear Earth woman, we wish to mate with you. It will be easier on your personality if you do this willingly."

Apparently their cosmic pick-up line worked, because Sheldon admitted that she was suddenly highly sexually stimulated and, without knowing why, wanted to fuck them all. The humanoids quickly undressed her, spread her out on a bench and took turns having their way with her. They told her it was all "in the interests of science," which didn't matter to Sheldon, as she said it was the most "exciting

SCREWED BY THE ALIENS

sex she had ever had, with feelings of unnatural delight mixed with shame and revulsion."

After everyone was finished, the UFO occupants told Sheldon that this was all an experiment to see if humans were genetically compatible with their race and they hoped that one of them managed to get her pregnant. The story ends with Sheldon stating that, despite her hopes, she never became pregnant. Somehow I don't think she was being all that truthful in saying that. Imagine how difficult it would have been for her to go home and tell mom and dad that their grandchild was the result of a wild, one-night-stand with a group of naked spacemen. It's not exactly something that you would include in the family Christmas newsletter.

The interesting part of these stories is the fact that everyone almost always states that they find themselves becoming sexually excited even though the situation is so strange and terrifying. This is especially significant when we take a detailed look at encounters between men and amorous, unearthly creatures.

NO PROBLEM GETTING IT UP

The wave of "alien abduction" cases starting in the 1980s brought out a number of alleged forced sexual experiences between men and their alien abductors. (Women as well, but we will concentrate on experiences as related by men in this section.) So many of the sexual abduction cases came out as a result of hypnotic regression, rather than a conscious recollection of events, that it is difficult to tell if the events actually occurred in physical reality.

It has become clear that many hypnotic sessions to uncover abduction experiences were conducted by people with little to no training in proper analysis hypnosis. Leading questions from the hypnotist and contamination from popular media resulted in bizarre stories that appeared to have been tapped from the subjects' subconscious on a fundamental archetypical level. It is no wonder then that so many hypnotically regressed individuals "remembered" incidents that involved horrifying sexual situations conducted by creatures dredged from the shadows of humanity's worst nightmares.

Nevertheless, it is not necessary to throw out every abduction case simply because personal beliefs intruded upon an investigation. Even the most sloppily-conducted investigation can provide valuable information if one knows where to look for it and is willing to put aside any and all preconceived notions. This becomes extremely difficult when abduction researchers are heavily invested in the whole "alien hybrid" scenario. As Abraham Maslow said in 1966, "I suppose it is tempting, if the only tool you have is a hammer, to treat everything as if it were a nail."

The late Budd Hopkins uncovered a plethora of abductees who thought that they had been abducted by extraterrestrials for the purpose of creating a human/alien hybrid race. In his book "Intruders" Hopkins details the experiences of "Ed

SCREWED BY THE ALIENS

Duvall" (pseudonym) from Wisconsin who had a series of sexually-related UFO abduction experiences beginning in the early 1960s.

Under Hopkins' direction, Duvall underwent hypnotic regression in January 1986. He recalled that a blinding light lifted him out of his pickup truck and into a hovering UFO. The beings inside were the typical big-eyed greys, but what really shocked him was the fact that he suddenly woke up from what he thought was a bad dream, only to find himself inside an object with curved walls that hovered above the precipice of a rocky cliff. Duvall was naked and with him was a naked female humanoid with long, silvery-blond hair.

Duvall describes the creature as tiny and "attractively unusual." She had large, intense eyes that "she used to get him extremely aroused by filling his mind with all sorts of erotic imagery." Even though the circumstances were extremely unsettling, Duvall said that he had no trouble performing and found the experience very fulfilling. His strange partner also told him that he was "very good" and that he had given her "a good sample."

Duvall admitted to Hopkins that he considered his experience to be a form of rape and was disturbed as well as curious on how he had managed to get and maintain an erection during the weird encounter. His statement harkens back to the 1957 Boas case when he was inside the craft and first approached by the nude woman: "I began to get excited... I think that the liquid they had rubbed on my skin was the cause of this. They must have done it purposely. All I know is that I became uncontrollably excited sexually, a thing that had never happened to me before."

Another South American case that is practically unknown in the U.S. revolved around a 21-year-old man named Antonio Carlos Ferreira from the city of Mirason in Brazil. Ferreira worked as a night watchman for the Transmoveis Fafa factory when on June, 28 1979 he observed a bright light that appeared to be coming down over the yard of the factory. Before he could react, he was suddenly surrounded by three small human-like beings who were dressed in one-piece coverall jumpsuits. Their heads were enclosed in opaque, round reflective helmets that prevented him from seeing their faces.

One of the humanoids pointed a red light at Ferreira's face and he was completely immobilized. In this paralyzed condition he was floated to a small, disc-shaped craft that had landed inside the south fence in the yard of the factory. Once inside, the creatures forced Ferreira to sit on a small stool while the ship ascended and it eventually landed inside a larger craft which contained other small ships like the one Ferreira was in.

The mother-ship was crewed by two types of humanoids. Both were small with heads twice the size of a human and their eyes were large and "pulled up" on the outside, similar to Asians. Some had skin near the color of light chocolate and

SCREWED BY THE ALIENS

their hair was long, a light reddish color and was coiled in ringlets. The other group had green colored skin with fine straight black hair and their eyes were green with the same slanted appearance. Both groups had jutting, sharp chins and large pointed ears that stuck out.

Ferreira was then approached by a small female who was completely nude. He described her as having chocolate colored skin, an immense head, coiled red hair, black slanted eyes and a straight large mouth with thick lips and white teeth. As with any man, Ferreira noted that her breasts were relatively small and her pubic hair was red in color.

The strange woman tried to kiss Ferreira but he said that her breath smelled bad, her skin was cold and he thought that she was extremely ugly. However, when he tried to push the woman away, other crew members grabbed him and ripped his clothes off. They then rubbed a dark, amber colored oil all over his body, including his penis and testicles.

The humanoids picked Ferreira up while the woman positioned herself on a type of couch and spread her legs. Ferreira was then held over her and she grabbed his penis with her hand. The man was shocked when he became instantly erect as the woman raised her hips to impale herself on his dick. Even though he was being held in place on top of the woman, Ferreira's penis now seemed to have a mind of its own and it quickly ejaculated into his other-worldly lover.

Afterwards, Ferreira was told by his abductors that they came from another planet and were here conducting experiments to produce a child of an Earthman for future studies. They said that they would return again later so that he could know his child. This statement proved to be true, as Ferreira met up with his abductors at least 16 times over the next ten years. During one of those meetings he got to see his daughter, who he said was named Azelia. Ferreira said he felt affection towards the little girl, but this was tempered by the extreme dislike towards the mother, whom he surmised had chosen him specifically to father their child.

This story is indeed odd as Ferreira had told his mother what had happened to him as soon as he was returned from this first encounter. At her request, he allowed Professor Ney Matiel Pires to conduct hypnotic regression to extract more details of the event. This early sexual abduction case has many similarities to other cases that would occur years later, especially the part where Ferreira said that he had met with his "hybrid" daughter. This motif would later become a central point in a lot of abduction cases investigated by Budd Hopkins and Dr. David Jacobs. What also makes the Mirason case stand out is the fact that Ferreira had no previous knowledge of the UFO phenomena and there was little if any media contamination dealing with UFO abductions in Brazil during the late 1970s.

Several other interesting points about the Mirason case are eerily similar to

SCREWED BY THE ALIENS

the Vilas-Boas abduction. Like Vilas-Boas, Ferreira had to be swabbed down with an oily liquid before he could perform sexually. As well, even though the creatures described by Ferreira looked different from those described by Vilas-Boas...both men found the "alien" women ugly and noticed that they had bright red pubic hair.

WHAT THE HELL?

The stories in this chapter are just a few of the many fascinating cases that have been collected over the years, both in paranormal and UFO research. Myth and legends basically tell us that humans are just plain hot and everything out there wants to come here to get a piece of the action. Possibly the stories about aliens trying to create a hybrid race either for the sake of research or to save their dying species, is just a big pick-up line in order to try and score with the luscious woman and men of planet Earth.

The "Earth People are Easy" scenario makes a lot more sense considering that a so-called alien species wouldn't be compatible genetically to produce viable offspring with Earth humans. A true alien race would have just as much luck breeding with a kangaroo than with a human. This leads to another point...why are these UFOnauts so human looking anyway? If intelligent life developed on a world in another solar system, they wouldn't have evolved to look almost exactly like Earth humans, including having compatible genitalia.

The late writer Otto Binder, in his book "Flying Saucers Are Watching Us!" points out that human penises are gigantic for our overall size and height. Our junk is far bigger when compared to other primates such as gorillas and chimps. As well, with the exception of the Spider Monkey, humans are the only primate that does not have a baculum, a penis bone. Binder suggests that the human race is not entirely native to this planet...this may explain in part why so many UFOnauts look so human...they are our cousins. This makes the whole sexual abduction thing even more disturbing, sort of a cosmic incest thing going on with our creepy uncles from outer space sneaking around to try and get into our collective pants.

Unfortunately, there are no easy answers to any of this. The phenomena discussed in this article are complex and we are trying to explain it all by using logic and reason. Perhaps the human brain, while efficient to look for danger across a grassy savannah, is not able to grasp the mysteries of the universe and its realities by using human reasoning. Not only are we not asking the right questions...we are simply *not capable* of asking the right questions.

SCREWED BY THE ALIENS

Extraterrestrial Seductress.

Demonic spirits of sexual perversion were known as succubus and incubus. They would haunt men and women during the night in order to seduce them into sexual activity. (Painting: The Nightmare, by Henry Fuseli)

Ancient mythologies often tell of women and men who were the objects of lust by various deities, demigods, angels and other ethereal creatures.

SCREWED BY THE ALIENS

Elisabeth Klarer claimed that in the 1950's she went to live with extraterrestrials from the planet Meton for four months where she gave birth to Ayling, her space child.

Portrait of Akon, Elisabeth Klarer's lover from the planet Meton.

Science Fiction magazines have long used the motif of aliens from space carrying off beautiful woman for purposes of seduction and other lascivious activity.

Possibly the first non-fiction book written about UFOs and their sexual connections. It was written by sci-fi author George Smith under the pseudonym Jan Hudson and was published in 1967 by Greenleaf Classic.

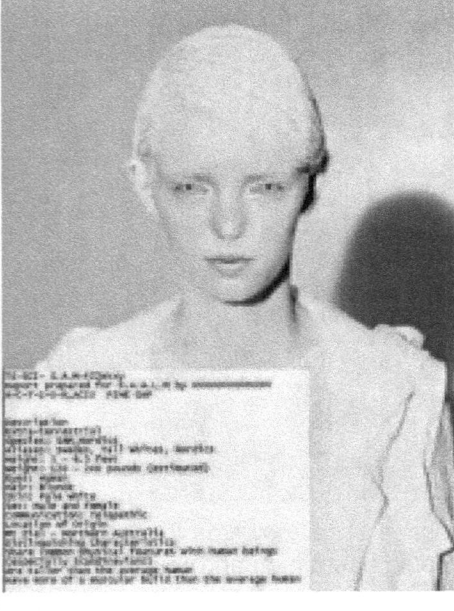

Alleged photograph of a "Nordic" type extraterrestrial, thought to be involved in the project to breed a hybrid race with humans.

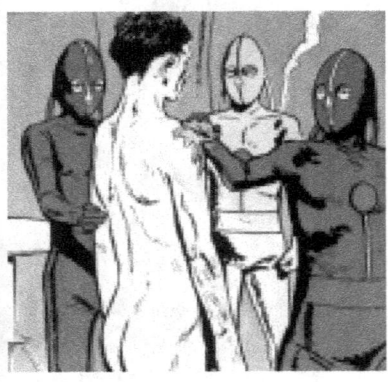

Illustration showing Antônio Vilas-Boas being swabbed down with a strange, oily substance just before meeting his other-worldly lover.

SCREWED BY THE ALIENS

The humanoids from the Villas-Boas case.

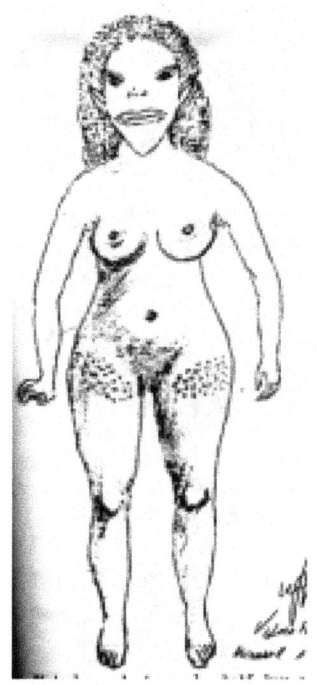

Illustration of the ET woman, done from Ferreira's descriptions.

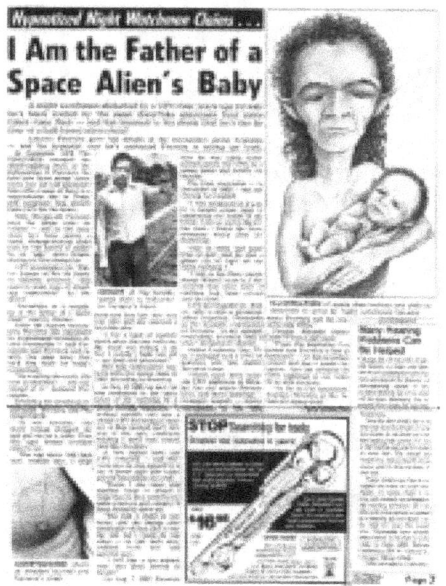

National Enquirer article about the Ferreira abduction.

Hallger+ur Hallgrímsdóttir, author of the book "Please YoursELF - Sex with the Icelandic Invisibles".

Bridget Nielson, 27, says that she was chosen to be the mother of "hybrid" alien children because she is young and fertile with strong genes. She says that her offspring lives with their father on giant spaceships, but say's she doesn't regret being chosen because the sex was the "best she had ever had". (Picture by Solent)

SCREWED BY THE ALIENS

Tim R. Swartz is an Indiana native and Emmy-Award winning television producer & videographer, and is the author of a number of popular books including The Lost Journals of Nikola Tesla, America's Strange and Supernatural History, UFO Repeaters, Time Travel: Fact Not Fiction!, Men of Mystery: Nikola Tesla and many others. As a photojournalist, Tim Swartz has traveled extensively and investigated paranormal phenomena and other unusual mysteries from such diverse locations as the Great Pyramid in Egypt to the Great Wall in China.

He has also appeared on the History Channels programs "The Tesla Files"; "Ancient Aliens"; "Evidence"; "Ancient Aliens: Declassified"; and the History Channel Latin America series "Contacto Extraterrestre."His articles have been published in magazines such as Mysteries, FATE, Strange, Atlantis Rising, UFO Universe, Flying Saucer Review, Renaissance, and Unsolved UFO Reports. Currently, Tim writes a column about high-strangeness in Indiana for the magazine "Daydrifter." As well, Tim Swartz is the writer and editor of the online newsletter Conspiracy Journal; a free, weekly e-mail newsletter, considered essential reading by paranormal researchers worldwide. Tim is also the host of the webcast "Exploring the Bizarre" along with Timothy Green Beckley, kcorradio.com

SCREWED BY THE ALIENS

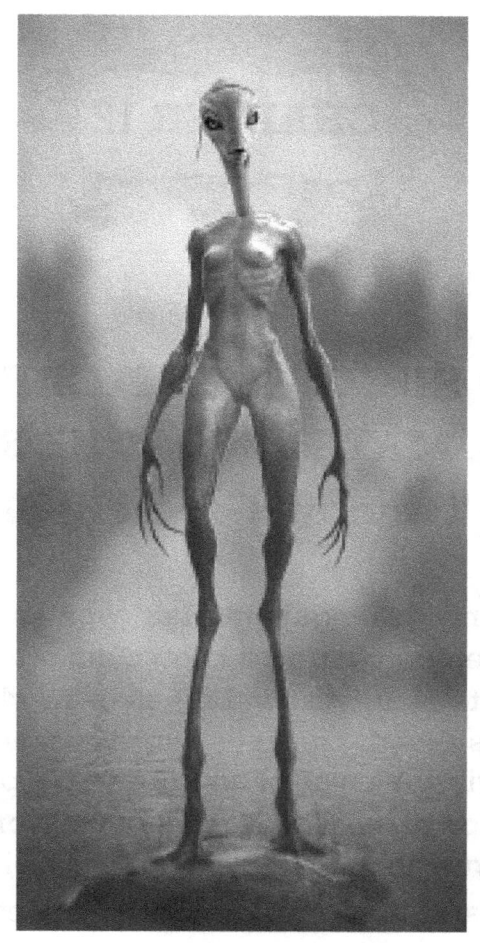

SECTION FOUR - CLOSE ENCOUNTERS OF THE PERSONAL AND PRIVATE KIND

Chapter Twelve: David Huggins and Crescent Soul Mate From The Stars

Chapter Thirteen: Raven de la Croix Abduction Seduction

Chapter Fourteen: Deanna's Abduction

SCREWED BY THE ALIENS

CHAPTER 12

DAVID HUGGINS AND CRESCENT SOUL MATE FROM THE STARS
By Timothy Green Beckley

Until recently most of my dealings with alien "women" and sex from outer space have been through a talented chap I've known quite a few years. And, actually, since I have long respected his artistic abilities even when I thought sex with Ultra-terrestrial beings was a totally crazy – utterly insane – bonkers idea, I always appreciated David Huggins because of his flare with a paint brush, even if he was a bit strange in the opinion of most of the rest of the world. Dave is a graduate of the NY Art Students League, though he confesses to being mainly self-taught.

A real "Shape of Water"-type guy, Hoboken, New Jersey, resident David Huggins appeared on my weekly podcast to tell co-host Tim Swartz and myself, along with special guest Adam Gorightly, how he dropped his pants at a very early age when he first met Crescent, the space gal from another time and place Listeners to "Exploring the Bizarre" (broadcast live every Thursday 10 pm Eastern/7 Pacific over KCORradio and archived on YouTube) must have been flabbergasted as we were to learn that this genteel, gray-haired artist lost his virginity not to a teenage heartthrob or even a hooker, but to someone who arrived in this dimension through the walls of his apartment many times over the years since this very important "coming of age" transgression took place.

To date, Huggins has stroked Crescent over a hundred times – that is on canvas of course. Many of his otherworldly portraits have been displayed at several galleries in the metropolitan area, but the best ones are permanently on display at "Balance," a rather avant-garde hair salon in Jersey City, New Jersey, that has been dubbed the Mothership by its owner, Carla Anderson, who was co-host of an older podcast that can still be found archived as part of our YouTube domain.

With headphone on we delved into this very controversial – but tantalizing – topic, batting around the general concept and basic history of crossbreeding

SCREWED BY THE ALIENS

between the Ultra-terrestrials and humans, which some experiencers have found to be an uplifting, Utopian experience. Meanwhile, others involved in what can be considered to be an unprovoked unworldly crime, dare to cry "Rape!" at the top of their lungs.

Regardless of your point of view as to what sort of phenomena we are dealing with, it is an historical fact that "crossbreeding," or however you wish to define this cosmic enigma, it does apparently take place even though we have no clue as to how this might be happening. Looks like ETs could see earth as their "Red Light District," whether we relish the idea or not. At the very least, they are using some highfalutin' genetic experimentation, perhaps, to repopulate their own race(s) somewhere out in space – or in another dimension. It begins to sound as if we were thumbing through a pulp-era science fiction novelette.

As unusual as his experiences with sexually dominate spacewomen may seem to the more normally lovelorn, we have allowed Mr. Huggins to do most of the talking so as not to dwell upon our personal opinion on such matters. I did start out the show by confessing that I had once walked off of a panel consisting of abduction researcher Budd Hopkins and three elderly ladies who claimed, in all seriousness, that they were fond of what they perceived as a regular sexual frenzy with their reptilian partners.

I couldn't grasp the principles upon which such cross fertilization might be possible or pleasurable for either reptilian or earth woman, but then there is no accounting for taste. I know Adam and Eve were supposedly confronted by a snake in the Garden of Eden, and a snake is a reptilian, but I don't think God set it up so that it would be possible for there to be a meeting of the genitals, because snakes have no genitals. But that's a problem for another chapter, and, besides, Dave's heavenly lady was not a serpent at all, but a full-blooded spacewoman. A warm blooded "creature" and not some coldblooded amphibian.

Give me a close-shaven, stellar lady like Antonio Boas was set up with and I will be more than happy.

Unlike most of these cases where the "parents" never get to hold – and sometimes cannot even see – their offspring, David maintains that he has fathered several ET children with his lover Crescent. She certainly is no "Creature from the Black Lagoon."

INTERVIEW

QUESTION: Isn't it true that you consider your relationship with Crescent to be a beautiful relationship that has blossomed into an interspecies romance that has lasted for decades and has resulted in Crescent bearing your children?

HUGGINS: That would be an accurate description of the ongoing experience.

QUESTION: Would you say that you had a rather typical childhood?

HUGGINS: I would say so. I was born in Norfolk, Virginia in 1943. Then, when

SCREWED BY THE ALIENS

I was about a year old, we moved to Portland County, Georgia, where I grew up on a farm. When I was about eight years old I went behind the barn. I heard someone call my name. The sound seemed to be coming from under a nearby tree. And so I turned around and there behind me was this little hairy guy like the character Elmo coming straight toward me. I thought it was the boogeyman or something, and so I screamed as I turned back around and ran straight back through the barn and out of there.

But I did return to the area sometime later and I saw this little fellow hanging out under the trees. I think of the word hairy when I see him in my mind even to this day.

QUESTION: So are we talking about a miniature version of Bigfoot or a dwarf?

HUGGINS: I don't really know what to call him. He did have glowing eyes if that helps any in the identification. When I first saw him I felt like for an instant I was inside his eyes looking out at me. Then that emptied – that stopped – and then I remember, you know, like I was running back to the barn.

QUESTION: Would you say that this was part of the extraterrestrial contingent you were to meet up with from time to time?

HUGGINS: It would seem to be since he was there several times when I was with the other beings. One was a giant insect-like being similar to a praying mantis. It really scared me.

QUESTION: And when did you start meeting up with the more pale being that we see in the vast majority of your work?

HUGGINS: It was around the same time. It was hot in August, so I went through the woods down by the lake and there was this person who was seated beneath and I became very aroused and she had me remove my pants. She got on top of me and I had a climax. Actually, it was rather painful, but it was at the same time quite ecstatic. And I'm looking up and into her eyes and then I passed out and woke up about maybe fifteen minutes later with my memory mostly erased.

QUESTION: Did you tell your parents?

HUGGINS: Well, I tried to, but they didn't want to believe me. Finally my mom gave me a real whipping and told me I was imagining this all and to stop talking about it. The next day I went behind the house and there was this woman there and I told her my mom and dad didn't believe me. She said something to the effect that I should probably just stop talking to them about it. Whenever I had an encounter with these beings later on I never said a word. I just kept it to myself.

QUESTION: Could you tell us in more detail what this woman looked like?

HUGGINS: She had black hair, large almond-shaped eyes and a very pale face, and she wore like a very dark blue cloak.

QUESTION: Well, if you saw her on the street, say, in a pair of blue jeans, would

SCREWED BY THE ALIENS

you say there was anything unusual about her? When you paint the space person or persons, they seem to have a pointed chin and a slit for a mouth and slightly resemble a grey that maybe is doing a bit of shape shifting. Is their depiction accurate or are you taking some artistic license?

HUGGINS: This is the way they looked. I don't know why there faces weren't the same pigmentation as the rest of their bodies but it was different.

QUESTION: You say your memory faded. When did it start to return and under what circumstances?

HUGGINS: 1987 or so. I was feeling very distressed for some reason and I went to look for a book by Whitley Strieber which I had heard about. There was another one written by Budd Hopkins. It was called "Intruders." I went to one bookstore and they didn't have it and I went to another place and it wasn't on their shelves either. Finally, a woman approaches me and says she has the books. I started reading one of them and there was something in there about having sex with an alien. At this point my experiences began to come flooding back into my mind.

QUESTION: Were these experiences of a regularly recurring nature? Monthly? Less frequently? More frequently?

HUGGINS: Well, I had left Georgia – I loved Georgia – and was living up on Washington Street and had an apartment for $90 a month near Central Park. You can't find a place like that any longer. I was working in a hardware store, Manhattan Hardware, commuting a short distance to New York City. And one day during a transit strike these two individuals I had never seen before caught my attention. So I go over and ask if I could help them and they don't pay any attention to me. So I ask again if I can be of assistance. They don't say a word.

Suddenly, for some reason, they quickly turned and walked out of the store. Well, anyway, that evening when I left for home it was raining cats and dogs and I thought to myself this is gonna be one wet walk. As I crossed 72nd Street and held out my thumb, there is this big black car, I don't know what kind it was, it looked more or less like a limousine. And a woman asks me where I am going and tells me I can get in. I gave her my destination. We didn't talk very much, hardly a word. When I got near to where I wanted to go, I told her she could leave me just about anywhere.

She just looks at me oddly and lets me out at the curb. That night I go to bed and I have this very weird dream of a woman's face. Her eyes are closed but she is coming toward me, and that is all I remember. There must have been more to the dream but I forgot.

QUESTION: So did this experience tie in somewhat with your having an affair with Crescent the spacewoman?

HUGGINS: I am certain it did. These were some of the unusual things that were

SCREWED BY THE ALIENS

happening to me. That's all I can say for sure. I don't consider myself anything special or anything like that. It just happened and that's pretty much all I can be certain about.

QUESTION: You have to admit it's a strange story. You tell us you had this sexual experience with an alien woman who is of another species, but it's also a kind of love affair. Not just a one-sided sexual attraction on either yours or her part.

HUGGINS: I would have these visitation and she told me that she would be back. And she did continue to return throughout my life.

QUESTION: We have to ask – at any time, did you feel you were going insane? That this couldn't possibly be real?

HUGGINS: There were little things that I could feel and touch that showed me this was real. One evening I'm walking up to 87th Street and I pass a florist and in the window there is some pink cyclamens. It's a beautiful plant. Anyway, I thought to myself, "Okay, if she is real, this plant is for her." Before going to bed that night I put the plant on the bookcase and when I got up in the morning it was gone. Someone had to take it during the night and there was no one else in the apartment. The memory of this experience also faded but it came back later on and I realized that I just could not have imagined all this.

QUESTION: You've stated that often they come as a couple, the alien woman and this insect-like being.

HUGGINS: I can't be sure. I'm not saying he's an insect but he does remind me of a praying mantis. I have seen them different sizes at different times. Sometimes larger than me. I have tried to communicate, and on one occasion I remember seeing an owl in a tree out the window. And these little gray guys came in and took me out of my room and floated me up to something in the sky.

I'm with a little boy and a white/gray "person." And I'm looking at both of them and ask if that is his mama and he just winks back and the woman smiles. She has a long thin rod in her hand and she is pushing it up my nose and I am telling her in no uncertain terms that she is hurting me and to make the pain go away. She touches my nose and the pain vanishes. But that day, when I see other people, they ask me why my nose is so inflamed. And what can I offer as an explanation?

QUESTION: So do you sometimes go to their craft? Do they take you up somewhere when you go into this other dimension through your wall?

HUGGINS: One time the wall in my studio opened up and there was Crescent and she told me, "David, my baby is dying." And I asked her, "What baby? Our baby?" I follow her and some others into another room, and this room is full of babies. I try to reach out and touch the one I think is mine and I get a shock like static electricity. I ask what I am doing there and whose babies these are and I'm told they are all mine.

QUESTION: The landscapes you paint seem to suck a person into the painting.

SCREWED BY THE ALIENS

I know we were at Carla's studio in Jersey City at a recent gallery showing she had for you and I'm looking at the paintings and it's almost as if the person viewing these works can be easily drawn into them. Very unworldly! I am reminded of the Icelandic stories about little people and humans disappearing and never coming back because they have gone on to this other world to live and to take wives – or husbands – and to marry. They may try to return to our world but most likely they are not permitted to do so. And even if they do stumble back here the children must grow up in this parallel dimension.

HUGGINS: I believe I have traveled there. It's like I'm inside a mountain and there are vehicles inside and I have no idea where I'm at but I know that the soil is very red.

QUESTION: In the movie "Love and Saucers" there is a sequence where it is explained by one of the beings that you are to have sex with a room full of alien women and that they will all become impregnated. Are you some sort of stud for ET females, would you say?

HUGGINS: No. Like I said, I just totally flipped out. There is no way I can make out with 30 or 40 women, there's just no way. The overseer, as I refer to him, led me onto a roof where I was expected to ejaculate into a bowl as one of the mantis beings watched. And I remember saying, "You want me to make love in a bowl, no hugging or kissing?" And I like hugging and kissing. And two space women came near me and started to hug and stroke my body and I ejaculated into the container.

QUESTION: Any other unusual sexual experiences you care to relate?

HUGGINS: Well, one time I am with this group of women and they are holding babies. One of them takes out her breast and for some reason she cannot give milk. So I tried to stimulate her breast by nursing on it but nothing at all happened.

QUESTION: So, to your way of thinking, were these sexual intimacies cold and clinical, for breeding purposes, or did they convey any sort of emotional feeling?

HUGGINS: I felt that their conception of what is emotional to us doesn't convey the same feeling to them. They have different grades of emotions. They don't have the same sensory value, but Crescent has touched my heart and portrayed herself as being as human as another species can possibly be.

QUESTION: Well, David, thank you for your time. We recommend that people go to Carla's gallery, "Balance," in Jersey, and grab a copy of the movie that has been made about you.

SCREWED BY THE ALIENS

HUGGINS: You're quite welcome.

SUGGESTED READING

LOVE IN AN ALIEN PURGATORY: THE LIFE AND FANTASTIC ART OF DAVID HUGGINS

Love and Saucers is now available for VOD streaming on iTunes, Amazon, Vimeo, Google Play and YouTube.

David Huggins and his cosmic love Crescent hold alien baby as Praying Mantis lurks in background

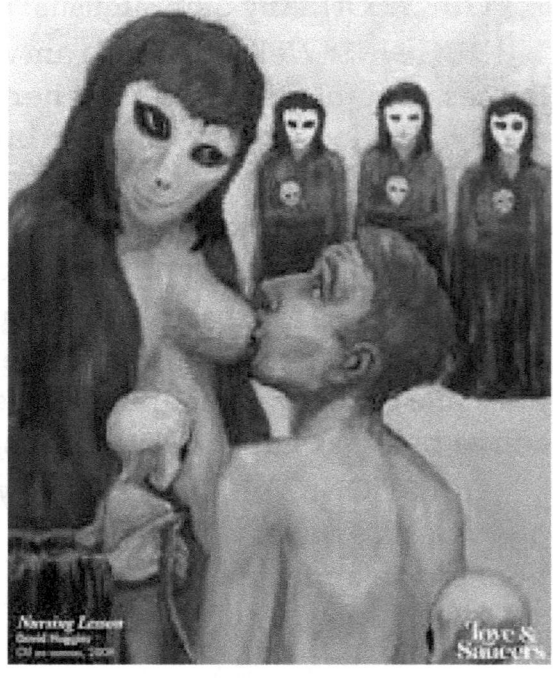

David Huggins nurses on an alien female.

SCREWED BY THE ALIENS

Travelers to Jersey City will find several of David Huggins' paintings hanging in the Balance Hair Salon and Gallery, as displayed here by head curator Carla Anderson, an unusual talent in her own right.

A little bit of tenderness — ET style.
   Painting by David Huggins.

Poster from Love and Saucers.

SCREWED BY THE ALIENS

CHAPTER 13

THE CLOSEST ENCOUNTER OF THEM ALL
THE ABDUCTION SEDUCTION
OF RAVEN DE LA CROIX

EDITOR'S NOTE: I was thrilled like a little boy in a candy store when I received an email that Raven de la Croix was going to attend one of my lectures in Tucson as well as make a presentation herself on the topic of UFOs and her philosophy of metaphysics.

Raven had never spoken publicly about her UFO experiences before, which she told me during the course of our initial conversation started out at a very early age. She was living in an apartment building where from her bedroom window she could see the brightly lit George Washington Bridge, which spans the Hudson River between Manhattan and Fort Lee, New Jersey.

Raven admits that her memory of this childhood event is rather limited — perhaps having been erased at least partially from her mind?

"We lived on the top floor of the eight-story walkup and I'm in bed and I can remember I'm just feeling kind of numb. My sister is in the room with me and she was on the way into the kitchen and I asked her to get me a cold glass of milk."

Raven says she must have seen something out the window as she recalls giving a silent scream.

"The room turned white and there was a distinct smell of sulfur, which I learned later is often associated with experiences that have an interdimensional nature."

Raven says she had to contend with a flashback when she went into the hospital as a kid for minor surgery. The doctors used ether on her to knock her out. The feeling of being suffocated was very reminiscent of her first "encounter."

The talented performer, who now resides beside a vortex in Sedona, AZ – the capitol of the "New Age" and everything strange in America — says she often found herself drawn to the roof to look up at the stars.

"I was seeing their ships, and somehow I felt I didn't belong here. That I had a

SCREWED BY THE ALIENS

mission that I needed to fulfill."

Before finding out what her mission was, Raven made a name for herself in the entertainment business, becoming well established as an actress and exotic dancer probably best known for her lead role in the 1967 Russ Meyer film, "Up." When Meyer first discovered her at Joe Allen's, a hangout in West Hollywood, California, she had no acting experience. Years later, Owen Gleiberman wrote that she "...may be [Meyer's] most spectacular siren." And while she recognizes the fact that UFOs exist, she has another tie-in with the "high and the mighty," that being that she is the granddaughter of aviation pioneer Lieutenant William Knox Martin. Before leaving Hollywood for the red rocks of Sedona, De La Croix produced and starred in "The Lost Empire," a camp spacey ode to the lost world genre doubtlessly inspired by a much earlier 1930s film by Sir Arthur Conan Doyle where dinosaurs still roam the jungles of the South American highlands.

From the patio of her home she is able to peer out into the heavens through a telescope and enjoy the nighttime view that only the red rock inspired atmosphere of Sedona can afford. When called upon, she speaks freely of her cosmically inspired adventures and performs her "Sonic Alchemy" with her performance art troop. The following story of her interrelation with an interdimensional alien is both provocative and profound.

* * * * * * * * * * * * * * *

THE ART OF A REAL CLOSE ENCOUNTER
By Raven De La Croix

I remember an evening in particular . . . which started in the waking state. I had been painting "The Raven & The Serpent," my personal metaphorical transformation for the integration of the light and the dark, in this never-ending spiral of awakenings. I felt the evening was early and decided to impeccably groom – as if for a special honeymoon. Why that thought crossed my mind in that way I had never explored until I began "the remembering."

Every inch of myself was glowing, oiled, glittered, scented and decorated in my usual Goddess Sacred Dancewear. Nine or so rings, including a toe-ring, six earrings, headbands, swords, candles, and the most magical sacred music, including veils. I was alone. Or so I thought.

Just as if on stage, I "showed up" as the real thing. "Layering In" essence of Goddess. I danced and breathed myself into oneness with myself and "all that is." Suddenly, there was an acute awareness that it was being experienced and recorded from an "outside" point of aesthetics. Who and what is this "outside" space invasion phenomenon? This sexuality is experienced as a total mind/body/soul explosion which can only be described as a continuing river of velvet purple aqua water in slow motion . . . like Dolphins flowing together and apart, always in synchronicity, yet independently creating.

SCREWED BY THE ALIENS

That was the ideal. Feeling this ethereal "partner" as physically present, I experience sheer delight for our timeless connection and full recognition of the sacredness and the eternal nature of this ancient/future union. I was the song played. I was the dance . . . the place where you say "yes" . . . and it is golden and divine.

The ecstasy is something no words can harness. Find me in the realm of the Sacred . . . the honor of "conscious" experience.

My Personal Side: This painting felt unique to me, as I knew this "experience" wasn't a dream. I had evidence of interaction and a higher awareness of Divine Tantra, and clear telepathy that came up while in my higher conscious state after this episode. I became aware of a very insightful and "new to me until then" aspect of the abduction phenomenon. I became aware of the inter-dimensionality aspect and how layered it was. All of a sudden, I understood "Alice in Wonderland" for the first time. All wasn't how it seemed to be!

The layered dimensionality of the experience was frightening at first, but more for the disorientation than the perception. At that time I had also just read the Jane Roberts "OverSoul 7" trilogy and it brought the hologram awareness right into present time! The flexibility of it all!

Then there was left for me the Great Mystery, and a yearning for what I could not remember from this interaction that haunted me until the next encounter . . . which is another story in my upcoming revelations of this ongoing series of paranormal unfoldings to date.

So be it.

Visit Raven's Cosmic Portal

www.RavenCosmicPortal.com

Author, Publisher and UFO researcher, Tim Beckley with Raven De La Croix

SCREWED BY THE ALIENS

A poster from Raven's best known film, "Up," produced by the late Russ Meyer."

No wonder the aliens found her hard to resist (photo from the movie "Up").

Many fans would love to get lost with Raven and the girls from the classic "The Lost Empire."

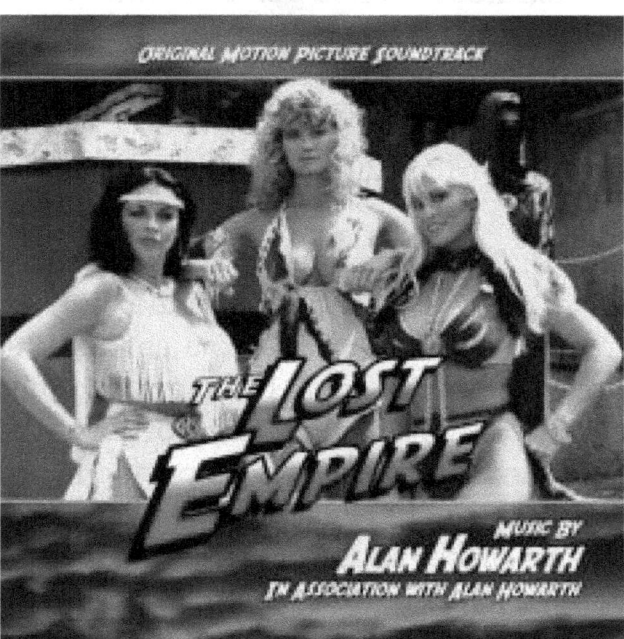

Painting "The Raven and the Serpent," Ms. De La Croix's personal metaphorical transformation for the integration of the light and the dark.

125

SCREWED BY THE ALIENS

AN AERIAL MOLESTER
By Paul Dale Roberts

EDITOR'S NOTE: In the majority of cases those having a negative alien encounter-sexual or just "ordinary"-can look at the event as a traumatizing experience, or they can see it as a "learning experience."

Molestation in childhood is most often a horrifying event, something not easily erased from one's memory; though often the trauma is so bad that the memory becomes distorted to the point that it is difficult to recall exactly what happened. Some believe that having sex with an alien is a cover for something that is almost certainly more earthbound in origin. Others believe the aliens themselves try to cloud the minds of those young people they have "messed with." This story told by veteran researcher Paul Dale Roberts illustrates how it is possible that such a state of affairs can lead to an opening of consciousness – as in the case of Deanna, who takes us along in the various stages of her psychic development.

* * * * * * *

My wife, Deanna Jaxine Stinson, as a young girl in Auburn, California, saw a mysterious "eye in the sky."

This Eye in the Sky most likely was a UFO. Auburn is near the Green Valley Vortex and is part of the UFO Gold Country Triangle. In and around the Sierras, Bill Birnes of History Channel's "UFO Hunters" referred to this area as the UFO Gold Country Triangle because UFOs are sighted in this area. It is theorized that the UFOs are attracted to the gold deposits. As for the Green Valley Vortex, mysterious entities have been seen there. And, believe it or not, it was reported in the Auburn newspaper that two high school boys were chased by robots that came out of a UFO. Auburn is definitely a mysterious place, and, from the way Deanna has described the Mysterious Eye, I do believe it had extraterrestrial origins.

Now that Deanna is an adult, she has reoccurring nightmares of floating up to a craft and things being done to her body. As a child, she remembers being molested by a human adult, but could it be that she was experimented on by extra-

SCREWED BY THE ALIENS

terrestrial entities that have fogged up her mind? Could it be that they have implanted misinformation into Deanna, causing her to forget experiments being conducted by extraterrestrials and setting the ground work for her to believe things were done to her by an adult male? See the last paragraph of this story. Meredith received misinformation from extraterrestrials and I believe Deanna received misinformation from extraterrestrials. Deanna now feels she has a strong connection to UFOs; she can feel the presence of a UFO. Deanna has the ability to uncloak UFOs. So, I definitely feel she has a strong connection to the UFO phenomenon and I believe she was abducted. The experience that occurred to her when she was a child comes back in reoccurring nightmares. It bothered her so much, she made a drawing of it.

My wife tells her story in more detail below:

When I was a young child, in Penryn, CA, I can't remember the exact age that I was, I believed in the world... I believed that there was no evil when I was just blind to it. I had black hair as a young girl. I remember that I was wearing shorts because it was in the summertime. I was spinning around in front of the door to my daycare talking to my spirit guide. I stopped dead in my tracks because I felt something staring down at me very hard. It took me a minute to look up but when I did I saw something incredible. At the top of my viewpoint is a pine tree that often dropped many pinecones. The lawn it was in was strange.

You could find a four leaf clover anywhere in this grass. I was paralyzed with fear. It was a giant eyeball that was the size at least of a tall building. It looked like it opened an invisible curtain. It was blue on the lids and in the pupil. When the eyeball saw me I couldn't quit staring so it rolled its self back into its lid and it sounded like boulders rolling down a mountain. Then, it was if someone closed this invisible curtain and pulled the eye backwards. After this event I heard the gate to my daycare swing open and there was a white man with black hair staring at me. He had glasses and he seemed young, like in his 20s maybe, I am not sure. I was sexually abused right then by him. So, obviously, I have tried to heal from this experience my whole life and I am still searching. The thing about the eye is that it could be many things and maybe the same thing all at once. It means different things in different cultures and ages throughout the world. So, here are the clues I have collected throughout the years:

SYMBOLOGY:

Four Leaf Clovers: The four leaf clover has four green petals. Many are mistaken for a four leaf clover but it is the green ones without any discolorations. The leaves are full and round. This clover has a huge problem with mistaken identities. In the Irish symbology (where they seem most important) the petals of the four leaf clover equal the holy trinity: One each for the Father, Son, Holy Ghost and the fourth represents God's grace. In America we consider them tokens of

SCREWED BY THE ALIENS

good luck.

Eyeball: The eyeball that I saw was blue in color. Of course, the whites of our eyes were also the whites of this eye. I could not tell you if it was a right or left eye or just a single one on its own. The eye is considered to be "all-knowing" and called the Eye of God in mystical practices. The theory is that the eye knows and sees all. The act that was committed on me was evil and the Egyptians regarded it as a protective symbol. I was not protected from the evil but maybe I could have been kidnapped and killed had it not shown up? I cannot know.

As a child, I was very psychic. I learned not to talk about what I was seeing because my sister had shared a ghost experience and my family had started considering her crazy. The only things that I could not hide were my psychic dreams because I often woke others up from my shouting and crying. One time I caught myself levitating in a white light above my bed in the middle of the night. Then I started to wave my legs frantically and freaked out until I was slowly lowered down as if by moonlight, which was also shining through the window...

Or is this a UFO? I found my husband because I was looking for some spiritual guidance and I called him and asked him about it and his first reaction is that it is a UFO. He had worked military intelligence before (Paul Dale Roberts) and saw photos of UFOs from the government. The sounds that it made and the weird rolling motion was almost mechanical when I thought back to this instance. Could there be a royal race of magic aliens? It seems incredible but then I think back to that night in the moonlight was that also a spaceship and then I have misplaced memories from childhood about a doctor and then it's in the middle of a K-mart and the curtains are clear and I'm naked and then it doesn't make sense. My mom was there in the memory but she cannot remember what I speak of. Also in the room where I levitated was this electronic black horse I called Black Magic. He would turn on in the middle of the night, frequently power off and on, and it was loud so it would wake me up. Was this an electromagnetic field or a haunting? Then that invisible curtain that I saw must have been a field wrapped over Earth that it penetrated deeply.

THE ANCIENT DAYS

The Eye of Horus is a symbol of protection, royal power and good health.

The name for the eye derived from the eye of a cobra. Hence, seeing that a cobra rose in protection, ancient sailors would paint this eye on their ship for their own protection.

When I first saw this my first thought at the time was that it was a giant's eye. Was this a Cyclops looking into our dimension, and did it enjoy the misery I went through? Why was there only one eye staring at me? Was that all it had or was there more?

One thing that I know is that it has been seen and worshipped before. I do not

SCREWED BY THE ALIENS

know how the conclusion came upon ancient peoples that it needed to be worshipped but it is causing me great speculation and I am not satisfied with the answers because I am looking for the truth. The truth is out there!

You can see more of the story at this link: www.costaricantimes.com/tag/the-psychic-power-to-uncloak-ufos

Deanna explains the Mysterious Eye here:paranormalhorror.com/2016/01/14/great-mysterious-eye-deanna-jaxine-stinson/

UFOs Appear in the evening sky.

Below: Deanna rendered her UFO experience as art.

Deanna

SCREWED BY THE ALIENS

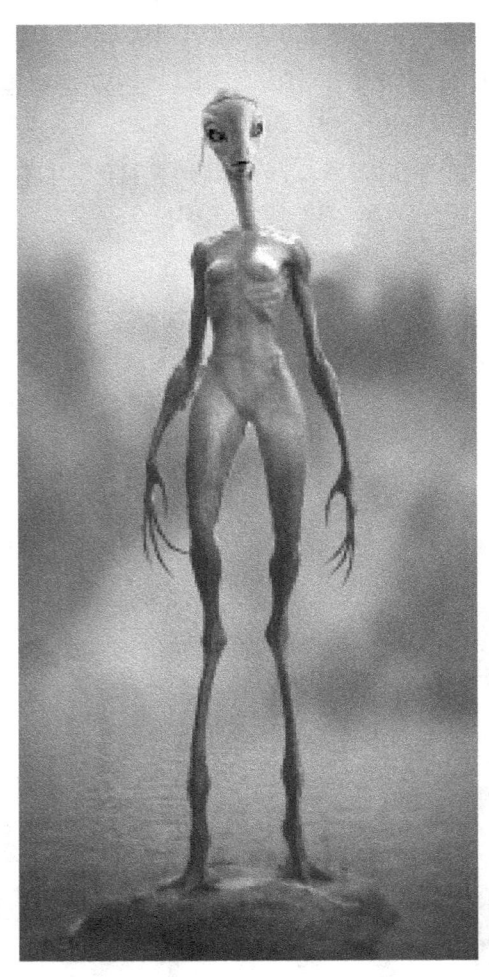

SECTION FIVE - ALIENS IN THE CINEMA
THE CINEMA, SEX AND SAUCERS

SCREWED BY THE ALIENS

ALIEN SEX CINEMA – CREATURE COUPLINGS
By Timothy Green Beckley

Science Fiction on the big screen has always managed to capture the essence of the sexuality of the extraterrestrial. From the very beginning of our confrontation with aliens, we earthlings have been poked, probed, impregnated and forced to abandon any sense of decency when traveling out among the stars. Aliens have forced themselves upon us, or if necessary have used the very powerful human tool of seduction to get their way – usually trying to prevent their far off race from dying out. To do so, they often employ a scantily clad crew of star maidens to do the bidding of some evil alien warlord.

To the issue of scanty pantied (if any?) aliens, Flashbak.com offers some thoughts:

"Whether it was the micro-mini skirt uniforms on Star Trek, the sex slaves of Logan's Run, Barbarella's see-through spacesuit, or the Moonbase girls on UFO, science fiction, more often than not, featured eye candy for the primarily male audience. Even the black and white films of the 1950s were prone to feature alien ladies in bikinis or skimpy attire. Indeed, the first appearances of the miniskirt on the big screen came via Dale Arden on the old Flash Gordon films and Ann Francis in Forbidden Planet. And in the late 1960s, sci-fi kicked things up a notch… rather, a dozen notches. As censorship laws and cultural taboos relaxed, cinemas were flooded with sleaze. As the censors fell asleep at the wheel, more and more graphic material gravitated to the big screen… and sci-fi was no exception. A number of 'X-rated' and adult-oriented science fiction flicks arrived at local drive-ins and midnight shows across the western world."

On the other hand, they also show us the far-flung possibilities of sexuality that may seem extreme to us currently, but which might become quite "normal" once we blast off out of here. There are, after all, many alien races and a multitude of possibilities that we will be faced with. There could be an endless lineup of temptations, though I can't imagine picking up anyone hanging out at the "Star

SCREWED BY THE ALIENS

Wars" bar. But, heck, you can never tell. You just never know.

Discover Magazine online seems to have a firm explanatory grasp on the situation.

"Science fiction knows how to play around with sex and gender. The free-lovin' of 'A Stranger in A Strange Land,' Commander Shepard's bisexual proclivities, and William T. Riker's seemingly universal interspecies compatibility are constant sources of entertainment.

"And the fun doesn't stop with organic entities. Androids, cyborgs, and robots make gender all the stranger. Why is Data fully functional? Isn't it curious that, of all the characters in 'Ghost in the Shell,' the two most heavily-cyberized characters, Motoko and Batou, are hyper-feminine and hyper-masculine respectively? And, my favorite: as a robot Bender has no gender, so if Bender bends his gender, what gender does Bender bend?"

AELITA: THE QUEEN OF MARS

By today's standards, Aelita could never win a beauty pageant, but she could easily be part of the "Me Too" women's movement as she is the undisputed ruler of the red planet. With an exposed midriff and a top that shows off even more of that Martian flesh, Aelita found her earthman through a telescope (a weird type of dating), and he promptly took off in a rocket to hook up with her. Made in Russia in 1925, Aelita had to use her feminine wiles to her best advantage in this silent science fiction classic. Indeed, she might have been the first sci-fi vixen. No "War of the Worlds" or "Close Encounters," but hell you have to start somewhere.

FLASH GORDON, BUCK ROGERS
AND THE SATURDAY AFTERNOON CLIFFHANGER

I actually met Flash Gordon. Well, sort of. I once was handed an assignment by the National Enquirer to interview Buster Crabbe, an Olympic Gold Medalist who played Tarzan, Buck Rodgers and Flash Gordon in the mid-1930s on the big screen in the Saturday afternoon cliffhangers which normally ran 13 episodes. Actually, Tarzan goes back to 1918, but there was very little sex portrayed (blame it on the restrictive morals of the time), not only in the movies, but most places on the planet. We all know about Jane of "Queen of the Jungle fame," a character which several actresses played. And while they might have been early cinema sirens, they were not space babes, so we must leave them being chased by Cheetah swinging from vine to vine.

But Buck Rogers and especially Flash Gordon were another core of the apple!

"Science fiction movies have been a good excuse for bare midriffs since the late 1920s," confirms Bikini,Science.com, "and Universal Pictures dishes up a rich helping of them in the Flash Gordon serials.

"Jean Rogers and Pricilla Lawson are both former beauty queens, and, like Muriel Goodspeed (Zona), maintain bare bellies throughout the science fiction

SCREWED BY THE ALIENS

series." The moviegoer is treated to both actresses being "clad in bare-belly tops, with long hair, and high heels that are quite racy for the 1930s." For those who like the thought of women being held in captivity on a distant world, you might discover a thrill or two in the remastered versions of these old black and white epics.

ONLY THE BEST HOLLYWOOD HAS TO OFFER CAN SAVE US

They – the movies – come in all shapes and sizes, just like the aliens themselves do. From the lowest of budgets to films that took millions to shoot, like the "Alien" franchise starring Sigourney Weaver.

In the handful of instances where sex between humans and humanoids takes place, the majority of the aliens are monstrous pests, perverts, or just plain galactic rapists and molesters. A few get off easy with their intergalactic charm – like Jeff Bridges as Starman and Jane Fonda as Barbarella.

No other movie in this breeding-with-aliens genre has gotten as much attention as Ridley Scott's "Alien." Few critics have failed to note the movie's preoccupation with sex, from its central rape theme to its obsession with alien reproduction – not to mention the erotic symbolism of the alien design itself. It is without a doubt one of the most harsh, barbaric depictions in a mainstream movie. Close to "Alien" in its intensity, but well below it in budget, is Roger Corman's "Humanoids from the Deep," where aliens who come out of the ocean besiege an entire town brutally raping its women right in the middle of a Fourth of July celebration.

FROM BLUES BROTHER TO BLUE BALLS

Probably the most "explosive" scene between an earthling (Dan Aykroyd) and a smoking hot Nordic-type alien (played by Kim Bassinger) can be found in "My Stepmother Is an Alien." Coming a long distance from a world that is light years ahead of us, the beautiful space maid isn't quite sure what sex is all about. She has to consult with a penis-like representative of her home planet to find out the basics. She kind of goes for the idea and ends up with Aykroyd in the sack, and together the earth tilts and the universe spins. As SYFY WIRE enthusiastically points out, "The alien turns out to be really nice and never tries to lay eggs in anybody (a huge sign of respect in alien culture)."

In your spare time get busy on the Internet and track down some of the more obscure films of this notion. It's good for interplanetary relations I would say!

FORBIDDEN PLANETS

The universe is teeming with life – given that certain astronomical statistics alert us to the fact that some nearby planets might be populated – which could also mean they are home to some pretty unsavory characters. Future star voyagers will have to do more than check the content of the atmosphere before landing on some unknown planet. They should send down a scout ship with heavily armed forces like in the movie "Flesh Gordon."

SCREWED BY THE ALIENS

Some planets should be marked on star charts as FORBIDDEN! These are our picks for those that we would warn future space travelers about venturing too close to. These are the "Rotten Tomatoes" of the cosmically-endowed cinema. No big budgets here. Definitely for adult star troopers. Some are funny; a few might take themselves seriously. But the posters that hung in front of the drive-in theater where most of them played back in the Sixties and Seventies are certainly eye openers and collectibles today.

1. STAR BABES —

This 1977 production reveals a top secret government project where the Star Angels are sent to the planet Phallus to prevent a takeover of Earth.

2. INVASION OF THE LOVE DRONES —

Released in the same year, one viewer said there is a great scene where a female agent is forcefully "droned" by a weightlifter-type alien as she is held down by multiple drones.

3. EARTH GIRLS ARE EASY —

A Valley Girl befriends three furry humanoids in a Hollywood swimming pool. Shot sometime in the mid-Eighties. There was even a short lived TV series.

4. 2069: A SPACE ODYSSEY—

Sexy gals from Venus rocket off to Earth in order to grab some sperm samples which will resuscitate their dying planet, but what good will it do for us after viewing this 1974 "classic"?

5. FLESH GORDON—

I remember giving this a good review when I was Hustler's movie critic. Instead of giving a film one or four stars we invented an erection scale. This adult spoof of Flash Gordon was entertaining and for its day had some fairly good animation sequences. Made in 1974 for $700,000, this adaptation has Flesh Gordon trying to protect the planet from an evil alien emperor who is bombarding Earth with a sex ray to stir up the groins of the populace.

6. NUDE ON THE MOON—

A 1961 release all about a wealthy scientist who organizes a lunar landing and discovers a plethora of naked women.

7. SPACE THING —

"Visit the planet of the rapes," the poster screams as the theater empties around us. Think I saw this on a triple feature circa 1968.

8. THE INCREDIBLE SEX RAY MACHINE/SEXUAL ENCOUNTERS OF EVERY KIND —

"Great" double feature that reaches out from the outer limits to the inner depths of depravity.

SCREWED BY THE ALIENS

9. STAR VIRGIN —

A futuristic (made in 1988) robot teaches a space virgin by way of several "explosive" vignettes, what sex is all about – giving her the wrong idea along the way.

10. ALIEN EROTICA

Complete with name change, this cinema epic depicts three beautiful women who find themselves unwilling subjects of an alien scientist's sexy experiments . . . so what else is new in this day and age?

Aelita is getting ready for the arrival of "her man" via rocket from Earth.

Flash Gordon's space rovers had the greatest gams in Hollywood – oh, sorry, I mean on Venus.

Buck Rodgers is the consummate space traveler who receives a radio message that the Tiger Men from Mars are about to attack. I think we will win as they are too busy fooling around with Earth women.

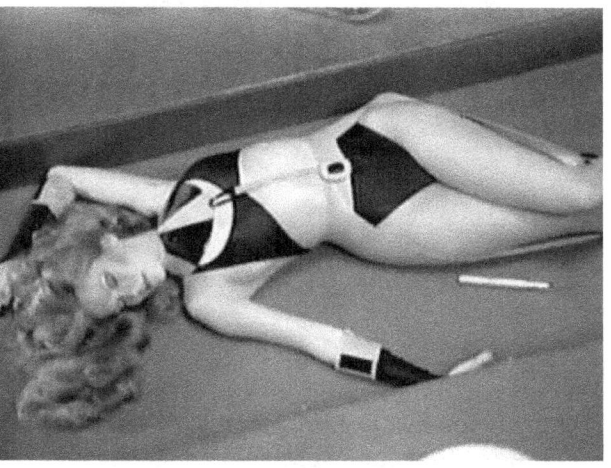

In "Starship Invasion," a farmer gets pulled off his tractor for an Antonio Boas-like experience. The alien breeder is the hottest thing this side of the sun.

SCREWED BY THE ALIENS

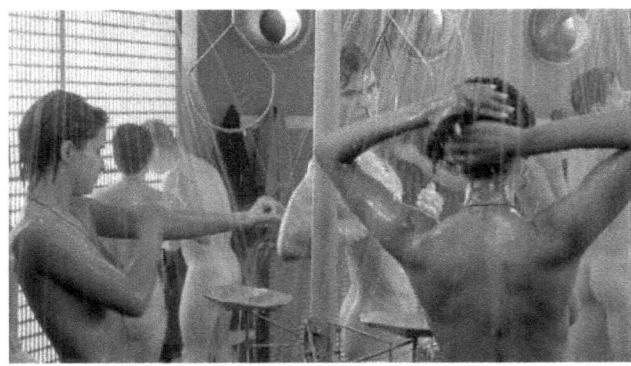

They supply the soap and the bare bodies in the best — if not the only — shower scene on the way to Mars in "Starship Troopers."

All the sex in space doesn't have to be crude and hurried. Ask the gentleman who is getting some well-deserved attention in "The Queen From Outer Space."

Loren Velquez is about to get her comeuppances in "Ship of Monsters," a 1960s el cheapo space opera filmed in Mexico.

Jane Fonda in "Barbarella" is getting an orgasmic tuneup from a hunk of a spaceman.

SCREWED BY THE ALIENS

With a face and body only a "mother" could love. Carting off the Earth maiden in "They Want Your Women." Is there no decency in outer space?

An alluring space vixen banned in 16 galaxies. Looks like she would like to get her tentacles around you.

The cyborgs want you. What a cute couple. She's a hottie – "he's" all nuts and bolts.

Jane Fonda as Barbarella has her hands full with an orgasmic ray gun. Best representative for sex with a space alien yet!

SCREWED BY THE ALIENS

Hog-tied bondage altar scene from "Fire Maidens From Outer Space."

Aliens take women by force in "Humanoids From The Deep."

Kim Bassinger has just arrived here in a UFO, and Blues Brother Dan Aykroyd sees this as a potentially explosive – orgasm-wise — situation. Don't bother to call out MJ12, Dan, they will only muddy the waters.

SCREWED BY THE ALIENS

SCREWED BY THE ALIENS

140

SCREWED BY THE ALIENS

SCREWED BY THE ALIENS

SCREWED BY THE ALIENS

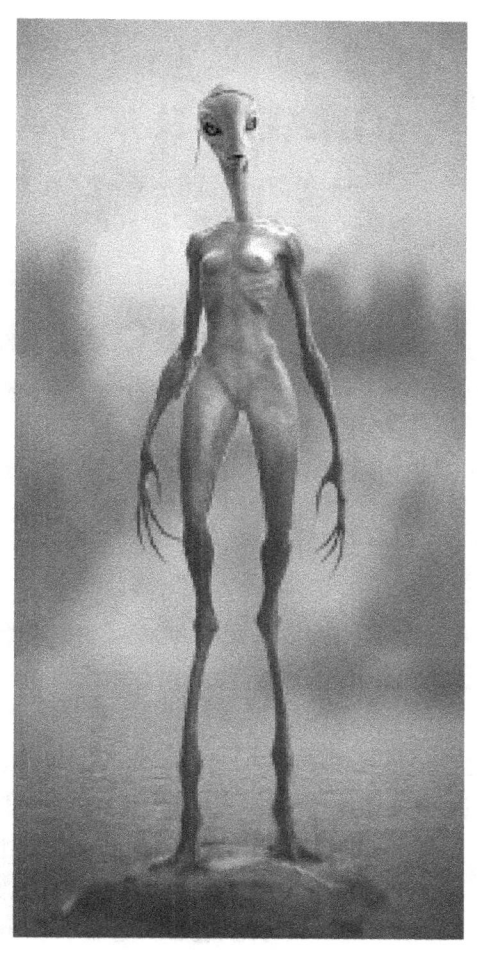

SECTION SIX
AN INVESTIGATION INTO THE RIDDLE OF THE "LOVE BITE"

Chapter Fifteen: The Anomalous Work of Eve Lorgen

SCREWED BY THE ALIENS

CHAPTER 15

PROJECT ALIEN LOVE BITES
THE ANOMALOUS WORK OF EVE LORGEN
By Timothy Green Beckley, Sean Casteel
and Eve Lorgen

Warning! This material is of a highly controversial nature, but is as well documented as this type of information can be, according to the principle subject of this chapter.

"Alien abduction research is NOT for the faint of heart. My associates and I have been under surveillance for years. And if we tell you the details, you will think we are paranoid, but that's what the aliens and their human supporters want you to think. They want to discredit everyone who even speaks about this topic in casual conversation. They want the topic itself to be of no value."

Working in close association with other researchers, Eve Lorgen – who holds a Bachelor's degree in Biochemistry from San Francisco State University and a Master's degree in Counseling Psychology – has taken part in studies that are beginning to shed new light on the various aspects of the abduction phenomenon, particularly those that are of a sexual and relationship-related nature.

And despite the "high strangeness" of many of the accounts that have been related to her, Lorgen is convinced that over 50 percent of those participating in what can only be described as the eeriest – and sometimes most terrifying – encounters are telling the absolute truth.

Throughout history these beings we call aliens have been manipulating the human race – "through the use of techniques that can only be described as 'Brainwashing,'" Lorgen believes.

Since the late 1980s, she says, thousands of credible witnesses have been coming forward with accounts of abductions by aliens. Their accounts included details of mind-control, chemical dosing, dream manipulations, surgery and implants. If we were to categorize this group, we might say they were all victims of a

SCREWED BY THE ALIENS

kind of rape, a "psychic rape."

And, she adds, "Even more alarming is that when investigated, many of these credible people, report having been handled badly, abused, victimized and mistreated. Horror stories of actual rape and sodomy came out and many of these reports were accompanied by the suggestion that the aliens were determined to inflict emotional pain. Many of the stories, collected from different parts of the world, had similar subtexts and began to sound like the aliens, if they existed at all, were not as compassionate as we might have once thought."

Now, even though what Eve has to say may sound quite hard to believe in the extreme, she claims to have credible proof that aliens exist and are interacting with a larger portion of humanity than we may have been led to believe. Her proof comes in what she calls the "Afterglow Phenomenon," which she credits to a discovery made some years ago by the "alien hunter" Derrell Sims. *(Sims website: http://www.alienhunter.org)

"He started telling abductees to get a black light and start looking for different marks because he had found that many of them had fluorescent marks on their skin following an abduction."

The marks were in many different colors, including blue, green, white, pink red and orange. *(See: http://evelorgen.com/wp/news/evidence-for-alien-abduction-fluorescence-body-marks/)

"It seems to be, in most cases, an irregular splotching," Lorgen says. "It's from handling the aliens. Some people have remembered the aliens taking them by the hand or by the arm during the experience. And where the aliens touched them, they would have fluorescence."

As an example she said one woman who went through the standard abduction scenario was handed a hybrid baby.

"The woman later had this bright orange fluorescence all over her chest and some on her neck and hands," Lorgen continued. "In her experience, she recalled being given one of those alien children to hold and to hug, and the places where she touched the child were where she had the markings on her body."

And she notes that there is also a kind of "branding" that often takes place.

"Almost as if people are stamped or marked for a particular reason. It looks like it's a definite tattoo sometimes. But unlike the fluorescence it does not fade with time."

* * * * *

So who is this Eve Lorgen whose body of work we are so determinedly delving into?

The UFO community is usually peopled by researchers, therapists and experiencers who act out their well-defined roles without much crossover be-

SCREWED BY THE ALIENS

tween the various areas of expertise. But occasionally – very rarely – someone comes along who embodies all these fields of endeavor and who moves easily between the differing demands of each perspective on the UFO phenomenon.

Lorgen was initially drawn to the UFO field in 1978 and found herself wanting to focus on anomalous trauma.

"I wanted to learn more about and work with people who were abducted," she recalls. "That's one reason why I got my Master's Degree in Counseling Psychology. At the time I held more interest in anomalous trauma than in research biochemistry."

Two years later she started a support group for UFO experiencers while also carrying out independent research in the fields of Oriental medicine, the paranormal and the occult, various religions, the Bible, Satanic ritual abuse, and people suffering from unusual forms of trauma.

One of the reasons Eve is adept at getting others to talk about what has transpired in their own lives is because she considers herself one of them.

"I am an abductee, too," she says. "And I find that people are more open to others who have a genuine interest and compassion for them than, let's say, just a staunch researcher out to get them for their information. I find that I get good, authentic information. People tell me all kinds of things that other researchers either don't get or are perhaps not trusted enough to get that information. So I find that it's better to empathize where they are and to accept them as they are. Because I, too, am one of them.

Eve said her experiences go back to when she was about three and a half years of age when she sighted a very large, physical craft.

"Growing up there were UFO sightings in the neighborhood and at one time later something came into the house – initially I thought it might be a dream – and I woke up screaming. Before the aliens come I get a prodromal sense of their presence and I'll know it and I'll just get really anxious. You keep waking up all night long and they will still be there."

"BITTEN" BY THE ALIENS

In "The Love Bite: Alien Interference In Human Relationships," the reader is presented with an entirely new assemblage of material that we guarantee you will not find in any other book on the UFO topic.

Lorgen told journalist Sean Casteel in an exclusive interview that, "The aliens have the ability to mess with our minds. They often engage in what I refer to as 'detraction efforts,' in an attempt to keep their abductees under control and to prevent them from learning too much about what is happening to them.

"What I've found in my life and with other people I've worked with," she explains, "is that the moment when someone becomes really interested in studying the phenomenon – to the point of getting to core memories where one might want

SCREWED BY THE ALIENS

to get a hypnotic regression, seek counseling or work with a researcher – sometimes when that happens, it's like there's an emotional triggering effect. Probably orchestrated by the aliens, either directly or indirectly, to prevent that person from getting that information. They'll re-abduct them so that they have mixed feelings and anxiety compelling them not to meet the researcher or the hypnotherapist so that they don't get to their memories. So that they can't get to the truth. The aliens want to keep them in ignorance so that they can believe the false memories or whatever ideas they want them to believe."

The detracting efforts by the aliens not only happen consistently, they can sometimes be truly frightening.

"Not just feelings of anxiety," Lorgen said. "It can be really blatant, like car accidents and sudden illness. Or all of a sudden their spouse will get into a fight with them before they go to the group. All these minor, delaying annoyances and things like that that prevent them from getting to a certain place or a certain researcher. Even black helicopters hovering over their home and being directly threatened and all kinds of 'insane' stuff that is thrown at them from out of nowhere."

Still another factor that often continues and torments abductees is what Lorgen calls the "Alien Love Bite."

"One other thing I have focused on was the phenomenon of relationship manipulation that the aliens do to people, to get them matched up with partners or spouses of a particular kind. That could be either for breeding or for purposes of genetically putting certain combinations together. But it also seems they put people together and create situations and orchestrate dramas for whatever reasons.

"It could be to get emotional extremes out of people. They do this particularly with people's love relationships. 'The Love Bite' is a term for when two people are set up together. They pre-bond them in earlier abductions or virtual reality scenarios and encounters. And then, when the two people meet, they just have this magnetic attraction for each other and they have flashbacks of having been together before. A lot of paranormal and psychic things happen between the people and it's almost like a love obsession. But usually one of them is switched off emotionally and leaves the other one unrequited. It's really devastating for some people. But it's been a consistent thing that's happened over and over."

Sometimes, according to Lorgen, the emotional manipulation also serves as the familiar detracting effort.

"For example, one person in my group," she told Sean Casteel, "was starting to get involved with doing more in-depth research and really go full steam to find out. It's like she got hit over the head with a love obsession, which detracted her from doing the original thing she had intended doing. It kept her from being able to work on more personal growth because of this manipulated love obsession.

SCREWED BY THE ALIENS

"It's amazing," she went on. "It happened to several people I have worked with. It sounds crazy, but it's the truth. You would think they would put people together to make them really happy. But it seems like they usually switch one of them off, which seems really cruel. And it's been reported by so many that I know there is something to it!"

THE REASONING

Eve says from what she has gathered, "The aliens spend a great deal of time tracing blood lines and researching the human genome. I suspect they are farming, like we would raise a hybrid horse or dog, but the sadness and grief they generate points to the farming of a certain type of human energy; that energy which results from love obsession, broken hearts and unfulfilled relationships."

Eve says she found an entire litany of problems with experiencers.

"I found substance abuse in many cases. In others, I found people suffering as if they had just come back from Vietnam or Kosovo. It was as if these people were at war with themselves and the aliens, as if they were engaged in a kind of 'Spiritual Warfare.'"

In the worse scenario cases, the author/researcher says, "Murder is suspected, but not proven. Suicidal fixations, on the other hand are well documented amongst abductees. I took a count of the case histories, and tried to break them down into categories. I asked which ones dealt with rape and incest, heavy familial occult involvement, or alcohol and drugs and so forth. Some patterns emerged. I could see that obsession and tendencies toward addictions were common to people with unresolved abduction issues. Kidnapping victims, if they survive, always report separation anxiety, but what role does obsessiveness play? That's when I knew I had to publish my findings. The psychic and real scars found on abductees have been sugar coated in the UFO literature for far too long."

* * * * * * * *

With her kind permission, we have retrieved some of Eve's personal files to bring you two examples of "Love Bites." *(See: http://evelorgen.com/wp/news/the-new-predator-2/ and https://www.sovereignki.com/single-post/2018/06/03/The-New-Predator)

I THOUGHT HE WAS MY TWIN FLAME –
I WAS OVERWHELMED BY A COSMIC PREDATOR

Here is a more in-depth explanation of my experience with P. I was living on the [EL: non specified for confidentiality sake] island and immersed in one of the most powerful feminine awakening journeys of my life thus far in a facilitated journey known as Womb Wisdom. This was the beginning of my awakening to the world of hyper-dimensional realities, spirit influence, ancient feminine mysteries and my initiation into the (false) Christ Lineage teachings. My teachers were all women but the main man and masculine pillar who brought forth this work was

SCREWED BY THE ALIENS

named P.

I revered him as a man with great power, wisdom and love. When I met P for the first time, we hugged and my entire body activated with energy and it felt like my body was melting into him. He held me as I cried for hours, releasing pain and trauma from my body all while pulling me in closer to him. It felt like I was home in his presence. He was then later invited over to the retreat space I was staying at by the owner – who just so happened to be friends with him. Later that evening, P shared with me that we were lovers in Egypt and as he touched my leg, energy shot through my entire body and I felt the truth of this karmic resonance flow through me. He brought me to my room to share a story with me. As he spoke of the ancient temple in Egypt and the massacre of the Priestesses, he weaved his words in a way that made me become convinced that I had something to do with the betrayal of him and the murder of the priestesses. He claimed he was the Priest and I remember crying my eyes out looking into his eyes, seeing his face change into the man I once knew. He kept asking me who he was, telling me he was my Beloved. I gave him my will and became convinced he truly was my Beloved and that we had found each other again, after all those lifetimes. I was shaken at the core and so entranced that this man with such great power and depth was coming onto me. I was bewildered, startled and completely placed under his spell.

He then kissed me and quickly moved himself on top of me. It was the most passionate, intense experience I have ever shared with a man. The way he placed himself onto me was overwhelming, and I could feel pain shooting inside my mouth as he kissed me with intense vigor. I was so surrendered and, even though it hurt, I didn't have enough within me to tell him to stop. I was powerless and weak underneath him and a part of me had always wanted to experience a man with this much passion and desire and so I didn't resist. I surrendered and moved with him as my body began to open in ways I never felt before. I began experiencing profound tantric bliss like never before. The next morning I woke up with swollen lips and a gut feeling that something was not right. I tried to understand what was happening but I couldn't. After that encounter we were constantly pulled to each other. I was entranced and wanted to explore what was unfolding. He told me I was his "soul mate" and spoke of having premonitions of going to my home country as he felt my soul calling to him. He kept sharing stories from Egypt, weaving archetypal energies into my experience and tying me into a mythical storyline of truth weaved in with inflation and deceit.

We experienced the most amazing highs, blissful and ecstatic connection from the very beginning. Then crashing lows that would tear me apart and leave me feeling completely physically and emotionally drained. Many nights I was literally on the floor in shambles, crying my eyes out as his abusive and minimizing words attacked me. As I received this harsh energy I believed it was helping me evolve. I believed this pain was breaking my heart open to the truth of myself. I

SCREWED BY THE ALIENS

believed that the hurtful things he was saying about me were true because he was a highly evolved being who had vast precision, awareness and great consciousness that saw through everything. His manipulations had me inverted and emotionally controlled to feel that I continuously needed him. Even though he was abusive, I could not leave him. I was veiled. I could not see how his light was false. I thought it was the Guru's way. I thought I deserved this. I felt that without him I would not be able to live. I allowed myself to be robbed of my voice and my personal power. I trusted him completely and put my heart fully out on the table to continuously have it smashed by patterns of destruction. Something felt off within me, but I believed I had to be humble and take it all in without talking back or standing up against him, as he was serving my soul and had my greatest interest in mind.

Over time, we became even closer. The psychic connection grew incredibly strong. I felt like he was watching me when I was alone. I felt that he could hear my thoughts. I remember one night I woke up in terror as I felt this dark and heavy energy over me. When I became conscious, I realized it wasn't human. Moments later he showed up at my door saying he could feel me. He was so tuned into me. Sometimes I felt I had no privacy in my own space. When I was pulling away, he would show up saying all the right things to bring me back into his life. I was also very connected to him and experienced feeling what he was feeling. I could especially feel him desiring me sexually and would know when he would want to make love, as I could feel his presence pulling on my body to be with him. It felt that my sexual energy was literally being siphoned at times.

As time went on the abusive patterns kept increasing and the extreme highs and lows intensified. I became more and more drained as I was continuously rejected and then pulled back into this "love bite" agenda. It was like I was being emotionally whiplashed. He would push me away and then would show affection again, opening himself up sexually. I was so cast under a spell and, because of my own vulnerabilities and wounds, I could not get away. I felt such deep love with him and was so addicted to his charm and alluring, strong presence and also had a deep yearning to make love with him as it was like nothing I had experienced before. My entire body was being awakened and I felt my chakras and sexual centers opening in the most profound ways. I was so deeply influenced, believing that our relationship was one of the greatest blessings of my life. I believed that all his harshness and anger was the tough love I needed to help me evolve. That these highs and lows were a normal part of being with a man like this.

When we would come back together after the many intense separations, it was the most passionate, deeply blissful, ecstatic love I have ever experienced and he would share with me how much I meant to him and how I was the most beautiful woman he has ever been with and how I am his soul mate and that he would take care of me and be in my life forever. My heart was so open to him and

SCREWED BY THE ALIENS

so trusting that I believed him. I trusted that somewhere within him, he must truly love and care for me. Yet, every time we separated or spiraled into a drama, it was so intense and it felt like all his words would go shooting down the drain, holding no meaning at all. I would dive into the darkest places. At times it felt like I wanted to die. I wouldn't be able to get out of bed. I had no energy at all. It felt that without him I was hopeless, meaningless. My life had no substance and I felt completely paralyzed. No matter where we stood, his presence would always consume me and I could not let him go. Even though his words would cut me down, making me feel like I was nothing, portraying me to be a small, stupid and worthless girl compared to the "powerful, intelligent, and evolved Christ-ed being" he was, time and time again I would keep opening myself to him.

It was like I was possessed. I couldn't see clearly. My solar plexus would tighten and I could not be without him. I would do anything to win him back after he would treat me this way. My solar plexus was in so much pain feeling like it was being tied into a tight knot and pierced with a flaming red needle time and time again. I would think of him and cry so deeply it felt my heart was turned inside out and then he would call me saying he felt me and would somehow make me feel like everything was okay again. He would apologize, or hear my apology, and I would feel safe again, and I was right back in, opening my heart again. It felt like I was literally walking on egg shells with him. I had to watch my every move because I did not want to trigger or upset him in any way. I got incredibly used to always feeling pain in my chest, not having any security in my life, but somehow continuously trusting that I was in good hands. I worked myself to complete exhaustion doing all the practices and rituals he asked me to do. It felt that I had to do everything under his watch and approval and that if I didn't he would reject me. He would prescribe me practices that made me believe he really cared for me but now I wonder if it was just a way to fulfill his own needs and story. I worked 4 jobs at once to save money to travel across the world in a very short period of time to be with him, only to be sent back home in despair and heavy guilt and shame feeling it was "all my fault" and would completely gaslight me time and time again. I picked up and completely moved my life twice to fly across the world to be with him, only to last 2 weeks in his presence before another intense drama would play out.

I allowed myself to become the puppet on his string. I put him before everything in my life. I alienated myself from my family and my friends to be with him, I quit my business and jobs and put my finances in extreme jeopardy to be with him, only to arrive and be manipulated by his aggression and abused by his unpleased behavior, as I was never "enough" for him. I even remember him saying that the only thing I was good at was making love. His mannerisms were completely incongruent with his message and desire to support women. It was months of this back and forth abuse until some of the women in the work began to catch

SCREWED BY THE ALIENS

onto his harshness and behavior. After my trip to ********* to be with him, I felt completely paralyzed and frozen from the trauma I experienced. I spoke with (*****) and then herself and another woman came out in public about his narcissistic tendencies, psychopathic behavior and false light cult constructs. Later that day I received messages written from multiple women who had experienced things with P that were out of alignment. He had been visiting other women in their dreams, touching them sexually, sharing how he had past connections with them in Egypt. He created situations that tore people apart, casting spells with his words.

He stole other women's work, taking their teachings and using his intelligence to expand and twist them for his own agenda. (EL–This "copycat" plagiarizing behavior is common for these predators.) The spirits moving through him were feeding off of and manipulating a list of powerful women across the globe. After becoming aware of this, I completely left my body. It was like I was high on Ayahuasca. I was hallucinating and was experiencing strange body perceptions. I understand now that I was so traumatized from what I had been through that I left my body completely. Everything was swirling around me and I didn't know what to do other than ground into Gaia. I began cutting cords and focusing on really separating from him for good. I became very sick and my energy was very weak. I was beginning to understand the severity of the spirit influence and how entangled I was with him. As I began to disconnect, he began messaging me, telling me how he could feel me sexually and that he was receiving pictures of me in his mind.

I did not respond to him, but then, shortly after, I was strung in and felt called to share how I was truly feeling in hopes to bring this all to an end. He received me and apologized for his behavior, taking ownership of the spirits moving through him that caused him to minimize me and treat me like I was dirt and nothing to him. It felt like it was a real breakthrough and that he was finally owning himself and his darkness. He humbled himself and shared with me that I was his teacher of love and said all the right things to win me back again. (Now, I understand that it was just his – or the being moving behind him-'s way of making sure I did not add to the fire these women were bringing forth, because, if I had, then surely his veils would have come undone and the spirits moving behind him would have lost even more power.) Instead, being my love-drunk, addicted and forgiving self, I opened my heart back to him again. This time I could tangibly feel the spirit influence moving us together. I heard in my head, "You must go back with him to help him" as simultaneously my sexual energy was being turned on by a force outside of myself that was not natural. It was like my sexual energy was hijacked, but I was so aroused by the rush of energy that I agreed to see him again to work on healing together.

He came to visit me in my home town and within no time he slipped right back into his patterns of verbal and emotional abuse. He blamed me for being the one who provoked the women to turn on him. He belittled me again, telling me it was my fault and that if I hadn't spoken to them about my experiences in the other country, none of that would have happened. He reverted back to shaming and "guilting" me and playing the role of the "beautiful victim celestial boy" who was hurt and was justified due to his distorted thinking and blaming. He denied that any abuse occurred and reverted back to claiming that if it wasn't for what I did, he would not have gotten mad at all. He could not take ownership for the ways he was really abusing me and psychically feeding off these other women. I became the "Judas" and the one who betrayed him and another huge drama played out. He had a way that was so good with words that I believed his words to be true and I was immediately draped with an immensity of guilt and my solar plexus and heart were taken through another stabbing, tight sensation episode of great pain. These narcissistic ploys sucked more and more emotional strength from me and it felt like I was slowly killing myself.

When he left my space after we separated for the final time, it was then that we became aware of the "Love Bite" dynamic in our relationship. We both read Bernard's Blog post about Eve Lorgen's work (See: https://veilofreality.com/2014/11/22/the-dark-side-of-cupid-hyperdimensional-interferences-in-love-relationships/) and knew right away that this is what was playing out between us. Immediately he told me I had to heal this within me, implying I was the only one who carried this host or entity. I began detaching myself and was still experiencing deep pulls on my solar plexus but it wasn't as intense. As soon as I received the awareness, it was like a massive cord was cut, and I could feel myself coming back into my own energy. I took space from my teachers and the work and began my healing journey and research into this phenomena. Months later, my teacher reached out, inviting me back into the work. As soon as I was in contact with her, I had a dream where I was in a room by myself and P's voice was in my head speaking to me and the "entity of force" I had felt before was trying to make love to my body. I was trying to escape, but this energetic spirit kept touching me and caressing my body. I woke up instantly knowing that this was just another sign of the energies moving through him and that I had to cut myself off from the teachers connected to him and this work.

>>>>>>> P uses a facade of being involved in the Christ Council. Nothing could be further from the truth. He made me believe I was the center of his world and then, after becoming triggered, would tell me I am nothing and that I don't deserve him. To this day I still feel I am being watched as I unplug myself from the programming and the cluster of spirits moving behind him that weaved into my life. My solar plexus still feels pulled on and my nervous system is still rebuilding itself. P is overshadowed by a demonic psychic vampire and I wish that no one goes through what I experienced again. I hope that sharing this helps warn others.

SCREWED BY THE ALIENS

From the files of Eve Lorgen
EASTERN EUROPEAN WOMAN REPORTS ORGASMIC "THRILLS" FROM AN ALIEN AFFAIR

I want to share my experience with you if I may? I am looking forward to any input, if you want. If not, I'm sorry for bothering you, really.

I have met a man and we connected instantly. I realize now that, at the time, I was a stupid newbie to spirituality and naive. He helped me to solve all my troubles.

He hypnotized me in the woods and I was in a trance state with him, feeling orgasmic just by looking at him. I do not know how to call him, pagan, (black) magician, shaman or charlatan – but he looked like a demon, or some alien, and both of us started acting crazy, feeling the amazing dark, sexual energies of some entity. I froze from fear and cried and begged him to let me go because I thought he'd kill me. It felt like I had sex with some entity, not with the man, because it wasn't physical sex. It felt like bones in my body were twitching and I was doing something really creepy, almost levitating in several positions spontaneously, that would be painful to do without being in a trance. After that, we felt like we were weightless.

When I was in a trance he took me on an astral journey or projection just by putting his hand on my belly button. Or maybe it was kundalini. And I saw Earth, as a huge astral body (50 times larger than Earth, I thought it was God, lol), universe, rainbow (was that was my astral cord?), and some beautiful place on some planet that felt like heaven and I felt oneness. Or was it all just in my soul memory, my home? He has been evoking visions of occult symbols in me too. We had a telepathic connection. It felt like I was enlightened. No drugs were involved in all this, at all, I swear. I don't have mental illness in case you wonder.

Physical sex was amazing. He works with meridians points. He put his hand on my head and deleted my thoughts and went into my mind and all I saw was bright light and I was drunk on that energy. He has many lovers and wants orgies too and I was up for it. He says he has sex with people to liberate them. But he blew me off. He said we can't continue until my consciousness rises or else I will fall apart.

He showed me mind-blowing things and suddenly disappeared. Though he promised me he would teach me everything and called me his student. He recommended to me some occult books, as he initiated me into it. I was glamorized by it but felt just used for sex. I had never experienced any of it before. I didn't even know about any of this. He talked about our past lives and how we are soulmates. I thought he was my twin flame or guru. There were so many signs and synchronicities.

He left me with no explanation of anything. I've been possessed with some entity (or was it his energetic hooks?). I can channel some stupid threats in Latin that I didn't even know how to speak, but I translated it later online. I feel very

SCREWED BY THE ALIENS

depressed and heavy if I try to repress it, but if I express it in the hope it'll go out from me, it doesn't solve a problem either. I even tried doing exorcism on me, but that didn't work either.

In our last encounter (I begged to see him) I told him I love him and he told me it is all my fault because I expected us to be a couple and I need to solve it on my own, or I should kill myself. He was very mean to me before, too; he basically raped me mentally and I won't go into nasty details and really dark parts of the story. And I can't believe I actually wanted to help him.

Anyway, he suddenly discarded me by cutting all physical contact and kept contact only online until I stopped it. I've never wanted to play games. He rarely contacts me, but I ignore it. I have no idea what he wants from me. I live in a quite big city and sometimes I see him somewhere every few months. Weird coincidence or not? He just stares at me and then sends me negative energy. Not to sound paranoid, but I hope he's not stalking me. I even avoid going to places where I saw him before so he's out of my sight. So I don't know – how does this keep happening?

I don't know what kind of energy work has he done to me and how did it all happen? He last texted me that this is how I see it: it's all an illusion and we'll see each other when needed, when I'll be ready, and how nothing is over. And that he is with me all the time, but not physically. I ignored him by all means, from then on.

I don't know how to fully stop telepathy with him. I don't want to have dreams about him, but even in lucid dreams he gets in somehow or takes a different form. He puts his belly button on my belly and sucks my soul out and I find it very hard to wake up. Telling him to stop it doesn't help. I even see his future in my dreams and it turns out to be completely true. I get attacked by demons in the astral. I don't know – is it him too? He also projected in my bedroom with his friends – witches. He or some entity pulled my soul into the astral against my will. He or his evil spirits can change energetic blueprints around me and shape-shift things and play with electromagnetic fields so I really see my reality changing. Sometimes I'm so tired of it and it feels like I'm going crazy. Is this supposed to impress me or scare me? Not working. It's stupid. I'm not paying attention to it, but I still see it.

I think he has schizophrenia and a narcissistic personality disorder and thinks he's a god. He has a harem of woman and does what he did to me to many women. Though he told me I'm the first one he got to do so much with, and I'm the closest to what he wants in a woman because I'm open (I think he meant my aura is open). Since I don't want anything to do with him anymore, he's mad at me and maybe obsessed because he failed in whatever he wanted. He talks bad about me to other people and tells lies. Whatever.

At this point, I've worked with many healers. Some saying that he is draining

SCREWED BY THE ALIENS

me, that I'm in severe pain, and some say that I have someone's soul stuck inside me, or that he took fragments of me for himself. They tried to help, but it never worked in the long-term.

I cut cords many times and cleaned chakras but I still don't feel he is fully out of my system. I built many types of shields. I went meditating in nature and surrounded myself with wonderful people. I don't masturbate on thoughts of him. I deleted and blocked all his contacts. I pray to god and angels. I'm indifferent about him and I let go. I burned in fire the things connected to him and I cut my hair off to symbolically start fresh. What more can I do? I want to be free 100%, but it doesn't work. I'm ok for a few weeks and everything comes back again. Why? It's the same if I do a lot and try to help and fight back, and it's the same if I just live and do nothing. What exactly did he use me for and how likely is it that he will give up on me forever? Or is it me, is it all just in my head? If I accept this, I'll be suffering like this forever. It's still the same, it doesn't go away. I work on my inner child wounds and traumas. I got into this mess with him in the hopes that I'll learn how to heal others with energy and I got tricked by false light. I've forgiven him and myself, I love another man now and I'm in a healthy relationship. I want no harm to anyone.

I normally worry about other people he's abusing with his messiah complex but I can't do anything about it to stop it. I just live my life good like I normally do as if I've never met him, honest and decent I hope, trying to be happy and kind to people. I don't drink, I don't smoke, I don't eat meat, but I'm not a saint. I'm a normal person, but my inner life looks like what I've described, not peaceful. I know there are worse things in life than this. I may sound ungrateful, but it is what it is.

EL – In response to correspondence about the difficulty of receiving any kind of help or understanding in the "world of normals" who don't have a clue of what is really going on:

I know what you mean. About academia and "normal world" institutions. My guess is that such people are just not aware, they haven't woken up yet. So if they are in a place of high authority, such as in academia, mental hospitals, or any other system, it's very hard to be heard and be taken seriously, practically impossible, if your position is "below" them. They are the ones that lead. I'm sure that some of them are intelligent enough to know more, but they are afraid about their reputation (such as my mentor). So it is very hard to get across these barriers, especially in countries such as mine unfortunately, where everything revolves around politics an selfish interests, and we're far beyond that.

The letter writer resumes:

I forgot to say something important when you asked how he chooses his victims. He operates online mostly and he has many accounts on many different sites,

SCREWED BY THE ALIENS

such as forums about psychology, medicine, video games, spirituality groups on Facebook, dating sites, and so on. He then contacts people who seem to have some sort of trouble, or manipulates them into contacting him, and he offers them free help. And the rest is history, as you know.

When I found out he does this on a web-page made for teenagers, I wanted to report him to the police, but I don't have any evidence that he is having sex with minors. He's not violating the law by being on that site. (EL Note: With the New Predators, the "pedophile programming" often is part of their game at some point.)

He also plays a guitar on a street and preys on people who are into music. Then he starts his brain-washing program on them. He has some band and they play music all over the country so he meets new people that way too. You know how some sensitive girls are into musicians.

(He gets into all sort of projects for a good cause. It's scary. He talked to me about wanting to volunteer with kids in some art classes, as he has a Master's Degree in Fine Arts. So, basically, sadly, you get the picture: he is practically everywhere. But he is such an actor that people have no idea who he really is and they are either being tricked, or they stepped on the dark side to work for him.

Another form of predation he uses to entrap people is, for example, he takes home abandoned cats on the streets, takes pictures of them and puts them online, so people call him to adopt kittens. It's sick how there are countless ways he uses to get close to people and to appear as a nice person.

So, yes, of course, I would be thrilled if my experience could save or help at least one unfortunate soul somewhere. Please, go ahead and use it. And thank you.

*EL Note: After a few months she sent me this email about her newfound protection in Jesus Christ:

"The only thing that worked against evil spirits is quitting everything that is connected to New Age or the occult (meditations, visualizations, channeling, readings, lucid dreaming, astral projections, reading books about aliens, pseudo-science, psychology, hypnotherapy that embraces elements of New Age). I got rid of all such books and things with symbolism in my home. I completely and honestly surrendered my life to Christ, repented for my sins, invited him in my heart, and he restored me through the Holy Spirit. It helped immediately! I've read the Bible and it gave me answers to all questions I've had. This simple and free solution helped many and I wish I had found it out sooner. I recommend checking ex-New Ager Steven Bancarz, who explains this in depth, and other Christian testimonies. I understand not everyone agrees with this, and no one is to be judged, but those who truly search for God will be set free by this, and will get a new heart. I hope this helps someone."

SCREWED BY THE ALIENS

About Eve Lorgen

Eve Lorgen is a dedicated counseling and hypnotherapy professional, author, anomalous trauma researcher, Hatha yogi and Taoist Chi Gong practitioner. She began her pioneering work with alien abductees, "milabs" and mind control victims while earning her Master's Degree in Counseling Psychology in 1992. She also holds a BS in Biochemistry and worked in the Biotechnology industry for seven years. Eve started a support group in 1994 in San Diego County, CA, for experiencers of anomalous trauma and continues to consult with anomalous trauma clients worldwide today. She was a close associate of the late Barbara Bartholic and is dedicated to continuing and expanding the work of the late Dr. Karla Turner.

Anomalous Trauma is defined as traumatic events that are out of the normal range of human experience. These experiences may include alien abductions, near death experiences, shamanic initiations, military abductions (milabs), mind control, spiritual warfare, demonic and psychic attacks, cult involvement and narcissistic abuse. Early on in her career counseling alien abductees, she discovered a plethora of unusual experiences that often accompanied those who reported alien encounters and milabs. The most prominent aspect of Eve's counseling and support is with those who are experiencing some form of alien or paranormal-orchestrated love relationships.

SUGGESTED READING

THE LOVE BITE: ALIEN INTERFERENCE IN HUMAN LOVE RELATIONSHIPS

THE DARK SIDE OF CUPID

VISIT EVE'S EXCELLENT WEBSITE AT: evelorgen.com

The New Predator: https://www.sovereignki.com/single-post/2018/06/03/The-New-Predator

SCREWED BY THE ALIENS

ALIEN TATTOOS

Color of Fluorescence	Body Site Found	Designs, Markings	Illustrations (not drawn to scale)
Brilliant yellow-green	behind ear	"J" shape, crescent, 1" long	🌙
" "	arm, shoulder	2.5" bar with 3, 0.5" tick marks below	
" "	chin, chest, clavicle	10" triangular isoceles triangle, point of chin to tops of clavicle.	▲
" "	vaginal opening	irregular splotching	?
" "	breasts	irregular marking, splotching	?
" "	Backs of calves	" " "	
" "	Dog hair	splotching	
" "	hand, palm	dime size circle, diffused into hand & fingers w/ massage	●
" "	inside mouth	irregular splotching	
" "	tops of feet	"splatter marks" topical and subdermal. Some wiped away, some diffused into skin	
Very light blue-white	inside right bicep	non descript m	......
Light blue	inside mouth	irregular splotching	
	tongue	2" lengthwise strip in center of tongue	
Blue	arm	4" heart shaped mandelbrot	♥
Lavendar	left forearm	3/4" long, 3/16" wide rectangular mark	▬
Pink-red (hot pink)	fingers, neck	spots, irregular splotching	
Orange	tongue, nostril, face	irregular splotches	
Orange	chest, pubic areas face, neck, tongue	lasts several months, recurrs irregular diffuse dots	

SCREWED BY THE ALIENS

Art by Wes Crum

SCREWED BY THE ALIENS

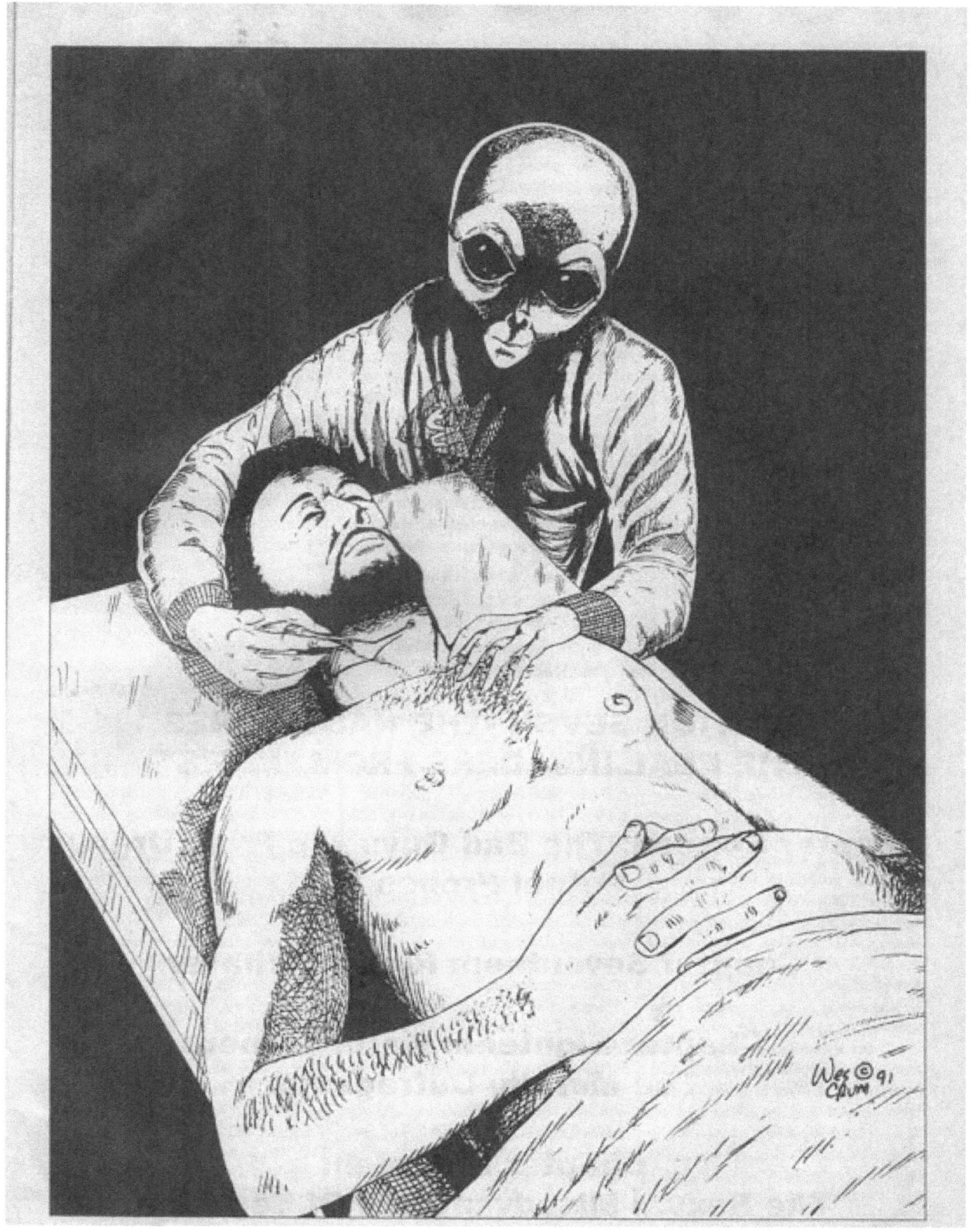

Art by Wes Crum

SCREWED BY THE ALIENS

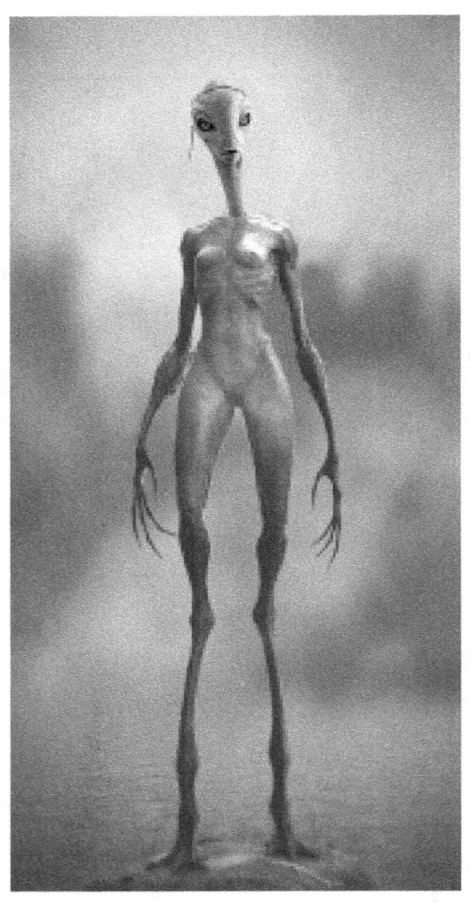

SECTION SEVEN - THE NASTY ONES
THE REAL INVADERS FROM "MARS"

Chapter Sixteen: The Bad Guys Are From Uranus
Anal Probes

Chapter Seventeen: Richard Shaver

Chapter Eighteen: Karla Turner
The Morally Outrageous

Chapter Nineteen:
The Sexual Misadventures Of Ted Rice

Chapter Twenty: John Stuart
Rape Of Aussie Researcher

SCREWED BY THE ALIENS

THE BAD GUYS ARE FROM URANUS
By Sean Casteel
(With input on the occult aspects from Tim Beckley)

In a world of scoffers and unbelievers, the concept of the "anal" or "rectal" probe has come to mean that anyone claiming abduction by aliens is either laughable, feebleminded or both. Like the "tinfoil hat" first introduced in the 2002 alien invasion movie "Signs," written and directed by M. Night Shyamalan and starring Mel Gibson, the anal probe is often referred to with a giggle or a sneer meant to telegraph the notion that "we all know only fools believe aliens are real."

Those who have been part of the UFO community long enough to remember the excitement stirred up in 1987 by abductee Whitley Strieber's number one bestseller "Communion" will likely agree that the anal probe ridicule started with his frank admission of what he believed happened to him.

I was a struggling freelance journalist at the time and I considered it a major boon to my career that I was able to wrangle a phone interview with Strieber. I submitted the interview to "Rolling Stone" on the chance they might be interested. It was the autumn of 1989 and the movie version of "Communion" had just been released, so an editor at "Rolling Stone" forwarded my call to Peter Travers, the magazine's film critic.

Travers told me that he had just seen "Communion" with a preview audience and that the mention of anal probes had the crowd, predictably, laughing. Meanwhile, Travers had been impressed by the movie's group therapy scene, where abductees sought out others like themselves, because it meant that the abduction experience could happen to anyone. Travers seemed to feel the anal probes undermined what could have been a good movie otherwise. [In case you're interested, my interview with Strieber was rejected by "Rolling Stone," but it was still cool to talk to Travers.]

But the anal probes joke soon demonstrated it had a life of its own.

SCREWED BY THE ALIENS

"Anal probes by aliens has certainly become part of the culture," says author/editor Tim Beckley. "If it happens to you, obviously it may feel like you've been punched in the gut. But if you like UFOs for their entertainment value – and you have to admit a lot of people do, try not to be cranky about it – you might find the probing of an earthly anus or two by deviant aliens of 'a strange kind' grotesquely funny."

Ten years after "Communion," the pilot episode of the popular cartoon series "South Park" was entitled "Cartman Gets An Anal Probe" and depicted one of the major characters as "farting fire" and having a satellite dish emerge from his anus after recounting an abduction experience which we are led to believe was just a dream. This is one of many examples where Strieber's compulsively honest admission about what happened to him had spiraled out of control and into the pop culture "joke" mainstream.

Not much further removed than "South Park" would be an animated skit on "Comedy Central." In a two-minute clip posted to YouTube, we see aliens abduct a drug smuggler, do an anal probe and find bags of coke. They snort the white powder, enjoying themselves to no end – so much so that they abduct hundreds of others and do an anal cavity search, looking for more cocaine. Party goers beware: that might keep you away from the "drug of choice" for most rock and rollers.

"Some jokes and puns are better, more refreshing than others," Beckley explains. "Hellboy, for example, is a well-known comic character that has been transferred to the big screen. In a comic panel, he is restrained and bent over as aliens grope him while commenting, 'Greetings, Hellboy. We have traveled millions of light years to explore new planets, and now we seek to explore Uranus!' How charming. That comment deserves a big boo!"

Likewise, on the boob tube there is the series "Castle," which has been canceled after a successful run of nine years. In one episode, the main character, Richard Castle – a crime novelist with a wild sense of humor turned a freelance NYPD investigator – is getting strange hate mail. He shows NYPD detective Kate Beckett one such letter which shows him being violated by an ET.

Enough you say? Hardly!

MEANWHILE, ON THE BIG SCREEN

"On the big screen anal probes seem more menacing than you can imagine," notes Tim Beckley. Readers, he says, might find particularly offensive the opening sequence from a British film "Evil Aliens," directed by horror mogul Jack West. "It's a film full of parody of the abduction experience. And it is exceedingly over the top, content-wise. One critic said he was very disturbed by the scenes involving sex and nudity. He warns that it is truly the definition of 'freaky,' not only showing a female alien deflowering a geeky guy, but also a pretty graphic scene

SCREWED BY THE ALIENS

where a bunch of aliens surgically impregnate a strapped-down, naked news reporter. Talk about seeking revenge for 'fake news!' In addition, there is probably the most horrendous of anal probe scenes, utilizing a surgical instrument that twists and turns while being inserted where our sun does not shine of its own volition."

No one has done a survey on how many times anal probes have shown up in feature films – both those aimed at commercial venues or those with an adult rating (to be discussed in another section).

Beckley says he has been told by those who troll the adult sites that there are now camcorder girls who are dressing up like aliens and conversing with fans on the other side of the Internet portal. On offer are private exhibitions for those who want to pay for a private "chat" with "a naked and supposedly horny alien space girl." Beckley maintains that one of those who enjoys such odd companionship is convinced that there is at least one gal who is not a model, but the real thing. "He says her skin is slightly green and anatomically she is not correct."

Beckley says he tried to explain to this person that with makeup today and tampering with the video process it's possible to add on special effects to a live conversation and that it is more difficult to detect than ever before.

WHERE DID THE ANAL PROBES BEGIN?

In an online posting, author and editor Jason Colavito asks the question, "Who was the first person to receive an anal probe?"

"I know this is a silly question," Colavito writes, "but silly questions often end up revealing hidden layers and secrets. And I have not been able to find a satisfactory answer to what should have been a simple question. Anal probes are now such an established part of the UFO phenomenon that you'd think there would be a clear answer. Many UFO books refer to it, and many assume that it's just a given during an abduction, but I can't find a catalog of anal probing or a timeline of when they supposedly started."

Colavito turns the clock back to the Barney and Betty Hill abduction incident from 1961.

"The interesting thing is that Barney Hill actually did claim to have been anally probed," Colavito recounts, "but because the claim was not included in 'The Interrupted Journey' (1965), the account by John G. Fuller of the hypnotic regression performed on the Hills, this claim was not generally known until a 1965 report by NICAP investigator Walter Webb was popularized much later. In that report, Webb stated that during the hypnotic regression, Barney Hill stated that 'A cylindrical object was inserted up the rectum, and once again the witness believed something was extracted.' Fuller left this out of the book, along with a claim by Hill that a cup was used to extract sperm."

In a case researched by well-known UFO investigator Ray Fowler, two brothers and two of their friends were fishing in the Allagash Waterway in Maine when

SCREWED BY THE ALIENS

they saw a light in the sky – much brighter than a star – that hovered a relatively short distance away. The object moved closer to them as they waved flashlights at it. They panicked and headed back to shore. Upon seeing their campsite fire had gone out in the meantime, they realized they had lost a few hours they couldn't account for. Shortly afterwards, they began to dream about four-fingered alien beings with large heads examining them on tables.

The initial events happened in 1976, but it wasn't until several years later that the four men were subjected to regressive hypnosis. All four of them had had their clothes removed and sat naked in an examination room. They were forced to watch one another being humiliatingly probed and prodded, including invasive genital testing. Medical instruments were inserted brutally into all their cavities accompanied by the excruciating pain of anal probes.

After psychiatric examinations, all four men were found to be mentally stable and passed lie detector tests. The case is still considered unexplainable by conventional scientific means. Raymond Fowler's book on the case came out in 1993 and is worth tracking down if you want a more detailed examination.

STRIEBER'S ACTUAL WORDS

What did Strieber actually write that started the anal probe cultural phenomenon? Colavito points out that, while Strieber never used the phrase "anal probing" in "Communion," under hypnotic regression Strieber did discuss the aliens violating him anally:

"Soon I was in more intimate surroundings once again. There were clothes strewn about and two of the stocky ones drew my legs apart. The next thing I knew I was being shown an enormous and extremely ugly object, gray and scaly, with a sort of network of wires on the end. It was at least a foot long, narrow, and triangular in structure. They inserted this thing into my rectum. It seemed to swarm into me as if it had a life of its own. Apparently its purpose was to take samples, presumably of fecal matter, but at the time I had the impression I was being raped, and for the first time I felt anger."

Budd Hopkins later offered his own theory as to what had happened to Strieber. Hopkins felt the purpose of the strange alien hardware had not been to collect a stool sample but was instead a matter of "electro-ejaculation," with a device intended to collect a semen sample through prostate stimulation.

"Hopkins had become convinced," Colavito writes, "that the aliens had a reproductive agenda, not a scatological one."

In a posting on his website, "Unknown Country," Strieber talks frankly about what he has come to believe about the anal probe.

"On December 26, 1985, I was raped," he writes, "and yesterday [in 2009] I made yet another visit to the doctor to be treated for the consequences. The injury has long healed, but the body remembers, and every few years, the excruci-

SCREWED BY THE ALIENS

ating pain of it returns.

"At the time, it was mentioned in passing in a hypnosis session with Dr. Donald Klein as a 'rectal probe.' This sparked years and years of laughter, and I found myself to be the only publicly admitted rape victim in modern history whose suffering turned him into a laughingstock. This greatly added to the anguish, I can assure you. It is devastating to a person's well-being to suffer such a humiliation and then be laughed at for it.

"To this day, both the emotional anguish and the physical pain have stayed with me," Strieber continues, "and I think that it's well past time for this to be known. After my experience, there was no question at all but that I was physically injured. How, and how badly, were matters I kept pretty much to myself, especially when I saw the laughter coming in cruel waves.

"Our only recourse is to be dismissed as lunatics, called liars and laughed at? Really? That's the best response society has to offer?"

Strieber recalls the humiliation of Larry King laughing in his face on the air. Strieber also watched in horror as "South Park" made its aforementioned anal probe jokes, saying it was "like having acid poured down [his] throat."

"I relived the rape," Strieber writes, "as I watched, horrified, at what was being done to me. And it was being done to me specifically. The writers of the program were amusing themselves and their audience with my rape."

But Strieber has not surrendered to despair.

"So, here I am, finally admitting openly, with this latest bout of pain, that I am a rape victim. I suppose that this will encourage more laughter, but not in everybody. No longer. The number of people who respect those of us who have experienced – and suffered – close encounters is growing larger every day. As mankind gradually comes to face the reality of the visitors in a more mature manner, the laughter is dying away."

THE OCCULT SIGNIFICANCE

Most everyone with a sense of conscience would agree that anal rape is a terrifying experience. Just ask anyone who has been in prison and who has had to suffer such humiliation.

There are some "masters of the occult" who have long thought that practicing sex magick, particularly rituals involving anal sex, could act like a magnet to bring them great supernatural powers, powers which would bring them everything that they desired – from money to international status. It would allow them to control the weather as well as influence the minds of others whom they fancied dominating.

Jack Parsons, one of the founders of NASA, and L. Ron Hubbard of Scientology fame, were actively involved in a secret society known as the OTO, which considered sex magick fully acceptable. There was wife swapping, bodily fluids were

SCREWED BY THE ALIENS

shared and spirits, both good and evil, were invoked.

The man known as "the Beast," Aleister Crowley, whose number was believed to be 666 (as described in the Book of Revelations) was proclaimed by the media to be the wickedest man in the world. It was an "honor" he promoted himself and seemed to enjoy.

Crowley was also said to be an "Extraterrestrial Medium." Performing his occult rituals while safely inside a massive symbolic pentagram, Crowley would call upon an entity known as "Lam," who resembles to a tee the greys of today's UFO abductions.

Researcher Daniel V. Boudillion gives a more detailed account of Crowley's encounters with Lam and how the now famous portrait of the being from another dimension came about.

In January through March of 1918 Crowley began a series of magickal workings called the Amalantrah Workings in furnished rooms in Central Park West, New York City. These were performed via Sexual & Ceremonial Magick (his spelling) with the intent to invoke certain "intelligences" to physical manifestation. In actuality, the workings typically manifested as a series of visions and communications received through the mediumship of his partner, Roddie Minor.

Be that as it may, at least one such "intelligence" was brought into physical manifestation via the Magickal Portal they created. (A portal in this context is a "magickally" created rent in the fabric of time and space.) Crowley maintained the picture (of Lam) is actually a portrait and drawn from real life. This entity either called itself "Lam," or was named "Lam" by Crowley. Either way, he considered it to be of interdimensional origin, which was the term then for extraterrestrial. In communications with Lam, the symbolism of the egg featured prominently.

Crowley included the portrait of Lam in his Dead Souls exhibition held in Greenwich Villasssge, New York, in 1919. In that same year it was published as a frontispiece labeled The Way to Crowley's commentary to Blavatsky's The Voice of the Silence. Beneath the picture was the following inscription: "LAM is the Tibetan word for Way or Path, and LAMA is He who Goeth, the specific title of the Gods of Egypt, the Treader of the Path, in Buddhistic phraseology. Its numerical value is 71, the number of this book."

As for anal sex, Crowley and others who practiced sex magick on a regular basis said it could open the pathway to a person's First Chakra, making an individual more perceptive and raising their kundalini. Proclaims one adherent of the practice: "Even though the First Chakra has many masculine qualities, it is also the 'seat of the Goddess Kundalini,' and is therefore often associated with our relationship with with Mother Earth. The brainstem and the area immediately above it are called the reptilian brain, because all creatures from reptiles to hu-

SCREWED BY THE ALIENS

mans possess it. For reptiles, this area is their entire brain; but for humans, it is the base or stem of their brain."

Doesn't this sound suspicious being that many women claim to have been seduced or raped by reptiles?

While the O.T.O. included, from its inception, the teaching of sex magick in the highest degrees of the Order, when Crowley became head of the Order, he expanded on these teachings and associated them with different degrees as follows: masturbatory or auto-sexual magical techniques were taught, referred to as the Lesser Work of Sol IX°: heterosexual magical techniques were taught XI°: anal intercourse magical techniques were taught. Professor Hugh Urban, Professor of Comparative Religion at The Ohio State University, noted Crowley's emphasis on sex as "the supreme magical power." According to Crowley: The Book of the Law solves the sexual problem completely. Each individual has an absolute right to satisfy his sexual instinct as is physiologically proper for him. The one injunction is to treat all such acts as sacraments. One should not eat as the brutes, but in order to enable one to do one's will. The same applies to sex. We must use every faculty to further the one object of our existence.

What is implied here is that the aliens mind have found that it is easier to control us both physically and mentally through the use of sex, in particular anal intercourse. So it may not be a matter of their pleasure, though it could be, at least to some degree.

When asked her thinking on the subject of sex magick, the psychic Lady Morgana (LadyMorgana.com) added this to the conversation: "In magick we manipulate a certain amount of energy into a desired direction; for that we specify a goal, raise energy and point it into the wished direction (release the energy) to achieve a manifestation in our physical reality.

"In sex magick we basically focus on a goal by affirmation, visualization, etc.; we raise much energy through prolonged sexual arousal and we release the energy at the moment of orgasm. The goal in sex magick can be the achievement or attraction of anything wished for in the physical world, like a new house, a better relationship or a healing. It can also be the charging of magickal tools or talismans. And the goal can be spiritual development.

"This controlled form of lovemaking for higher purposes is often mentioned as the ultimate explanation of Crowley's famous statement 'Love is the Law, Love under Will.' By love, Crowley meant the uniting of the opposites masculine and feminine, active and receptive, and not so much romantic love. Orgasm is considered to be the moment when 'the gates of heaven open up'; for a while the barriers between the restricted physical world and the limitless heavens dissolve.

"During the precious orgasmic moments, we swing away our magical desire into the universe with enormous power, and a 'magickal child' is born. This magickal child is the astral effect of our magical action that will result in manifestation.

"The sexual fluids of man and woman are charged with powerful qualities because of their magick and they can be used for several purposes."

WHAT KIND OF SEX CAN BE USED IN SEX MAGICK?

Oh, but you ask what types of sex can we best use for sex magick? Morgana expands on her philosophy:

"In fact, any sexual activity can be used to work sex magick. It can be practiced alone, it can be practiced with a partner of the same sex or of the opposite sex, and in advanced sex magick it is also possible to work with more people. But a group sex magick ritual is never an excuse for a sexual orgy!

"It is a strong ritual in which several people dedicate their sexual forces towards a mutual goal. Magick is synergistic, which means that the power conjured up is geometric (1,2,4,8,16, etc., so a ritual with four people gives the energy of eight separate people!).

"Please remember that in no way this is an invitation to ever do a group ritual in your life unwanted, nor does it mean that joining a group ritual implies that you should also have sex with more than one partner in your personal love life. You can include all forms of sex in your ritual; it can be genital, oral or anal sex; it can be bondage, bizarre sex or whatever; as long as all partners included enjoy it and agree that it's okay."

THE ALIENS ARE PLAYING DOCTOR AND INSTILLING FEAR

Dr. Allen Greenfield, a Gnostic bishop, UFO expert and longtime friend of Beckley, sees the use of anal probes as a device to put fear into our minds so that we are more easily controlled.

"The phenomena of alien abduction and aliens having sex with the abductee is painfully ancient. Going back perhaps to Zeus abducting and raping Europa, through various fairy abductions, down to the famous Antonio Villasss Boas case and others associated with modern UFO lore. It has been a part of human folklore all along."

"What may be more interesting is how many abductees, contacteees and John Keel's so-called 'silent contactees' report what appears to be 'playing doctor' by aliens, ostensibly as an endless number of physical examinations but which conspicuously involve restraints, rectal probes and other aspects with broad sexual implications. I personally suspect that all of this is to induce fear in the hapless 'percipient,' as certain alien beings seem to 'eat fear,' as I have discussed in my own books."

A MORE "SCIENTIFIC" APPROACH

If you visit the doctor, often one of the first things they do is ask you for a stool

SCREWED BY THE ALIENS

specimen.

Now I know a few doctors whom I might consider to be "aliens" in their approach to medicine, but this is not always the case. Ask any physician why they collect a sample of your stool and send it away to the lab and you will probably be told that tests done on fecal matter help diagnose certain conditions affecting the digestive tract. These conditions can include infection (such as from parasites, viruses or bacteria), poor nutrient absorption or even cancer.

Almost reassuringly, if the aliens are probing and prodding "back there," they might send specimens to their space lab to see if we are up to the challenge of breeding or bearing one of their hybrids.

"Of course," wisecracking Tim Beckley notes, "they could improve their bedside manner. But aliens are aliens, and maybe they just don't give a shit!"

SUGGESTED READING

MODERN SEX MAGICK: SECRETS OF EROTIC SPIRITUALITY, by Donald Michael Kraig

MOONCHILD, by Aleister Crowley

COMMUNION, by Whitley Strieber

NIGHTMARE ALLEY, by Timothy Beckley

THE AUTHENTIC BOOK OF ULTRA-TERRESTRIAL CONTACTS, by Timothy Beckley

ROUND TRIP TO HELL IN A FLYING SAUCER, by Timothy Beckley, Sean Casteel and others.

Actor Christopher Walken played Whitley Strieber in the movie version of "Communion." In real life, the well-known author told of his anal rape by aliens in the bestselling book.

SCREWED BY THE ALIENS

Be mindful if you decide you would like to go to the next "Alien Orgy" (book available on Kindle).

Super hero "Hellboy" is open to intense pressure from alien probers. You would think with his contacts he would have better friends.

Album cover from the band "Sex Fiend." See what happens if you play it backwards.

A drug dealer gets his just desserts on Comedy Central when the aliens search for his smuggled contraband in a place where you wouldn't normally store your stash.

Aleister Crowley was praised as an Extraterrestrial Medium. He was accused of being a Satanist. He is said to have influenced bands like Led Zeppelin and the Beatles. Was the conjured spirit Lam a true Grey?

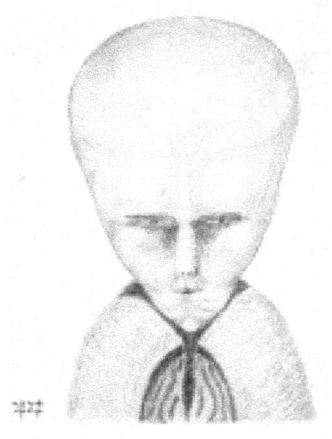

SCREWED BY THE ALIENS

An overpowering sex-with-aliens scene from the far-from-tame "Evil Aliens."

A scene from the campy "Love Witch" film shows how deeply ingrained the magick of sex has become in our culture. No sexual "misconduct" implied. Promotional still.

On "Southpark," in the episode "Stick of Truth," viewers were given the opportunity to examine the inner workings of the aliens onboard their craft.

SCREWED BY THE ALIENS

About Sean Casteel

Sean Casteel is a freelance journalist who has been writing about UFOs, alien abduction and many other paranormal subjects since 1989. Sean's writing appeared in many UFO- and paranormal-related magazines, including "UFO Magazine," Tim Beckley's "UFO Universe," "FATE Magazine," "Mysteries Magazine," and "Open Minds Magazine," most of which are now defunct but were a major part of a thriving UFO press in their heyday. Magazines in the UK, Italy, Romania and Australia have also published Sean's work.

Sean has written or contributed to over 30 books for Global Communications and Inner Light Publications, all of which are available from Amazon.com. Sean's books include "The Heretic's UFO Guidebook," which analyzes a selection of Gnostic Christian writings and their relationship to the UFO phenomenon, and "Signs and Symbols of the Second Coming," in which he interviews several religious and paranormal experts about how prophecies of the Second Coming of Christ may be fulfilled.

To view and purchase books Sean has written or contributed to, visit his Amazon author page at: http://www.amazon.com/author/seancasteel

SCREWED BY THE ALIENS

SEX, SHAVER, THE DERO AND THE CAVERN WORLD
By Timothy G. Beckley
With assistance from Richard S. Shaver

If you were a teenager back in the 1940s and early 1950s, there was no PornHub on the Internet to satisfy your juvenile cravings for illicit pornography. There might have been a few "stroke books" around, but you would have to get them in an adult shop. And if you were still wet behind the ears in the ways of the world, you were not going to be allowed through the doors of these rather sleazy establishments (not even the ones that lined Times Square).

So you had to get your kicks some other way and without your parents finding out. There wasn't even a copy of Playboy to hide under your mattress, so what was a poor boy to do?

Read Science Fiction!

Yes, that was perhaps the only game in town. Tales of half-naked, lusty ladies were welcome in the story lines of sci-fi pulp magazines, which you could purchase for a quarter at the local newsstand without anyone looking at you strangely or asking for ID – which no one had in those days anyway.

In the March 1945 edition of "Amazing Stories," editor Raymond A Palmer, who later published "Fate," "Flying Saucers From Other Worlds," and "Mystic," introduced the Shaver Mystery to the world. Richard S. Shaver was a freelance writer who, even though "Amazing Stories" was a science fiction zine, claimed his stories were all too true. Shaver says that he was working at the Ford Motor plant in Detroit when he began to hear voices inside his head every time he started to rivet one of the autos on the assembly line where he was employed.

Initially, Shaver thought that he might be going crazy.

But he wasn't.

In a while the voices began to come through clearly, and he realized he was actually spying on "someone" telepathically without them realizing it. But the

175

SCREWED BY THE ALIENS

sounds and the conversations he heard were maddening. They could only, Shaver figured, be originating from another person or a group of individuals. There were sounds of whips whooshing through the air and high pitched screams and the begging of tortured souls to be put out of their misery. It was a sadistic nightmare, something the Marquis de Sade would be proud of!

A RACE OF COSMIC SUPER BEINGS EXPOSED

Shaver began to realize that there were various encampments of beings and creatures living below the surface of the earth, the most dominant being the "Dero," whose hatred for any surface dweller was well established. The various groups existing underground spread throughout the underworld via an ancient system of caverns and rail cars, building elaborate cities in some cases and living in total darkness at other random locations. The Dero became the most dominant group, but they had become completely deformed, almost blind, and without a heart and soul. They were merciless in their efforts to kidnap humans and bring them underground to their chambers for their own perverse "pleasures," often ending in torture and, ultimately, a barbaric death.

Shaver's supposedly "true" horror stories were full of cannibalism, snuff and sexual perversion. Elements of S and M were established throughout his nightmarish tales of depravity, as blogger J.J. Marino

(https://joelmarino.wordpress.com)

points out::

"150,000 years ago, according to Shaver's 'racial memories,' Earth was colonized by god-like, long-lived super-human beings from outer space called "Atlans" or "Titans" who settled on the lost continents of Atlantis and Lemuria. The Titans created an advanced technological super-civilization, served by incredibly sophisticated machinery and by genetically engineered flesh-and-blood 'robots' of various types, some of whom became our own ancestors. About 12,000 years ago, the Titans discovered that the Sun had begun emitting poisonous radiations from heavy metals, causing them to age and die prematurely.

"At first, the Titans tried to escape the poisonous rays by building and moving into vast underground cities. Despite this, the "detrimental energy" which had contaminated the whole planet still poisoned them, causing early aging and death, and the Titans evacuated Earth, migrating 'en masse' to a planet around a still uncontaminated star. However, they did not have enough spacecraft to transport all the genetically engineered robots, as well as themselves, to their new planet.

"So many of the robots were left behind to fend for themselves. Some of the robots returned to the surface, adjusted to the Sun's radiation, gradually forgot about the cavern-cities underneath them, sank into Stone Age savagery, and became our own ancestors. Many other robots, however, remained in the cavern-cities. They were shielded from some of the detrimental rays from the Sun, but

SCREWED BY THE ALIENS

also from its beneficial rays as well. Like the surface-dwellers, they survived and reproduced, but most of them degenerated into a race of deformed, psychotic dwarfs, the 'detrimental robots' or 'Dero' – cruel, sadistic, sex-crazed midgets, sexually perverted versions of the 'Morlocks' of H.G. Wells' 'The Time Machine.' A few other cavern-dwellers, the 'integrative robots,' or 'Tero,' avoided the mental and physical deterioration of the Dero, and tried to do all they could to defeat the evil designs of the vastly more numerous Dero."

If you are wondering how humans ended up "downstairs," Shaver maintained that there were openings in various caves that you could get trapped in and never be found. There were even some elevators which went sideways after going to the basement of various skyscrapers in New York, Los Angeles, Chicago and Detroit; these led to some "warehouse" of humans far beyond our grasp or understanding.

J. J. Marino continues with his vivid description of the subterranean conclaves and the true nature of its inhabitants

"The Dero began using the marvelous machinery the Titans had left behind in the cavern-cities, still in perfect working order. However, they used the machinery for their own evil purposes, to bedevil both the Tero and the surface dwellers and to enhance their own pleasure in their almost continual sex orgies. The misused Titan machines enabled the Dero to watch scenes anywhere on the Earth's surface, to read minds, to teleport instantly from one point to another, to create seemingly solid 3-dimensional illusions, and to induce hypnotic compulsions, such as the strange 'urges to kill' of surface folk who heard voices. With the aid of the Titan machines, by means of rays and telepathy, the Dero were responsible for most of the world's catastrophes great and small – wars, fires, airline crashes, shipwrecks, traffic accidents, nervous breakdowns – they even tripped people walking down the stairs.

"The Dero ordered the crucifixion of Jesus Christ, inspired Hitler, designed the Nazi death camps, sliced the blood vessels in FDR's brain, killing him just as World War II was ending, and even stole copy from Ray Palmer's desk to stop him from printing any more exposes of their nefarious activities! The Dero also indulged (like sex-crazed versions of H.G. Wells' Morlocks) in cannibalism and the sadomasochistic sex-torture of hapless humans unlucky enough to blunder into their caverns! The sane, virtuous Tero did what precious little they could to foil the evil activities of the Dero, who vastly outnumbered them. Shaver himself had found a group of Tero who showed him 'thought records' enabling him to see his past lives in Lemuria."

Dog-eared copies of "Amazing Stories" and other pulps can still be found, with Shaver's diversely perverted tales, as this prime example certainly illustrates.

SCREWED BY THE ALIENS
A DERO'S FEAST – BY RICHARD SHAVER

Let us look at one of the greater "feasts" held by these Satanists under the domination of Lila Onderde, who has wrought the evil work of making sin paramount on Earth.

The hour of the feast has arrived, and about the great, gloomy rock chamber hang the decorations, nicely writhing in their niches from the wired strong currents flowing through their naked limbs. There is dancing and merriment and all forms of debauchery. There is no limit to the perversity that flows through the twisted, demented minds and bodies of these creatures from an all-too-real living Hell. The underground dwellers have been joined by some of the most wicked visitors from the stars, who have traveled light years to frolic with their demented Dero brethren in the most loathsome of perversions, regardless of whether it is against man or woman.

The terrific ancient carvings on the walls, nicely polished by slaves, and new looking, but smoked and darkened again in places from the many fires of the recurrent Demon feasts –and every feast an orgy of bloodletting for the inverted pleasure senses of Lila and her cronies.

Scrabbling, crab-like, the mighty body of Yahveh finds its horrible way across the stage in an awed silence of fear. For many of the Satanists think he is the true and immortal Devil-God himself – and with good reason, for many are his evil deeds done under Lila's constant control. Above, in her luxurious chambers, Lila sits at the great mech, controlling his tortured movements with the great ray, and augmenting the audience's awe with little diffuse stirn beams, so that the whole chamber worships this thing, Yahveh, her tool.

Yahveh takes his place on the great dais, his mighty, evilly twisted body becomes the center of the gathering, the focus of all eyes, the dominating background for all the writhing Hell that is to occur there today. Lila freezes his body in place with a shot of the epilepto ray that sets his great mutilated muscles in immobile position, and leaves the switch off the rayon until she has played her part in the program.

Then she takes a last look in the mirror, her body twisting sensuously as she postures her hips right and left in lewd suggestiveness. Her slave girls dust her with powder, adjust about her waist the tight jeweled cincture that accents the curve of her hips and the smallness of her waist, set the green emeralds flaming at her wrists and ankles, place on her head the great polished wooden mask that will proclaim her the Devil's chief handmaid, touch up the rouge of her cheeks under the curling locks that cascade down her nude back and shoulders – and Lila undulates down the stairs and out to the great dais before the painfully frozen statue of living flesh that is the mighty slave – Yahveh – become now the living reincarnation of Sathanas by Lila's subtle work.

SCREWED BY THE ALIENS

Flames were roaring now from a full hundred cooking fires about the walls, and over each revolved a spit, and on the spits were pieces of human flesh, of various ages, and both sexes, for it was to be the main delicacy of these feasts. Lila now, her near nude, provocative body posturing in a thousand subtle movements suggestive of desire and its gratification, writhed out from the wings of the dais, and, after a short ceremonial invocation to the black figure of Yahveh in the background, lay full length before him, belly upward – for the altar of Satan is traditionally the nude body of the high priestess of the Dark God.

Now a procession of dishes for the feast were placed upon her gleaming white body, for the blessing of Sathanas, and the great figure of the giant black man, under the watch and control of several concealed ray-warriors, nodded its head gravely and ceremonially over each of these dishes – some of which were the nicely browned bodies of babies.

Now Lila rides and postures before the terrible mutilated figure of black strength, the "Devil Incarnate" and begins the "dance of the She-Devil," which she is eminently fitted to portray. That dance of a soul becoming the Devil's ecstatic property – that dance, for sheer wanton lust of the flesh, for sheer all-out casting-off of all spiritual and moral restraint (such as lingers in all surface men's equivalent performances) can give the mind a view into the true fiery lure of Hell.

A feature of the dance is the slaying of some poor slave, and his living heart cut from his body. Lila offers the pulsing heart to Satan as a reward for the giving of herself to him forever. Satan (Yahveh under control by concealed ray-warriors) takes the heart from her hands and attempts to consummate the gift by taking the promised body of the She-Devil then and there. Lila, acting her part, feigns fear of the terrible strength and huge black fearfulness of the figure of Sathanas, then retreats about the stage with Sathanas in pursuit.

While the feast is being served, a number of slaves that have been saved from the roaring fires of the human roast know better than to refuse the gross sexual advances of those twisted who have gathered for the gala and who feed off of human misery almost as much as they do off of human flesh.

Because of the ancient ray devices stored in the cavern, they can go on for days without being sexually satisfied, their engorged organs swelling to massive proportions, the women with their enlarged bosoms and the males with phalluses of evil intent. Their equally demanding guests from the stars would certainly praise their hosts on their return trip all the way back to their home planet, with intentions to return soon to the pleasure palace in the caverns below the Earth's surface.

SCREWED BY THE ALIENS
EXTRATERRESTRIAL BEINGS AND A TASTE FOR HELL
BY RICHARD SHAVER

EDITOR'S NOTE: A persistent theme was that the Dero were responsible for almost all our troubles – from surface wars, murder, natural disasters and even airplane crashes and the sinking of the Titanic. Women especially were sought out and brutalized. Shaver claimed that the Deros sometimes traveled with spaceships or rockets, and had dealings with equally evil extraterrestrial beings. Shaver claimed to possess first-hand knowledge of the Deros and their caves, insisting he had been their prisoner for several years.

Shaver is hardly what you would call "New Age." He was not particularly a religious or spiritual person. Didn't seem to believe in spiritualism (levitation, table rapping and full body apparitions was a Dero trick) and at one point professed that he was a communist. He said there was no Heaven or Hell, but that Hell did exist in the caverns and had been misinterpreted by Christians. This is a perverse description of Shaver's idea of Hades:

****

"There is so much to tell you, to teach you, that I hardly know where to begin. But first of all you must know whom it is that we must battle against. Come!"

She led me to the great hall where I had first met her and paused before one of the mechanisms. Her hand on the control, she swung a huge distance-ray beam and almost immediately upon the visi-screen a scene of utter horror became visible. I could hardly believe my own eyes' evidence.

That was a Hell, a real Hell, I looked upon. Men and women – especially beautiful women – hung swinging from hooks, boiled in fluids, writhed on racks, thirsted in the stocks, sat on spikes, tugging to get off, lay under hammers that crushed them inch by slow inch, or slid inexorably into machines that sliced them gradually with the thinness

"Since there is no logical reason for anyone behaving as they (the Dero) do, none of the motives that animate surface people being evident in such activity, they can't believe any tale of a modern Hell. Even if you show them projections of the things that go on in the evil caverns, they are sure that it is a concoction made up to frighten them, from motives wholly mischievous. The truth is, almost none of the surface people believe in the existence of evil ray groups from antiquity down to the present day. They don't even understand the detrimental robotism which is the underlying cause of such a horror. And there is no way to tell them, short of taking them there. Even if they knew, what could they do? They have no weapons to fight an ancient ray weapon; nothing they could do would atop the thing. Since most of the victims come from among us cavern people, surface people never miss anyone without having a simple explanation for the disappearance."

Many go missing and are never accounted for. The helpless, the vagrants, the

SCREWED BY THE ALIENS

ladies of red light parlors. They traffic in flesh and brutality. The pain and suffering is never ending. She twirled a dial on the great apparatus and swiftly the picture on the screen swept through the beautiful caves and came to rest on a group of things that should not live.

"Do you see them?" she demanded. "Those things that could not live but for the beneficial rays they bathe in perpetually? The worst thing about them is their fear of technical men. They are so stupid they think that modern science might produce weapons effective against their mighty antique mechanisms, so they particularly persecute and obstruct modern scientists on the surface, although the truth is, it is improbable that men can produce anything equal to the ancient work in even centuries of effort."

Nydia explained the horror, and I got at last the full significance of the ancient legend of Hell.

"You see, they will not allow their victims to die, but keep them alive through every torment by the use of beneficial rays. They keep them alive for sadistic purposes and train them to service them sexually, both men and women. Not only do they use the ancient devices, some of which were brought to her by the hunters from space, but they brandish whips with metal tips for their prolonged gratification, keeping themselves in a state of excitement and frenzy.

"When a person is nearly dead, they place them in one of the revitalizer machines for a day or two, and they are healed up completely. Then they start going through the same thing again. Do you see those shriveled bundles at the side? That is how the victims look when they finally do die."

We watched in horror for a space and Nydia concluded, "Some of those have lived in that torment for twenty years. This is our enemy's pleasure palace; a Hell for helpless victims of their lust for blood and pain. From immemorial times, they have had such Hells in the underworld, and it has never ceased. You see, you surface Christians are not so far wrong in your pictures of Hell, except that you do not die in order to go there, but wish for death to release you once you arrive. And they are very careful about letting a victim die, for that would end the fun. There has always been a Hell on earth, and this is one of them. Every man or woman who falls into their hands, from the caverns or from the surface, faces one of these torments to the death you witness. It never mentions such things in your newspaper, does it? That misbegotten spawn fears all living men."

"Do any surface men know of this thing?" I asked her.

"It's impossible to tell them of such things," she answered.

* * * * * * * * * *

Richard Shaver and Ray Palmer are long since deceased, but their legacy lives on. We have probably more books on the Inner Earth than all other publishers combined. Not all stories of the cavern are so salacious. Shaver seemed to pretty

SCREWED BY THE ALIENS

much have the Marquis in mind when penning some of his stories, while with others he did not. But it certainly is a prime example of sex and aliens and robots and those evil things that keep us awake at night.

SUGGESTED READING

SUBTERRANEAN WORLDS INSIDE EARTH by Timothy Beckley

THE HIDDEN WORLD (a series of books about Shaver kept in print by our company)

REALITY OF THE INNER EARTH: RETURN TO THE CAVERNS by Tim Swartz

RICHARD SHAVER'S CHILLING TALES FROM THE INNER EARTH

INNER EARTH PEOPLE, OUTER SPACE PEOPLE by Rev. Blessing

MR. UFO'S SECRET FILES – OUR YOUTUBE CHANNEL

Richard S. Shaver, "creator" of the Dero.

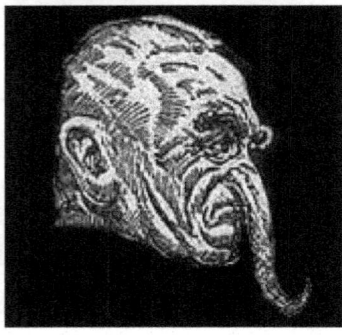

A deformed Dero.

SCREWED BY THE ALIENS

Artist Carol Ann Rodriguez depicts life in the caves and the various perverse activities that take place there.

SCREWED BY THE ALIENS

"Amazing Stories" often devoted their covers to graphic illustrations of half-naked women being kidnapped by aliens or held captive by the deformed Dero. Artist Stefan Poag (StefanPoag.com) brings out the brutality of Shaver's stories in his soon-to-be-released comic.

SCREWED BY THE ALIENS

THE "MORALLY OUTRAGEOUS" CASE STUDIES OF DR. KARLA TURNER
By Sean Casteel

On Project Camelot, a website created as a tribute to the late Dr. Karla Turner, she is described as an "intrepid human rights activist." Born in 1947, Turner earned a Ph.D. in Old English Studies from the University of North Texas. She and her family began their involvement with alien abduction in 1988, after which she would research the phenomenon for the rest of her life. Two traits, she would eventually conclude, characterized alien behavior above all: deceitfulness and cruelty.

Until her untimely death from cancer in 1996, Karla Turner was one of the most outspoken critics of the alien abduction phenomenon in the UFO community. When she died, some of her sympathizers were openly calling her death "murder" at the hands of the aliens.

In Turner's book, "Taken: Inside the Alien-Human Agenda," she writes about an aspect of alien abduction that outraged her more than any other: the sexual abuse by the aliens of innocent, unwilling human "specimens." That the sexual element is often swept under the rug, even by some major researchers, also bothered her.

"Regrettably," Turner writes, "much of what abductees have reported has not been publicized, for a number of reasons. In some cases, as with alien-human sexual activity, this may be because so many abductees are unwilling to talk about such intimate things. In other cases, it is the researchers themselves who are reluctant to expose some aspects of the events, fearing they will push the credibility of their audience, especially their desired audience of professionals and academics, too far. Some parts of this phenomenon, they feel, are simply not 'politically' acceptable, no matter what the abductees themselves insist they have experienced."

Turner next cautions her readers not to take the stories at face value.

SCREWED BY THE ALIENS

"It is important to remember that the aliens have superb 'virtual reality' capabilities," she writes, "and that without external verification it is impossible to know if the memory or dream of an encounter reflects an actual event. This is especially important when assessing reports of sexual activity with the aliens, for in some situations people tell of seeing celebrities, religious figures and even dead acquaintances."

ARE THE ALIENS CHILD MOLESTERS?

When reading about some of the sex-related cases that Turner has researched, it is easy to understand her outraged sense of violation.

In one case, a female abductee named "Polly" told Turner about what had happened to her child, "Sam."

"Sam just took me aside," Polly wrote to Turner, "to tell me about a dream he had last night. He said, 'Can I talk to you in private? It's personal.' He has a partial memory of this dream, or else the dream itself was a fragment. He was with some people approaching the entrance to a UFO. He went through an entry way which led to a place that was all white. He was in a line with other people and the person in front of him was older than he. This young man proceeded into the craft and approached a long, white tube. He put his penis into the tube. After a little while he apparently withdrew it and left by some way other than the entrance. Sam was next. He did the same thing with the tube as the man before him had done, but his memory ends at this point. He felt this had something to do with the aliens wanting sperm. He said there was no sound and he did not see any aliens. He kept asking me for reassurance, saying, 'That was just a dream, right, Mom?'

"He does not read adult-level books and I have never mentioned the sexual intrusions to him. It seems that just in the past year his experiences have become less agreeable to him. Previously he was the one of children who seemed to feel a need and desire for 'them.' That is not completely gone, but certainly some intrusive elements have been introduced. Damn it, Karla, something is sexually molesting my eleven-year-old boy!"

After pondering the situation for a while, Polly later commented, "I think the motive is not sperm gathering, but control. What affects the depths of the human psyche more than issues related to our sexuality? It is perhaps an unadmirable fact that sexual identity is probably the deepest, most primitive, most powerful identity concept that a human being has. Violate sexual identity in a situation where the human is made to believe that he/she is totally powerless, and you have gained a measure of control probably unattainable by any other single act."

POLLY'S OWN CHILDHOOD MOLESTATION ENCOUNTERS

After Polly felt more comfortable about sharing her experiences with Turner, she was able to address the sexual issue and the painful memories from her childhood.

SCREWED BY THE ALIENS

"The area of my psychology which I feel has been most damaged by 'them' or by some very early influence," Polly confided, "is the area of my sexual concepts. At approximately age four, I became obsessed with sadomasochistic sexual imagery. The images involved a little girl on a flat table similar to a doctor's exam table, but I think it may have been metallic-looking, silver metallic, a little grayer than actual silver. I remember being obsessed by these images day in and day out, and I would try to detach from them by saying that the little girl was not me, but yet at the same time I knew it was.

"Sometimes there would be one 'person' doing things to the little girl," she continued, "and sometimes several. There were generally those who observed. I had the sense of both males and females present. Occasionally a female would do a procedure, but more often a male."

The intrusive procedures included what Polly now understands, but did not understand at the time, to be her genital and rectal areas. She also recalled needles being inserted in her navel, which made sense to her later, as an adult, when she read about the same process happening to other female abductees. As a child of five or six, Polly would draw pictures of a little girl on the table with "people" and their intrusive machines gathered around her. She showed the drawings to her mother but can't remember her mother's reaction, except to say her mother didn't "shame" her about them.

"If I had been molested by adult family members," Polly reasons, "I don't think I would have had images of an exam table and needles associated with machinery, especially at ages three and four. I think these images had to have come from some source outside my own imagination. This early influence imprinted my sexuality with the dynamics of sadomasochism. I feel this imprinting set me up to be victimized and set me up to expect all sexual encounters to involve humiliation by a dominator."

Polly avoids sexual involvements now, in an attempt to regain control over the compulsions that have caused many problems for her in the past.

"I now simply stay out of any relationships of a sexual nature," she told Turner. "The sexual and 'psychic' energy in [the last relationship] was intense to the point of being ridiculous, totally 'directed,' and involved frequent telepathy and transference of feelings. I am in counseling for childhood incest, but there is only so far I can go with it because I don't have a human incest background."

HAVING SEX WITH AN 'AUDIENCE' PRESENT

Turner writes about a woman she calls "Lisa," who says that one of the first sexual situations she remembers happened in late 1989, beginning with her conscious awareness of the aliens' presence. Lying in bed, she woke up and saw a group of aliens standing around her and her husband, "Neal." One of the aliens held up a wand-like instrument. The tallest of the beings was touching Neal's chest.

SCREWED BY THE ALIENS

"I looked at them," Lisa recounted, "and told them not to touch him and to leave him alone. That's the night I got to see them for a few seconds in an unaltered state. Then they pointed the wand at my forehead, made me feel dizzy, and I was out. I believe that's the night they made me have sex while they watched."

The sexual interaction involved another abductee. Lisa said the man told her his name, even spelled it for her, and then told her he had been abducted since he was a child. "He was very sorry."

NOT EVEN BESTIALITY IS FORBIDDEN

In an account that may shock even longtime students of alien abduction, Lisa also recounts being forced to have sex with animals.

"These types of bizarre reports turn up less frequently in the research," Turner writes, "but they are not unheard of. She recalled the first episode as a dream-event, in which she and a gorilla-type creature were sexually engaged. Lisa woke up after having this 'dream' when the sound of a 'breathing device' brought her to consciousness. She saw a dim figure in the doorway step out of sight and then, as unlikely as such a response always seems in these situations, she went back to sleep. The action, however, was not yet over. At 3:25 she woke up again, flinging her arms about and trying to rouse Neal, who was completely unresponsive. She saw a lighted object outside the bedroom window and she could feel an energy controlling her body."

On another occasion, while lying down during the day, Lisa dreamed about a number of sexual situations. Something like a small horse was involved, as well as a "dolphin," some grays, and a "dark, leathery, scaly creature" whose features she couldn't clearly recall. In still other "dreams," she was placed in sexual situations with several animals, again while being observed. She also recalled an experience of having sex with a well-known public figure after which she saw a nebulous form move quickly across the room and disappear. Startled and frightened, it took her a long time to fall back asleep and in the morning she felt nauseated.

A HUMAN-LOOKING RAPIST

In still another case of nonconsensual sex, an experiencer given the name "Anita" told Turner her story.

"In the 1970s, Anita lived in Houston for a while," Turner writes, "and it was there that a number of events occurred. The most traumatic and terrifying was in 1972."

Anita recalled an encounter, a daytime event in which she was conscious. But, as in most abductions, her state of mind was soon altered as the strangers intruding into her home took control of the situation. She was lying on the living room couch when she became aware of "presences" there with her, and instantly her mind was clouded. She saw a man who appeared "human-looking in every way" bending over her.

SCREWED BY THE ALIENS

"I have never experienced such terror in my life," Anita told Turner. "I was like a dream, in that I knew the human was raping my body, but I did not feel anything at all."

The rapist had not come alone.

"I could see maybe three others," Anita recounted, "standing by the table, but it was like seeing them through frosted glass. I could make out their bodies but could not really see any details."

Anita had no idea, therefore, if the other figures were human-looking, like the rapist, or alien. She did recall that, after the forced intercourse, the man spoke to her about something, but the only communication that stayed with her consciously was his statement, "I'll be there to help you."

Anita doesn't remember what may have happened after that, but as soon as she was aware that the "men" were gone, she reacted in a very conscious state of mind. In a state of utter terror, she grabbed her children and fled her house immediately.

The trauma of the event had disturbing effects on Anita for a very long time.

"It is very embarrassing to say this," she confided in Turner, "but after that experience I started wearing a tampon twenty-four hours a day so they couldn't do it again. As if that would stop them."

TURNER'S CONCLUSIONS ON SEXUAL ENCOUNTERS

Turner writes that half of the women whose cases she researched for "Taken" reported being forced or induced to engage in mostly traumatic sexual activities with aliens, humanoids, or other abductees.

Some researchers have theorized that all such sexual scenarios are the product of mind-control – erotic images without substance – used merely to facilitate an actual event which involves nothing more than the taking of sperm or ova for the alien breeding program.

But there are problems with this theory, Turner warns us.

"For one thing," she writes, "although sperm-gathering can be accomplished via erotically induced orgasm on the part of a male, it certainly isn't necessary for ova-gathering. In fact, it is totally unnecessary. Nor does it serve a reproductive purpose for a female to be compelled to masturbate, as in some abductions, as well as in cases where a person feels 'switched on' for this purpose when no abduction is underway. Another problem is that sexual intrusions involving reproductively immature children are reported. And finally, there is clearly no sperm/ova gathering going on in those situations where abductees are forced into sexual situations together."

SCREWED BY THE ALIENS

SUGGESTED READING, BOOKS BY KARLA TURNER:
INTO THE FRINGE
TAKEN
MASQUERADE OF ANGELS

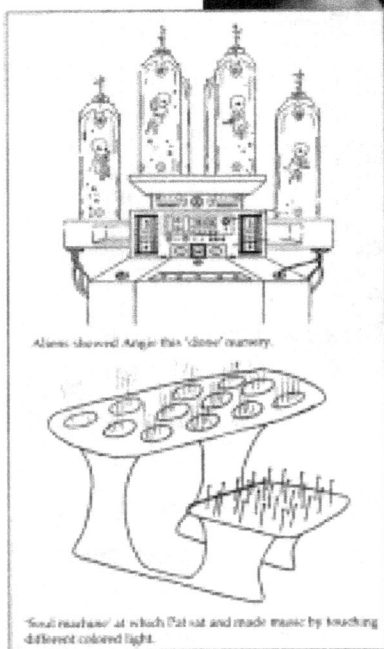

Above: Reptilians, says Dr. Turner, are here harvesting humans. (Still from the movie "Jupiter Ascending")

Left: Abductee saw a rather horrendous "breeding chamber."

Below: The hypnotist who worked with Dr. Turner on the Ted Rice abduction case passed away from a stroke well ahead of her time.

Above: Abductee Ted Rice told his strange and remarkable encounter while under hypnosis. (Photo courtesy Bruce Cornet).

SCREWED BY THE ALIENS

CHAPTER 19

THE SEXUAL "MIS-ADVENTURES" OF TED RICE
A PERFECT EXAMPLE
ANYTHING BUT PLEASURABLE

EDITOR'S NOTE: While conscious, surface memories often provide great detail, it is while under hypnosis that the grimmer, unadulterated, and perverse aspects of a close encounter will typically come to the surface. Karla Turner had to put one of her subjects, Ted Rice, at ease repeatedly, as he was provoked and prodded under hypnotic regression to recall what really happened to him during his encounter with a group of perverse alien intruders. Here is his story. The hypnotic session was conducted by Barbara Bartholic, one of Turner's closest allies in the field of alien abduction research.

The following is an excerpt from a hypnotic regression in which hypnotherapist Barbara Bartholic regressed abductee Ted Rice to recall events he began experiencing at the tender young age of eight. Barbara worked with Dr. Jacques Vallee for nearly a decade

Hailing from Tulsa, Oklahoma, Bartholic was a well-recognized UFO investigator and researcher who used hypnosis and regression techniques as analytical tools. When troubled people, who suspect UFO abduction in their pasts, learned of her work, they were relieved that there was someone whom they could call out to for help. Barbara passed away from a very untimely stroke. Some claim there is no rational explanation for her death once one has excluded the Reptilians!

****

Soon he began to get new images, also from his childhood, but this time involving his other grandmother, and himself at a slightly older age. Ted struggled to regain a clear sense of vision, but something – an induced block, perhaps, or his own reluctance – held him back. And then, as if bubbling up from somewhere deep within him, information began to trickle into his mind. His recollections started in the midst of a bizarre scene unlike anything Ted had ever consciously remembered.

SCREWED BY THE ALIENS

"Grandy is standing on something," he started again, after a long pause. "She seems hypnotized; she's not saying anything. They remove her nightgown, and they've got something like a little drill, touching to the back of her head. They've done something to her, and she's slightly different."

He paused again, as if listening.

"They're telling her she's very special," he resumed. "They put a white gown on her and make her look beautiful, or they're telling her she's beautiful. They dress her up and tell her that she's beautiful, and that she's coming to live and work with them."

"How old are you here?" Barbara interrupted.

"I'm ten years old," he said. "I remember this, the room, and these beings around her, and I'm watching. She's not in control, and they're all around her. They've loosened her hair and are showing her how beautiful she'll look when she lives with them. They're preparing her for this. That's all I seem to be able to see right now. And she does look beautiful, and young, too."

Ted stopped again, pondering.

"I don't feel like that's all exactly right, though," he admitted. A mental alarm went off, because the words felt false even as he spoke them.

"We want only the truth," Barbara said, "that's what we're aiming for."

"I suddenly felt like that stuff was what they told me I was seeing, but it's not really," Ted said.

"Clarify your vision," Barbara told him, deepening his trance, "and tell me what is really happening."

"She's complaining about the pain," he continued, "and they've brought somebody else in. I feel like they're antagonizing and torturing her. Somebody's come in who says he's my grandfather, but my grandfather is dead. She's arguing with him that it's not her husband, she doesn't care what they say. Somebody's angry. And that's all I can see right now."

"Ted," Barbara asked, "is this the grandmother you were with in bed the night you heard the voice in the room?"

"Yes."

"How old were you when that happened?"

"Ten."

"Let's shift your focus to that night," Barbara directed. "Feel the bed, you're in bed with your grandmother. Feel it, and your memory is perfect. Do you feel yourself there now?"

"Yes," he slurred, sinking deeper into the trance.

"On the count of three," Barbara continued, "you begin to tell me, with truth and clarity, what happened on that night. One, two, three."

SCREWED BY THE ALIENS

"I can hear her voice now," Ted responded. "She's demanding that we be taken home. She's complaining about the pain in the back of her head. She's telling them to get that thing away from her."

"How did this start?"

"I remember we were sleeping," he explained, "and somebody takes me out of the bed. Then the next thing I know, I'm at the side of the room, and somebody who's got a hood over their head is beside me. My grandmother's in the center of the room; they've taken off her robe and put another one on her and done something with her hair. She does look beautiful, but before that they did something with that strange drill to her head. She got very angry, and I think she hit one of them because they were hurting her.

"I'm beginning to see," he said after a short pause, "what she hit wasn't a person. It was one of those dark gray or brown looking men, like a lizard-like man, one of those reptilian beings. They're offering her something to make her young again, and she's angry, refusing to cooperate. She's demanding that we be taken home. This reptilian guy leaves the room, and he comes back with ...oh, this is making my grandmother very upset. They've brought in my grandfather, who's been dead a while. He looks young and handsome, and they're telling Grandy that she's to join him."

"How does she respond?" Barbara asked.

"She tells them that it isn't true, that they are lying, and that my grandfather is deceased. They're arguing, and she refuses to cooperate. I hear her calling out to Jesus."

He stopped again, listening.

"The reptilian man is talking ugly," he resumed, "and telling her that..."

He broke off abruptly.

"What is he telling her, Ted?" Barbara asked.

"He told her that they put something into her head," he said reluctantly, "and that if she doesn't cooperate, it would kill her, and only they can stop it. She still refuses."

"What did they want her to cooperate by doing?"

"I don't know!" he exclaimed, but Barbara directed him to program his inner computer for the truth and then to proceed.

"I can't understand it," he began again. "But it has something to do with sick people."

"Did your grandmother have anything to do with sick people?"

"She could make warts disappear, and things like that. She knew where to get roots and herbs in the woods and use them to make people well. They told her something about sick people coming to her, but she refused to participate. It wasn't for the right reasons, she said. She called on Jesus two or three times. I can hear her saying, 'No, no, I will not!' They're telling her that someone will come and teach her more, but she doesn't want to learn anything from them."

"Why would it be evil if they wanted her to cure people with their knowledge?"

"I don't know, but every time they tell her this, she tells them no. Then the reptilian man tells her she's going to die because she won't cooperate."

Ted became very sad, and then he caught his breath with a start.

"What is it, Ted?" Barbara asked. "What did you just become aware of?"

"He told her he would have my soul," Ted replied, "and they brought me to the center of the room where she is. They're doing something to me. No, she steps in between them. There are several beings around: me, Grandy, this reptilian man, my grandfather. He's standing there immobile, like he's in a daze. She steps in between me and the reptilian man, puts out her hand and stops him. She's telling him that she's not afraid of him, that she's met him before. I don't know after that," he sighed. "They do something, and we're back in the bedroom."

"Do you remember telling me you heard a voice that night?" Barbara reminded him.

"I feel like it was the voice of that man wearing the hood, but I'm not sure."

"She died not long after that, didn't she?"

"Yes, she died two days later of a massive stroke. That day I went to her because I remembered the talking that night in the room. I asked her about it, and she held me and started crying. She told me to forget about it, that it was the devil. Then she got my father to take her back home, and we all went. Less than two hours after we arrived, Grandy had a stroke in front of us and died."

Barbara listened to Ted describe the scene, and as he relived the events, his memory strengthened. He said once again that he had always felt some guilt about his grandmother's death.

"I kept thinking that something I did caused it," he finished.

"What made you feel that?"

"I guess because of what happened during the night. She was trying to protect me."

"Let's get it all out," Barbara said. "Go back and look at the situation."

"This reptilian man was talking about me, when we first got there. It had something to do with my being, and with the other group that had had contact with me. I'm not sure who the other group is. They wanted my soul, and Grandy protected me. She said, 'Jesus will not allow you to touch this child or take him.' That's when he told her she would die."

"Move back to where they're putting the gown on her," Barbara suggested, hoping that Ted's recollections would be clearer and more complete, now that he

SCREWED BY THE ALIENS

had begun breaking through the screen sequence. "What is the truth? Tell me the truth about what is taking place. Remove all the blinders, all the veils of deception."

Ted's chest began to heave.

"Oh, no!" he whispered in fright, shaking and panting for breath. "I don't want to look at that anymore!"

"You don't have to look any more," Barbara assured him soothingly.

"I don't have to look," he whispered even more fearfully, "because I know, I already saw."

Barbara led him into a more serene state of mind, reminding him of the protective energy he had built around himself. At last he began to breathe more normally, listening to her soft words.

"The reptilian man was wanting to have intercourse with her," Ted said, once he was able to speak again with any control. His voice was more sure, yet tinged with a deep note of sorrow and resignation. "But she wouldn't allow it. She told him she only did that with her husband, and he was dead. So they brought in the grandfather, and he was having sex with her. But when he got off her, it wasn't him, it was a reptilian man. And that's when she intervened. They wanted me next, I don't know, but I think it was sexual. That's when she jumped in front and blocked the reptilian man. They were arguing, and he told her she would die for that. And she did."

"It didn't seem to matter that she was older?" Barbara asked, referring to the sexual activity.

"They told her they could make her young again."

"Can you describe the situation more completely? How did they do it to her? Was it just the one?"

"There were several in the room, as well as the one with the hood who had been holding me back. I never saw his face very clearly, but when he turned it looked pasty white."

"Did they have her on a table or standing up?"

"Standing up, but leaning back on something like a movable table."

"Do you want to see the rest?" Barbara asked cautiously. "Remember, you said he started coming toward you?"

"Yeah, he wanted me for some reason."

"Do you want to go back and find out?"

"Yes," Ted sighed, "let's go back."

Barbara returned him to a deep concentration and then asked him to look at the scene again.

"What is your grandfather doing while intercourse is taking place?" she asked.

SCREWED BY THE ALIENS

"Is he aware?"

"He was doing the raping," Ted tried to explain, "but it wasn't really him. When they brought him in, he took her in his arms and started making love to her. They removed her gown, and she was immobile, not speaking. But when they were finished and he turns around, I can see him. It isn't my grandfather, it's the reptilian man."

"Backtrack a minute," Barbara suggested, "back to where they were telling her about the herbs."

"They were talking to her because she knew a lot about herbs. He tells her that he's got some herbs. Oh," he paused, "oh, they're wanting her to take some of theirs. He's telling her they can exchange information and for her to try his stuff. She takes something they put on her tongue, and I think they gave me some, too.

"They dropped it in our mouths. It was kind of clear, maybe slightly yellow. Everything seems to be centered around Grandy now," Ted described as he relived the event. "She refused to have sex with the reptilian, so they left and hurried back with supposedly my grandfather. By that time, my grandmother seems to be submitting to the sexual situation. She doesn't seem to be resisting. After he's done with her, another one's on her now. Then they take me and lift me up on top of her as if I'm supposed to be having sex with her. But I can't recall any stimulation."

"Does she respond to you?"

"She seems to be kind of out of control."

"That thing they gave you by mouth, did it affect you in any way?"

"I don't think I was sexually excited," Ted said, "but it affected Grandy, like they'd given her some kind of aphrodisiac."

"What's happening now?"

"There's more than one that has intercourse with her," he continued, "at least three. Then the one that looked like my grandfather comes over, and he makes me have oral sex with him."

"So does he have a penis?"

"Yeah, but it doesn't look like a normal man's. It looks more like a male dog, more shaped like a little gun. Instead of just getting an erection, it seems to come out of an encasement like a gun.

"They've moved my grandmother off the table," he said, "and they put me on it. It's flat now, horizontal. Then one of them has anal intercourse with me. They say something about the other group that has something to do with me, and it's like they're laughing about it. Like they're making fun of the situation."

Ted's disgust was evident, but he was also bewildered.

"I don't know what they're talking about," he admitted, "but it's me. They're

SCREWED BY THE ALIENS

doing this to get even, maybe, that's the only way I know how to say it."

"How do you feel while this is happening to you?" Barbara asked. "Are you able to think?"

"I'm crying out for Grandy," Ted said. "I can't seem to feel a lot of pain, but I'm terribly frightened. My hands are clamped down on something, and my ankles, too. When that reptilian came to take me and says they're going to keep me there, Grandy steps in between us. She says, 'In the name of Jesus Christ, I demand that you stop.' She says that for what they've done to us, he will burn in hell forever. He says there is no hell.

"She says, 'You're not going to have our souls.' She rebuked him, that's what made him so angry. She's got me close to her, and they're all standing back, and she says, 'You tricked me, you tricked us.' She's angry about the herbs and what they did to us."

After a brief pause, Ted concluded the recollection.

"That's all I can remember. We have our clothes back on, and he tells her, 'You're going to die for this, because that boy belongs to us.' And then we seem to be back in our bedroom."

"How do you feel now?"

"Repulsed somewhat," he admitted. "Angry. Hurt. Glad that I looked at it, but it was so hard to look at. The first regression came easier. They didn't want me to see this one. Old Volmo, my buddy, the reptilian who taught me all those wonderful things, I bet he's the sorry bastard who was doing that to me."

Ted shook his head, overwhelmed and deeply angry.

Excerpt from the book: "Masquerade of Angels," 1994, by Karla Turner, Ph.D. Kelt Works Publishing, Roland, Arkansas, ISBN 0-964089

SUGGESTED READING

ROUND TRIP TO HELL IN A FLYING SAUCER (Inner Light - Global Communications edition)

PROJECT ALIEN MIND CONTROL

EVIL EMPIRE OF THE ETs AND THE ULTRA-TERRESTRIALS

REALITY OF THE SERPENT RACE AND THE SUBTERRANEAN ORIGIN OF UFOs

SCREWED BY THE ALIENS

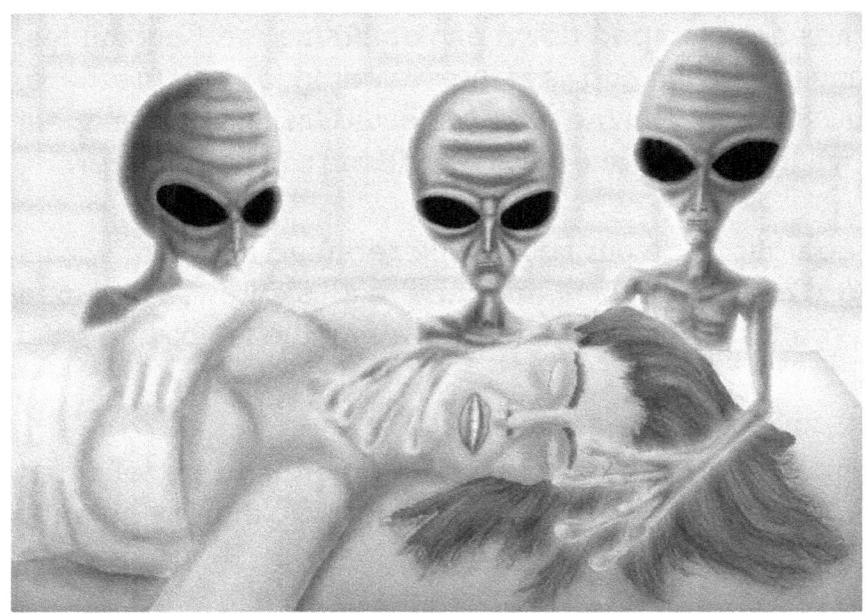

Sexual probes have been used on both men and women, often causing unusual pain and discomfort.

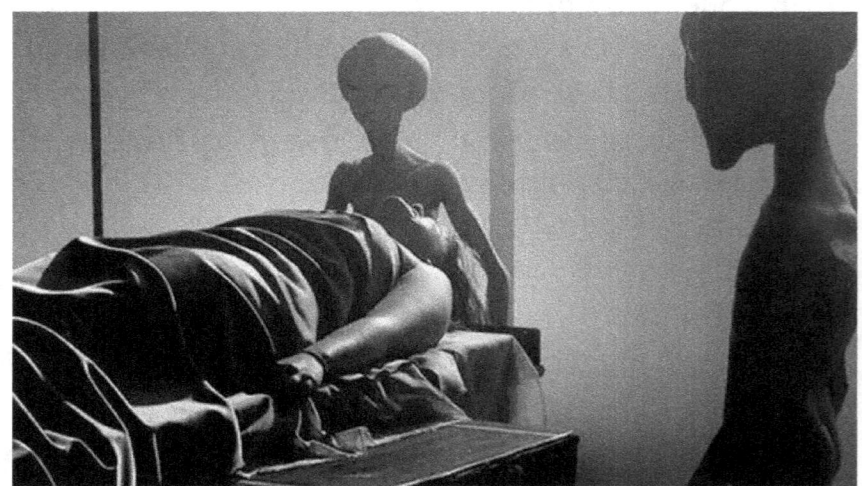

Under hypnosis, as in the case of Ted Rice, often the most barbaric aspects of the sexual molestation come to conscious recall.

SCREWED BY THE ALIENS

WILL YOU BE VICTIMIZED NEXT?
THE RAPE OF AN AUSTRALIAN UFO RESEARCHER
By John Stuart

EDITOR'S NOTE: At the same time Bridgeport, Connecticut, researcher Albert K. Bender was fighting off visits by the UFO silencers – best known as the Men in Black – his co-worker Down Under, John Stuart, was having to help prevent his staff member from being raped. An affiliate of the International Flying Saucer Bureau, Stuart's organization was besieged by the ugliest of ugly aliens who materialized before him and co-worker Barbara. The alien took a particular "liking" to Barbara, as you will read below. Very disturbing in its time – the 1950s – the incident was "one of a kind." Today there are many parallel reports that include rape among the methods the Ultra-terrestrials use to achieve their mysterious ends. No book on a disheartening subject like this would be complete without revisiting certain extreme events in the disturbing history of modern day contact between humans and aliens.

******

It was a beautiful evening. Clear and rather mild. The terror was closer to us now, and soon the pressure would increase to force us out of this research. But on this evening there was nothing to fear and we walked in the moonlight, still discussing the theory we had thought out.

We strolled along, lost in the world of mystery, and I was rather startled when Barbara suddenly came up with: "Do you really and honestly believe I am in danger from these things, Johnnie?"

"Yes," I answered grimly. "I do."

"And what are they likely to do to me?" she inquired, adding one terrible possibility.

I stopped and gripped her shoulders, staring down at her. "That could happen too!" I said harshly. "Doesn't that scare you?"

"I don't know, Johnnie," she replied. "I suppose that if it did happen I'd be

SCREWED BY THE ALIENS

terrified. But the thought doesn't worry me very much." She grinned at my serious expression. "Anyway, nothing has happened to me yet, so why worry?"

"Nothing has happened yet!" I echoed. "Can't you realize what could happen to you?"

"Yes, I do, Johnnie. And I refuse to be frightened!" she replied with some spirit. Then she said, rather strangely, "But I might like to meet a space man. I wonder what one'd be like?"

"Stop it!"

"I think I'd kiss him, y'know," she said with a grin.

"You might get one heck of a shock if you did see one of these things!"

"Something like a satyr?"

"Yes."

"The satyr and the nymph. Me, of course, being the nymph?"

"Barbara, I can't understand your silly talk about this! You don't seem particularly concerned about it all, do you?"

"No. Why should I? I haven't been hurt yet, as I have already said, and should they attack me, well, that is when the time will come to worry."

Her attitude rather frightened me, and that evening when I said good night to her I again warned her to take care.

"Look, Johnnie. I'm all right. Now stop being a silly goat! I'm not going to be harmed."

She was soon lost in the darkness as she moved away.

I SEE THE DISC

I stood there, pondering her strange attitude, and wondered if she were as relaxed as she made herself appear to be. I didn't like it at all. The fear was growing in me that they would strike at her. Would I be able to protect her? What would happen? When would it happen?

I began to feel that the attack was coming, and beads of perspiration formed on my forehead as I thought of Barbara being used as a plaything of some heinous thing. I was trembling. With a cigarette lit I felt a little better, and my wife just arriving from her lodge meeting brought a happy smile on my face.

"Hullo, you're out late, boy."

"Yes. I was just thinking of the UFOs, darling. I don't know if we're making any progress, but it could be that we have stumbled on something pretty big. Dunno yet."

I threw my cigarette away and lit another, and the action did not escape my wife's attention.

"What are you worried about, John?"

SCREWED BY THE ALIENS

"Nothing, dear," I lied. "Just tired, that's all."

I drew on my cigarette, and, looking up at the stars, remarked, "It's just the sort of evening to see a saucer. Y'know, darling, that's what I'd like to do."

"You've seen them before."

"I know. But I'd like to have a fair dinkum close look at one. Be rather interesting, wouldn't it?"

"For you and Barbara it would be very interesting. But I'm going to bed. Coming in?"

"Shortly, darling. I'll finish my cigarette before I do. Anyway, I may see a saucer."

I leaned against the gate staring upward, still thinking of Barbara's strange manner. I tried to force it from me, but the feeling persisted in my mind. She was in danger. But how to make her realize it?

I wasn't going to accept her claim that there was no fear in her mind that she would be attacked; but if such an attack did take place, what would happen? What force would be used? And what form would an attack take? Would it affect her sanity? Would she still be able to carry on our research? A thousand similar questions raced through my mind. Did she really have fears that an attack would take the form she suggested? It was almost too frightening to think about! But the fact remained that she thought they would attack her in such fashion. What if this should come about when I wasn't present? How could I protect her then?

My thoughts were interrupted by a light. I straightened up. It was very high and moving slowly. North to south. It must be all of 10,000 feet, I thought. It was now at an angle of about 70 degrees to my eyes.

Quite big, really. Not a meteor – not moving fast enough. It stopped, as I watched with some excitement. Now it was growing bigger and had changed from a reddish-orange to a duller yellow. Still very bright, though. Still bigger. I could now make out its shape. Bell-like. Still a dullish yellow. It was now down to about 200 feet! And still descending.

It descended to about 100 feet above me, or maybe a little higher. I stared at it. It was rocking slightly. I estimated it was about 30 feet across, and maybe slightly higher from rim to the round ring I could see on top. Up near the top of the object was a row of circular portholes, and from these a bright light shone.

It was pulsating a little, while a band, containing the ports, revolved slowly. Underneath I was able to make out three ball things, which I decided could be its landing gear. At the height where it was I decided it was a dark grey in color, although it was hard to be definite. I detected no sound from the object, but after it had hung there for about ten minutes (this again is difficult to be certain of, owing to the excitement I felt), it suddenly rose to a great height and raced away to the south.

SCREWED BY THE ALIENS

I stood there, trying to collect my excited thoughts, and made myself realize that I had seen a UFO at very close quarters. I was sorry that my wife hadn't heard me call to her. I hurried inside to tell my wife of what I had just seen, and my excitement was sufficient to prove to her that there certainly had been something there. I was very keen to find a witness, and discovered that there was one! I was safe now from ridicule.

The next night I related the details of the sighting to Barbara, and she questioned me closely. She was most convinced that I had actually seen it. We then returned to our Antarctica theory, this in turn brought us back to Bender's affair, and after discussing our previous view, we turned to Edward Jarrold of Australia.

"Who was Ed's visitor?" she asked.

"He might have been from Australian Air Force Intelligence," I replied. "He did tell us in his letter that he was onto something pretty big, and that he had been invited to meet a bloke from R.A.A.F. Intelligence. And you remember we have his report on the meeting. No, I don't believe it was an official from Air Force, Barb."

"H'm. Well, who the blue blazes was the bloke?" she asked impatiently.

"Haven't a clue on that one, I'm afraid."

"Harold Fulton might know, mightn't he?"

"Granted. But we can't ring Harold up and say, 'Look, Harold, old boy, who was Ed's visitor?' Can we?"

"Oh I know that, you idiot."

"Well, what can we do?"

Barbara shook her head. "Oh, I suppose we will have to leave it for the moment, eh? Let's have another look at this area..."

She stopped suddenly to look across the room with a strained expression. A frown crossed her face, and then her eyes turned to mine. I had also heard it. A kind of whisper.

I felt that it came from somebody who had been listening to our conversation and had whispered some comment to it! I was ready to face anything I could see, but when it came to something invisible, I didn't feel so confident! I tensed as Barbara held my arm in her hand, her startled whisper breaking the tension.

"What...was it, Johnnie?"

I sensed the fear she felt, and to calm her nerves, I tried to laugh, failing miserably.

"Oh...I reckon we were just hearing things, my dear."

Her eyes roved the room, and she asked grimly, "Were we?"

Her hand was shaking as she held out her cigarettes. I took one and flicked my Ronson.

SCREWED BY THE ALIENS

"I'm frightened, Johnnie!"

"But I'll look after you, Barbara," I said, hoping my words would calm her.

"I...I...let me sit near you."

She moved her chair next to mine and I put my arms around her waist, feeling her trembling body. Did we hear the sound, or was it just a case of hearing things? Had just one heard the whisper, it would be different, but we had both heard it.

"What is it, John?" she asked fearfully. Have we discovered something? Something we aren't supposed to know? Is that it?" she asked me, her eyes demanding an answer.

"Yes," I admitted wearily, "I do believe we know more than is safe for us."

THE HIDEOUS THING

"Look, Barbara, you've got to get out before it's too late!" I warned. "It's you they'll hurt. You're a girl!"

"I refuse to give up!" she told me firmly, and again her eyes widened. Her slim body stiffened.

"What...what was that?" she whispered. A distinct sound of breathing came from across the room! And it sounded as if the breather had a serious case of asthma. Then it stopped, and I nervously lit a cigarette, not knowing quite how to tackle a problem such as this.

I didn't try, for I realized I was doomed to failure before I even started. But my companion was afraid now, and her earlier words were forgotten. It was quite early when I said goodnight to her at the gate, my mind filled with thoughts of danger for her. This fear was to grow in intensity as the days went by, and would continue until the first of the horrifying attacks, only then to become greater! What was to be next? Had we known, F.S.I. would have closed down there and then, forgetting that there were UFOs to be studied. But we didn't know.

So far the attacks, if they were caused by our research, had not been too serious. They had shaken us considerably, a lot more than I was prepared to admit. I was almost at the stage where I was looking over my shoulder at each step. My health began to suffer. Barbara looked wan and tired, and I knew she was afraid, too. But we persisted in our research, and soon were to be sorry that we had not heeded the warnings.

The terror was about to strike! That Friday evening was much the same as any other, though I later felt most thankful that my wife had been out with a girlfriend. Barbara and I settled down to talk; then soon afterward she realized she was out of cigarettes and decided to go to the store after a pack.

I got myself a pot of beer, and sat down with it. The "sounds" still concerned me. I glanced at my watch. Ten minutes. I continued to think. Another look. Twenty minutes had passed, and still there was no sign of Barbara. I became anxious about

SCREWED BY THE ALIENS

her safety. Another look at my watch, and still another. By then I was very anxious. I got up and started to walk back and forth across the lounge. Suddenly the front door flew open, and a figure rushed into my arms.

Barbara said in a voice filled with fear, "There's something out there!"

Quickly releasing her, I hurried outside, stopping on the top step as a terrible stench struck me. I almost fainted in terror. It was like burnt plastic and sulfur. I stood there for a moment, and then walked down to the front gate, neither seeing nor hearing anything. I retraced my steps, seeing Barbara was on the upper step, watching me. I searched the rear of the grounds, finding nothing, and had just started to return to the door when I heard distinct sounds behind me. I stopped and shone my torch. There was nothing there.

I walked on. The sounds followed. I stopped and the sound stopped. I moved. It moved. Again I stopped, was amazed and startled when "it" kept on! The peculiar shuffling, scraping sound went past me, and I felt something solid brush against my shoulder!

This was the first indication I'd had that "they" were solid as I! As the sound continued toward the front gate, I slowly walked to the door, joining Barbara. I asked her if she had heard it.

"Yes, Johnnie. It was the same as I heard outside when I came from getting the cigarettes."

I saw fear living in her eyes and I wanted to send her away. But now it was too late. I poured two brandies, and told her I was going out for another look around.

"I'm coming, too, Johnnie," she told me firmly.

I shook my head. "You're going to stay here!"

She came closer, and tried to smile. "But, if I'm with you, Johnnie, I'll be safer than here on my own, won't I?" she asked with logic.

"All right," I agreed. "Only stay close to me!"

"Yes, Johnnie," she said, a little meekly.

I felt her hand on my arm as I walked along the path to the rear of the house. I turned the corner, stopping in horror, feeling, more than seeing, Barbara move to my side. We stared at the evil thing which faced us about 27 feet across the lawn. It was loathsome. Hideous. Evil. Disgusting. Horrifying. It was about eight feet in height. I don't profess to be a hero, nor am I a coward, but this thing was sufficient to cause me a lot of natural fear. We stood transfixed, staring in complete horror at the monster in the exceptionally bright moonlight.

I felt a desire to take Barbara and run as fast as possible from it, but I discovered I had no will-power to move a finger. I was helpless! I forced myself to pay some attention to its appearance, wanting to hold my companion close in protection, for even at that moment I had some premonition of what was to come.

SCREWED BY THE ALIENS

The monster's head was large and bulbous. No neck. A huge and ungainly body supported on ridiculously short legs. It had webbed feet. The arms were thin and not unlike stalks of bamboo. It had no hands, the long fingers jutting from the arms like stalks. Its eyes were about four inches across, red in color. There was no nose, just two holes, and the mouth was simply a straight slash across its appallingly lecherous face. The whole was a green lime in color, and it was possible to see red veins running through its ungainly form. The monster was definitely male. Barbara's eyes opened wide in fear and shocking horror at the sight of this monster.

She was not moving in any way, and I felt she was held powerless as was I. We were at the mercy of the odiously base thing. I almost wept with distracted terror, as I understood the intentions of the hideous thing. I strove frantically to move, inwardly moaning that I was held in the power of the terror before us.

It was now moving toward us, its filthy eyes fixed on Barbara's slim body. I shuddered. Completely frantic now, I tried to pray, but the words just would not come. Still closer, its spindly arms lifted toward her body. I felt the sweat trickle down my face, my chest and my back. The fingers were now almost touching her shirt. I tried to yell her name as Barbara seemed to come into complete mental control of the monster, and I will spare the reader Barbara's actions.

This wasn't my little friend! She was a stranger! She had to be! She seemed to be waiting for the filthy hands to touch her! The arms lifted more and only a hair's breadth now separated her body from its fingers. I saw all this in the moonlight as I watched helplessly, knowing I couldn't stop it carrying out its hideous attack. I could only watch in terror.

It was our master and it was making Barbara obey its instructions. It was the only answer! It had to be the answer. But just at what seemed to be the critical moment, the thing withdrew its hands from her and moved slowly back to where it had been standing when we first saw it. Then it disappeared from sight. Barbara moaned and fell into my arms, and she shook uncontrollably. I got her into the lounge, eased her into a chair and got her some brandy.

Her lips were moving, but there was no sound. I knelt in front of her, holding her hands, feeling with my free one for some cigarettes.

"What....what was it, Johnnie?" she whispered in terror.

"God above knows, dear! I don't!"

She nodded slowly, and then said in a strained voice, "You saw...what it made me do?"

Tears overflowed now, and her young body shook.

"Yes," I told her miserably, "I know."

"I'll be all right, Johnnie," she whispered. "I got a fright, that's all."

SCREWED BY THE ALIENS

"I'll take you home, Barbara."

She nodded. "Home. Home to what, Johnnie?" She smiled grimly. "Home to another attack? Maybe it will come back. Yes," she continued as if in a daze, "it might come back again. This time I won't escape from it."

Her words stopped as she saw the expression of terrible fear in my eyes.

"Please, Johnnie," she whispered. "Nothing is going to happen.

"I'm not leaving you alone!"

"It won't come back. Take me home," she asked. "You certainly can't spend the night in my room," she grinned bravely. "Look, Johnnie, I'll be safe. Dinkum, I will."

"All right. Come on."

I walked along with her, amazed at her efforts to sound quite normal as she chattered to me. It was an act. But a very brave one. She swung her hand as it gripped mine, and said brightly, "I'd like to kiss you, Johnnie. Shall I?"

"Would that make you feel any better?"

"Very much better," and she pulled my head down and kissed me on the cheek warmly.

At the house I had to leave her alone, but the rest of the night was long, and sleep was far away from me. I was too afraid that the telephone would ring and I wouldn't hear it. At last, though, dawn broke and the birds sang as I told my wife of the shocking attack.

After breakfast I sat in my chair, my thoughts chaotic and grim, and later I sat on the front step. Questions tumbled through my mind with a speed that left me breathless. What was it? Where did it come from? Why did it attack us? What was behind it? Would it return? Was Barbara safe from another attack? How could I protect her?

I lit another cigarette and walked to the corner, staring across the lawn to where it had stood, almost again seeing it, in my mind's eye. I shuddered and returned to the steps, still deep in thought.

I jumped as a voice greeted me, and I looked up at the strangely beautiful girl who faced me, a look of curiosity in her lovely eyes.

"Hullo, Terry," I smiled and rose to my feet.

"You're very grave this morning, John," she said in her lilting voice, and sat on the step.

"I...I would like to talk to you. Do you mind?"

"I feel deeply honored that you have joined me, fair lady," I murmured sincerely.

She appeared nervous, and at last said, hesitantly, "John ...Would....oh! Listen, did you see anything on your back lawn last evening?" she hurriedly asked.

SCREWED BY THE ALIENS

I stiffened and lit a cigarette, lifting my head in surprise. "What was there?" I asked tensely.

She drew a small pad from her pocket and quickly sketched. She handed it to me. "This!"

I stared at the very same "green thing" Barbara and I had seen. Terry had drawn a remarkable likeness, almost as hideous as the actual thing. Hardly a detail was missing, and I knew she had seen the same thing.

"We both saw it, Terry. It...it was absolutely hideous," I said, forcing the words from my tight throat. I told her what had occurred, right from the start, and found it made me feel much better.

"It was going to...do something awful to Barbara," she gasped in horror, her slim hand on my arm.

"Yes, Terry, that is about what it was going to do when whatever controlled it, and God knows what that was, called it back from her. I was in a terrible fever the whole time, and did everything I knew how to break the power it held me under. I had to stand there and watch it all."

THE CREATURE RETURNS

"Hullo, Johnnie. You look all in," Barbara greeted me.

"You are the one who should be ill, Barbara, but I feel terrible."

"You look it, too, John! Did you tell your wife?"

"Yes. I told her as I lay in bed at dawn. It was so strange to be telling her of the terror while outside the birds sang happily. Nothing further happened to you? No troubles?"

"None, Johnnie," she told me. "I took some aspirin and went to bed. I slept right through the night." (She didn't tell me that she had taken so many tablets that she had put herself into a drugged sleep. I did not learn that until much later.)

"Terry came over to see me this morning. She saw the thing too."

Barbara gasped. "She...saw it too?" Her eyes were wide. "But...if she saw the thing, she must have seen everything!"

"No, she wasn't able to see us. Just the thing."

"Strike! What a shock for little, sweet Terry."

I nodded. "Yes, it was a shock, but it didn't stop her from making a sketch of it. Every detail was there, and it proved that she saw it."

"Strewth!" was Barbara's reply. "What a girl!"

We talked about the thing because it had to be discussed. We had to talk about it to find some answer, to find some defense against another similar episode.

"Well, as Terry saw the thing, it proves it was there, doesn't it? It was fair

SCREWED BY THE ALIENS

dinkum, alright," nodded my companion.

"Of course it was fair dinkum! It wasn't a nightmare we had last night, girl!"

I almost yelled at her. "And, my dear, you're going to pull out before it's too late!"

Her head turned, and she stared at me in amazement.

"I'm going to . . . what?" she gasped. "Look, if you think I'm going to be scared out of this business, you've got to think again! I'm in this, and in it I'm going to stay!"

She lit herself a fresh cigarette. "Pull out! Just because that ugly thing appeared and did what it did! It's not enough to frighten me out of all this! I'm not a coward!" She almost shouted.

"I didn't say you were a coward! But I'm not going to stand by and see the same thing happen again!"

She looked down at her cigarette. "I'm sorry, Johnnie! You couldn't have helped me, even though you had tried."

This was in answer to the inference that I stood by and couldn't help her. I knew we hadn't seen the last of this thing, and I knew somehow that she would be in danger again. I was terribly afraid for her safety, but deeply shocked as I saw again and again that I would be powerless to save her.

Whatever we might have anticipated regarding the next attack, it should have been what actually happened! It was one affair I will always remember for its ferocity, and for the harm they did to my young friend. I know that somewhere in our research we stumbled onto the truth, and they were determined to frighten us sufficiently so that we would be silent.

I pointed this out to Barbara a number of times over the following evenings, but she was adamant that we were going to carry out our efforts. As she gradually recovered from her terrible fright, we found we could discuss the attack with a calm outlook – but we never did arrive at any particular answers.

Then, one evening, just before the end came, I again escorted Barbara home, amused at her chatter of happiness. There was nothing in the air to show us there was anything to fear, and she even facetiously remarked that one evening perhaps she would meet a spaceman in her room. I told her not to talk like that, but she only laughed delightedly.

At her door, however, it was different, and she asked me to search the room for her. I found nothing, and it wasn't until the following day that I remembered the very slight, but most peculiar odor I had detected. There had been the usual feminine odor of powders, perfumes and the usual makeup, and these registered in my mind. But there had also been the other smell, like burned plastic or sulfur. My overlooking this was a terrible mistake, for it was that night when they struck

SCREWED BY THE ALIENS

again. And they struck while she was alone!

I left her and walked home, unaware as I lay in bed reading that she was undergoing a terror such as a human had never known! And it was not until many hours later that I learned of the hideous attack they launched upon this defenseless girl. When I did learn about it, I marveled at the manner in which she managed to retain her sanity in spite of the horrors she had known.

I saw her the following day, and was uneasy when I detected she was walking in some sort of daze – or a horror-filled dream. And that evening she told me all that had befallen her after I left her alone.

I saw the vile scene as she spoke! A terrible coldness gripped my stomach, and I wondered how any girl could have endured such horror and remained sane! She sat at my side, her hand resting on mine, and there was a slight trembling, but her voice was surprisingly calm. She seemed to be quite unmoved, but I was aware that she was on the verge of hysterical tears.

After she had related the ghastly details of the attack, she typed a report on it in ghastly completeness. I read it. It was all there. A shocking testimony of fear!

I will abridge this report in presenting it to the reader, for only a few could peruse it without becoming ill – if it were presented as Barbara wrote it: "When I entered my room last evening I immediately noticed a peculiar odor, but decided it came from outside. Also I did not want to mention this to Johnnie for fear it would unduly alarm him. I undressed and drew on my dressing gown, planning to have a bath before retiring. On my return from bathing, I removed my gown and sat down on my bed to smoke a cigarette. It was a very warm night.

"Suddenly I had the impression that I was not alone, that unseen eyes were studying me. This impression was so strong that I searched the room, finding nothing. I returned to sit on the bed, and to go over in my mind some of the research John and I were doing. The impression of unseen eyes persisted, but I forced myself to ignore it, preferring to think of our investigative tasks.

"I crushed my cigarette out and turned to pick up my pajamas, freezing as someone touched my shoulder. I jerked upright, my eyes closed in fear. I found that I was unable to move. I gradually mustered the will power to force my eyes open to see my attacker. I almost fainted away! I could see nobody in the room! Whatever or whoever it was, it was invisible!

"Hours seemed to pass, during which time I seem to be able to remember all details. I tried to think of my friend, John, and his grin, but all I could think of was the horror that I was experiencing.

"Finally the horror was gone. The attack ceased as suddenly as it had begun. I dragged myself to a sitting position and stared at my body, shuddering as I saw the fine scratches I was covered with. With a trembling hand I lit a cigarette and looked at my watch. Two and a half hours had passed! I tried to think clearly, and

SCREWED BY THE ALIENS

eventually forced my mind to accept what had happened to me. Sleep was far away and I tried to find an answer to this new development in the UFO research I had embarked upon.

"I concluded that the thing had been solid, even if invisible. There was, of course, no way of knowing exactly what it was like, and I tried to form a picture in my mind to fit it, but I gave up in fear. I got into bed and eventually fell into a deep sleep filled with nightmares. With the light of day, I again looked at my body and shuddered when I saw the scratches. It had really happened after all! I felt sick, but I knew I would have to go to work, for to remain in my room all day would drive me completely mad!"

I listened to all Barbara told me in silence, almost petrified with horror at the bestial terror she had experienced at the hands of this invisible thing. I was not particularly keen to question her, but realized it was the only way we might solve the identity of the thing.

When I asked her if she felt well enough to answer some questions, she nodded. "Yes, Johnnie, I'm ready."

"What size would you estimate the thing to have been?"

"Much taller than you. Well over six feet or more."

And in reply to the texture of its skin, she replied, "It was like sandpaper. Very rough."

"Did you notice any particular odor?"

"About the same as we noticed the evening we saw the green thing. A little."

"Would you say it was anything like the green thing?"

"I couldn't say. It was invisible."

"Was there any sound?"

"None. Except for my own breathing."

"Did you notice any shadows?"

"Yes, when I first opened my eyes I saw a faint shadow against the wall at the head of my bed. It was a shadow of a man, only it was clearer below the waist."

"You had no trouble in seeing this?"

"None, because I was partly facing that way."

"You say you attempted to force it from you. Will you show me your hands? Palms up?" (I looked at her hands and there were fine scratches covering the skin.) "I see." I watched as she stood up, pulling her shirt free from the waist band of her slacks.

"What are you doing, Barbara?" I asked her apprehensively.

"Forgive me, John, but this is something you must see!"

She faced me, calm, unmoving, and I stared at her, appalled at the scratches

SCREWED BY THE ALIENS

which covered most of her body. I looked at her ribs closely, noting two brown marks about the size of an American 10-cent coin.

I mentioned these, and she told me, "They appeared there after the thing left, Johnnie. I don't know what caused them."

She slowly dressed and sat down again, her voice now telling of the fear she felt. "What was it, Johnnie?" She almost whispered. "Why did it do it?"

"God above knows that, my dear," I replied a little lamely. "Just one last question," I added. "You say it seemed to be only clinically interested in you, despite what it did? When did you get that impression?"

"It didn't seem to be very sensual. Just curious, that's all."

During the following weeks, I saw the fight had died within her, and I knew there was little hope of our continuing this research to which we had dedicated ourselves. The months had taken their toll of me, too. And the fears that I had known, and the strain of too little sleep, had combined to undermine my health.

I realized the time had come to rest completely. Only after such a rest would I be able to return to my investigations with any vigor. Barbara informed me she was returning to her home, and I encouraged this, for to have made her change her mind could have been fatal to her. I felt lost without her to talk to, but I told myself I would return to the research alone. But it was not to be. "They" were to have the final word in this strange drama.

It was a monstrous figure that attacked the female researcher, giving off an offensive odor.

Those looking for further information on the case should be steered toward the book "Curse of the Men In Black: The UFO Terrorists."

Australia has a rich history of UFO research. The last printed UFO magazine in the English language was UFOlogy magazine published by an Aussie as was this UFO zine among the first on the scene circa 1952.

SCREWED BY THE ALIENS

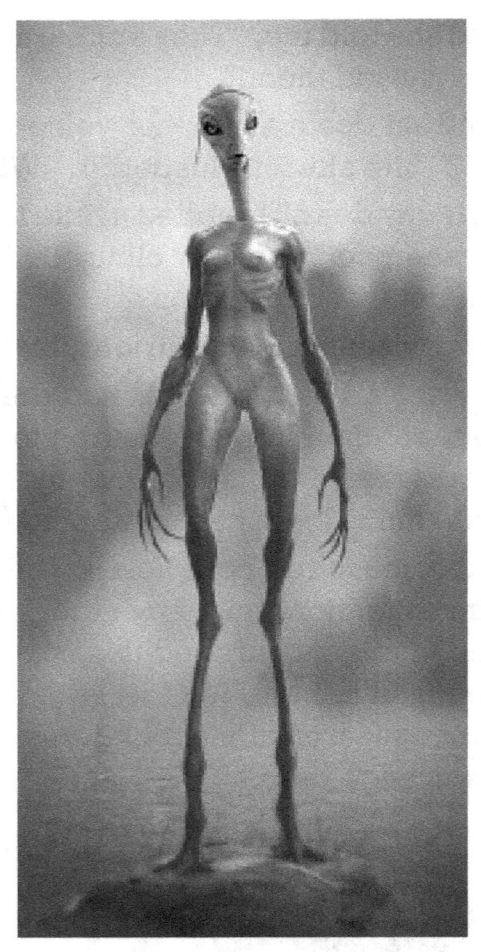

SECTION EIGHT - NO FLYING TACOS PLEASE ONLY IN SOUTH AMERICA

Chapter Twenty One: Antonio Villas Boas
By Scott Corralles

Chapter Twenty Two: Brazilian Abduction
By Dr. Buhler

SCREWED BY THE ALIENS

CHAPTER 21

AN ALIEN HEAT:
CHRONICLES OF SEX AND SAUCERY
By Scott Corrales

It is an unquestionable fact that sex has played a pivotal role in a number of UFO cases and has become the mainstay of the abduction phenomenon, whose literature centers around the non-consensual aspect of these goings-on. But these are merely the latest facet of a phenomenon that goes back to the very start of human history and myth. Who can forget the Greek gods and the numerous guises they assumed to seduce humans? But the Mediterranean cultures were hardly alone in their beliefs. Hindu deities were equally proficient at seduction: the Bhaghavata Purana tells us of the exploits of the divine Krishna with mortal milkmaids. Hardly a culture in the Americas lacks a story concerning a sky maiden who fell to earth, married a mortal, and then returned to her people after having had offspring.

The notion of sexual congress has also played heavily in science fiction and other speculative writing as far back as Edgar Rice Burroughs's "John Carter of Mars" stories, where the human hero fights all manner of alien beings on the Red Planet and wins the affections of the alien princess Deja Thoris (Burroughs's Martians were oviparous, so in the course of time, we can imagine that Carter's alien lover laid an egg).

THE CASE TO END ALL CASES: ANTONIO VILLAS BOAS

Many researchers and writers have agreed that were it necessary to sum up ufology in a single case, the one involving the strange experience of Brazilian farmer Antonio Villas Boas would more than likely be the one to choose.

Veteran Brazilian ufologist Fernando Cleto reminisces about the surreal days of this most unusual case: "…being a friend of Joao Martins, I already knew enough about the event in his own words. On one occasion, I read letters written by Villas Boas and even managed to see a small model of the 'flying saucer' and of one of its occupants – small rustic statuettes whittled out of wood by Villas Boas himself. I also recall that Joao Martins was completely opposed to making this case known

SCREWED BY THE ALIENS

to the public, for which reason it was disclosed much later. After Irene Granchi disclosed the case overseas, I published my own opinion in this regard in a Belgian or British magazine – I can't remember which. I made an observation which greatly favored the Villas Boas case."

As if the incredible AVB required any further bolstering, Fernando Cleto managed to show that there had indeed been sightings of the same elongated oval vehicle elsewhere in Brazil prior to the date of the events in the AVB case.

"I remember," says Cleto, "that a few days prior to October 15, 1957, there was a case in the interior of the State of Goiás. A car was forced off the roadway by a force issuing from a 'flying saucer.' The driver described something which bore a strong connection to what Villas Boas had seen. He compared the UFO to a helicopter, at first, with the power to exert traction...and to have seen occupants similar to those seen by Villas Boas. There is no doubt that on November 6, 1957, Colonel Ivo Gastaldoni, who was on the way to the hospital to see his newly born daughter, was summoned by his commander to see a UFO hovering directly over the Cumbica Air Base. The colonel remarked that the object was high up in the air and well out of the reach of the base's fighters. His overall impression was that it resembled some sort of egg-shaped craft with a helicopter blade spinning over the ovoid fuselage.

"The event with the driver before October 15, 1957, when added to the November 6 case," writes Cleto, "coincided with the description given by Villas Boas for his own object and impressed me greatly. It was as if a certain model of UFO carrying a very special crew complement had been operating in a given region of Brazil for a given period of time while on a special mission."

Ufologist Cleto notes in his memorandum regarding the AVB case that Joao Martins' reluctance to disclose the particulars of the astonishing event was to keep mentally unbalanced individuals from conjuring up similar scenarios.

But what exactly happened to Antonio Villas Boas?

The deposition taken by investigator Dr. Olavo T. Fontes and subsequently delivered to Brazil's Ministry of the Navy remains the cornerstone of research into the case. It was taken in Fontes' office on February 22, 1958 and witnessed by journalist Martins himself.

Villas Boas began by stating that he was 23 years old at the time and was a farmer by profession. He lived on a fazenda on the outskirts of Sao Francisco de Sales, Minas Gerais, not far from Sao Paul and came from a large family composed of two brothers and three sisters who all lived in the immediate area. The young farmer explained that it was their custom to work two shifts during the planting season: one at night, which he was responsible for, and another by day which was handled by farmhands.

On October 5, 1957, Villas Boas went to bed at 11:00 p.m. following a party at

SCREWED BY THE ALIENS

the farmhouse. He shared the room with his younger brother Joao, and they were both witnesses to a strange nocturnal light which lit up the entire room and had its source in one of the animal pens on the farm.

It was ten days later – on October 15 – that Antonio Villas Boas would have his historic experience. While driving his tractor, he noticed a shining star that increased in brightness as if descending to earth. "In a matter of seconds," he told his interviewers, "it turned into a very shiny oval object headed straight for me." He tried to escape from it by speeding up the tractor, but the object had already landed some 10 to 15 meters ahead of the tractor. "It got closer and I was able to see, for the very first time, that it was a strange device with a slightly rounded shape, encircled by small lights and with a large, enormous red light in front, from which came all the light I could see when it was higher...the machine's shape was now clearly visible. It resembled a large, elongated egg with three spurs in front." AVB added the curious detail that "something appeared to be spinning at high speed on top of the vehicle and gave off a reddish fluorescent light."

Seized by terror, Antonio jumped off the tractor in hopes of eluding his pursuers on foot, but the furrowed terrain made a speedy getaway impossible. The next thing he new, someone had seized him by the arm. It was a figure much shorter than he, wearing a "strange outfit" and a helmet. The farmer pushed the figure away and managed to knock it to the ground, but three more similarly-dressed figures turned up, seizing him by his arms and legs, and bore him off to the waiting craft.

Villas Boas indicated that he did not go off meekly to whatever fate awaited him: he kicked, screamed and hurled insults at his helmeted captors. Given the narrowness of the vehicle's access stairway, the farmer managed to break away from his captors, but he was overpowered once more by their uncanny strength and superior numbers.

The humanoids dragged him into the craft, where he was stripped naked and subjected to several indignities. His captors drew a blood sample from his chin using a chalice-like device, and after slathering him with a strange liquid that covered his entire body, he was taken to a room – unfurnished but for a couch – where he was left alone for some twenty minutes, by his count. At this point, a mixture of fear, nausea and coldness, coupled to the stench of a strange gas that was pumped into the room, led him to vomit in one of the corners.

"After a long time," Villas Boas said, "a noise at the door startled me. I turned in that direction and was shocked to see that it was now open and a woman was entering the room, walking toward me. She was approaching slowly, perhaps amused at the astonishment that must have been visible on my face. My jaw had dropped and with good reason. This woman was completely naked, as was I, and barefoot. She was also pretty, although different from the women I'd known. Her

SCREWED BY THE ALIENS

hair was an almost whitish shade of blonde, as if peroxided, straight and not very abundant, neck-length and with the ends curled inward. Her eyes were blue and large, more narrow than round and slanted outward – like the pencil-painted eyes of those girls who fancy themselves Arabian princesses and make their eyes look slanted; that's what they were like. Only it was a completely natural effect, since there was no paint at all involved."

The strange liquid which had been spread over his body, apparently some sort of aphrodisiac, began to work as Antonio felt less tense as the small woman began to caress him, ultimately seducing him. "It sounds incredible," he confessed to Fontes and Martins during the interview, "given the situation I was in. I believe that the liquid they rubbed on me was the cause of it. All I know is that I felt an uncontrollable sexual excitement, which had never happened to me before. I forgot about everything and held the woman, returning her caresses with my own. We ended up on the couch, where we had relations for the first time. It was a normal act and she responded like any woman. Then came a period of more caressing followed by more sexual relations. In the end, she was tired and breathing quickly. I was still excited, but she now refused and tried to get away. When I noticed that, I cooled down too. That was what they wanted from me, a good stallion to improve their stock."

The door opened once more and two of the "crewmen" appeared, summoning the woman away. Before leaving, she turned to the farmer and pointed at her belly, then pointed at him, and finally at the heavens. Curiously, Villas Boas took this to mean that "she would return to take me from where it was she came."

After having served as breeding stock, Antonio was unceremoniously led off the vehicle, which took off immediately. Returning to his tractor, Villas Boas learned that the time was now five-thirty in the morning. Estimating that it had been around 1:15 a.m. when he was abducted, his entire experience had lasted some four hours and fifteen minutes.

"My mother told me I shouldn't become involved with those people again. I didn't have the courage to tell my father, since I had already told him about the light that appeared over the pens, and he didn't believe me, telling me that I was seeing things," Villas Boas concluded.

After his traumatic experience, Villas Boas withdrew from public life to pursue his studies, earning a law degree and becoming a practicing attorney in the city of Formosa, Goias, while running a small business on the side. He died in late 1992 in the city of Uberaba, in Brazil's Triángulo Minero.

In June 1993, the late Dr. Walter K. Buhler, president of the Sociedad Brasileira de Estudios Sobre Discos Voadores (SBDEDV), disclosed the fact that, between 1962 and 1963, his organization had received an anonymous letter from the U.S., inviting Villas Boas to visit this country in order to examine a recovered flying

SCREWED BY THE ALIENS

saucer in the possession of the American military. This letter was sent to Formosa, state of Goiás, by Dr. Buhler. Allegedly, Villas Boas's son advised him that his father had indeed visited the United States to inspect the object but had kept silent the rest of his life concerning the visit.

IN THE WAKE OF AVB

On March 3, 1978, in the small hours of the morning, eighteen-year-old Jose Inacio Alvaro, studying to be an electrician at a vo-tech in the Brazilian town of Pelotas, noticed a strange glow pouring in through one of the windows of his house. Alvaro, who had been up at that late hour studying, felt an unusual torpor seize him at the very moment that a thin blue beam appeared out of the light. The next thing he remembered was waking up on the street at a considerable distance from his home. Casting a frightened look at his wristwatch, Jose Inacio realized the time was now four o'clock in the morning: he had no recollection of what events had transpired in the intervening two hours.

Jose Inacio's case attracted the attention of Brazilian ufologists who urged him to undergo hypnosis. The sessions were conducted by a number of faculty members of the University of Pelotas and at one point even included the college's chancellor.

Under hypnosis, Jose Inacio recounted an experience that rivalled the classic Antonio Villas Boas case: at a given point, he found himself in an unfurnished, circular room and in the company of a naked, dark-haired woman that was much taller than he. At that point, the student realized that he, too, was unclothed. The woman approached him, placed a hand on his forehead, and told him not to be frightened since no harm would befall him. She immediately began caressing Jose Inacio, who at first had misgivings about the situation but eventually relented. They ended up having sexual intercourse on a structure that he described as "a net."

The details of his carnal experience were intensely graphic. The hypnotists' report states that the subject's words and movements clearly indicate he was reliving the experience under trance. For the sake of decorum, the researchers allegedly erased the recording of the session.

Unlike the AVB case, there were witnesses to Jose Inacio's return from his odyssey. One resident of Pelotas claimed having seen the student lying on the street at that time of the morning; upon approaching to offer assistance, the Good Samaritan alleged that Jose Inacio stood up like an automaton and began to walk away from the scene. Other local residents claimed to have witnessed the passing of a disc-shaped flying object in the air above Pelotas which caused disruptions to the power grid as it passed overhead.

The experiences of AVB and Jose Inacio Alvaro were not to be unique: theirs would soon have to share the spotlight with those of a third Brazilian man by the

SCREWED BY THE ALIENS

name of Juan Valerio.

On the evening of November 30, 1982, Juan Valerio da Silva went out of his house in the rural town of Botucatú to get some water and did not re-enter the structure. Three hours later, he was found unconscious in his backyard, naked and covered in what appeared to be oil.

Having no conscious recollection of what happened during the three-hour absence, hypnosis was again employed to ascertain his whereabouts during the "missing time" period. Valerio claimed that he was taken to a strange place by unseen captors, stripped of his clothing and placed beside a dark-skinned naked woman with long black hair who forced him to engage in sexual activity. A series of "strange tattoos" were etched upon his body.

While lacking the lurid descriptions that made his predecessors' experiences famous, the importance of Valerio's story lies in what we could term the postscript: the abductee developed a number of psychic abilities, most notably telekinetic powers. He has also had repeated visits from his non-human hosts, and was led to believe that his eldest son, Reginaldo, was also the product of genetic experimentation by these alien entities.

THE EVENTS AT MIRASSOL

Mirassol is a city of some thirty-two thousand inhabitants in the state of Sao Paulo, Brazil, which has earned its place in ufological history due to the events which allegedly took place there in 1979, regarding the experiences with non-human entities lived by Antonio Carlos Ferreira, who was 21 years old at the time and working as a watchman for a large furniture manufacturer in town.

At three o'clock in the morning on June 28th of that year, Ferreira witnessed a large shining light descend from the darkness on to the ground not far from where he stood watch. As he concentrated on the bright light, he then noticed that three diminutive entities were approaching: their heads were covered by opaque helmets and their bodies were encased in form fitting suits with what the young watchman took to be "breathing devices." Before Ferreira knew it, one of the beings fired a beam of red light which left him paralyzed. Then he was conveyed – in this state of immobility – toward the painfully bright light, which turned out to be a small disc-shaped craft that shuttled Ferreira and his captors to a larger vehicle in space.

Once aboard this craft, the frightened watchman was surprised to notice two different sorts of beings milling about: one having dark skin and curly red hair, and the other with lighter complexions and straight black hair; both non-human species had large slanted eyes, wide mouths with thick lips, well-defined chins and lacked eyebrows or eyelashes. His own abductors proved to be some sort of "mechanical men" who returned to their stations against a wall after delivering their captive.

SCREWED BY THE ALIENS

Had nothing else occurred, Antonio Carlos Ferreira would have merely been a South American Travis Walton – a stranger in a strange place filled with non-human entities. But the most harrowing part of his unearthly experience was still to come. The humanoids transferred the watchman to a small room and told him to lie down on a couch after giving him multiple assurances by telepathic means that he would be returned home unharmed.

Feeling more at ease, Ferreira complied until another being appeared in the room: it was a naked female of the darker skinned alien species. Under the hypnotic regression preformed by the late researcher Walter K. Buhler, Gullermo Pereira and Ney Matiel, Ferreira described his would-be sex partner as downright repulsive, having an unpleasant breath, an overly large chin, small breasts and icy cold skin. The detail of red pubic hair, which had first emerged in the Villas Boas case, resurfaced in Ferreira's experience.

A struggle with the aliens – also reminiscent of the AVB case – would take place as three of the creatures tore his clothes off to prepare him for the act. Ferreira was outraged and told the female not to come closer since "her ugliness was repulsive." A slightly taller alien gave Ferreira an injection that caused him to lose strength and brought his combativeness to an end. They then covered him in a dark, amber-colored oil and placed the repulsive-looking female on top of him. The sexual act was rapidly consummated and the aliens fussed over him again, bathing him in the strange oil once more. His captors informed him they came from "another planet" and that their mission was to secure human offspring for future research; he was told that he would be contacted once more in order that he could meet his hybrid offspring.

At one point, Ferreira complained of an inability to breathe and his abductors gave him an unpleasant-tasting liquid that appeared to remedy the situation. Similar "cordials" (for want of a better word) have also been described in other Brazilian cases, such as the one involving the soldier "Jose Antonio," who was abducted by strange dwarves while fishing on a riverbank.

Ferreira apparently underwent other abduction events of which he had no conscious recollection whatsoever – the second in January 1983 and the third in April of that same year.

ONE DAY WHILE CHASING KITES

This case takes us from subequatorial Brazil to the Caribbean, where, in 1934, a teenager identified only as "Julio" became the protagonist of an episode that would scar him for life. It was first investigated by Puerto Rican ufologist Sebastián Robiou (mid-70s), then re-investigated by Salvador Freixedo (late '80s). The witness has since been interviewed once more by Magdalena del Amo-Freixedo (1997).

One morning, while flying a brand new kite on a slope outside the city of

SCREWED BY THE ALIENS

Mayaguez, Puerto Rico, before going off to school, young Julio was startled to see his kite being sucked in by what appeared to be an air-pocket or vacuum of some kind. He pulled on the string and noticed an inordinate amount of resistance from the wayward kite. Upon looking up, he was amazed to see a ball "like a ball bearing," but measuring some twenty feet across and having the same coppery hue of a BB. A light issued from the object and he felt himself being raised into the air. Before he knew it, he was inside the strange flying object.

"On one side, I saw a girl," Julio indicated during the interview conducted by Robiou, "and on the other was a guy looking at a some sort of giant emerald. He wore a tight-fitting olive-drab suit that looked like plastic. I couldn't see his face, because he was minding the device. He gestured at the girl...the girl had a pinkish complexion and wore a silvery suit. She was small, like one of our six-year-old girls, with platinum blonde hair. I don't remember the color of her eyes."

Julio explained that the child was holding his kite in her hands, and that he made all possible efforts to tell her that it belonged to him. The girl not only did not surrender the kite, but instead gave him a small box, from which images could be made to appear. He did not remember how, but the object returned him to the place from which he had been collected, and returned him abruptly to the ground. He suffered a sprained ankle as a result of the experience – but he had the curious little box with him.

Further details would emerge during Freixedo's re-opening of the case. "Julio," now a hardened man in his early sixties, informed the Spanish ufologist of the ultimate fate of the little box he'd been entrusted with.

The box measured some 20 x 20 x 20 centimeters, and when its "user" placed his or her hands upon it, a "kind of vapor made up of lights" would spin on its surface, causing an entity – a small ape-like creature no more than one meter tall – to appear in the room. According to Julio, the entities materialized in such a manner would not speak and appeared to be surprised to find themselves in an alien environment. The girl-child on the strange object had successfully caused the "little apes" to return to their native surroundings or "back into the box," as Julio put it. Only the hapless boy was not so good at this final aspect: the diminutive simians would materialize and vanish at breathtaking speed out the window, many times in the presence of his classmates who had asked him to perform the "neat trick" with the box. The apported entities were not at all pleased, claimed Julio, with their new condition. They would frighten children and dogs, and appeared to prowl the surroundings of Julio's family's house. "Believe me," he told the researcher, "I would just like to die. I'm tired of seeing strange things." The supernatural primates had apparently been the source of a number of mysterious deaths which had occurred in his corner of southwestern Puerto Rico over the decades.

SCREWED BY THE ALIENS

When Magdalena del Amo-Freixedo re-opened the case as part of her book, <u>Abducciones</u> (Bell Book, 1998), a further wrinkle appeared which has a direct bearing to this article.

Now willing to go on the record by his real name – Juan Rivera Feliberti – he explained to Del Amo-Freixedo that his contact with the alien "girl" had not stopped after the incident of the wayward kite. Many years later, now a married man with children, the experiencer moved from Mayaguez to Sabana Grande, P.R. and took his family to the beach one day. While the children frolicked in the water, "Julio" decided to go fishing. He suddenly realized he was not alone: a beautiful woman had appeared right in front of him. A wave of remembrances washed over him as he realized her blonde hair was identical to that of the girl in the odd circular vehicle so many years ago. He asked her where she came from, and she allegedly replied "from far away, from the stars."

Male figures soon appeared, clad identically to the one he remembered seeing back in 1934. "They were the lady's companions...they were identical to the ones I'd seen as a boy. Suddenly, I don't know what she did, but she was completely naked. She didn't tell me anything, but I understood in my mind that she wanted to have relations with me. I didn't want to...I wanted to run away. Besides, my wife could catch me if she happened to come around." Although hesitant to describe his unusual experience to a female investigator, Del Amo-Freixedo eventually convinced him to elaborate. Uncomfortably, "Julio," now in his seventies, continued the story: "Look, I didn't want to at first, but you know how it is. I was young and the woman was very good-looking. She began caressing me all over, and we ended up like men and women do when they're both unclothed."

"Julio" bashfully added that his alien lover's body was not exactly like that of a human female: her breasts appeared to be placed lower on the torso and her pubic area was hairless. He made the curious observation that her skin, while soft, was somewhat scaly. These anatomical differences did not deter him, however: "We [had sex] several times. I think four. Back then one was full of energy and recovered quicker." In subsequent years, he would return to the scene of the events in hope of seeing his unusual sex partner again, but never did.

As if to bring the events in the long, strange life of Juan Rivera Feliberti to a full circle, at around three o'clock a.m. one day in 1995, he saw the same girl who'd stolen his kite once more, standing outside his house.

CONCLUSION

Regardless of whatever stance we may have regarding the UFO phenomenon, and provided that we are willing to suspend disbelief, the information which can be gleaned from these cases is of considerable interest: absent from the scene are the Greys, Reptoids and Nordics that seem to populate the abductee chronicles. We have beings of an entirely different taxonomy engaged in an operation or

SCREWED BY THE ALIENS

mission that appears to be taking place largely within the confines of Brazil, the South American giant. The commonalities of the experiences – the oily liquid applied on the abductees, which serves as antiseptic and aphrodisiac at once; the beverage that relieves human discomfort; the choice of intercourse rather than artificial insemination – link them together while separating them from the coldly clinical abduction phenomenon in the northern hemisphere.

The fact that this libidinous aspect of the UFO phenomenon appears to have a strong preference for Brazil has led to jocose comments on the appeal of Brazilian virility to non-human intelligences. The fact remains that somewhat similar situations have occurred elsewhere in the world and in our own country as well.

In October 1974, oil worker Carl Higdon took a day off from work and went hunting near Rawlins, Wyoming. Coming across an elk (an astonishing piece of luck in itself on the first day of hunting), Higdon pulled the trigger on his rifle only to see the bullet issue from the weapon in slow motion and land fifty feet away from him. To his astonishment, the hunter realized that time was standing still all around him and that a chinless, jawless alien being was looking at him. Higdon was apparently abducted and hooked up to strange devices aboard "a cube-shaped UFO." The hunter attributed the reason for his return to Earth by his captors was that he had had a vasectomy performed a few years before the abduction and was therefore useless for the "breeding program" that his captors appeared to be pursuing.

SCREWED BY THE ALIENS

Scott Corrales became interested in UFOs as a result of heavy UFO activity while he lived in both Mexico and Puerto Rico. He was also influenced by Mesican UFOlogists Pedro Feniz and Salvador Freixedo, a former Jesuit priest who advocated a paranormal interpretation of the phenomenon. In 1990, Scott began translating the works of Freixedo into English, making the literature and research of experts and journalists available to English-reading audiences. This led to the creation of a SAMZDAT journal in 1993 and his collaboration with Mexico's CEFP group, Puerto Rico's PRRG and the foremost researchers of Spain's so-called third generation of UFO investigators.

In 1965, Corrales documented the manifestations of the entity popularly known as the Chupacabras in three works. the Chupacabras Diaries, Nemesis The Chupacabras at Large, and Chupacabras and Other Mysteries. In 1998, the SAMDAT bulletin was replaced by the Inexplicata The Journal of Hispanic UFOlogy as the official publication of the nascent Institute of Hispanic UFOlogy. In addition, Scott has been a guest on numerous radio shows and his articles have been featured in publications all over the world. His forthcoming book on "Alien Blood Lust" will be published by Tim Beckley's Inner Light - Global Communications.

SCREWED BY THE ALIENS

CHAPTER 22

ALIENS RIP OFF ABDUCTEE'S CLOTHES
A BIOGENETIC EXPERIMENT IN BRAZIL
By Dr. Walter K. Bühler and Guilherme Pereira

EDITOR'S NOTE: While this case has been touched upon in several places, it still merits reprinting the official report as investigated firsthand by a team of dedicated Brazilian researchers led by the late Dr. Walter K. Buhler (he transitioned in 1996) with whom we exchanged information for many years. Buhler was president of the Brazilian Society of Flying Disc Studies. The SBEDV went so far as to put out an English language newsletter, although the original material was published in Portuguese, naturally. He was highly respected among his peers in South America and was known worldwide. In this instance the clothing was forcibly ripped off the UFO abductee, as if the aliens did not know how buttons or zippers operated. The material was translated by Col. Wendelle Stevens, himself a dedicated investigator of contact cases.

* * * * * * * * * *

The story Antonio Carlos related to his mother of the incredible experience was considerably incomplete and lacked certain details. Though elaborated in logical sequence, the narrative lacked specifics, such as the dress of the extraterrestrials, their physical appearance and the equipment they carried. He did not mention to his mother, (picture of her below, together with the watchdog) the interior of their ship, how he was immobilized or transported, and the vague sort of communication they used with him. He couldn't remember the instant of leaving or return or how it was done.

In short, his exterior conscious memory did not contain all the details of what had happened. There were fragmented, indecisive scenes that seemed incomplete. He could not remember exactly what did happen in all of its details, and this worried his mother even more.

Hypnotic regression back into the incident seemed to present a way to overcome this problem. In fact this form of therapy did break the mental block and

SCREWED BY THE ALIENS

then allowed Antonio Carlos to remember consciously. There was an initial sensitivity test conducted on 5 August 1979 to check his receptivity. He proved to be a good subject and it was possible to obtain from him a complete account of the fantastic adventure experienced. We will see the orderly sequence of the account as it progressed in these sessions summarized here, but reported in more complete detail later in this report as questions came up and were further clarified. The word for word transcriptions of this and succeeding sessions may be studied in great detail later in this work.

THE BASIC STORY

At 03:00 in the morning of 28 June 1979, Antonio Carlos Ferreira, a young night guard at the Transmoveis Fafa plant, on the edge of Mirassol, marched his rounds every 15 minutes as was his custom. He was walking with his guard-dog, at the particular moment, from the bath-house of the plant toward his next check-point when, from a position near the bath-house, in mid-stride, he observed the bright light of a strange object that was lowering over the yard of the plant. He wondered what it could be, and what was it doing so low in the sky over the sanitary area?

Then suddenly Antonio, who is 1.75 meters tall, found himself with three human-like beings of very small stature, a little over one meter tall, who were dressed in a strange sort of one-piece coverall jumpsuit in a strangely scintillating white color that covered their whole body. The head was enclosed in a kind of opaque, round reflective helmet that impeded his observation of their faces and features.

Honge, the shepherd dog that routinely accompanied him on his rounds, became aroused and was running ahead near the bath-house when Antonio was confronted by the strange beings. The guard-dog went for the strangers and was immediately subjugated by them in some way, falling as though in death. One of the three small humanoids pointed a red light towards the face of Antonio. It was projected from a small box about 15 centimeters square. It had two small orifices of about 3 centimeters diameter in the front face from which the luminous red ray was projected. At that instant the youth was completely immobilized. In this paralyzed condition he was transported to the ship parked inside the south fence in the yard of the plant. He could not feel his feet touching the ground and seemed to be floating in the air. Later investigation showed that a few meters from the bath-house his steps on the ground disappeared in such a way that it seemed like he went out and evaporated into thin air. There were no other steps besides his.

As they got closer to the machine, Antonio noticed that it was of circular disc-form around the base with a curved conical upper surface. It was of small size, about two meters diameter at the base by 2.5 meters in height. The color of the exterior surface was light ash grey metallic with some degree of luminosity. There it was, parked in the yard of the plant, and it rested on three legs in a three-pod arrangement of which he was unable to observe details. He could not see more because a small rectangular port of low height opened and he was passed inside the ship.

The internal part was illuminated by a diffuse reddish light. He could see a control panel covered with many buttons and control apparatus operated by two of the crew. The seats were small stools of circular shape with three legs, all of the same ash metallic color and without cushions.

In a moment the small airship took off. Antonio Carlos could hear a muffled buzzing – something like a transformer in operation – and a cold chill swept over his body.

The three small beings, who wore a tiny insignia on their suits, did not address a single word of communication to him at any time during the ascent. They held him seated on two of the small stools. The youth could not remember how much time it took for this flight nor how this small ship entered the bottom of another larger ship, believed to be a mother-ship with other smaller ones aboard.

He noted that they took him into a large room of sober aspect with different kinds and colors of lights, blue, maroon, and fiery color. He now saw that the small transport ship did not sit on the floor of the mother-ship but floated a few centimeters above it. It was in the big room with him. This larger room contained diverse apparatus of many kinds. Antonio Carlos saw various of the beings of small stature there. They were all dressed in the same type of white shiny jump-suit that covered their bodies to the neck and the hands were covered with white gloves.

This larger ship had two different race-types of crew personnel aboard. They all were about 1.20 meters tall with an abnormally large head, almost double the size of that of an Earth human. Some had skin near the color of light chocolate, eyes large and "pulled up" on the outside, like those of Orientals, without eyelashes or eyebrows. They had a large flat nose, a little turned up on the end, like a pug nose. Their mouth was wide and had more or less thick lips, a pointed chin that jutted forward and a short strong neck. Of these the hair was of a light reddish color and was coiled in ringlets and was quite long. They had very large ears that stuck out and were pointed, almost double the size of ours. The other race-type aboard had skin of a greenish leaf-color, fine straight black hair, large nose also but smaller than the others, green slanted eyes, and a large mouth with finer lips and the same jutting pointed chin. They also had the large pointed ears that stuck out.

It seemed like this room Antonio was in had various divisions. The walls were shiny metallic and in one of them was set a large panel covered with green and red lights.

In the other wall he could see a small circular window protected by a kind of glass of a reddish color. Twice when Antonio Carlos came near this window, he

SCREWED BY THE ALIENS

felt very truthfully horrified to see the Earth "very small and distant" – where he could make out small lights, very dim, that he thought might be cities. They never told him what this was.

Antonio observed also through this window, a part of this mother-ship he was in, something that rotated at high speed, emitting a greenish glow. He also noticed some perpendicular motion outside of the ship, and he could see an immense green light rotating above the surface.

The wall opposite the window had an enormous square panel with exquisite designs in a brilliant green color, something like a large map. They blocked his view when he looked toward it. He wondered why it was so secret. The room was profusely illuminated with what looked like fluorescent light. In the central part of the ceiling he saw a great yellow light. He remembered that the floor of this room was of a dark color in sharp contrast with the white shiny metallic walls.

Of the great quantity of apparatus in the large room, Antonio Carlos paid particular attention to one unit, of rectangular form with five buttons of green color and topped by a round green light from which many colored wires emerged. That apparatus somewhat resembled a TV set except that it had more the characteristics of a projector. Antonio was placed in front of this apparatus to, according to his own words, "take my photograph," though everything indicated that this device detected his thoughts and reactions, too, because they always directed it toward him. Two of the beings manipulated the buttons and controls on it.

In another section of this room there was a convenient low rectangular table with various banks of rectangular formations on it and some round ones of a dark maroon color, almost black. They were on a slightly inclined panel.

Near this apparatus there was a kind of divan. Antonio Carlos was taken to this divan by the extraterrestrials and there followed the most unusual of the fates in this strange series of occurrences. The youth saw in front of him one of these small beings completely nude, clearly demonstrating her intention to take his hand.

According to the information elicited, this young crew member of the spaceship was the taller of the females seen. Her height was between 1.50 and 1.55 meters. She had chocolate colored skin, an immense head, red hair more or less coiled, black slanted eyes, long turned-up nose and a straight large mouth with thick lips and white teeth similar to ours. Her breath had a disagreeable odor. She had a pointed, jutting chin, small breasts and red hair in the pubic area, and a very cool skin temperature.

At that moment the nude extraterrestrial woman spoke something to Antonio Carlos. She demonstrated with gestures of affection that she wanted him to kiss her. She did this several times when they were together.

Antonio Carlos considered the female Ufonaut very unattractive and did not like her. When he touched her body it gave him a considerable shock and her

SCREWED BY THE ALIENS

skin was cold. (Consideration must be given to the possibility that this shock could be partly psychological as well as real due to the repulsion felt by the youth over the alien-ness of the relationship with this woman.)

After taking Antonio Carlos to the divan, three of the extraterrestrials began to pull off his clothes. He resisted. He shoved and struck at the entities but they were strong and treated him with disagreeable roughness and finally subdued him. His clothes were forcibly ripped from him and his body was scraped and scratched in the process.

Later, on cross-examination on this particular aspect of the abduction experience, more light was shed on this peculiar mistreatment. The Ufonauts were trying to strip Antonio's clothes off from the top down without bothering to undo the closures such as buttons and zippers, possibly lacking familiarity with these features. This may also tell us something about how they get in and out of the one-piece bodysuits that they wore and the elasticity of the material.

SEXUAL CONGRESS WITH THE NUDE SPACEWOMAN

Then the nude young woman tried to come near him again and sought to take hold of his hands. Antonio was violently repelled by what was happening and exclaimed to the woman that she was very ugly, that he did not want her near him. At that point a taller extraterrestrial gave him an injection in his right arm and he lost all his strength and will to resist. On his left arm they placed an apparatus that is difficult to describe and the youth watched them attach it.

Then, following that, the extraterrestrials rubbed a dark ember colored oil all over his body, his legs, his sexual organs, his belly and his back and chest. After this operation they held him in position on top of the other party to the experiment and made him consummate a sexual union with her.

It did not take him long with the girl. After that he resolved to get rid of the apparatus on his left arm and get dressed, but they applied the dark-colored oil to his body again before handing him his pants.

During this whole time the crew members conversed between themselves in a language that was completely unknown to him. However, when they directed words to him he could understand perfectly what they said.

They reassured him that he need not be afraid, that nothing bad would happen to him and that they would take him back to Earth. They told him that they came from another planet and that they were here conducting experiments to produce a child of an Earthman for future studies. They said that they would return again to see him so that he could know his child. When they said, "To see him," they marked him with a symbol on his body. They told him that the symbol was their mark. Then they allowed him a moment, as he felt out of breath. They gave him a dark, disagreeable, exotic tasting liquid to drink after that.

After these experiences, Antonio Carlos was lifted and carried into a dark room,

SCREWED BY THE ALIENS

where he could see nothing for lack of illumination from any source. The room was very dark as the youth was re-positioned in another transport ship for return to Earth.

The next thing he remembered, the small ship had disappeared and he was once more standing outside the bathhouse, in nearly the same place from which he had been captured.

Portions of this material were first published in the Portuguese language in Brazil under the title "O CASO DE MIRASSOL" -Livro Branco Dos Discos Voadores, by Dr. Walter K. Bühler and Guilherme Pereira, in 1984.

IN THE AFTERMATH OF THE ALIENS' VISIT

Some days after this, a flying small green ball of light came near him and seemingly left him a message: "They followed him, and would try to help him improve his life."

In that timeframe, UFOs were seen by many people in this region in the following months.

Yes, their mission seems to have involved using this man as a seed-delivery source for a genetic experiment, and out of his sexual interbreeding with this UFO-woman came a child that he was allowed to see on many of the later visits onboard their ship. Yes, they later came back many times to show him the child he had "made" on the extraterrestrial woman. Remarkably, Antonio was given a garment on the ship with which he could "walk" ABOVE the floor, apparently. He was shown around on the mothership and guided. And the ETs knew that he was hypnotized after each contact by the local investigator to bring forth as much info as possible.

It seems out of the hypnosis session that he had had more sexual breeding experiences with more alien women, but under hypnosis he remarked that he didn't like it and was not attracted to those women, really. Yes, just abhorrence, he seemingly felt. Out of the account obtained through hypnosis, it seems he was "beamed" up into the UFO when he was walking on the railroad track to/from his work. He says (under hypnosis) that the UFO was much bigger than a house.

One day, some years later, while at work at another location nearby, he sat for lunch, but suddenly felt an urge to go outside. This was January 1982. There – in a wood nearby – he suddenly met one of the spacemen, who reminded him of his first contact in 1979. And in that encounter he was told that that an ET-child he had given seed to under coercion was a girl named AZELINA.

SCREWED BY THE ALIENS

The late Dr. Walter Buhler, whose team of investigators reviewed this sensational abduction case for many months before releasing their findings.

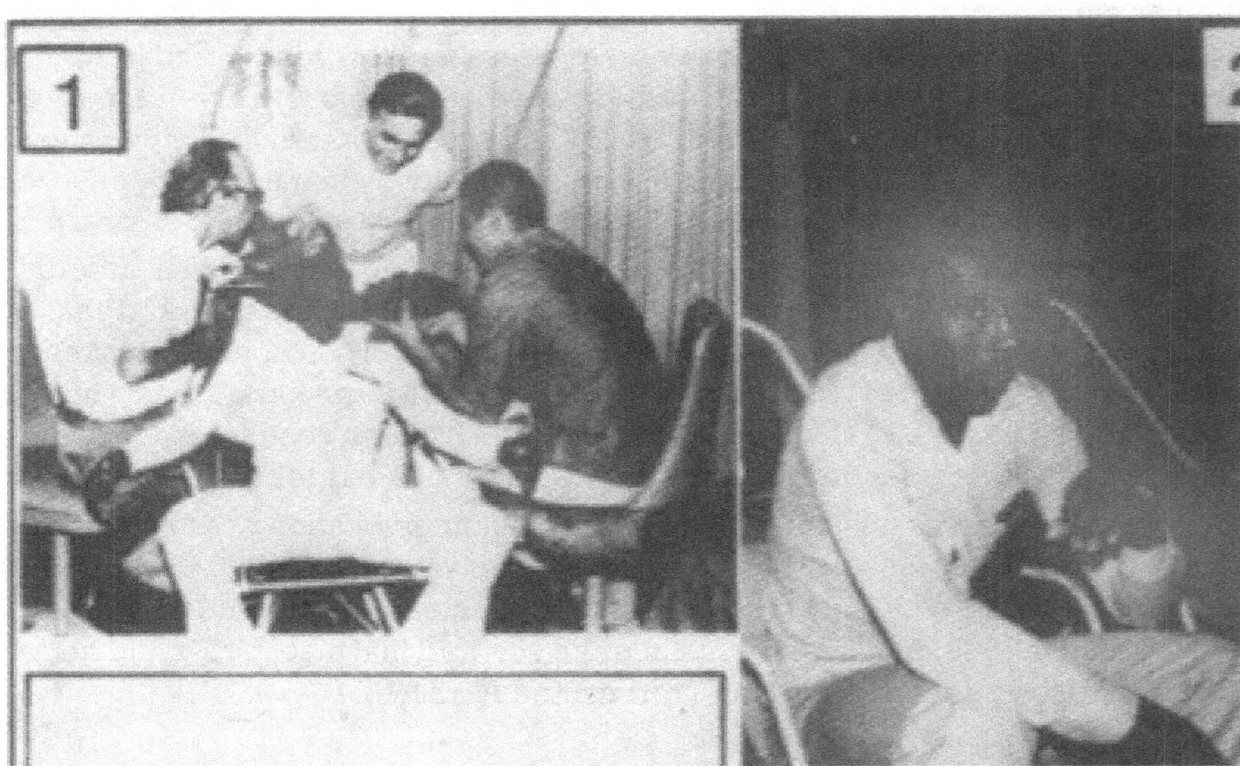

The case was one of the first of its kind to receive attention both in the local Brazilian media as well as in the supermarket tabloid The Enquirer in the U.S. providing a worldwide circulation.

The witness undergoes hypnotic regression from a capable team of investigators.

SCREWED BY THE ALIENS

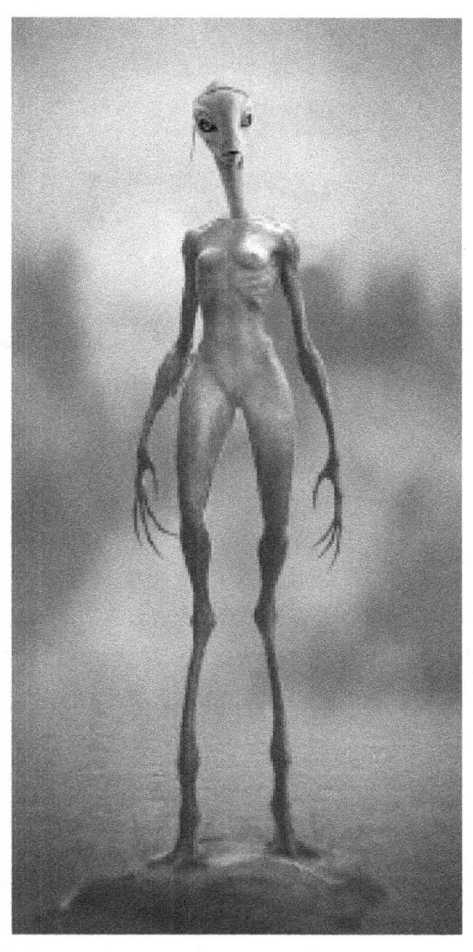

SECTION NINE
THE HYBRIDS AND THE PREGNANCIES

**Chapter Twenty Three:
Mysteries and Unexplainable Pregnancies
By Brad Steiger**

**Chapter Twenty Four: Birth of an Alien Hybrid
The Christa Tilton Story
By Timothy Green Beckley**

SCREWED BY THE ALIENS

CHAPTER 23

MYSTERIOUS – AND UNEXPLAINABLE PREGNANCIES
By Brad Steiger

NOTE BY PUBLISHER:

The late, very prolific author/researcher Brad Steiger was among the first to turn us on to the concept that the Ultra-terrestrials had more than an appropriate interest in human females. He had long seen the connection between the paranormal and human sexuality. His book for our publishing company, DEMON LOVERS, even told of how werewolves were copulating with females more for sadistic purposes than for breeding as the Ultras might be attempting to do according to his writings on the subject.

* * * * * * * *

Mary B. of New York is convinced that she has a special mission here on Earth, but she is very confused as to what it might be. She reports that she began having dreams about UFO people when she was only five years old. She would see a large ship hovering over her parents' home, and then, on a beam of light, entities would come into her room and look at her.

They did not speak, and their mouths seemed to be fixed in a permanent kind of half-quizzical smile. She was not alarmed; she was fascinated.

As she grew older the examinations seemed to continue. She remembers having these dramatic UFO dreams at least every three to four months. Shortly after she turned 10, she remembers the entities coming to her, taking her by the hand, and apparently lifting her out-of-the-body in a kind of astral dream. She remembers being taken to a lovely pink room where everything was soft, gentle, and loving. She recalls very pleasant music playing. She could not identify the music as any familiar tune, but it relaxed her, made her feel very comfortable. She felt somehow as though she were taken to a nursery.

Her most dramatic occurrence took place when she was still in her teens. She

SCREWED BY THE ALIENS

was visited in her room by the entities, who stood back in the corner, while a more human-appearing man approached her. She, in spite of her youth and her inexperience, knew that she was engaging in sexual intercourse. The man caressed her, but did not speak.

Within two months, Mary Anne claimed she was pregnant. She was frightened. She became very concerned. She could not work up the nerve to tell her parents. She considered telling her school counselor, but she could not bear the shame and humiliation.

She knew that she had not had any type of physical experience with any boy her own age or any older man. Her only sexual experience, she swears, came from the "man" who entered her room on a beam of light, the man who was accompanied by the same entities who had been visiting her since she was five years old.

And then she reports that the strangest thing happened. She had another dream in which the entities came to her room and again seemed to examine her. This time she felt a bit of pain and remembers lying as if she were paralyzed while they performed an operation on her.

"I wasn't pregnant anymore," she said. "It was really weird. A short time after that dream, my periods resumed; and I knew – I knew with all my being and my inner conviction – that I was not pregnant.

"Several months later, I had the last of my UFO dreams. I dreamt that I was taken aboard this craft. Once again I was in that beautiful pink room and this time I was looking at a baby, a beautiful baby boy. The entities smiled and indicated that I could pick up the baby. I did so, and I had the strongest feeling that I was holding my own child. I caressed and held him and said, 'I love you.'

"Everything then became hazy. The pink room seemed to get smaller and smaller, and I seemed to be covered with a pink mist. I awakened back in my room, and I have never had another UFO dream of that type."

"THEY WANTED TO INCARNATE THROUGH ME"

Shortly after Doriel of Chicago, Illinois, had seen a UFO, two beings appeared to her: "One, a female, was named Leita or Leia. The other, a male, was named Gamal. They told me that they wanted to incarnate through me.

"I asked them, why me? They told me because I was one of them. They said that I could provide the right environment for them.

"I have a daughter now. I gave her Leita for a middle name."

A BRIGHT LIGHT VANQUISHES STERILITY

Theresa of Manitoba is a 27-year-old accountant who reported that it was not until she had been out on her own, away from home for three or four years that her mother told her the following story:

SCREWED BY THE ALIENS

Theresa's mother had been decreed sterile, and in spite of repeated attempts to become pregnant, it was to no avail. The doctors had suggested adoption; and Theresa's parents were considering this very strongly.

Then, according to her mother, she was awakened one night by a strange buzzing sound which she described as something like a metallic bee. She looked up and saw a bright light about the size of a soccer ball moving across the bedroom. Before she could say anything, before she could shout, before she could express fear or alarm, she felt herself entering an altered state of consciousness. Dimly she remembered the light hovering above her husband.

At that point, the husband, although he was asleep, became animated, as if he were a marionette being pulled into sudden life. And although her husband never opened his eyes, he performed the act of love with her, and it was roughly nine months after that strange act of cosmic coitus that Theresa was born.

According to Theresa, her mother told her that on the way home from the hospital she became aware of a bright light in the sky above the automobile. As she walked in the house with the baby Theresa in her arms, the light seemed to hover at treetop level. The light, according to the mother, was witnessed by several neighbors and by Theresa's father. After hovering at treetop level for 10 or 15 minutes, the light seemingly disappeared – or according to the mixed testimonies of the eyewitnesses – moved into the night sky at an enormous rate of speed.

Upon hearing her mother's story, Theresa said that she felt a little uneasy about exactly who her true father might be. She admitted that ever since she was a small child she has had a fascination with outer space and UFOs. It was during such a discussion of various science-fiction and science-fact concepts and the possibility that extraterrestrial visitations could be occurring that Theresa's mother told her the strange account of her conception and birth.

SELECTING "THEIR KIND"

Sometime in 1975, Karen of Grand Rapids, Michigan, dreamed that she heard a voice coming from the hill behind her house:

"I got up and put on my robe and followed the voice that was calling my name. I walked over the hill, and in the field behind it was a UFO, a very large one. I saw three figures standing beside it. I walked up to them, but I could say nothing. I felt they had control over me.

"They explained why they were there and why they wanted me. They wanted me to give birth to one of their kind. I had been selected because I was of their kind, also.

"One of the three men, who was standing on my right, came up to me and slowly started slipping off my robe. I tried to move, but I could not. The man on my left stepped forward and started touching me. All I could do was cry. They told me that they would not hurt me, so I should not worry.

SCREWED BY THE ALIENS

"As they helped me with my robe, I could hear them speaking to me. Their mouths were not moving, so I knew that they were using telepathy. They told me that I could go back and that they would be contacting me at a later time. The next thing I knew, I was at my patio door. [In her communication, Karen added that her daughter, who was by then five years old, had been observed levitating. The child also spoke intimately of relatives, deceased before her birth, and she had already outlined her future life as a healer in a hospital.]

"These men were dark-complexioned with slightly slanted eyes. They were small of build and stood about five feet to five-feet-four inches tall. They wore a two-piece suit with a belt around the waist. They had boots on their feet with their pants legs tucked inside.

"On their belt buckles they had some sort of symbol. It looked like some kind of bird in flight."

JO ANN FAILS HER UFO PHYSICAL

In her boarding house in a small Arkansas community, Jo Ann had taken in a roomer named Ernie, who was a quiet chap but vague as to his personal background. Although she is a quiet person, definitely not the nosy type, Jo Ann still felt a strangeness about the man. But she asked no personal questions, and he volunteered no information. He got a job and made a down payment on a truck.

One night, after Ernie had moved from their boarding house, JoAnn had what she thought was a dream in which she saw Ernie come to the foot of her bed and motion her to follow him.

Without awakening her husband or her son, Jo Ann arose, put on her housecoat, and went with him. Before leaving the house, he apologized, but insisted that he must blindfold her. Ernie drove for miles before he stopped. He then led Jo Ann through weeds and up some steps before he removed her blindfold.

Jo Ann said that she was aboard a spaceship and was in a kind of laboratory. Entities around her wore long, dark cloaks and hoods, but their faces were indistinct. Jo Ann was placed on what seemed to be an operating table. Wires were attached to various parts of her body. After she had been examined, one of the creatures said to Ernie, "Didn't you know that this woman has had surgery so that she cannot bear any more children?"

Ernie answered: "No. I came to know her and her son. I thought that she had the potential to be a good specimen for artificial insemination. I thought she would be an excellent mother for our child."

Jo Ann was immediately released from the table. She was once again blindfolded, walked back to the car, and taken home. The next morning she awoke thinking about her strange, but vivid, dream.

Now comes the strangest part: Jo Ann's son was at that time [1966] in the Youth Air Patrol. A few days after her strange dream, he was called to an airfield for a

SCREWED BY THE ALIENS

meeting. When he returned home, he told her that there had been a group of government men checking a circular, burnt area on the other side of the airfield. The officials had put the youths to checking the surrounding area for anything they might find.

The investigators discovered where a car had been driven onto the field, parked, and left. The night of Jo Ann's "dream," a rental car had been taken from the agency at the airfield (no one knew how the key had been removed from the hook inside the locked building). The car had been replaced with twenty-five miles of usage registered on the odometer.

Jo Ann also learned that Ernie had disappeared from town that night. His truck was left abandoned on a city street until the police towed it away. When last she checked, three years later, she found out that the truck had never been claimed and had at last been disposed of by the police.

A BEAUTIFUL SPACE BABY

Mrs. Cynthia Appleton of Birmingham, England, appears to have passed her physical and become involved in a cosmic plan to develop a hybrid race of UFOnauts and Earthmen. Mrs.

Appleton's spaceman manifested right in her living room, "like a TV picture on the screen, a blurred image and then suddenly everything was clear."

The spaceman told Mrs. Appleton that a year later she would have a "space baby." Although she protested that she was not even pregnant, the "Venusian" told her that the child would be called Matthew.

A bit over nine months later, the spaceman had been correct in every detail with the exception of the date. Matthew had been born two minutes after midnight on June second. Mrs. Appleton was informed, however, that her worry over the date may have delayed the delivery.

Mrs. Appleton told newsmen: "Matthew has a lovely Sun look. He is almond-colored all over, and not a blemish. Of course, my husband, Ron, is the father, but really, the baby will spiritually belong to a race who live on Venus."

THE ULTIMATE ACT OF ALIEN INFILTRATION

One cannot help wondering how many other "space babies" there may be around the planet. Little children with almond skin, strangely slanted eyes or other less obvious and apparent physical anomalies, whose mothers had visions of spacemen or saints or ghosts shortly before or immediately after their sudden pregnancies. What a superb method of building a fifth column within a people and, at the same time, having the infiltrators being nurtured and maintained by the very men and women who are being infiltrated.

Infiltration by the ultimate physical contact may have been going on for quite some time. I refer to the sixth chapter of Genesis:

SCREWED BY THE ALIENS

"And it came to pass, when men began to multiply on the face of the earth, and daughters were born unto them, that the sons of God saw the daughters of men that they were fair; and they took them wives of all which they chose .... There were giants in the earth in those days; and also after that, when the sons of God came in unto the daughters of men, and they bare children to them, the same became mighty men which were of old, men or renown."

To the ancient nomadic Jews retelling such dramatic interaction with UFOnauts in their oral tradition, it is quite easy to see how "Space Brothers" from the skies could be evaluated

as "sons of God." And what man would deny his daughter the honor of marrying an angel so that a mighty son could result from their union?

THE PSYCHOKINETIC "SPACE KIDS"

Several years ago, the eminent parapsychologist Dr. Andrija Puharich and his associate Melanie Toyofuku told me of their research with the "space kids," who were sprouting up all over the world with demonstrable psychokinetic abilities and extremely high IQs. Puhrich said that these boys and girls very straightforwardly claimed to visit spaceships in their astral bodies.

"The funny thing is," Puharich said, "when two of them meet in a spaceship, they start swapping notes. It's really funny, and they're very cool about it."

Puharich told of an interesting experience that he had had in Mexico. He gathered six of the space kids and started teasing them with some equations and symbols that he told them "aren't known on Earth."

He wrote some things out and asked the kids if any of them recognized the equations.

"Yeah," said one of the kids, "but you didn't draw it right. There's a little thing that should go here!"

"Immediately the kids got into it," Puharich told me. "In one half-hour – and I have all this on tape – they'd gone through the various progressions.

"When I asked them later if they'd ever thought about these problems before, it came out that they had not. But somehow they remembered it, either from these classes aboard spaceships or preprogramming and getting it all together!"

BORN OF UNCERTAIN PARENTAGE

Shelly B. of Minneapolis, Minnesota, said she was born on June 15, 1950, at 1:00 A.M. to a mother who had had three previous miscarriages and who had to remain flat on her back for the first three months of her pregnancy to enable her to keep what eventually would be Shelly.

Shelly was told by her mother that at her birth she did not cry like the other babies did, but just uttered a few little sounds. Shelly wasn't red and bloody like the other newborn children were. Her mother said that Shelly refused to take her

SCREWED BY THE ALIENS

breasts, so she had to be put on a formula immediately.

Shelly was told by her mother that during her toddler years she never spoke much, but her mother always seemed to know what she wanted. She was late learning to speak, because she and her mother had developed telepathic communication. To this day, she and her mother "know what one another means to say and often will say the same thing simultaneously."

When Shelly was five years old, she experienced a very bright light in her eye which awed her so much that she called out to her mother in the middle of the night. Shelly asked where the light had come from, but her mother couldn't answer her.

She just didn't know what a light in the eye might be. Shelly continued to see night lights of different colors. At the same time, she became preoccupied with pixies, fairies, and elves; and she began to draw pictures of them. Since she exhibited a talent for drawing at an early age, some of the drawings were deemed so professional by her parents that they were displayed in art showings and in galleries in the local area.

AN "ADULT" BABY

Peggy of Dearborn, Michigan, gave me a complete report of her daughter Sara, who came from an unplanned pregnancy. She has now begun to question Sara's true origin or who the child's true father may have been.

Sara was closely monitored before and after birth because of the accelerated growth of her head. The doctors feared water on the brain because of the rapidity of the brain growth. Finally, at one year old, Sara was x-rayed. The doctor told Peggy that while Sara's head was adult-sized, there was no need to worry. She only had an excessively rapid brain development and was an exceptional child with potential genius ability.

In 1982, when Sara was three years old, Peggy was taking her out for an evening walk when Sara suddenly pointed out what looked like an extremely bright light in the evening sky. Peggy immediately scanned the sky for signs of the moon to see if this is what the light could have been. The moon was in its usual evening place.

Peggy grew intensely curious and began staring at the bright light. Peggy imagined all sorts of things such as weather satellites or balloons, but she knew in her heart that what she saw was none of those things. She grew frightened because what she was seeing was against all her conventional childhood teachings. She stepped up her pace, holding Sara's hand, until she was more or less dragging the child along.

Peggy continued to glance over her shoulder as the light seemed to follow them around a complete street block. She gauged its distance in the sky with the trees and the moon. She knew that it was moving and following them. It was at this point that she panicked, picked Sara up, and began to run.

SCREWED BY THE ALIENS

"The bright light followed us all the way home, and I ran into the neighbor's house, calling upon her to come and look at the light. I was then no longer afraid, as I had become aware that it had followed Sara and me for a reason. As people began to gather around and stare at the light, it continued to stay directly over our heads."

To prove the fascination that the mysterious light appeared to have for her and Sara, Peggy began to walk down the block. The light moved with them. Peggy went out of the house, later, around 10:00 P.M., and drove in the car in a northbound errand. The light followed until it finally disappeared into darkness. Shortly after that, faces began to appear to Sara in the night, and there seemed to be an assortment of unusual occurrences.

Two years later, Peggy had remarried and was now living in another state. Sara and she were on their way to the laundry room in the apartment complex in which they lived when Sara pointed to the sky and said, "Mama, look, there is our light again." Peggy looked up, dropped her laundry basket, and shielded her eyes.

"The light was so bright, it was blinding. It was directly over our heads. I knew that it was there for us again, but I wanted someone else to see it, too. We ran back toward the house, and I asked my husband to come out and look, also. There were several other witnesses.

"I felt a vibrant communication with this light during the whole time that it hovered above us. While no physical conversation took place, I knew I was receiving some sort of thought wave or implantation.

"My life and Sara's have never again been the same from that point on. I had actually welcomed the light this time and received something from it, as I am certain Sara did."

Peggy became convinced that she was a child of the light and that she was on a special mission here on Earth to help others. Sara and she suffered through many attacks of negativity during that period of time.

During that same period of time in 1984, Peggy reported, Sara also had contact with spiritual beings who gave her counsel and would take her aboard a space craft that she would crudely sketch for Peggy. Sara began to recite sequences of numbers and to draw sketches of what looked like spacecraft, containing computer keyboards, and people with strange names. The two entities who were seemingly the strongest contacts for Sara were Pencilava and Obta. Sara described them both to Peggy in great detail.

Pencilava was a very pretty lady with hair piled on top of her head and who usually wore a pink gown. Obta was a God-like figure with longish white hair. He was a very commanding authority figure who was strict in his ideas about Sara's future. He gave her spiritual teachings, and when she tried to block it out because

SCREWED BY THE ALIENS

it kept her awake at night, he would reprimand her and tell her that such was her destiny. He would let her sleep, but he would always return – for he was her true father.

"I honestly thought that this entity may have been her true father," Peggy said. She went on to say that Sara began to speak more and more of a new place to which she was taken aboard the spacecraft at night. Sara told Peggy that one day Earth would be fixed up just like new.

"Sara began to engage me in long conversations about our mission here on Earth. That we were to show people the way to the Light. Sara became concerned that so many people would be destroyed with the Earth as it progressed on the path of destruction on which it was set."

Peggy tried to tell her that those people would be given a choice whether or not to trust in the Light and to accept eternal life.

Sara could often take the pain out of the back of Peggy's neck. Peggy was on medication for arthritis. She went frequently to chiropractors, and she had sought all kinds of medical help.

For several years, she had lived with excruciating pain in her neck that would seem to intensify with humidity changes. Sara would be able to soothe it with her little hands until Peggy could feel the pain slowly fading.

"Sara has always been overly compassionate for the plight of others, and she cries easily when she feels that she has hurt someone. In general, she is extremely emotionally sensitive."

A PANEL OF ABDUCTEES SHARE EXPERIENCES

The abductees speaking at the Mutual UFO Network's Washington, D.C. conference in June of 1987 reported frightening and disorienting aspects of their UFO experiences. They said that they often remembered the experiences only in fragments and flashes until they underwent hypnotic regression. For the abductees speaking on the panel, the interaction with the UFO entities had seemed primarily to be negative. They told of the frustration of being partially paralyzed and taken without their consent to undergo medical examinations.

A woman in her mid-thirties said, "In a way, you can't blame the aliens for taking us. It would have cost them millions of dollars to get volunteers. If they had asked me, I definitely would have said 'No.' The thing that makes you angriest is that they don't care whether you want to go with them or not. They don't seem to have any understanding of the fact that we have a sense of free will here on this planet and that we think and act as individuals."

As reported in UFO, Vol. 2, Number 3, 1987, the woman went on to say that much of the anxiety of the abductee experience comes from the culture shock that it provokes. "You have to re-evaluate your value system because suddenly there is no longer just a possibility that there are other lifeforms, but a

SCREWED BY THE ALIENS

great probability that they exist – because you've met them. And not only have you met them, but you're not able to be equal with them because they're calling the shots."

Kathie Davis, the woman profiled in Budd Hopkins' "Intruders" as having been the nonconsenting mother of nine alien babies, reported that she had dealt with her experiences by denying them. "I can live with it because I don't believe it. I really don't. I mean, I'm from the Midwest. Maybe I could accept it more if I was from New York."

Reporting her experiences nervously, but with a sense of humor, Ms. Davis went on to say, "I don't know why I'm afraid, really. I haven't been injured. I don't think it's a terrible thing, and I wasn't left with a lot of anger. I didn't think it was a spectacular thing or exciting, either. I had more anxiety than anything else."

THE MYSTERIOUS PROCESS OF SELECTION

Over the past several years, hundreds of people who claim the abductee experience have contacted me, and I have often speculated about the process of selection involved in such alleged acts of cosmic kidnapping. Why would certain men and women be selected for what appear to be these remarkable encounters with alien lifeforms from other worlds or other dimensions?

It does seem as though abductions "run in the family." Intense investigations of the abductees very often reveal that UFO abductions seem to occur over several generations of the same family. And in the matter of the mysterious pregnancies, this would seem to be even more so the case.

It may well be that certain of our species are being developed to serve as some kind of intermediaries between "us" and "them." Perhaps a kind of shepherding of specific family lines has been overseen for generations, breeding humans to serve as appropriate "seed people" during the fast-approaching time of "Armageddon," the transition from one epoch to another.

We can only hope, of course, that it is not, as some more cynical UFO researchers suggest, that an alien intelligence is programming and cross-breeding certain of Homo sapiens to become living robots and Judas goats to lead our earthly civilization into servitude.

SCREWED BY THE ALIENS

ABOUT BRAD STEIGER

Brad Steiger is a world renowned author of over 175 books with over 17 million copies in print. His titles include: "Mysteries of Time and Space," "Real Ghosts, Restless Spirits and Haunted Places," "Conspiracies and Secret Societies: The Complete Dossier," "Touched by Heaven's Light," "American Indian Medicine Power," "Strangers from the Skies," "Project Bluebook," "The Rainbow Conspiracy," "Real Encounters, Different Dimensions and Otherworldly Beings," and many more. Steiger first began publishing articles on the unexplained in 1956; since then he has written more than 2,000 paranormal-themed articles. From 1970-73, his weekly newspaper column, "The Strange World of Brad Steiger," was carried domestically in over 80 newspapers and overseas from Bombay to Tokyo. He was born in Fort Dodge, Iowa, on February 19, 1936. He is married to Sherry Hansen Steiger, author and co-author of over 22 books. They have two sons, three daughters, and ten grandchildren. Keep up with Brad at his Facebook page,

https://www.facebook.com/Brad.Steiger.Author

or the Steiger website www.bradandsherry.com.

SUGGESTED READING:
CAT MIRACLES
GODS OF AQUARIUS
MEDICINE WALK
REAL MONSTERS, GRUESOME CRITTERS, AND BEASTS FROM THE DARK SIDE
HAUNTED-MALEVOLENT GHOSTS, NIGHT TERRORS, AND THREATENING PHANTOMS

SCREWED BY THE ALIENS

CHAPTER 24

BIRTH OF AN ALIEN HYBRID
THE CHRISTA TILTON STORY
By Timothy Green Beckley

She was a fascinating lady, but I never really knew what to make of her. Christa Tilton was somewhat of a fixture in the UFO field, though an enigmatic one. She had been married to animal mutilation researcher Tom Adams and, after they split, she hooked up with veteran UFOlogist Wendelle Stevens and tied the knot with him.

She was bright, attentive and attractive. Men thought she had a magnetic personality – and I would guess the aliens thought so as well.

I corresponded with Christa Tilton over a period of years, met her at a UFO conference and spoke to her in private. Before she vanished from the field, we published a book containing a quantity of material she had submitted for publication.

"Underground Alien Bio Lab At Dulce: The Bennewitz UFO Papers" dealt with a man by the name of Paul Bennewitz, who claimed to have photographed UFOs that appeared over a New Mexico military base. He had learned that the occupants of these craft had established a base under the town of Dulce (located on a Native-American reservation) and were generally thought to be "up to no good."

As verification of Mr. Bennewitz's revelations, Christa says she was taken to this bunker seven levels down into the Earth and was impregnated by extraterrestrials, who came in several forms, from very human-looking to the often dreaded greys.

Her ongoing series of encounters begins in the summer of 1962. According to a lengthy account published in the now defunct newsletter CRUX, which her husband, Tom Adams, published, "At dusk, ten-year-old Christa was looking for rocks in the desert of suburban Tucson. After watching a 'fireball' land or crash, she was approached by a five-foot-tall gray being who traded rocks with her, then took her onboard a craft. She was examined physically and to alleviate her fears was

SCREWED BY THE ALIENS

told that they were 'planting a garden.' Onboard she met a more human-appearing being she would come to think of as the 'Doctor' and would see him several times in future experiences."

This "Doctor" was what is often referred to as a Nordic – a space being said to be very Aryan in appearance.

Several other instances are reported in that same publication:

Tulsa, Oklahoma – Fall 1971: Gray aliens took her from apartment and onto craft, where she was implanted with fertilized ovum.

New Orleans – Early winter 1971: Hypnotic regression disclosed that gray aliens took her again, this time extracting the fetus prematurely; something had gone wrong. There was a taller gray that seemed to be in charge; about five-feet-tall, like the one in Tucson in 1962. This was the most disturbing, most traumatic of Christa's experiences. She was shown stacks of incubators containing fetuses. She also saw what was apparently a hologram of a human child, a girl of about ten-years-old. She was told this was the daughter she would give birth to in the future. Also onboard was the human-like alien, the "Doctor."

Tulsa - February 1976: Following a long period of no sexual activity, Christa was suddenly pregnant. Regression disclosed implantation of another fertilized ovum. She would later meet the father. The pregnancy resulted in the birth of a daughter who, at the age of ten, looked identical to the child she had seen in the hologram in 1971.

In an interview I did for "UFO Universe," Christa described in intimate detail one of her traumatic experiences, which she believes took place deep underground.

TAKEN CAPTIVE

My experience happened in July of 1987. I had about a three-hour missing time episode in which later, under hypnosis, I relived a most harrowing night. I remember driving to a deserted area, north of Tucson, Arizona, in the middle of the night. I saw a craft sitting up on a small hill and it was then I saw two aliens approach my car. I panicked and locked my doors. When they got closer, I heard a click and it was then I noticed my door had just opened. I began fighting off the two entities and, after laying me on my back, one grabbed one of my arms and the other did the same and they actually pulled me over the rocky terrain up to the craft. When onboard, I was given something to drink. The next thing I realized I was being led off the craft and I noticed I was in a different area than where I had been abducted. I looked around and noticed the craft was sitting next to an opening in the mountain. I saw what looked to be a tunnel that led into the side of the mountain. This time I was accompanied by a human who wore a type of military uniform like what a test pilot would wear. He was to be my guide for the rest of the trip.

SCREWED BY THE ALIENS

We entered the tunnel and I soon noticed the tunnel was illuminated with some type of artificial lighting. Another human with the same type of uniform approached us. I noticed he was wearing a strange looking weapon on the side of a large black belt. I also saw a strange symbol worn on a patch on his chest.

The guard did not seem friendly at all and when I tried to ask questions I was told not to speak. The guard asked me to step on something that looked like a large scale. I saw what looked to be a large computerized screen in front of me and two cameras were visible at that checkpoint. I was then told to clip on some type of identification card with holes punched in it. It seems as though they had me change into some type of uniform, but I do not consciously remember all the details.

It was at that time I saw a huge elevator that had no door. I heard strange tones inside this area and noticed strange symbols on the walls. There was a time in which my guide explained to me that we had just entered LEVEL ONE of the facility. I asked him what kind of facility this was and he replied that I would soon see.

It was like an underground city. I was amazed at what I saw there. We rode in some strange transit car that was rounded and looked as though it was connected someway to the side of the cavern. I noticed other people walking by and none of them even glanced my way. Some wore white uniforms and lab coats and others had the military-type of jumpsuits on. As I said before, the lighting was very strange. I could not find a source for it.

After exiting the vehicle, I was taken to a large area. So large that it looked as though a jet plane could fly and land there. It was then I saw the small alien craft parked to the sides. I noticed a large number of scanning cameras. They made me very nervous because I felt as if I was being monitored everywhere I went. I was taken down a long hall where I viewed huge computers and heard strange tones and frequencies. I saw cubicle areas where others worked. It was like a factory atmosphere. At times I thought that is where I was, but I would soon find out it was not a factory!

THE TANKS

The whole time I felt as though I was taken on a special tour, as if I was meant to be there for a specific reason. My guide argued with some guards at one point. They kept looking over at me, but I could not hear what all the arguing was about. It was at this point I was taken down on the elevator once again. It seemed like it took forever, but we arrived and, when I stepped into the secured area, a different set of guards approached us immediately. They were not friendly at all.

All of a sudden, an extreme sense of fear overcame me. My guide explained that as long as I was with him I would not be harmed. The guards were issuing orders right and left. My guide swiftly walked me down a long hallway. I heard a humming sound like a generator. We passed an area in which I felt as if I were

SCREWED BY THE ALIENS

going to be physically ill. I saw huge tanks with gauges hooked to them and an arm-like device was extending down into the tanks. They looked to be around four to five feet in height and, just as I started to go see what was in the tanks, I felt my guide quickly grab my arm and lead me out of this huge area. I was told that it would only complicate matters if I knew what was being kept in those tanks; I became very scared at this point.

At this point, if I had known what was in store for me, I probably would have started screaming and run for my life! I was led into what only looked to be a laboratory. I saw the back of a small alien's head as he was working diligently at a counter. I heard the clinking of metal and it was then that I remembered my training in the operating room in the late 1970s. I was beginning to get very frightened until I saw a man in a white lab coat turn around to greet us. He smiled and shook hands with my guide.

I remember it being very cold in this room and I started to shake. My guide smiled and patted me on the back and said he would be just outside and told me to relax and I would be finished in no time. I began to cry. I cry when I am terribly scared. The man was a doctor and he called for an assistant to come and help. This is when I saw the gray alien come in. The next thing I knew, I was very drowsy. I was told to lay on the table and I felt as if I were dying. My legs were positioned and I realized that I was being examined internally. The "doctor" rubbed something clear and cool on my abdomen and it seemed to calm me and make the pain subside. I could not believe this was happening to me all over again and in such a strange place. I felt more alone than I ever had in my life. I felt like a guinea pig and after I left this lab I became very silent. I was angry at this man for allowing this to happen to me. He told me it was necessary and told me to forget.

How could I ever forget?

THE FACILITY

The most bizarre part of this facility was an area we approached in which I saw the strangest thing. I saw what looked to be people of all different races standing up against the wall inside a clear chamber. I went up to one and touched it. It felt ice cold. The people looked like wax figures ... not real. I also went past some small cages in which I saw animals in a similar state of what I only could guess was suspended animation. I think the animals were alive though. For some reason, seeing the animals upset me more than seeing humans in the chambers. And every so often we would pass other technicians working. Never once did they turn around to acknowledge my presence. They looked almost like robots doing their menial tasks in an emotionless manner. It was all very disturbing to me.

It became very apparent that this facility was not run by just aliens, but a form of military also. The security was very high and it was impossible for us to get to LEVEL SIX. I was told that this level contained some things that might be upsetting

SCREWED BY THE ALIENS

and it would be something, at this time, that I would not be able to comprehend. It was then we started our ascent back up.

I was returning that evening to the area in which my car was parked. I walked back to my car and drove back to my aunt's home. I was still wearing my dirty nightshirt I had left the house in and must have immediately fallen asleep in my room, not waking my best friend. In the morning my friend saw huge long red scratches on my back and it was then that I realized something very strange had occurred the night before. It was too bizarre to believe.

MILAB INTERVENTION

EDITOR'S NOTE: At this point Christa begins to bring in the weird but ever-recurring relationship between the military and the aliens. Dubbed MILABs (for "military abductions"), numerous abductees who have been taken to their "chambers" say they have been molested or at the very least harassed by an unknown branch of what appears to be the government. Many times these agents show up later and continue to bombard the experiencers with their negativity.

Many people report abduction experiences, but there is an aspect of my account which is not common to most. Most abductees, whether they experience isolated or repeated incidents, are left to fend for themselves, often with no one with whom to candidly discuss their experiences. This often occurs without anyone offering corroboration or supporting evidence for their accounts, for whatever consolation that would be (and, in most cases, that would be substantial, trauma-dispelling corroboration). In the past few years of my own investigation into my own abductions, I have had communication by phone and in person with a military man who not only exhibits intimate knowledge of my abductions, but also my life in general. He is – or claims to be – an agent of the federal government. I refer to him as John Wallis.

The first inkling I had that the government was involved in my abductions is when I began to receive strange phone calls while I was staying at researcher Wendelle Stevens' home in Tucson in August of 1987. At first the man would tell me he knew all about my experiences and then he would tell me that it would be a good idea if I were to move back home and forget I ever had these experiences. Alarmed by these calls, Wendelle Stevens encouraged me to "keep the faith" and he continued to help me sort through all the details of what had happened to me. The next week I received a visitor at Wendelle's home, and when I opened the door, the man flashed what looked to be an official government card and asked if I would mind if he came in to ask me a few questions. Startled by his urgency, I said it was alright.

He stayed for approximately one hour and in that time he seemed to indicate to me that his agency was concerned about me and he wanted to warn me not to marry a certain researcher. I was shocked at his insistence. I asked him why the

SCREWED BY THE ALIENS

government would care about what I do. He stated that it was his business to know every detail of my experiences. He told me there was a government listing of people who had been abducted. I laughed and told him that our government could care less. He stated that that was not the case, as many people think. I asked him if he could show me any documentation about my abductions and he said the papers were in a file and it was all kept in confidence.

A few months later, he showed up on my doorstep in Tulsa, Oklahoma! This really frightened me. We had a rather heated conversation about my trip to New Mexico. He wanted to know every detail about what I saw,

What was really fantastic about the Tulsa visit is John Wallis' knowledge of the abduction I had in Tucson in July, 1987. He claimed there was a video tape of the incident and also photos taken. I was horrified! I demanded to know why he did not try to help me and he stated that they were aware of where I would be taken and knew I would be safe. I couldn't believe my ears! I made a note of the date and later was told by a man that worked in the Sheriff's office that a UFO was spotted in that very area that same night. I also found out later through hypnosis that in the facility they had removed another fetus from me.

There were discussions about emotions, hormones, and a chemical imbalance in my brain. And what was strange is that John Wallis had even admitted to me that he was present. Then I began to remember.

Whatever the reason, John Walls has maintained contact with me since 1987 and has not only asked information of me, but also volunteered prudent information to me. There seems to be an exchange program of some kind, but it is a mutual one. I do not believe John Wallis has been sent to do me any harm. He may be a pawn also in this game the aliens are playing with us.

EDITOR'S NOTE: When asked if she ever was able to find out where the man who questioned her lived or is stationed, Christa said yes she did! "He is stationed at a major military installation – one of the most sensitive in this country – and he has been there for quite a while. I know he feels it is his duty to keep these secrets (about MILAB). He is a very patriotic man. Be he has told me that there are several alien factions on earth and that some of them can pass for human. I spoke for a UFO group in Dallas and he was there in the audience. He was simply monitoring what information I was giving out to the public."

VIEWING CHRISTA UNDERGROUND
AN INDEPENDENT WITNESS COMES FORWARD
TO CONFIRM HER ACCOUNT

As is highly unusual in abduction scenarios, a man, a total stranger, came forward to verify Christa Tilton's story because he insists he saw her in the underground facility while he was being examined and mistreated there. The South Carolina man, whose name is Donovan Masters, was taken by a group of ETs where

SCREWED BY THE ALIENS

a series of bizarre experiments were conducted on him and during the process a small "tattoo" was even placed on the base of his back.

We published this testimony initially in "UFO Universe," but the case has since been covered by other media.

Masters admits he had a long time interest in UFOs and had sightings that verified his beliefs. His wife thought him a bit odd, but didn't push the issue until one day she was in the market and someone approached her and said he knew her husband and wanted to know what Mrs. Masters thought of her husband's UFO fascination. The woman wanted to know how this complete stranger would know of her husband's "hobby." She was told, "We know a lot about him. He isn't crazy, even if you think he is, and at the right time all will be revealed to him."

THE STORY MASTERS HAS TO TELL

The following is, I feel, a very real experience, which I believe ties in with the experiences of Christa Tilton.

Three of my friends and I were taken to what I perceived to be some type of underground installation or UFO base. I say "friends" because that is how I perceived them, although I had not met them at the time. I remember feeling as though I had been drugged, as if everything was kind of going in slow motion. We were placed on and strapped to a conveyor belt by our wrists and ankles. The conveyor was activated and, as it began to move, our bodies were passed through blocks of pure intense light. These blocks of light (perhaps laser scanning devices) were either green or blue in color. At each block there was what I perceived to be a robot controller. They also were either blue or green in color. Their color corresponded to the color of the light in front of which they stood.

Suddenly we were on a different conveyor belt or at the end of the first one. As the belt moved around a circular console, it stopped. There were two men, human in form and characteristics, seated at the console. One assisted the other. One of them picked up what I thought was a razor and shaved an area on my back left side, just below the waist line. I remember the spot bled considerably. I was released and then I observed them carrying out the same procedure on my friends. I remember thinking over and over, "What is happening to me?" Then I heard a reply from one of the aliens. "You have just been implanted with your government control extension number." I remember looking into a mirror and looking at the area that bled. The number "04" was there.

In a very upset manner I turned to a woman in a uniform and exclaimed, "You can't do this to me!" Incidentally, all the personnel in this facility wore uniforms. I then ran back to the console where they allowed me to leave. By that time, my friends had been released also. I hurriedly told them that I had discovered what was happening to us. As I was speaking, the two men at the console were gathering materials in a great hurry, in what seemed to me like an attempt to escape. In

SCREWED BY THE ALIENS

particular, I remember the man that had implanted the number on me had a computer printout list. He protected that list with his life as my friends and I ran after him and another humanoid. They escaped through a set of double doors.

This is what is strange.... that during the time I was there I sincerely believe I saw Christa Tilton in this same facility. I also do not think it was our first meeting.

Like Christa, I also have been plagued by intense, repetitive dramas of meetings and communications with what appear to be non-human, otherworldly beings. I am also continually frustrated by my inability to learn the truth about my experiences. Also, like Christa, I suffer from insomnia and the fear of what might happen if I fall asleep. I believe that I have been abducted countless times and it was one of those vivid times when I am sure I saw Christa aboard a craft.

I remember walking around a circular corridor, just sort of checking things out unattended when I came upon an open door. I walked just inside the door and there she was, just lying there on what seemed to be an examination table. She was surrounded by light grey alien beings, 1/2 to 4 feet tall. They were wearing what looked like close-fitting coveralls, almost like a second skin. I was then told telepathically that I was not to enter that area nor to ever contact her. I was not only asked to leave, but also escorted out of the room and down the corridor. At that very moment things became very hazy and I fainted. That is all I can recall from this experience.

TILTON PICKS UP THE STORY
"YES, I KNOW MASTERS WAS DOWN THERE WITH ME!"

Masters says much of what he saw underground cannot be discussed because some of what happened remains too painful for him to speak about. In "UFO Universe," I detailed my numerous experiences which took place in an underground UFO base located under the community of Dulce, New Mexico. I saw an array of conveyor systems in this underground facility and at every checkpoint there was a computer console. Also, Donavon saw what he could only call "a computerized elevator," which correlates with the magnetic elevator I was taken on. There is also the matter of the pungent smell when he came close to the large barrels.

We both saw human entities and small grey aliens working in the same area. What is the purpose for them to be working side by side? Researchers still have found no answers to this enigma.

What is unfortunate is that Donavon's marriage broke up because of his obsession in finding out what had transpired. I, too, have loved and lost because of my obsession with what really happened to me.

For the most part, the aliens seem oblivious to our emotions. Can you imagine how horrifying it must have been for Donavon to be shackled down to this conveyor system and actually feel the tattoo being embedded into his side? The tattoo is apparently only visible under some special type of lighting the aliens have.

SCREWED BY THE ALIENS

It brings to my mind our branding and tagging of animals to track them. This is exactly what I believe happened to Donavon Masters.

Donavon has had other abductions, but this one particularly stood out in his mind because he recognized me as being onboard and he felt helpless because he wanted to try and assist my escape.

Another interesting aspect to this experience for Donavon is the fact that the people he labeled his "friends" were all of a different culture. He remembered being especially close to a black man who was also experiencing the same tattoo. They both were angry because they had no control over the situation.

But while there have been certain negative aspects to this encounter, overall these experiences have had a positive impact on Donavon's life. In many ways, he feels different and special.

On March 30/31, 1987, I had a strange abduction south of Tulsa, Oklahoma, where I was taken onboard a UFO and given another physical examination. I remember looking to the left and seeing a young blond man just standing there with tears in his eyes. I telepathically heard the head alien tell the man to leave immediately. I have to wonder, could that young man have been Donavon?

Donavon sent me some of his medical records in which it stated that there was some type of strange object found under his skin. It still haunts him to this day.

I have to wonder just how many of us have had similar experiences and have never reported them to anyone? Maybe sharing the experiences will help all of us. I know it helps me!

THE NEVER ENDING STORY

It would be nice if Donavon's experiences ended here, but unfortunately – for him – they did not. Soon after he reported seeing objects in the sky and this strange man approached his wife asking far too personal questions, Donavon began noticing a black car driving around the trailer park he owned. This man poses as a man working in conjunction with the government and even began scaring the neighbors. No one knew who this man was or where he really came from. In a small town like Liberty, South Carolina, everyone knows what is going on with all their residents. He never approached Donavon, but would park across the road in his black car and just sit there for hours.

Scared and confused, this is when Donavon contacted me at researcher Wendelle Stevens' home. I tried to comfort him, but it is difficult when you truly feel your life is in danger. Then mysterious, unmarked, black helicopters began flying low over the trailer park. Donavon felt they were of government origin, but could not be certain. Donavon began to feel weak and his health deteriorated during the next few months. I received a letter from him the other day which bordered on the bizarre. It was as if Donavon was not writing the letter, but I knew it was his handwriting. He had never come across as being overly religious in any

SCREWED BY THE ALIENS

sense, but the letter was quite the opposite. Maybe this is Donavon's way of dealing with his experiences. I know I have a closer relationship with God because of my experiences. But again, men-in-black activity haunted him for quite some time. It is too bad that more has not been written on the subject of these strange MIB. More investigating is certainly required if we are to understand and help the victims of unwanted harassment by the strong arm of some unknown agency.

POSSIBLE GENETIC TAMPERING

When first interviewing a man about his alien examinations, I always try to allow them to tell me "all" the story. Sometimes, for a man, revealing things of a sexual nature to a woman he has never met can be quite disconcerting. So I spoke to Donavon on many occasions before he ever mentioned the possibility of genetic tampering with him.

This reminds me of the case of Jocelino de Mattos from Maringa, Brazil. Jocelino was taken to an exam room inside a UFO and laid down on a table. The beings examined him, taking sperm samples with a tubular device and placing the specimen in a clear package. Later, Jocelino and his brother Roberto had sexual relations with two of the beings onboard the craft.

For Donavon, I believe, something such as this may have happened to him and it is being suppressed by his subconscious. Donavon has often showed interest in trying hypnosis, but in the years gone by, I believe the thought is just too painful for him to dredge up at this point.

At some stage, I believe there was some speculation on Donavon's part that he and I could possibly be lined in such a way. I try to play this down because even though it could be humanly possible, it would be hard to prove that both Donavon and I were on the same craft or in the same underground facility at the time this happened to him. For now, Donavon is happily living alone. His wife divorced him right after these strange events and Donavon has chosen not to marry again. He seems happy and has not had any events occur recently, although the aliens have been known to wait for years before contacting their subjects again. I believe the tattoo might be the answer to many of our questions.

The puzzle of the underground facility still remains. At the time Donovan reported his experience to me, he had not read any material on the underground experiences of others. I think that many of us here on Earth are herded up like cattle and maybe given some type of invisible implant underneath our skin in the form of a number. In Donavon's case, he had only one implanted, if true. But, in my case and in many other instances, we remember numerous implants placed in many areas of our bodies. What do these implants do for the aliens? What do they do for us? The study will continue and there will be many more like Donavon who have these encounters with beings from another world.

We are being manipulated by some force outside of our realm of understand-

SCREWED BY THE ALIENS

ing. Maybe by reporting more stories such as Donavon's we can place the pieces of the puzzle together. The best we can do for now is give support to our friends who do not understand. An update may be warranted in the future, but let us hope Donavon will be left in peace. For this is all we want here on Earth anyway, PEACE.

Donavan's real name is Samuel Paul Holcombe. This is an update dated 2005 from his web site. One of the more recent inexplicable events is as follows, September 28, 2005. I left my friend's house driving home at 11:00 pm. As I was approaching a roadside park, which is 4.4 miles from my friend's house, I was thinking that I needed to stop by my post office box and pick up my mail. That was my last conscious recallable memory until I was standing in my bedroom with a nose bleed and my friend's truck was parked behind my house. I looked at the clock, it was 1:30 A.M. I was feeling as though I had been drugged and went straight to bed. The following morning I didn't wake up until 11:30 A.M., still feeling as though I had been drugged. That feeling lasted for about three hours after I awoke, and my legs were weak and unsteady. It is 4.4 miles from my friend's house to the aforementioned roadside park, and 5.3 miles from that park to my home. A trip distance of 9.7 miles which would have normally taken no longer than 20 minutes, lasted for more than two and one half hours, with absolutely no recall of what happened from the roadside park to my home. Consequently, I never did stop at the post office to pick up my mail that night.

SUGGESTED READING

UNDERGROUND ALIEN BIO LAB AT DULCE: THE BENNEWITZ UFO PAPERS, by Timothy Beckley, Sean Casteel, Christa Tilton and others.

UNDERGROUND ALIEN BASES, by Commander X

SCREWED BY THE ALIENS

  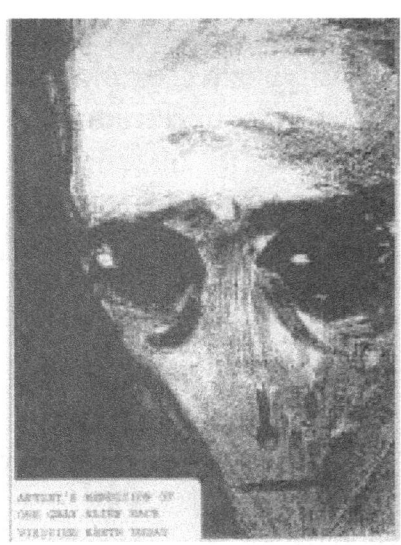

Abductee Christa Tilton.

Artist's rendering of "The Doctor," which has been a part of Christa Tilton's life since the age of ten.

Artist's rendition of one Grey alien race visiting Earth today.

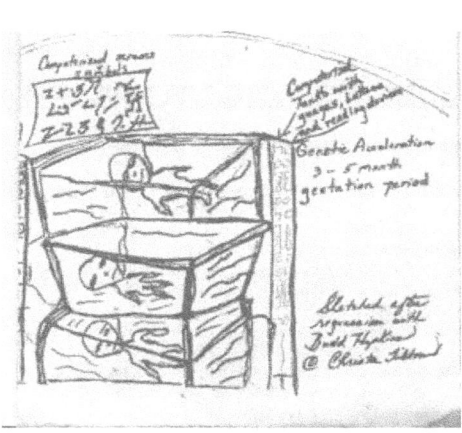

Fetuses and incubators seen on board a craft by Christa Tilton in 1988. She was not allowed to touch anything in the chamber where she found herself.

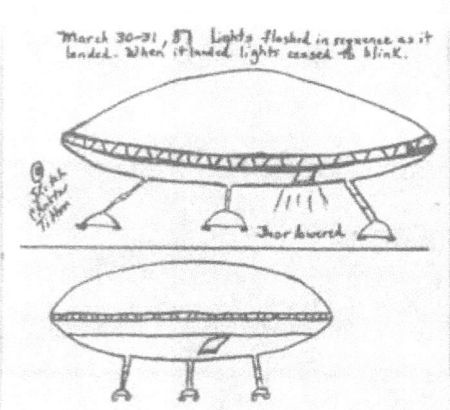

Craft seen by Christa in the early morning of 3-31-87 twenty-eight miles south of Tulsa and compared BOTTOM to Ashland, Nebraska, policeman Robert Schirmer in the fall of 1967.

The hybrids are growing in number. Some of the offspring of the mating of humans and aliens are remarkably human in appearance; some are brilliant and downright attractive.

SCREWED BY THE ALIENS

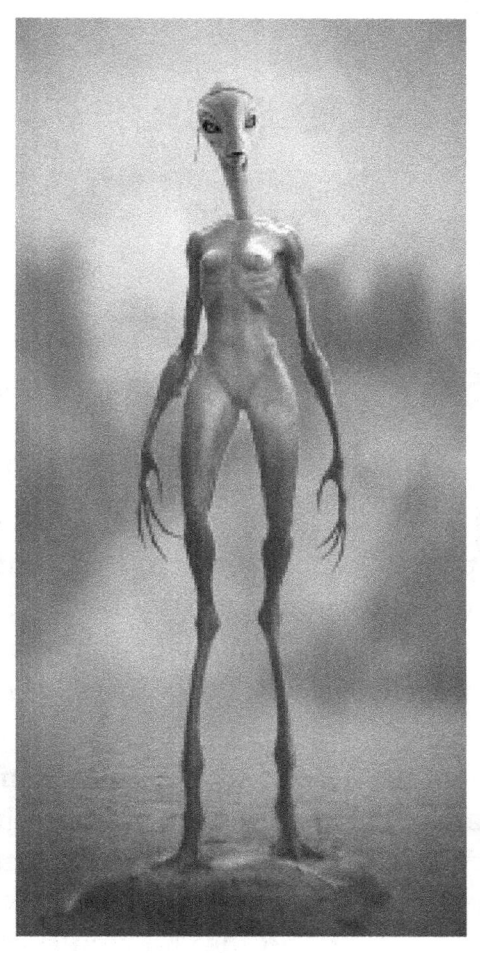

**SECTION TEN
IT'S ALL IN THE DNA!**

**Chapter Twenty Five: Hair of the Alien
By Tim Swartz**

**Chapter Twenty Six: Screen Memories
By William Kern**

SCREWED BY THE ALIENS

DNA EVIDENCE!
THE PROOF IS IN THE HAIR SAMPLE
By Tim R. Swartz

Skeptics of the UFO phenomenon repeatedly point out that there is no tangible evidence to support the claims made by both witnesses and researchers. There have been, however, a number of cases that may dispute the debunkers' assertions, such as the bizarre event of July 23, 1992, involving Peter Khoury in Sydney, Australia.

Peter Khoury was no stranger to the strange world of UFO abductions. Khoury was originally from Lebanon and moved to Australia in 1973. On July 12, 1988, Khoury was lying in bed when he suddenly found himself paralyzed and surrounded by three or four figures wearing dark robes with hoods on their heads. He was told telepathically to relax and that he would not be hurt. Two of the figures came close enough that Khoury could see that they were a golden-yellow in color, tall and thin with big black eyes and a narrow chin. The one closest to him brought out a long needle-like, flexible crystal tube which was inserted into the side of his head, causing him to lose consciousness.

When he awoke, Khoury found his father and brother asleep in front of the TV. When he woke them, they were dazed and believed that only 10 minutes had passed, but it was actually more than two hours. At that point Khoury was not familiar with UFO abduction cases and he battled with anxiety and confusion because of his strange experience.

BEDROOM INTRUDERS

By 1992, Peter had married and was living in Sydney. On July 23, he stayed home for the day because of a work-related injury. After driving his wife to the train station, he returned and went back to bed. Khoury would later tell UFO researcher Bill Chalker that around 7:30 AM he awoke suddenly, realizing that he was no longer alone in the house.

SCREWED BY THE ALIENS

"I was trying to wake up, put my senses together," Khoury said. "I noticed there were two naked females on the bed. The one directly opposite me was a blonde-looking woman and she was sitting with her legs tucked under her. The one on the other side was dark-haired and oriental-looking. She was kneeling on my bed, kind of sitting upright a bit."

Khoury said that the blonde woman appeared to be in her mid-thirties with white, almost translucent skin. Her hair was thin and wispy, but was curled "something like Farrah Fawcett, really exotic." The shape of the face was long, like it was stretched out, with an extremely pointed chin. She had high, protruding cheeks, with a long nose. Khoury also noticed that her eyes were two to three times bigger than normal eyes.

"She looked humanoid," Khoury said. "But I knew I wasn't looking at a human female."

The other woman, Khoury remembered, seemed to be around 5 foot 8 inches tall, but her features weren't completely human either. Her skin was dark, like an Indian. She had straight, stiff black hair that went down to her shoulders. Her cheekbones looked Asian, but they sat up too high on her face and were puffy, like she had been "punched by Mike Tyson."

"Her eyes were large and dark, almost black. I don't remember seeing white in the eyes."

"THIS ISN'T THE WAY IT'S SUPPOSED TO HAPPEN"

The blonde seemed to be in charge and Khoury had the impression that she was communicating telepathically with the dark-haired woman. The blonde woman then reached forward, cupping her hands around the back of his head, and pulled him to her breast. He would pull away, but the woman would pull back even harder, trying to force her nipple into his mouth.

Khoury told Chalker that, in his panic, he bit down hard on the woman's nipple, accidentally swallowing a piece of it. The bizarre thing he said was that the blonde woman did not cry out or act like she was injured. Nor was there any blood. Instead, the expression on her face was one of shock or confusion.

"She looked at the Asian one," he said, "and looked at me like, this isn't the way it's supposed to happen. You've done this wrong."

Involuntarily, Khoury swallowed the nipple and it caught in his throat, causing him to have a coughing fit. When he looked up, the two women had vanished.

Continuing to cough, Khoury went to the bathroom for a drink of water, but realized that something was hurting his penis. When he checked, he found to his dismay that there were two long strands of thin, blonde hair wrapped tightly around his penis underneath the foreskin.

As the pain became an intense burning sensation, he finally he managed to removed the hairs and immediately put them in a small, sealable plastic bag.

SCREWED BY THE ALIENS

"The reason I did that was because I knew that there was no way, no way at all, that a hair that size and wrapped around the way it was should have been there," Khoury said. "Thinking of these women, the thing in my throat, the hair, something bizarre had just happened."

Fortunately, Khoury hung on to his bizarre evidence and eventually Bill Chalker was able to enlist the help of a group of friends that included scientists from the biochemical field. Chalker's circle of friends were interested in UFOs, but insisted their involvement would be on a strictly anonymous basis. Chalker became the public face of the UFO "invisible college" which called itself the Anomaly Physical Evidence Group (APEG).

The hair samples were examined by Dr. Horace Drew, who had worked for decades as a head research scientist at The Commonwealth Scientific and Industrial Research Organization (CSIRO), Australia's leading scientific research organization. As well, Dr. Drew co-authored the authoritative reference book "Understanding DNA: The Molecule and How it Works."

It was noted that the hair samples did not resemble any of the test samples taken from Khoury or his wife. In fact, according to Chalkers 1999 paper ("Mitochondrial DNA Sequence Analysis of a Shed Hair from an Alien Abduction Case"), the hair was "extremely thin and almost clear, and that further investigation...by high-resolution dark-field microscopy showed it to lie at the lower end of normal human hair thickness, and also to show a pronounced 'mosaic' structure, perhaps due to the near-absence of melanin."

Dr. Drew's PCR (Polymerase Chain Reaction) DNA profiling of the hair revealed that it came from someone who was biologically close to normal human genetics, but of an unusual racial type – a rare Chinese Mongoloid type – one of the rarest human lineages known, that lies further from the human mainstream than any other except for African pygmies and aboriginals. Even more bizarre, the mitochondrial DNA profiling revealed a rare Basque/Gaelic-type DNA in the hair root, along with the indications of the CCR5 gene deletion factor – indicating possible viral resistance against diseases such as HIV and smallpox.

The incredible finding of the DNA study seems to show human genetic manipulation on a scale not yet accomplished by modern science. There is also the disturbing indication that the "humans" that supplied the hair sample have been genetically altered to be resistant to sexually transmitted diseases such as HIV/AIDS. This is an interesting development considering the stories that have been circulated for decades about a possible human/extraterrestrial hybrid program being conducted by some unknown group(s).

HUMAN DNA

Even though Bill Chalker book is titled "Hair of the Alien," the DNA results, while extremely unusual, show that the owner of the hair is human. Caution must

SCREWED BY THE ALIENS

be taken not to jump to any conclusions on the origins of the hair that Peter Khoury found...no matter how bizarre the circumstances were prior to its discovery. That being said, there is no doubt that the DNA tests show that the owner of the hair is a highly unusual person whose genetic makeup is like nothing ever seen before.

In 2012, Chalker wrote in his Oz Files blog that the "Asian mongoloid sequence, found in the Khoury sample, is only found in the DNA signatures of an isolated group of people – the Lahu, who are limited to the region of the southern Chinese province of Yunnan, and the immediate regions bordering that locality – northern Thailand, Myanmar (Burma), and Laos." He also adds that ancient Lahu mythologies recount visits from the "sky beings" and today the region is rich with UFO and unusual light phenomena.

The question of human bioengineering, along with the centuries old tales of sexual interactions between humans and "nonhuman" entities, is maddeningly complex. We are looking at a phenomena that has been effectively hidden from us, with the exception of the occasional slip up. Unfortunately, those slip ups always bring up more questions than answers.

A TEACHER OF HUMAN SEXUALITY

Peter Khoury was no stranger to the abduction phenomena. The UFO-related incidents that he had vague memories of could have been just a small part of possibly many incidents that had been wiped from his memory. It is no wide stretch of the imagination to say that what happened to him in his home in Sidney did not just happen out of a vacuum.

Looking at Khoury's experience, it could be that at some time he had been tasked as being a "sexual guinea pig" or even an instructor of human sexual habits to young, non-human (or hybrid) entities, that are learning just what it is to be human. Given that shortly before his 1992 bedroom event, Khoury had been injured in a fight and was on medication, it is possible that his injuries, along with his prescribed drugs, had negated any earlier mental programming, allowing him to not only be aware of his bizarre visitors, but to remember them afterwards.

Khoury recalled that when he violently resisted the "Nordic woman's" efforts to draw him to her breasts, she look surprised. As well, there seemed to be a telepathic communication to the "Asian woman" indicating that his reaction was wrong, that it wasn't supposed to happen that way. Was she surprised because Khoury had been previously "programmed" to respond correctly to the sexual stimuli but instead responded in fear and violence?

As with other abduction scenarios, there were similarities with Khoury's experience on July 23. The women seemingly were able to instantly appear and disappear from his bedroom. Also, there was obviously some missing time with this particular event, as Khoury was not able to recall how the two strands of hair ended up wrapped around his penis. This leads to another unanswered

SCREWED BY THE ALIENS

question...why were the strands of hair left behind in the first place?

A HIDDEN AGENDA

The UFO/Abduction phenomena have operated under the radar for possibly centuries, maybe even longer. Whatever the source of the phenomena, it has worked under the strictest of secrecy. As was mentioned earlier, there have been the occasional mistakes that have left suspicions of some sort of covert activity taking place. However, in regards to the hair samples left with Peter Khoury, they were not left behind by mistake. They were deliberately wrapped around his penis in such a way that they would cause pain and quickly draw attention. Considering the history of secrecy surrounding abductions and human/hybrid sexuality, this breach in protocol is indeed baffling.

The extremely bizarre nature and methods of the creatures involved with abductions suggests that traditional ideas about hybridization between humans and extraterrestrials are woefully inadequate. The events of July 23, 1992, show a shocking sophistication that goes far beyond the ideas and theories that have been entertained so far. One aspect of this sophistication comes from the discovery in the hair samples of the CCR5 deletion factor, which enables viral resistance to human sexually transmitted diseases such as HIV/AIDS, and possibly Smallpox. This mutation is relatively young, appearing possibly no more than 5,000 years ago.

The appearance in Khoury's hair samples may indicate that this particular mutation may be the result of bioengineering, and not natural evolution. This mutation could provide one reason that the "aliens" involved with human sexuality programs are able to interact physically with humans with impunity. This mutation may also be passed on to any descendants of these sexual interactions, thus producing hybrids that are more and more resilient to the potentially dangerous viruses that infect our species and ecosystem.

Throughout this article I have resisted the implication of "aliens/extraterrestrials" as the main player in the abduction mystery. I think that the idea of interplanetary visitors may be too simplistic to explain the mysteries surrounding UFOs and abductions. Considering that UFO occupants are often reported as humanoid in shape and behavior, it makes me think that unless the human shape is ubiquitous throughout the universe, the likelihood of an extraterrestrial race(s) looking almost exactly like us is extremely small. Yet, time and time again, we get sightings of humanoid UFO occupants. Why is this?

"Alien Hunter" Derrel Sims has suggested that we have never actually seen the extraterrestrial intelligence behind the UFO/abduction mystery. Instead, he says that the creatures that interact with eyewitnesses are biological constructions using earthly DNA so that they can safely operate on Earth. The so-called "Nordics," "Reptilians," "Insectoids," even the big-eyed greys, are bioengineered robots and not the true "Aliens."

SCREWED BY THE ALIENS

The humanoids encountered have similarities that are often reported across the board. They are often described as having larger than normal heads and eyes. In fact, the eyes are often said to wrap around the sides of the head. Their faces are seen as having high, prominent cheekbones and their chins are long and unnaturally pointed. Their skin color ranges from extremely light, almost white, to dark with an olive-tinged color. Again, it is odd that beings with very large eyes, high cheekbones and pointed chins seem to predominate with these occurrences. Why are these physical features so often reported and what is it about the strange shape of the head and eyes?

Again, there is no telling who or what is behind the UFO/abduction mystery. I cannot rule out time travelers or visitors from alternative realities because, whoever they are, they have an intimate knowledge of humans that seems to go beyond the traditional belief system of beings from other planets.

The suggestion made by some abduction researchers that an alien race is trying to save their species by integrating human DNA into their own gene pool to create hybrids sounds like the plot for a science fiction movie. Experiencers who claim to have met these human/extraterrestrial hybrids say that for the most part, the hybrids look more human than alien. If an extraterrestrial species is trying to save their gene pool with borrowed human DNA, I doubt that they would be happy with the results looking more human than their own species.

We cannot dismiss, though, the disturbing fact that this program, whatever its motives actually involve, has possibly been in operation for thousands of years. This kind of long-term methodology will continue to stymie us until the time that the operators finally decide to reveal themselves. The question that we have to ask is, do we really want to know what is going on, or are we better off living our lives in ignorance of a possibly soul-shattering reality?

SCREWED BY THE ALIENS

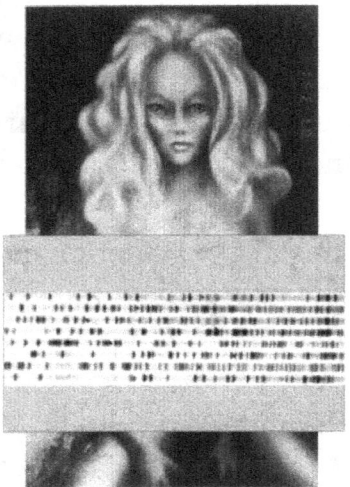

IS THIS A STRAND OF ALIEN HAIR?
Bill Chalker first published the results of the "alien hair" DNA results in the April, 1999, edition of "International UFO Reporter" (IUR), a quarterly magazine put out by the American UFO association, CUFOS.

One of Khoury's bedroom visitors was described as "Asian with high cheekbones and black eyes."

DNA tests confirmed the hair came from someone who was biologically close to normal human genetics, but of an unusual racial type - a rare Chinese Mongoloid type - one of the rarest human lineages known.

Peter Khoury and Bill Chalker look through the book "Hair of the Alien" which accounts Khoury's bizarre bedroom encounter.

SCREWED BY THE ALIENS

STRANGE ENCOUNTER WITH AN ALIEN FEMALE AND POSSIBLE DNA TRANSFER
By William Kern

William Kern is a retired career Navy enlisted man who has worked on countless books for Inner Light/Global Communications as a typesetter, layout artist and writer. In the following chapter, he talks about meeting a young alien female he may have been used to impregnate. Along the way, Kern offers some strikingly original theories about interbreeding among reptilians and humans and why the reptilian form is more useful in space travel. We've never seen the hard science involved expressed in exactly this way before.

******

It is a grand and terrible thing that the hero should be the only one to see his heroism from the inside, to see into its very vitals, and that everyone else sees it only from the outside, in its external features. It is for this reason that the hero lives alone in the midst of men and that his solitude serves him as comforting company.

— Unamuno

During a period when some men were claiming to have been visited by beings in nuts and bolts flying saucers filled with computers (IBMS? Macs? Linux? Cray?) and all sorts of furniture, including medical examination slabs and other devices and debris; when these same people were claiming to have traveled to Venus, Mars, Saturn and beyond with beautiful, scantily-clad, robust, voluptuous Caucasian blond females who looked like 1950s movie stars, and who spoke perfect English or Spanish or Italian or German or Russian (but never Reptilian); when women were claiming to have been abducted by aliens and raped, impregnated and abandoned by badly behaving alien males, (believe me, it could not happen) there came this formerly unreported encounter from a career military serviceman (the reason why it was not reported for almost 50 years).

SCREWED BY THE ALIENS

THE EVENT

In mid to late August 1968, I was standing the 2400 to 0800 security watch at a top secret intelligence facility in Southeast Asia during the Vietnam conflict. I had called the OD at 0600 to report all secure and decided to step outside to get a breath of fresh air, something I had never done before that night. The two story concrete building was behind me. To my right (south) was a range of low mountains obscuring approximately 20 degrees of the southern sky. To my left (north) was (a bay) and the South China Sea. I was facing east where, about 20 miles away, another range of mountains obscured approximately 5 degrees of the sky.

NOTE: I am reasonably certain about the date of the sighting because, as I recall, the USS Ajax, AR6, had departed for Japan two or three weeks earlier, around the last week of July or first week of August, 1968. . Ajax, having arrived near the end of June, had been in port to repair gun mounts aboard the USS Boston. The repairs, as I recall, took approximately seven to ten days. A former shipmate served in Ajax and he had invited me aboard for an hour or so.

I "felt" the presence of another object (like the touch of fingers on my neck) and turned toward the bay to see an identical object gliding at the same altitude, direction and speed as the first. The second object sighted made a sharp right turn; not a sweeping turn but a vectored immediate right angle deviation, glided overhead at an altitude calculated to be 1000 to 1500 feet, passed behind the first object and disappeared from view beyond the mountain.

A NOTE:

Speed, altitude, separation and sizes of aerial objects having no spatial references are extremely difficult to estimate and, so, are subject to great errors. The sizes, speeds, distances and altitudes related here are simply my first impressions and may be completely wrong.

CONTINUE:

The first object sighted continued eastward at approximately 10 to 15 miles per hour. Both objects were as bright as a 1,000 watt street light as seen from a distance of 200 feet. Neither object made any noise and neither object displayed any normal aircraft running lights. The objects were the size of a dime as seen at arm's length. I estimate their size to be 40 to 50 feet in diameter and spherical rather than elliptical in shape.

The first object was in sight for approximately 1 hour and 45 minutes. It did not deviate from its eastward course, nor did it pulsate or change colors. Its speed appeared to remain constant throughout the entire sighting.

I stood transfixed and was unaware that an hour and 45 minutes had passed until the morning crew began arriving for duty at approximately 07:45. At the sound of automobiles approaching from my right, I turned abruptly, astonished and frightened, and I rather felt myself explode violently downward into my body while

SCREWED BY THE ALIENS

experiencing a strong pressure against my eardrums, something like slamming the door of a Volkswagen with all the windows rolled up.

It seemed only a few minutes and now the sun was rising! At that time (7:45 A.M.) the east-bound object was a pinhead size bright light still visible on the face of the rising sun! Oddly, I found myself in a small field of grass and weeds where two roads diverged about fifty to sixty feet farther east from the building than where I thought I had been standing on the macadam carpark while I observed the TLOs. The field was a very poor vantage point from which to observe the east-bound TLO because it (the field) was laced with weeds and knee-high grass, and scrub trees at 5 to 6 feet or more. Some, at that time, were even taller, although not in the line of my sight of the object. I was disoriented and confused for a brief period until I realized where I was and what had transpired.

I calculate that the object was approximately 20 to 25 miles away at the time I returned to the building. Of course, it may have been much farther than that.

I signed over the duty log, relinquished my sidearm and went back outside. The object was still visible on the lower edge of the rising sun which was approximately 10 to 12 degrees above the horizon. But the spell was broken. After only moments of observing the tiny dot, I went to my car and drove to my quarters.

I later remembered that the duty crash cameras, a 4x5 Speed Graphic and a 16mm Cine Special camera, were inside on the floor beside my chair and I had not even thought to take a picture!

I had been in the Navy for 12 years, the entire time as a photographer, a portion of that time as an aircrew member. My MOS was Photographer but my job was processing and printing overflight surveillance and intelligence film from U2s, RA3Bs, RF101s, RF4s, and other (at that time) secret reconnaissance aircraft. I had been around aircraft, both civilian and military, for fourteen years. I learned to fly in an Aeronca Champ at an unpaved, uncontrolled field in southern Indiana when I was 16 years alive.

I cannot explain what I saw but I believe they were not fixed wing or rotary wing aircraft, not weather balloons (one turned, the other did not) and they were not celestial bodies or atmospheric phenomena. My original assessment, although the objects appeared to be identical, was that I had seen two different things, one perhaps a weather balloon, the other a slow flying aircraft of some kind. Neither, however, displayed the movements or identification lights one would expect for either object. I no longer consider this as a possibility.

Weather balloons, when blown by the wind (there was none that I recall) wobble and bob through the sky. Instrumentation packages or RAWIN Targets swing below them, causing them to change shape and direction. Additionally, weather balloons are not lighted from within nor do the instrumentation packages carry such bright lights.

SCREWED BY THE ALIENS

Helicopters can certainly fly at 10 to 15 miles per hour, however, none known at that time could fly silently at 1000 to 1500 feet and then to 10,000 feet or more. Neither of the TLOs emitted engine sounds or exhaust trails or displayed navigation lights.

Rotary wing and fixed wing aircraft, particularly military aircraft, have all sorts of lights on them which are on at night to alert personnel on the ground and other aircrews the direction the plane is going. There are colored lights, port wing tip red, starboard wing tip green, strobe lights, tail beacons and formation lights. While some aircraft may have a brilliant light similar to the TLO, it would be a landing light visible only from the front of the aircraft and used when taking off or landing at night. One would not see a "landing light" when an aircraft was flying away from the observer, and especially not after 20 or 30 miles.

When seen against the sun, even at a distance of approximately 25 to 30 miles, no hull shape or fuselage could be seen. The glowing orb seen against the sun appeared to have traveled in a straight line; that is, not following the curvature of the Earth. At last sighting, I estimate the altitude of the object to be 10,000 feet or higher above the ground.

Because of my background in photography and my experience as an aircrewman, I feel I objectively calculated the altitude, speed and size of the objects, however, as noted above, airborne objects having no spatial references are difficult to measure and, so, are subject to great errors.

The descriptions of the two TLOs do not fit any known aircraft or weather balloon. They do, however, perfectly define the objects known as Transient Luminous Objects, which have been shown to glide silently and slowly for long distances, change directions with apparently intelligent purpose and emit no sounds or exhaust trails.

TLOs do not display any overt signs of hostility or covert curiosity. None that I have observed, that is. They do not damage objects or affect the environment in any apparent manner. They simply appear, move about the skies for a time, then glide away or vanish, leaving stunned and confused witnesses to wonder what they have observed.

Unlike the objects known as UFOs, which seem to have destinations and purpose, and are solid and three-dimensional (or more), TLOs are truly unexplainable, having no observable substance or core, no common size or brightness, no common speed or direction. They may forever remain a mystery to those of us who have been fortunate (or unfortunate) enough to observe them.

CHANGED

This event changed me in ways I cannot easily explain. It has left me uneasy and suspicious; at times even fearful and anxious. I returned from Southeast Asia with an illness and dis-ease that no one would validate and the sighting of the

SCREWED BY THE ALIENS

TLOs was constantly at the back of my thoughts. I could not sleep in the house so I placed a thick piece of plywood across two sawhorses under a Mulberry tree in the back yard and slept outside with a loaded .30 caliber M1A-1 carbine fitted with a 30 round extended clip. I could not shake the dreadful feeling that someone was going to come for me and I didn't want to be trapped inside the house.

I feel certain my reaction to the event contributed significantly to my divorce from my first spouse a few years later. She just thought I was mad, of course (who can deny it?). Sadly, when others think you mad, they usually run away with the house, the car, the kids and the bank account. I harbor no ill feelings although I was homeless for nearly three years, living under a tool cover on the back of my old Chevy pickup truck.

ONLY THE LIGHT

When one is engaged in any activity, whether watching a boat race, a football game, children playing or when raking leaves from the yard, one is aware of many other concurrent events, such as aircraft and helicopters flying over, birds flitting from tree to tree, the smell of fireplace smoke, autos passing on the streets, cats and dogs, people talking and jogging by and many other things, including an awareness of one's self as a participant in the drama of life.

But while observing the two TLOs I had absolutely no awareness of myself as a living being. Moments after the second object vanished behind the mountains on my right, I became aware only of the remaining TLO. I do not recall seeing or thinking of the night, the trees, the building behind me, the ships in the bay, my abandoned duty post, heat, cold, wind, comfort or discomfort. I had neither awareness of myself nor the will to look away from the light.

There was only the brilliant globe. I was possessed by it. I was entranced and enraptured, so engrossed in the light was I. I simply could not tear my gaze from it and, indeed, did not even think of it. There was only the light. Only the light.

And it is this very loss of identity and awareness of self, my loss of will and singleminded fixation with the light that has troubled me for so many years. I simply did not exist in this time and space for nearly two hours. I do not recall having "gone" anywhere or encountered anyone or any thing. I do not recall being inside any vehicle and do not recall being questioned or examined or instructed.

I was simply entranced by the TLO. There was only me and only the light, the observance of which for nearly two hours had released me from all physical bonds of will and all memory of earthly existence. It was a sort of empty awake sleeping death. In my mind...as I recall it now...there was only the unwavering light that I was somehow compelled to watch.

But I am unable to explain how or why I wandered into the field although I feel there must be a wholly logical explanation for it.

I have been asked by several investigators if I believe I might have been ab-

SCREWED BY THE ALIENS

ducted, given that I experienced a period of "missing time." And I think not. I did not feel at the time that I had gone anywhere or encountered any beings during the sighting. I still think not today although I have experienced some rather odd "dreams," especially in the early years following the sighting, which I will recount anon.

AFTERMATH—THE DREAMS BEGIN
A STRANGE ENCOUNTER AND AN ANALYSIS OF THE "DREAM"

Last night while climbing up the stair
I met a man who wasn't there.
He wasn't there again today;
Oh, how I wish he'd go away!

The events that occurred in 1968 still haunt me in 2018 and I suspect I will never be able to forget what happened that night. I began to have strange dreams around 1970 or '71, when I was 34 or 35 years alive. I was working on the manned space program at the time. Occasionally—after I was enveloped in the "light," I would see a fleeting small figure just at the edge of my vision. I was always startled by the apparition but never frightened. But I could not see the figure when I looked directly toward it.

Then about 2015 I began to have frequent "dreams" of being led through an old abandoned farmhouse or warehouse. There were lots of people watching or following me as I made my way through the dusty rooms. It was not particularly dark but neither was it brightly lighted. There were stairways and endless hallways leading to room after room.

In one "dream" I was standing in one of the empty, softly lighted rooms when quite suddenly there appeared before me, only 10 feet away, a small, fragile being, not more than five feet tall. My first impression was that the being was a female. It had shoulder-length, russet-orange hair; not garishly orange but auburn, soft and tousled. It had a smooth, delicately sculpted face with pronounced female lips, naturally colored. They were not painted. It had a slightly protruding lower jaw, looking as if it were about to blow out a candle.

THE BEING

That's about the best I can describe it. Other than the russet-colored hair on its head, I saw no other body hair, not the slightest or thinnest. No eyebrows or lashes.

It had no breasts, and no nipples. It had no navel. There was no visible or apparent pubic mound. Its body was as featureless, physically, as a plastic doll. Its covering or skin or epidermis was smooth and free of blemishes. It was of uniform color—a pale amber-brown—and, except for slight shadows, did not vary in hue or tint from head to toe. The being did not have fingernails or toenails. Its

SCREWED BY THE ALIENS

limbs, unlike the others who were present, were firm and normal looking, humanlike rather than thin and long. If I had passed it in a public place, clothed and wearing sunglasses, I could not have known it was not human.

It did not look around the space; its gaze was fixed straight ahead. Until it walked away, it did not appear to look towards me at any time. And, yet, it seemed to be alive, a living being. Its eyes were all black—or extremely dark. There was no white in the eyes and no visible iris or pupils. It never blinked once during the entire time that I observed it. The eyes were the size of a human child's eyes, wide but not the excessively large, wraparound eyes that are so often reported with "grays." It did not move its appendages, although I could see that it was "breathing." It did not speak or swallow or wet its lips.

It was unclothed and I realized that I, too, was unclothed, although I can't remember how or why or when I had removed my clothing. Other beings in the space seemed to be there only to observe my reaction to this fragile, lovely, dainty creature. My reaction was one of wonder, astonishment, surprise, enchantment.

PHYSICAL CHARACTERISTICS

It had three fingers and an opposing thumb on its hands. The fingers were jointed similar to a human's fingers and they were tiny, childlike, and very feminine. There were webs between all its fingers up to the first joint from the palm, much like the web between the thumb and forefinger of a human hand, only more expansive. The webs were thin and nearly transparent. I could not see small details but I imagine it had no fingerprints as we know them.

It had four small, nearly equal length toes on its feet. It seems there might have been webs between the toes as well, but they were small and short and may not have been webbed. I don't recall having purposely looked at its feet.

I thought, briefly, that the being was an automaton or android but its later movements were too agile and flowing to be those of a machine unless it was a rather remarkable marvelous machine.

After brief minutes—no more than two or three as I recall— it quite suddenly turned and walked toward a portal that had appeared in the empty space behind it. It moved with the same fluid motion and purpose one would expect from a human female child of ten or eleven years, walking swiftly and silently, swinging its arms, and just before it reached the portal, it turned slightly to the right and peered over its shoulder to steal one last half-second glance at me. It was an exact motion, precise, natural, and normal. I think a machine could not or would not have done that; however, that thought might be completely incorrect.

ALONE AGAIN, NATURALLY

And then the portal closed, it was gone and I found myself alone in my house in darkness, standing beside my bed in my skivvies, wondering if I had dreamed it all or if I were going mad. My skivvies, I later discovered, were on backwards.

SCREWED BY THE ALIENS

(This is not wholly unusual. I have several times put my skivvies on not only backwards but inside-out beginning from the time I had a fatal reaction to morphine in 2013).

LOCATION

I want to describe the space where I encountered the being. It was opalescent white, misty, endless, boundless, empty. There was no furniture, no machines, no computers, no walls or doors, except for the sudden portal that appeared in the space behind it just before the being turned to walk away. But the portal was not a "door" in the sense that we know them. It may have always been there but not visible until it was to be used for the departure of the being. I will call it a "not there."

There was no deck or overhead, no bulkheads, no lights, although the space was softly lighted evenly throughout. The surface beneath my feet did not feel solid and I could faintly see through it—or imagined I could— to the soil or earth moving below. This effect caused some vertigo at first but it passed quickly. I was warm and comfortable. There were no noticeable sounds or noises or odors. There was no movement of air. I felt as if I were suspended in space so I could participate in their little game. It was peaceful. I felt no anxiety or fear. I could not see anything beyond ten or fifteen feet other than the pervading misty white emptiness that seemed to go on forever.

As for the being itself, it had, as I have said, a fine, fair, feminine face, full lips and mouth and a rather featureless, hairless body, save for the hair on its head. I later wondered if the hair might have been a wig or a mental image that might not have really been there. At the first impression it seemed real, authentic. Because the sides of the head were concealed by hair, I could not see if it had human ears.

WAS IT A HYBRID?

It had no visible reproductive or nurturing organs, but I only assume it was a female. The pudenda was smooth and curved inward without a visible cleft or opening, which leads me to think that the being, because it had a mouth, might have had as a reproductive organ and a method of disposing of body wastes, a cloaca—a vent—such as might be found in reptiles, birds, monotremes and some fishes here on earth. If so, it may deposit eggs like a bird or, more likely, a reptile.

Now, that is not to say that my assumption is correct no matter how compelling the evidence might be. Just because I could see no reproductive organs doesn't mean there were none.

In the first place I wasn't close enough to clearly see such details, which might have been less apparent than on a human. And, besides, I really hadn't a lot of time to closely examine it. I was more interested in its facial features and expressions (there were none) and any movements or gestures that would provide evidence that the being was alive rather than a machine or holographic projection.

SCREWED BY THE ALIENS

As far as I can determine I was observing a young, childlike female being, perhaps ten earth years old, who may have hatched from an egg and who may have been incubated in a nursery of some sort.

As a general rule creatures with cloaca do not bear live young (the Anaconda is one remarkable exception) and I cannot imagine that any of the other beings who attended the viewing would be content to sit on an egg until it hatched.

Except for reptiles, the eggs of surface dwellers— birds and monotremes in particular—are kept warm at nearly constant temperatures by creatures with feathers or fur and these beings had neither. That is to say nothing of the physical structure of the aliens' bodies which most certainly were not designed for sitting on an egg. But it was not a mammal in any sense of the word. It simply did not have the proper plumbing.

So...was this being male, female, neither or both? There were no obvious physical signs that the beings, including the observers, could participate in any kind of sexual activity with which earthlings are familiar. And yet...they had to have come from somewhere.

LIGHT YEARS

The age of the beings is completely impossible to determine. The being I observed appeared to be about ten earth years old. The others in attendance (who, incidentally, looked so much alike that they might have been clones or replicants) appeared to be about the same age. If they moved through space at or near the speed of light they could have been hundreds or even thousands of earth years old. If they were accomplished enough to manipulate time (and of that I had no doubt) they could have lived for eternity. It is the nature of time travel. One just goes back to the beginning and projects again.

Having proposed that I encountered a being such as I have described, two immediate questions arise: First: Did I actually encounter such a creature or was the entire episode nothing more than a screen image projected by the visitors (intruders) to deceive me? Second: What do they really want?

RECURRING EVENT

The dream of being led through a strange dwelling recurs in slightly different scenarios. There are always people I do not know and houses with wandering passageways and empty or sparsely furnished rooms. The people always touch me or lead me to different spaces. Always, in every dream, I am massaged or stroked by a being or beings I cannot clearly see. It is always behind me and I seem to be unable to turn so I can see who or what it is. During the time that I am being touched I am unable to control any movement of my own body.

In the dream—if that is what it is—this touching does not last very long. Although it is not the same, I can compare it to a cursory physical examination by a human doctor. Throat, neck, underarms, groin, wrist, fingers, knees, feeling for

SCREWED BY THE ALIENS

lumps and tender spots.

Not the same, but something like that. Again, are these screen memories or just parts of a disjointed, poorly remembered dream?

I have never awakened with cuts, bruises, scratches or scoop marks on any parts of my body that I can see.

BUT WHAT ARE "DREAMS?"

Dreams are not fantasies created by the mind from nothing; they are memories, even if they are recalled improperly and in pieces. The right side of the healthy human brain stores everything that has ever happened during its existence and it can recall every episode exactly as it occurred when necessary.

I don't know if the observation I have described was (or is) a dream or not, and I worry that I may never know the answers to my questions.

SO, WHOSE FACE IS THIS?

One thought is that the creatures who crew modern UFOs might not be from another planet, but might have been genetically cultured and incubated right here on earth in one of those secret underground laboratories, and not by aliens, but by human tinkerers. Suppose the future astronaut is not a warm-blooded mammal (human), but a coldblooded intelligent reptile (saurian) who can tolerate cosmic radiation better than humans and who have been shown to be able to survive mass extinctions with little change or effect in their subsequent behavior and evolution.

Suppose the saurian is not only a creature who lived before us, but is the creature, by genetic manipulation, some of us will one day become. Some reptiles, remember, have an uncanny ability to regenerate lost parts, often two or three parts. This would prove a real benefit for explorers on a planet several billion miles from home base where spare arms and legs are not readily available. Some reptiles can survive days, months or even years between meals while warm-blooded mammals can hardly exist more than a few hours!

Some reptiles appear to be unaffected by cosmic radiation that is killing human beings by the thousands. Some reptiles can hibernate for months and years in Arctic conditions without suffering adverse effects.

Perfect lifeform for the constant space traveler! Have the visitors learned to use the DNA of saurians not only to advantage but also to their detriment, having sacrificed their ability to easily reproduce in order to become proficient space/time voyagers?

THE CLOACAL KISS

Creatures with cloaca do not achieve penetration during mating; they usually merely touch cloaca, very briefly—referred to as the cloacal kiss. This touching stimulates the female to produce a fertilized egg, which it soon deposits. The fe-

SCREWED BY THE ALIENS

male then sits on the egg to incubate it or, in the case of some reptiles, buries it, until it hatches, at which time—particularly in the case of reptiles—the newborn may at once be an independent creature, eating and walking and sleeping or crawling, finding its own way and its own food and caring for itself without the need for any nurturing from the parent. Fowl, of course, must be cared for briefly.

An exception is the Volcano Bird, a large megapode found on the Island of Sulawesi. She digs a hole, deposits her egg, covers it with warm sandy volcanic soil and lets the volcano keep the bird inside alive until it hatches. It then digs out and is at once an independent creature, usually flying in a few hours.

Birds, fish and reptiles do not have teats with which to nurture their young. They do not have navels. They do not have the sex organs that are common to mammals. Female birds often will spontaneously deposit an egg when there are no males around to stimulate her. These eggs are often—and usually— simply abandoned. They are not fertilized and will, therefore, produce no offspring. Birds seem to know that.

But suppose, without my knowing or understanding it, the female was somehow stimulated to produce an egg because sperm was introduced to her cloaca during or prior to the very brief encounter.

I seem to remember only that she appeared very suddenly. What happened before she appeared? Other than some aimless wandering through a dark building, I have no memory of leaving my bed or of arriving at the place where the encounter occurred.

There was no apparent touching, no fondling or foreplay, no conversation, neither verbally nor telepathically. She appeared, stood immobile for two or three minutes and then turned to walk away.

If some kind of fertilization did not occur, the encounter just seems totally pointless, unless it was, as I contend, nothing more than a strange dream (most of which are often totally pointless).

But most hauntingly intriguing was that last glance over her shoulder as she exited the scene. She looked directly at me as near as I could observe, as if to say silently, "Now I have you in me. Thank you and goodbye." I was a rather cold glance; not warm or affectionate. I did not feel that at the moment; it was only later that the impression came to me.

Then, too, I first realized I was nude during the encounter and later partially clothed when I found myself back in my home standing beside my bed. What happened to my clothes before the encounter? I never found them.

And there was that sudden, mysterious portal that appeared in the air or space behind the being just before she turned to leave. I get the creepy feeling that it was a portal to another dimension or another time. I believe it opened and she stepped out and that is why she seemed to have appeared as if by magic. And

SCREWED BY THE ALIENS

when she stepped back into the portal she seemed to have simply vanished.

Was it a time portal or a doorway to a parallel universe? The concept is almost too deep for me to comprehend. The portal was not there. Then it was there. And then it was not there.

WHAT INCUBATES THE EGG?

Now suppose those hybrid creatures people claim to have seen floating in great bubbling vats in those secret underground facilities are not all human babies stolen from the wombs of impregnated human females, but are, in many cases, the nurturing containers for the alien eggs.

If the alien offspring could live inside an egg until it hatched, such incubators would not be necessary. But these are hybrids and the aliens apparently have no way of bringing them to term by themselves. If they have chosen to have their females fertilized by human males, they would need a way to keep the offspring alive until it was able to eat and breathe of its own volition. Hence: incubators.

So, do the aliens have more than one method of producing offspring? It seems unlikely and, indeed, impossible, that a "male" alien could impregnate a human female since they have no apparent sex organs. Even if we and they are biologically compatible, would it not require some kind of surgical extraction of the male alien sperm and artificial insemination?

I suspect that those exact procedures are also used to obtain human sperm for impregnating the alien females. There most certainly could not be physical sexual union between a human male and the alien female I encountered.

Perhaps some aliens are really taking human embryos and cooking them in their incubators to produce their own type of hybrid children.

It would make sense that they probably would not depend on a single method (which might often fail) to produce their future starship crews. Backup systems are always a good idea.

Hybrids cannot reproduce themselves; they need outside help—the tinkerers— to introduce all the ingredients into the mix that makes good soup.

WHERE ARE THE CHILDREN?

After 50 (or 5,000) years of abductions and forced fertilizations, one would think there might be tens of thousands of hybrid children on the loose somewhere out there. Where are they?

Do we see them as a matter of daily routine? Are they living among us, unseen, unnoticed? Or are they now living among the stars? What does a civilized species do with so many children? Are they forever young, eternal time fiddlers? Or have some of them grown old and feeble, facing the inevitable end common to all human beings? They do, some of them at least, after all, have human DNA.

Without parents, how do they learn all they should know in order to survive?

SCREWED BY THE ALIENS

Is their knowledge gleaned from telepathic sources? Or is it some kind of inherited genetic encoding?

We believe they are mortal, that they die or can be killed. So, do all hybrid children survive long enough to reach adulthood or do they have an unusually high mortality rate, necessitating the aliens' constant gardening and husbandry?

Perhaps these are perplexing questions best saved for later examination.

A REEXAMINATION OF THE EPISODE

After the passage of some time, during which I have had the opportunity to reexamine the strange encounter presented here, I have theorized that the "being" (if not purely a fantasy dream image) was probably clothed in a tight-fitting epidermal-like fabric of some sort which may have hidden any physical features such as breasts or pudenda. That would, however, create a distinct barrier to any sexual contact as we humans know and understand it.

And I will leave that conjecture unexplored further.

AND A WHISPERED CONVERSATION WITH A DOCTOR

I recently had an interesting conversation with a doctor concerning DNA and blood transfusions. I asked if a person receives a blood transfusion during major surgery, does the DNA of the donor get mixed with the DNA of the recipient?

Yes, she answered, definitely. Also the DNA of a bee from a sting, the DNA from a mosquito or an ant, or any other biting or stinging creature. The mixture of DNA is permanent. Donor DNA is not "absorbed" by the recipient's DNA; therefore, the recipient is thereafter forever two persons, or three, or four, depending on how many donors contributed to the patient. DNA is the stuff of life. DNA is the stuff of consciousness from which dreams and memories are produced!

And then I asked if the recipient could possibly experience the memories of the donor or donors. Could the strange, bizarre and unexplained dreams some people experience be those of another person whose blood now courses through the recipient's body?

Blood is living stuff. It passes through the entire body many times every hour of every day. It passes across the corpus callosum into the right and left temporal lobes where memories and dreams are produced, whether they are experienced as fantasies or total recall.

The doctor was intrigued (and a little unsettled) by the thought, and she admitted that she knew of no scientific investigations that might prove or disprove the theory, but she was inclined to believe that it was certainly possible for a transfusion recipient to begin experiencing the dreams or memories of a donor. Because donor identity is confidential, it would be extremely difficult, if not impossible to learn if the donor ever had an abduction experience or observed a UFO.

I did not mention abduction or UFOs because I did not want her to call the men

SCREWED BY THE ALIENS

in white coats to come and hustle me off to a padded cell.

My dreams or "memories" began in earnest after a recent major surgery. I felt at the time that I had awakened in a totally different universe. My wife says I have changed. I KNOW I have changed. I feel that I am a different person, neither completely alive nor completely dead, neither completely here nor completely there, neither completely me nor completely another.

For whatever reason, whether from the NDE or from the infusion of blood from an anonymous donor or donors, I am certain I am not the same person who went into the OR in 2015. I even mentioned the changes to the surgeon soon after my recovery but he had no response, which I thought a bit curious.

What do the aliens actually do to captive humans when they are strapped to examination tables? When abductees claim the aliens extract fluids and skin tissues, are they mistaken? Perhaps instead of taking samples, the aliens are actually pumping DNA into the abductee. That might explain the strange, bizarre and unexplained recurring dreams that begin shortly after the human is returned to Earth (or to their bed, as the case may be). Such DNA manipulation would certainly explain occasional rapid evolutionary progress in the human animal. It could also explain "junk DNA."

Someone might begin an investigation of these episodes and try to determine if my theory has any merit. It could be your next book or motion picture script.

William Kern, Briefly:
Served 20 years in U.S. Navy. Photojournalist with Great Lakes Bulletin; Documentary Motion Picture Cameraman. Participated in many NASA unmanned and manned space missions. Served 10 years in the intelligence community prior to and during and following the Vietnam conflict. He is currently the layout artist and ad designer for "Conspiracy Journal"," edited by Tim Beckley.

In the early 1960s he was assigned to VAP-62, a heavy reconnaissance photo air group at NAS Jacksonville, Florida. Flying RA3B's, this squadron, with others, was charged with the responsibility of obtaining intelligence photos of Soviet missile emplacements in Cuba, evidence of which led directly to the "Cuban Missile Crisis."

Prior to the Vietnam conflict, he was assigned to Defense Intelligence Agency in Arlington, Virginia. DIA is the military counterpart of CIA. Revelation of his duties while at these facilities is still classified.

During the height of the Vietnam conflict, he was assigned to the Fleet Intelligence Center, Pacific Facility, where over-flight intelligence information from SEATO was gathered and disseminated to friendly nations and to U. S. Intelligence Agencies. He received special training as a Courier and qualified with both the .38 Service Revolver and the .45 Model 1911 semi-automatic Service Pistol; and qualified with the .30 caliber M1A-1 Carbine. He was authorized to use deadly force to safeguard highly classified overflight materials which he transported for dissemination to Civilian and Military Intelligence Agencies of the United States, Australia, New Zealand, Canada and United Kingdom.

SCREWED BY THE ALIENS

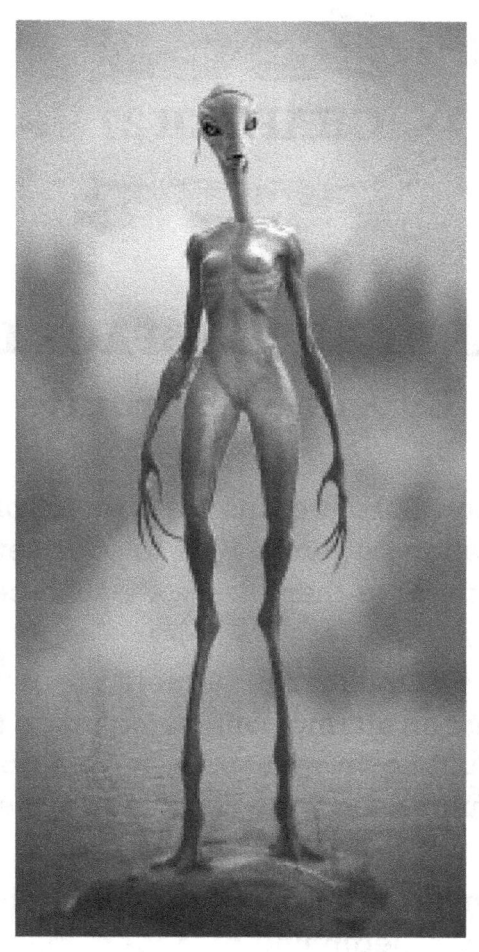

SECTION ELEVEN
EXAMINING THE PATTERNS AND SYMBOLS

**Chapter Twenty Seven: Planet Earth Space Lab
By Aileen Garoutte**

**Chapter Twenty Eight: The Symbolism of Alien Sex
and UFO-related Pregnancies
By Michael Grosso**

SCREWED BY THE ALIENS

CHAPTER 27

PLANET EARTH SPACE LAB!
By Aileen Garoutte

EDITOR'S NOTE: Aileen Garoutte was the director of the UFO Contact Center International, an organization begun in 1984 to offer services to those who were abducted by UFOs. At one time there were 64 such centers set up around the world.

Aileen was well aware of the many uniquely problematic aspects of the UFO phenomena, including that an attempt was being made to breed a special race of humans/aliens for some unknown reason. Is there a possibility this will happen more extensively in the future and we will see actual stellar babies being born?

****

The question of genetic manipulation has been with us for some time now, perhaps even from the beginning of modem man, if we choose to go back that far.

Previously in our group's newsletter, "The Missing Link," we wrote an article on genetic engineering, describing our research and the data we had accumulated. We inferred that "extra close" encounters regarding sexual contacts have been on the increase, or have we just noticed this because of the unique position we at UFOCCI find ourselves in? Information comes from everywhere. Through this information, a pattern gradually is beginning to emerge.

ANGELIC IMPREGNATION IN THE BIBLE

Some persons get very upset to think we might have been tampered with genetically. It could be that it has always been that way, and what we didn't know, didn't upset us. For example: in the Old Testament, Abraham's wife Sarah was approximately 92 years old and had never conceived. After a visitation by angels, she bore a child.

Elizabeth, cousin of Mary, was visited by an "angel" (which means "messenger") and had her "womb opened." She and Mary had similar experiences which left them both pregnant. Many examples are cited in the Bible of "angels" ma-

SCREWED BY THE ALIENS

nipulating women sexually. Why should it be shocking today? Why, because we haven't heard of it in this day and age.

In our files we have records of unusual babies that have been born. The following are but a few examples. Think about it with open minds. Man is not unique – there are varied life forms throughout the universe. Because we have not had open communication with the aliens that are contacting persons on a one-to-one basis, does not mean they aren't making regular visits to planet Earth from many different places. Because of the environment they have evolved in, they probably will not look like us, but then, some may!

THE SUPERBABY WITHOUT INTERNAL ORGANS

In an article entitled "Superbaby," a report from Nepal states that after many UFO sightings scientists have found a "Superbaby" they believe was fathered by a creature from outer space.

"The child, outwardly, is a perfectly normal human being – but any resemblance to a human ends right there," said Dr. Wah Singh, head of the expedition. Dr. Singh said X-ray studies show the child does not have human internal organs – other than a stomach-like tube terminating in another tube similar to human intestines.

"The youngster has no heart, kidneys, appendix, pancreas, lungs – nothing," he said.

"Instead there is a single mysterious organ about the size of a walnut in its chest. We conclude it is a combination of all the necessary organs and glands."

Dr. Singh, a noted lecturer at European universities, including the Berlin Institute of Research, said the Superbaby and its teenage mother were found living alone in a hut outside a mountain Villasssge.

"The young woman had been expelled from the Villasssge because she became pregnant out of wedlock," the scientist said. "She delivered the baby herself and supported herself and the child by begging."

The girl told Dr. Singh and his assistants of a nighttime visit by a beautiful, strange man.

"She said she became unconscious and has no memory of the sexual encounter."

Dr. Singh said the region in which the Superbaby was found is one of the busiest UFO areas in the world: "We were simply gathering information on these objects in the sky when we heard of the baby," he said. "Villasssgers spoke of a white baby, hardly six months old, who never cried, walked as easily as an adult and spoke a strange, unknown tongue," Dr. Singh said.

THE COUPLE WHO SHARED A DREAM

A couple in Princeton, British Columbia decided to drive to Penticton, British

SCREWED BY THE ALIENS

Columbia. A drive that normally takes one hour took three hours after driving steadily. Later under black light in their bedroom they noticed two spots over her ovaries and similar spots over his sex organs. Shortly thereafter they learned she was pregnant, although they had been using two kinds of contraceptives.

Several months later, at a friend's home, he mentioned some strange dreams that he had been having. She was very surprised that most of the dreams were very similar to what she had been having over the last few months. The substance of the dreams was that each was laying on a table undergoing a medical-type of examination. Each recalled being given some kind of a funny drink to avoid becoming ill. They both felt that the beings that were around them "spoke" to them inside their heads, and that the "voices" sounded metallic. The beings around them were tall, with pointed heads and metallic silver robes.

Nine months later they had a baby girl. The child appears normal, except that she is anemic and underweight. She should be about 24 pounds, and she weighs only 12 pounds.

Since then there have been two other cases in which people driving cars in the same area have had similar experiences. In one of these cases, the woman involved also became pregnant within a short time after the incident.

A BABY BORN "BETTER-THAN-NORMALLY" DEVELOPED

Another case in Longmont, Colorado, November, 1980, involved the birth of an extraordinary "space baby," according to a renowned university researcher.

The mind-boggling episode where an American husband and wife were taken aboard a UFO was reported by hypnotic regression. The most extraordinary result of the encounter was the birth of a better-than-normally developed baby to the couple after doctors had predicted that the infant would be a brain-damaged, sickly, undeveloped child.

On the day following the encounter, which neither Michael nor Mary remembered, Mary noticed a strange mark on her lower abdomen in the shape of a rectangle with a white line around the outside.

Two weeks later Mary was taken to the hospital where seven doctors fought to save her from streptococcal pneumonia. It was while she was there that she discovered that she was six weeks pregnant.

Doctors expected her to lose the baby and she delivered it two months prematurely. To the amazement of her doctors the child was born more developed than a normal, full-term baby and has since that time shown signs of high intelligence and physical precocity.

The encounter came in November 1980, when the couple was driving to their home in Longmont, Colorado late one night. They saw a strange light, heard a loud whooshing sound, and were mentally confused. After what seemed like seconds later, the light and sound disappeared, and they discovered that over an

SCREWED BY THE ALIENS

hour and ten minutes had passed. They had no memory of what happened to them during that time.

Under hypnotic regression, Michael revealed that:

· He and Mary were taken aboard a UFO, stripped naked, and subjected to some sort of examination.

· He felt a burning pain at the site of the deadly melanoma growths on his legs from which he expected to die and which have since miraculously begun to disappear.

· He communicated with an alien being who he described as "a nice guy," and expressed hostility to two others he called "creeps" who he said were emotionless robots. · His memory was "stolen," but later returned to him filled with astounding amounts of new knowledge that changed his life. They have since moved away.

BORN WITH A SONG IN HIS HEART

A newborn tot who talked and sang just hours after being born has stunned experts who have long believed such an event was impossible.

The phenomenal baby boy, now just three months old, has been shielded from public attention by his parents, for fear that he could become the target of exploitation or even kidnapping.

The boy was born last August. The doctor who delivered the child said that the birth was quite normal. He noticed nothing unusual about the infant. But just a few hours later, as a nurse was making her rounds of the maternity ward, an incredible occurrence took place. She reported that, as she passed the ward, she heard a voice speaking. It was too high to be an adult. She thought a small child might somehow have gotten in.

As she walked down the aisle of cribs, the talking continued. Then just as she passed the next to last bed, she clearly heard the word "mother." Thinking someone was trying to trick her, she looked under the cribs but found no one. Then she looked at the baby boy in the bed. He turned to her, smiled, and said "mother?" as though he were asking a question.

Shocked and frightened, the nurse fled the maternity ward and called for the doctor on duty. By the time they returned to the crib, the amazing infant had begun singing a simple Chinese folk song similar to "Baa Baa Black Sheep."

The doctor, scarcely able to believe his eyes or ears, called for a psychologist – an expert in the field of child development – and called the child's parents and tried to explain what had happened. The psychologist and the parents arrived at the hospital at about the same time.

Meanwhile, the young doctor took several pictures of the infant and the maternity ward to record the historic event under wraps.

SCREWED BY THE ALIENS

The psychologist, who admitted he was baffled by the child's ability to talk and sing, administered a battery of oral tests to find out how extensive a vocabulary the child had. It turned out the boy had the word knowledge of a normal seven-year-old – but unlike a child of that age, the baby was not able to read.

Shortly after the test, which lasted most of the day, the parents were advised to remove the child from the hospital and care for him, with nurses, at home. They wanted to protect the baby from the furor that would certainly result if word got out of a talking, singing, newborn. The parents took the child and left the hospital. Currently, their whereabouts are known only to the psychologist and one of the pediatricians who attended the test sessions.

The above events present our case well. Think about it and do some studies on your own. Perhaps you will have a new insight concerning where we all originated from.

Have aliens been tampering with the DNA makeup of humankind since the beginning of life on Earth? Abduction researcher Aileen Garoutte feels strongly about such issues.

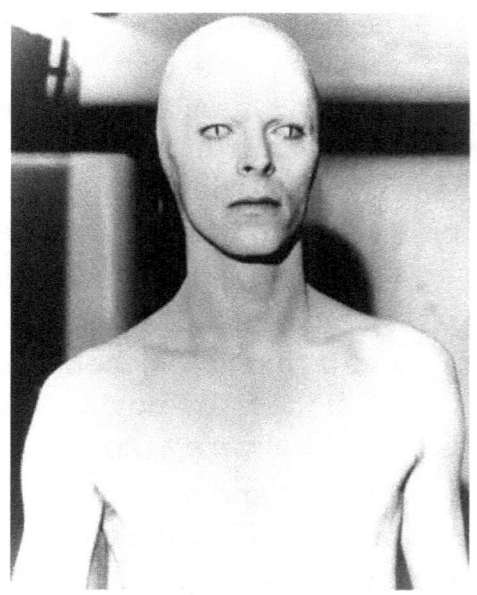

Is an attempt being made to breed a special race of human aliens for some unknown purpose? Is it possible we may appear more like "them" than like "us" a hundred years from now? (David Bowie – "The Man Who Fell To Earth").

SCREWED BY THE ALIENS

Throughout Biblical texts, angels would appear to Earth women and later they would be "with child" without having been impregnated by a human male. Many female abductees are reporting similar experiences today, after being taken onboard alien spacecraft.

Is it possible that the space people visiting here since ancient times have also helped create such beings as Bigfoot in some sort of genetic experiment?

SCREWED BY THE ALIENS

CHAPTER 28

THE SYMBOLISM OF ALIEN SEX AND UFO-RELATED PREGNANCIES
By Michael Grosso, Ph.D.

ABOUT THE AUTHOR:

Michael Grosso, Ph.D., is an independent scholar and part of an ever-growing group of scholars and thinkers critical of the prevailing materialistic view of the world. He has taught humanities and philosophy at Marymount Manhattan College, City University of New York, and City University of New Jersey. "The Man Who Could Fly: St. Joseph of Copertino and the Mystery of Levitation" is his sixth book.

EDITOR'S NOTE:

What is the strange symbolism to be found behind the sudden increase in UFO abductions and the phenomena of "alien" sex and mysterious pregnancies among female UFO witnesses? In this work we have presented many startling cases and fascinating studies of this intriguing – very complex – enigma. Is there more to the claims of those who profess to have been taken inside UFOs and examined at the hands of aliens? Michael Grosso is an established researcher who several years ago had a transformational experience of his own which involved the sighting of several craft over a church in New York City. You can hear him discuss this mind-altering episode on our YouTube channel "Mr. UFO's Secret Files" by searching for "Dirty Ghost Box and the Flying Saint" on our channel.

****

The UFO mystery has taken a sharp turn lately. Suddenly, at least in the United States, UFO abductions have come into prominence. Thomas Bullard ("On Stolen Time") has done a careful comparative study of over 300 claimed UFO abductions; he concludes from his study that the stories, taken en masse, are internally consistent. Bullard cites eight common stages to the abduction experience: capture, examination, conference, tour, otherworldly journey, theophany, return, af-

SCREWED BY THE ALIENS

termath. This is an idealized pattern, but enough data supports a definite structure and sequence to the experience.

But the basic mystery remains. Knowing the experience has a structure doesn't tell us what is causing the structure. Near-death-experiences show a coherent structure; but this by itself is proof of nothing. For instance, it doesn't prove life after death. It may only prove that the human mind has been programmed to produce certain kinds of images in life-threatening situations. How to interpret the images is another question.

One theory of abduction experiences is the most obvious to abductees, and the most shocking and alarming. This is the extraterrestrial theory. According to Budd Hopkins, large numbers of human beings are being abducted for alien purposes.

The aliens are either extracting genetic material from us to solve a problem in their species' pathology or breeding a hybrid species, mixing human and alien gene pools.

At this point, there isn't enough evidence to decide on the ET theory. It may be we are under siege from aliens; it may be we have been for a long time and not known it. New and more compelling facts may force us to accept this frightening possibility.

However, in the meantime, we should feel free to explore other theories. Too much is at stake to get locked prematurely into any one hypothesis. For one thing, there is the danger of investigator bias; the investigator tends to notice only data that confirm his hypothesis. It is very easy to do this in UFO studies. Exploring alternate hypotheses can help us to look at the data in fresh ways. In the case of UFO data, which are so complex, paradoxical, and often contradictory, this needs to be done.

So right now I want to focus on the symbolic nature of abduction stories. While not ruling out a face-value interpretation, I do find it hard to believe that a technical civilization with the ability to negotiate interplanetary expedition should not have the ability to solve its own genetic problems. It seems highly likely that a civilization's biomedical technology would be on a par with its space-travelling technology. If the latter is very advanced, so would the former.

In any case, it is revealing to look at the abduction stories as symbolic. Now, of the eight motifs make up these stories, the one most likely to give us clues to the purpose of the abduction is what Bullard calls the Examination. Abductees report being scanned by mechanical eyes; specimens of their blood, skin, tears, gastric and spinal fluids are taken. The abductors focus on neurological matters, in 13 recorded cases removing or inserting tiny objects in the brain. (As far as I know, there is no hard medical evidence for this.)

On the symbolic level, nevertheless, these brain insertions are intriguing; they

SCREWED BY THE ALIENS

remind one of shamanic initiations where candidates have rock crystals stuck in their heads by otherworldly beings. This is part of the shaman's dismemberment whereby he becomes a man of power. Transpersonal psychologist Ken Ring likens the UFO encounter to an initiation experience. Is the abduction experience an initiation? But into what? And who or what is doing the initiation?

What now of the reproductive motifs that unmistakably crop up during the Examination? Examinations include pregnancy tests, extraction of sperm samples, groin probes, observations on hysterectomies and vasectomies, and sometimes actual sexual intercourse with aliens. One woman was allegedly cured of barrenness. (Odd, in light of the aliens' problems with their own fertility.) Budd Hopkins reports cases of alien impregnation and theft of hybrid fetuses. Clearly, the aliens are concerned with our reproductive facilities.

The question is why? Hopkins, in an interview in "UFO Magazine" (see UFO: 3.2, p. 17), says:

"We don't ultimately know if a hybrid species is being produced, although I think the evidence for that is incontrovertible." However, Hopkins asserts, it's not just our genetic material they need; they also need our psychic and emotional "richness." So, we're also being psychically and emotionally raped by the aliens. The abduction experience is curiously holistic.

The aliens themselves confess their infertility, that their planet is dying or the victim of some cosmic disaster. The images of the otherworld they supposedly come from evoke themes of barrenness, dimness, ruin and devastation. "The beings themselves," Bullard sums up, "have gray, unhealthy skin and large eyes indicative of life in a dimly lighted (underground) environment." The denizens of this otherworld look like they might all be emigres from

Plato's Cave! – that classic symbol of enslaved, unenlightened humanity.

Let us assume the abduction experience is an extraordinary type of dream. The coherence of the experience shows it's not a private but a collective dream. A dream, perhaps, of the species mind. Produced by the species mind, like any dream, it is about the dreamer. Perhaps about the dreamer's future.

What we need here is to practice a little planetary depth psychology. One point to start with is timing. UFO abductions begin in the late sixties with the classic Betty and Barney Hill story. They come to a focus in the 1980s. Why now, at the end of the second millennium? Millennial thinking is quite strong in other quarters, and Christian fundamentalists yearn for the Second Coming and for the Rapture. In I Thessalonians, Paul writes: "Then we which are alive and remain shall be caught up together with them in the clouds, to meet the Lord in the air."

Significant portions of the American populace, brooding or at least vaguely worried about the coming of Armageddon, nourish, somewhere in their minds, the vision, the hope, possibly the expectation of divine abduction. This fact needs

SCREWED BY THE ALIENS

at least to be noted in any attempt to assess the condition of the collective mind nowadays, especially the American mind. (Most abductions seem to be taking place in America.)

Another timing factor: the late eighties is uneasy about sexuality. First, the AIDS epidemic, which, psychically speaking, forces us to associate the fear of death, barrenness, cancer, etc. with sex. Second, public attention is on child abuse as never before; images of perverted sex are daily pumped into the collective consciousness. Finally, bioengineering is sending new and strange signals to the collective mind; the idea that science can manipulate the gene pool of living species is brand new to us. Activists like Jeremy Rifkin are warning that such biological experiments contain many unforeseen dangers.

The model of natural sex – never an easy thing to keep in focus – seems totally out of whack. Images of erotic monstrosity constantly flash on TV into collective consciousness. The other day I watched a medical report about a man who injected cocaine into his genitals; as a result of this rash experiment, the man suffered for three days with priapism, which led to gangrene. His legs and a finger had to be amputated and, finally, his penis fell off.

The collective psyche, daily bombarded with such dismaying images, is being primed to have assorted sex-related nightmares. The aliens – sick, gray-skinned, vampirish – it's easy to see them as psychic projections of ourselves. In other words, we have become alien to ourselves. The abduction scenarios, viewed this way, could mean a lot of different things. (Dreams have multiple meanings.)

For instance, the cold and calculating way the humanoids deal with us is a mirror image of the cold and calculating way we exploit nature and each other. The dim, wasted otherworld well symbolizes our own wasting environment, polluted by de-immunizing toxins, threatened by deforestation, the hazards of a punctured ozone layer, the menace of atomic radiation, and so forth.

Read the abduction experience a symbolic conversation with the species mind, and several messages come across. That we are being examined – against our will – seems like a forceful reminder that we who are making nature sick are pretty sick ourselves.

What of the main idea that the aliens are here to produce a hybrid species? Taken literally, the reason perhaps is to revitalize their ailing stock. Taken symbolically, the idea of hybrids would be about our need to be revitalized; the need to enhance our gene pool. It certainly makes sense to say that we need to embark on evolutionary experiments, to mutate ourselves. In other words, if we interpret the symbolism of the abduction experience as a strange kind of species dream, the message is that our world, symbolized by the otherworld, is a dying wasteland and that we have to evolve into a higher (and hence more adaptable) species.

SCREWED BY THE ALIENS

Once we look at abductions symbolically, they fall more readily into place with contactee experiences. The contactee experience, which came into prominence in the '50s and '60s, is also about the threat of doomsday and the need to regenerate the human species. The difference lies in the way we decode the message. In the contactee scenario, the Space Brothers are idealized projections of the higher species we need to become (tall, blond, long-haired, white-robed). In the abduction scenario, the gray, sickly diminutive humanoids are symbolic projections of what we are – needy, ruthless, etc. The same meanings are coded, but in different ways for different purposes. According to Jung, all archetypes (symbols of the collective unconscious) are bipolar; they have high/low, bright/dark sides. Gray dwarves complement tall luminous beings; the former want something from us; the latter have come to help us. The core wasteland motif, and need for regeneration, stays constant.

In fact, a strict separation of contact and abduction reports is hard to sustain. The Andreasson affair, one of the best documented abduction stories, is loaded with contactee (spiritual transformation) elements. Many of the classic '50s contact stories contain typical abduction items. Orfeo Angelucci found mysterious burn marks on his body, experienced missing time (a week), and underwent a sexual (albeit sublimated) episode with a female ET. In 1951, a Frenchman, Pierre Mormet, was taken on board a spaceship, examined, and operated on to "regenerate" him – the symbolism neatly bridging contact and abduction stories. In the shift from contact to abduction stories what's changed is the tone: from lofty and benign to sinister and cruel. Instead of visionary dreams, designed gently to draw us upward to the Light, we are exposed to jolting nightmares, designed, perhaps, to manhandle us to change. The shift might only reflect worsening, more desperate, circumstances.

Again, I want to stress, we can't be certain about any theory of UFOs. But abduction stories offer rich material for a symbolic approach. Of course, this approach raises lots of tough questions. First, who or what is producing the symbols and why? And second, what about the physical or physiological affects?

The "why" question seems easiest to answer, on the ET or the symbol theory. Whether it's us or aliens, sickness is the problem and healing the goal. Suppose it is the aliens. This fact would be of monumental importance for the human race. It would mean that humans are part of an extraterrestrial gene pool, and that we're part of an experiment in interplanetary biology; even if we are being victimized by a ruthless alien species, we can accept the challenge to neutralize their danger and then to learn from them. For all we know, the hybrid species the aliens may be trying to produce may not only be useful to the aliens but also to ourselves. Looked at in this light, the alien and symbolic theories could turn out to be complementary. In any case, the "why" seems clear: this cosmic coitus is about regeneration, survival, evolution.

SCREWED BY THE ALIENS

But who or what is projecting the symbols? Several possibilities come to mind. In the order of the least fantastic: they could be coming from our own species mind. (In my book, "The Final Choice," I call it "Mind at Large.") I believe it is possible to make a good scientific hypothesis for the existence of such an entity. The species mind, built up over millennia of human history from the telepathic linkage of individual minds, would be the psychic reservoir of ghosts, gods, goddesses, elves, fairies, angels, archetypes and innumerable psychoid entities known to us from experience.

A second possibility is that they emanate from some super-technical, extraterrestrial civilization. It is possible that a highly advanced civilization is sending out signals of transformation – modulated by some psychotronic system – and picked up on a quasi-random basis by receptive beings. It may be a cosmic routine that a civilization goes through a cycle where it mutates

beyond its self-destructive technical phase – or perishes. There may be a set of standard signals of transformation that become available to the endangered species at a critical time.

This total system – the species mind – thinks, but not quite like an individual person. This is the hard part for us. Its concerns, its interests, its goals are transpersonal. It deals with the adventures of the species. And the system is highly unstable nowadays because the species is going through wild times. The threat of extinction hangs over it as never before. Since long-range survival of the whole is at stake, it's no surprise that individuals get hurt, become psychically inflated, and dark powers are released.

At the moment I incline to the less fantastic theory of a species mind, but I wouldn't rule out the possibility that our species mind is telepathically linked with a larger system of Mind at Large – intergalactic or even "interdimensional" (whatever that might mean).

But how could the symbol theory explain the physical effects in abduction stories? The answer is it would have to belong to a larger parapsychological theory. If UFOs are symbols of transformation, they have to be understood as part of a whole system of unknown creative energies. In other words, the physical side of UFOs is what forces us to build a radically new paradigm. In my view, UFOs are part of a family of anomalies that, taken together, point to a system of transformation. I believe that this system, the creative aspect of the species mind, can change the structure of reality.

UFO craft that temporarily appear on radar, modify soil chemistry, produce photographable or video-tapable photons, interfere with electromagnetic function, produce physiological changes, (harmful and helpful), produce psychological, psychic, and conceptual changes (also harmful and helpful) are real, but only part of the workings of a total system of transformation.

SCREWED BY THE ALIENS

This, in my opinion, is the ultimate challenge of UFOs. They force us to look for the total system of evolutionary energies, for the connections among the whole family of anomalies – ghosts, UFOs, levitation, apports, Virgin apparitions, poltergeists, psychic healing, demonic possession, materializations, and so on. Part of this challenge is to set up a creative dialogue between ourselves and the species mind. In the past, it was done haphazardly by magic and religion.

Of course, the individual mind is mystified by the logic of the species mind. It's a problem of communication, and it's obvious that straight rationalism, trapped in the premises of mainline materialism, is not very helpful here. We need a figurative language for this kind of communication. One way of talking with the species mind is to try to crack its symbolic thought processes. The point to remember about symbols of the species mind is that they can transform physical reality. Once we grant that, we have a big clue to the UFO mystery.

SUGGESTED READING:

THE MAN WHO COULD FLY

EXPERIENCING THE NEW WORLD NOW

THE MILLENNIUM MYTH: LOVE AND DEATH AT THE END OF TIME

SOUL MAKING

FRONTIERS OF THE SOUL

consciousnessunbound.blogspot.com/

Michael Grosso contemplates the New Age of consciousness raising.

SCREWED BY THE ALIENS

Far from monstrosities, the creation of Indigo Children has been spoken about as being the hybrid results of relationships between the Ultra-terrestrials and humans.

< Early 1950s contactee Orfeo Angelucci claimed he met a beautiful spacewoman during a midnight encounter in the desert.

Though he never went into detail, Angelucci alluded to having had an ongoing relationship with the beautiful space captain. Aura Raynes' likeness has been captured by artist Carol Ann Rodriguez. >

The late Budd Hopkins (right) was an early pioneer in alien abduction research who often likened the involuntary aspects of the experience to rape. Hopkins was also among the first to popularize the idea that the sexual machinations of the experience were part of an alien hybrid breeding program. Hopkins is seen here with journalist and author Sean Casteel at a California MUFON meeting sometime in the mid-1990s.

SCREWED BY THE ALIENS

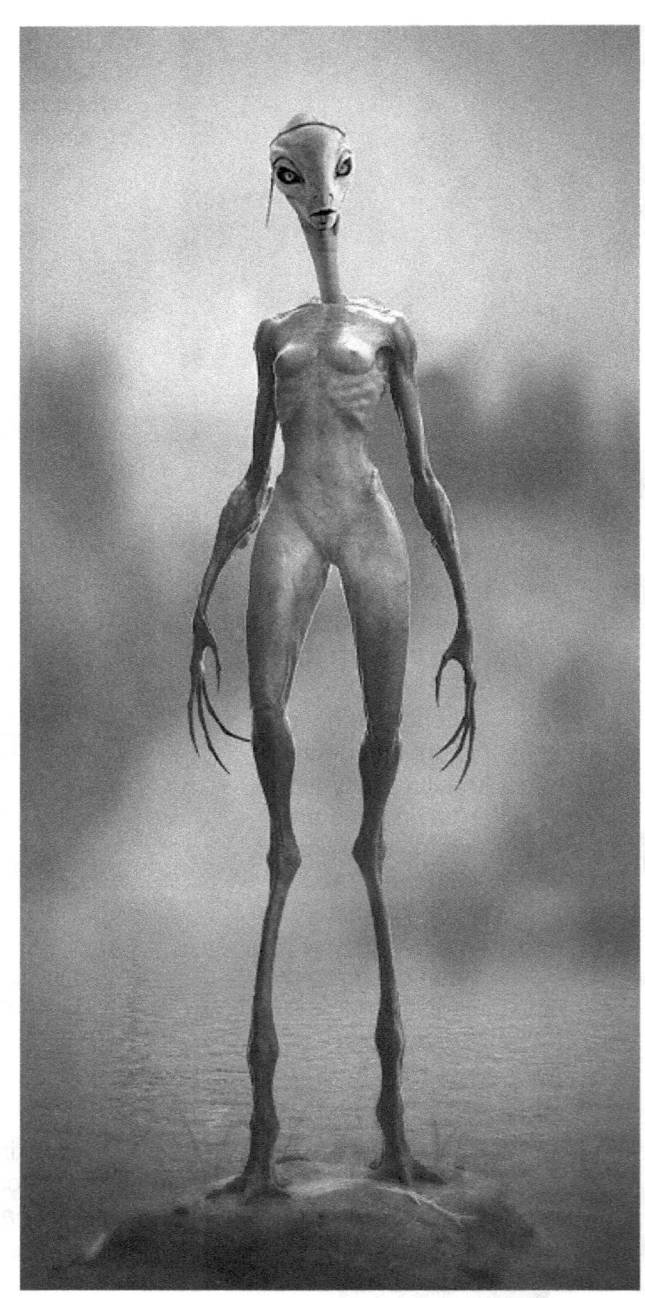

CONCLUDING WORDS
By Barbara Bartholic

SCREWED BY THE ALIENS

A REMEDY FOR PREVENTING THE FUTURE ALIEN SEX "TRAFFICKING" AND MOLESTATION OF HUMANS
By Barbara Bartholic

Quotes from: "The Story of a UFO Investigator" by Barbara Bartholic, as told to Peggy Fielding.

Barbara says:

"There is a distinct possibility that they created us for their own self-serving agenda. They could be our creators, and we could be their resource, you know, but must we be their puppets? It's time we become powerful, strong human beings in our own right, rather than pawns in the hands of the intruders. We can each take charge of our own lives when we resist the temptation to cooperate with those UFO creatures who seem to love the darker side of our civilization. We can waken to the facts and quit feeding them what they long for. Begin now to turn off any negative frequencies or activities or fantasies, which you know will bring negativity into your life. Concentrate on nature, gardens, plants, flowers and herbs, which you can plant or which you can simply enjoy as the creation of someone else. Participate in activities that bring you joy. Soften your voice and lower your tone. Stand ready to do good and heroic deeds for other people, even for unknown persons, no matter how small or how large the deed may be. Stand ready to do good and heroic deeds for yourself. Treat yourself well in ways that uplift your spirits. Clean, groom and protect your body from harmful contacts. Do the same for all living beings under your roof, including your animals. Teach your children to display kindness toward all other living beings."

Specifically, Barbara recommends the following remedies (see her book for further details and preventative practices):

"Eliminate activities that destroy and degrade. Fighting, cursing, violence, drug use, racial hatred and molestation of others, rape or cruel sex of any kind, abuse of any kind... all are meat and drink to the watching aliens. If mother and father fight while the children watch, that fight is opium to the aliens who are privy

SCREWED BY THE ALIENS

to the destruction. All pain and cruelty is a euphoric drug to these beings. They live on our anger and fright and pain. A battle in Bosnia or Iraq or anywhere at all is delectable to the aliens. They must have our darker energies to function. Sexual pain, war, brutality, hatred, fear and anger are all craved food for the intruders."

exopoliticshongkong.com/uploads/Barbara.pdf

Barbara Bartholic

SCREWED BY THE ALIENS

THOSE SALACIOUS ALIENS
Pulp Magazine Covers
From The Collection Of Nomar Slevik

Even before Playboy there were pin-up magazines. But they were nothing like the men's magazines that flooded the newsstands in the Fifties, Sixties and onward. Sex has always sold (or at least we are told). And obviously the publishers of pulp science fiction magazines realized this early on and almost always depicted nearly naked, hot earth babes being harassed – and far worse – by aliens – of one sort of another – on their priced-at-a-quarter magazine covers.

Some of the stories inside the pulps were truly bizarre. Some were good. Some were horribly written. But in some cases you could never find in the magazine anything remotely related to the cover. Or maybe the cover was done first and a writer getting paid a penny a word by Ray Palmer would come up with a story that would closely approximate the plight of our damsel in distress. Maybe the artist of this period knew something about these alien combatants that has only

SCREWED BY THE ALIENS

come to the forefront in more recent times.

Writer and musician Nomar Slevik possesses a collection of "salacious alien" covers, as I like to call them, and agreed to share them with us. "I have been fascinated by all things paranormal since early childhood, beginning with a UFO encounter I had at 4 years old. I am now 40 and my life's passion has been to research, investigate and write about UFOs and alien encounters from everyday people and to share those stories with as wide an audience as possible. The reason for this is three-fold: I want to share the older stories with today's readers and keep them alive for years to come, and to archive the new stories whenever they become available." Nomar is the author of "UFOs Over Maine" and "Other Worldly Encounters," and contributed a chapter to "UFO Hostilities – And The Evil Alien Agenda."

SCREWED BY THE ALIENS

SCREWED BY THE ALIENS

SCREWED BY THE ALIENS

SCREWED BY THE ALIENS

SCREWED BY THE ALIENS

SCREWED BY THE ALIENS

SCREWED BY THE ALIENS

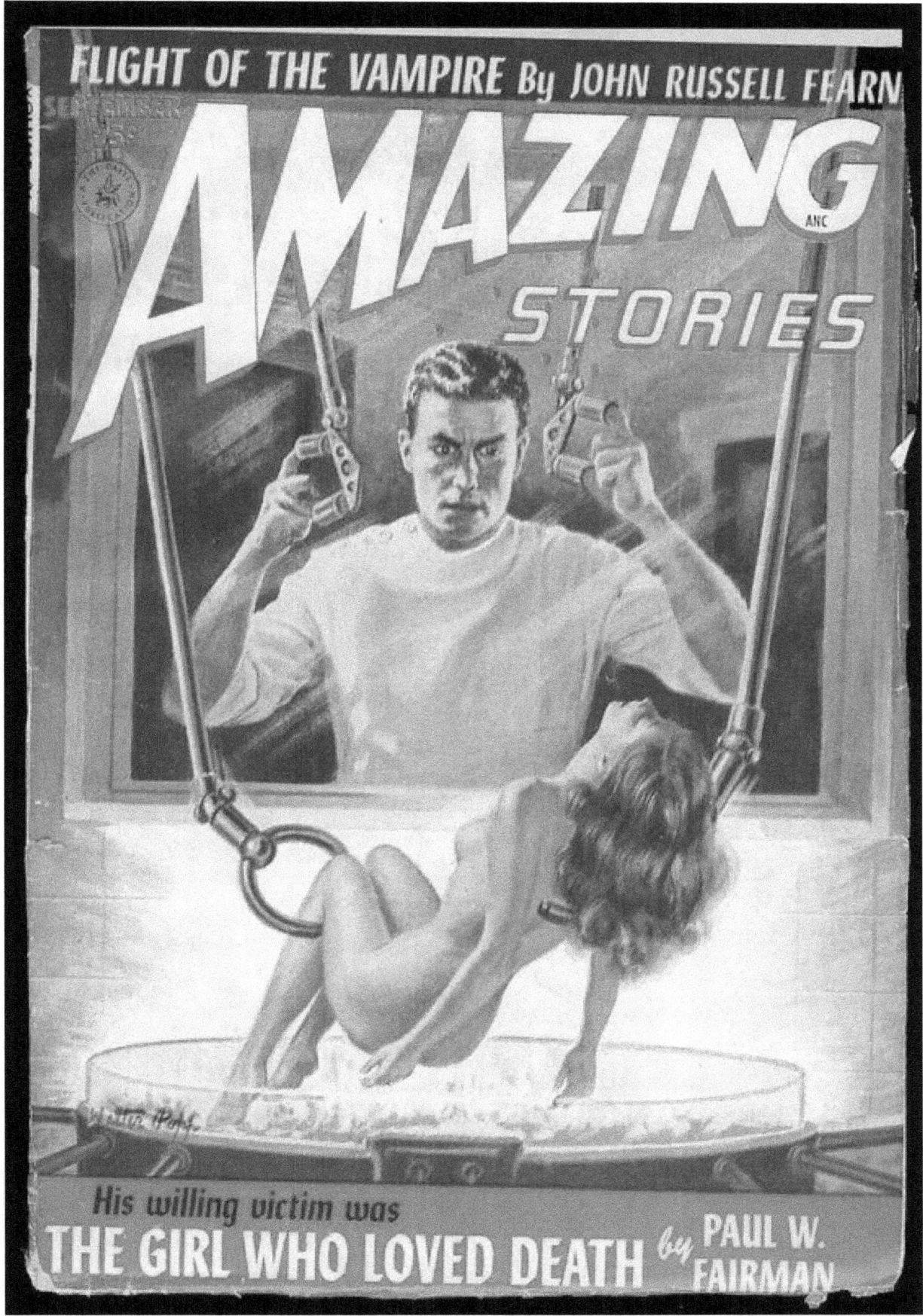

SCREWED BY THE ALIENS

SCREWED BY THE ALIENS

SCREWED BY THE ALIENS

SCREWED BY THE ALIENS

SCREWED BY THE ALIENS

SCREWED BY THE ALIENS

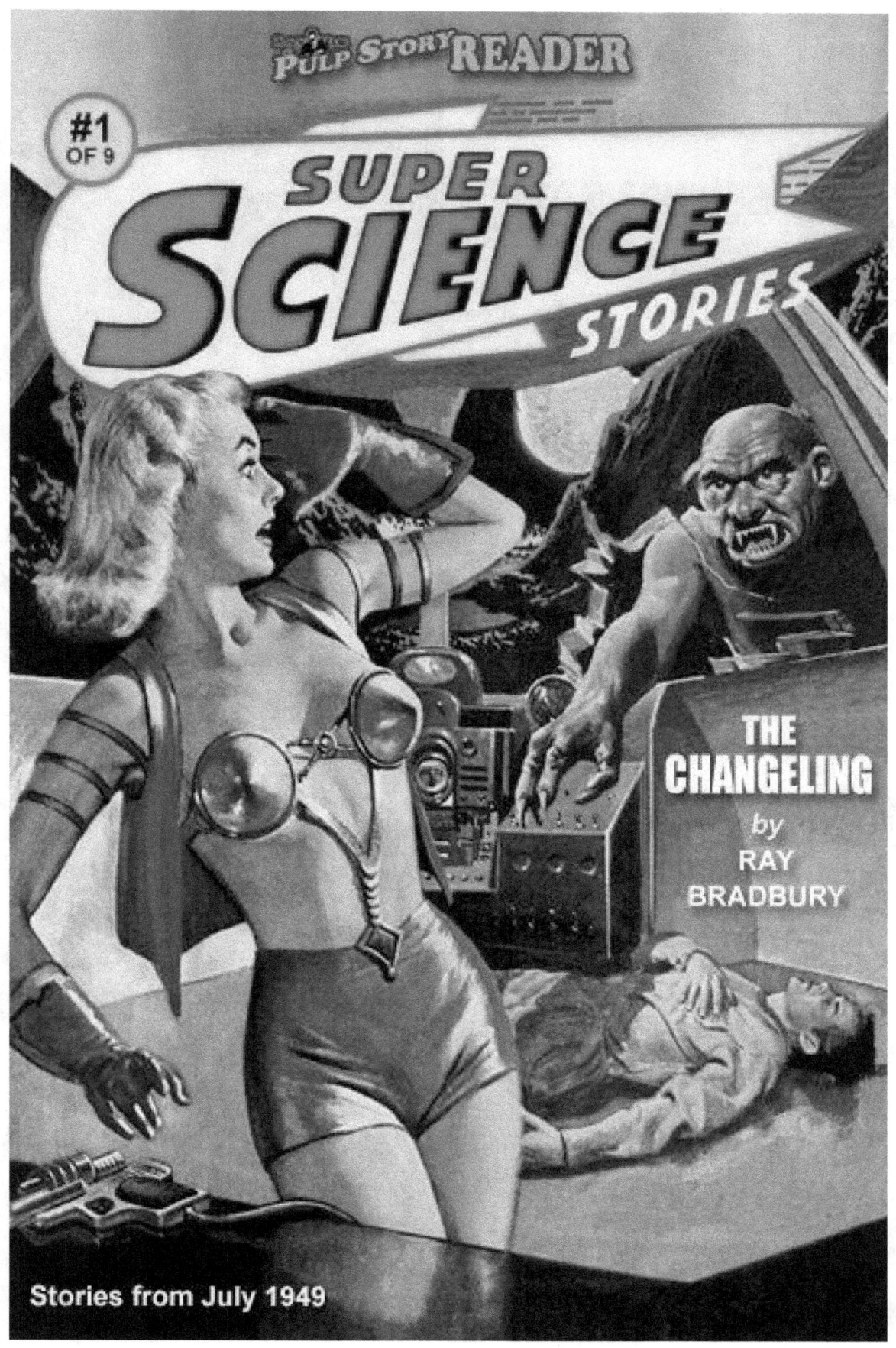

SCREWED BY THE ALIENS

310

SCREWED BY THE ALIENS

SCREWED BY THE ALIENS

SCREWED BY THE ALIENS

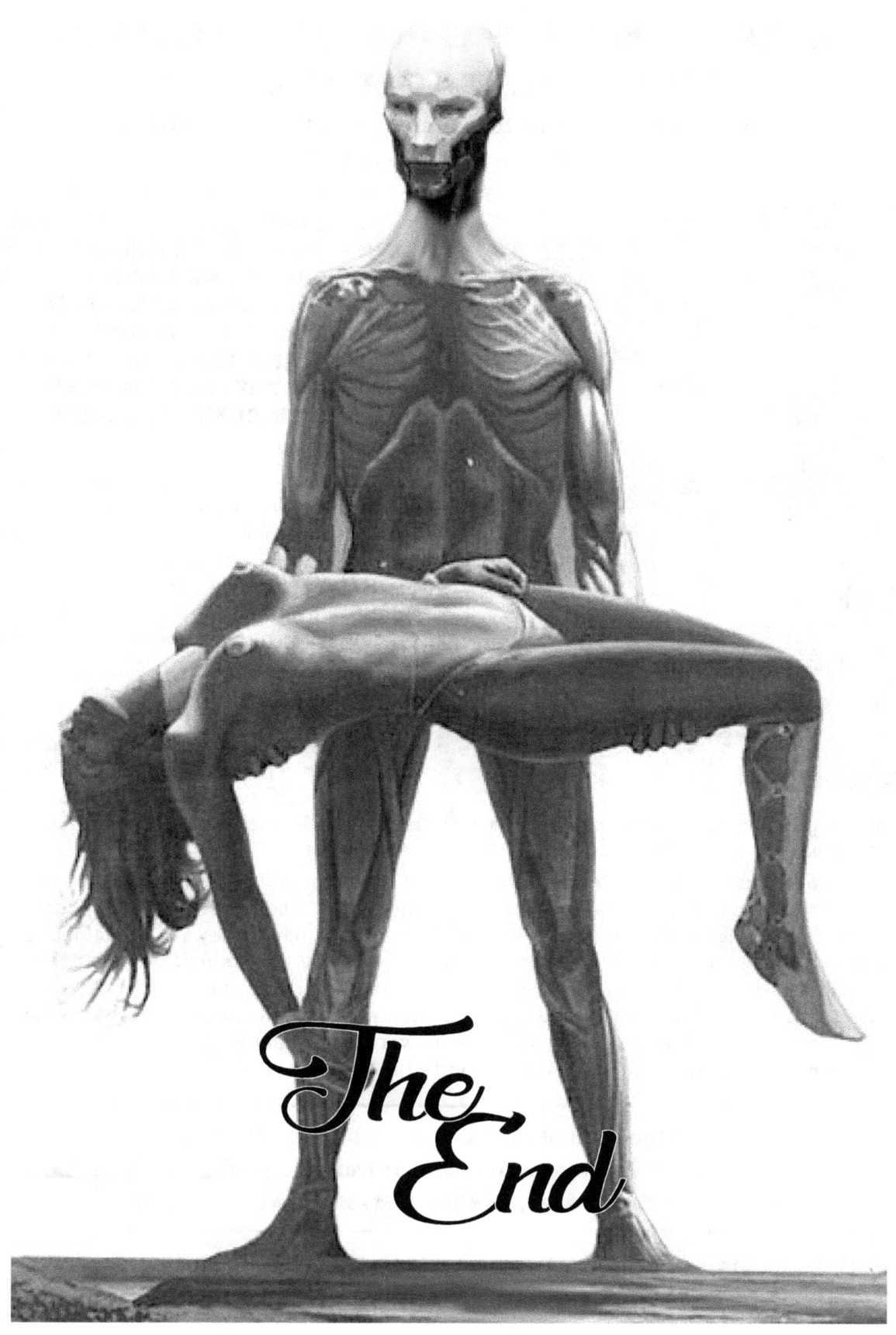

ADVERTISEMENTS

CRAVE MORE UFO HOSTILITY? UFOS ATTACK EARTH

From The Wondrous Research Of HAROLD T. WILKINS

Edited by Sean Casteel

HERE ARE SOME OF THE MOST DISTURBING CASE HISTORIES OF THE STRANGE AND UNKNOWN THAT YOU WILL EVER ENCOUNTER! PROOF THAT THERE ARE UNSEEN REALMS AND THAT THE UNIVERSE IS MORE PERPLEXING THAN WE EVER CONTEMPLATED!

It may have a long title, but the works of Harold T. Wilkins are nothing to sneer at. Noted historian Timothy Green Beckley has proclaimed Harold T Wilkins one of the most important writers on the paranormal of ALL TIME, "who immersed himself in tales of Atlantis, lost civilizations in the jungle of South America, haunted treasure troves of infamous pirates, and prehistoric creatures which may still be alive. In the 1950s Wilkins became mesmerized by the earliest flying saucer accounts, and his works FLYING SAUCERS ON THE ATTACK and FLYING SAUCERS UNCENSORED became popular hits because of their controversial nature. Here are electrifying reports of the unknown...

Recounted is the history of a militant race of Atlantean warriors who could only be killed by stones or wood because they were invulnerable to steel. And read a terrifying account of a fire breathing monster which emerged from a UFO in 1952. Witnesses say a half-man/half-dragon creature, 10 feet tall with a red/orange face and green body was seen floating just above the ground! And do exotic creatures still exist in the deepest jungles of the world? Read about a brave reporter found ripped to shreds by a King Kong-like monster, and the native women who coupled with large "apes." Also included are the world's most mysterious creatures: Unicorns, the Abominable Snowman of the Himalayas and a bird with the head of a monkey.

Large Format - 180 pages—ISBN: 1892062984
Order From Amazon.com or from the publisher
Timothy G. Beckley, Box 753, New Brunswick, NJ 08903

$15.00 + $5 S/H   646 331-6777 FOR CREDIT CARDS AND
MRUFO8@HOTMAIL.COM FOR PAYPAL INVOICE

ADVERTISEMENTS

EXPOSING THE UFO FEAR FACTOR!

DANGER LURKS ALONGSIDE OF US IN THE DARK! THE ULTRA-TERRESTRIALS TAKE ON A VARIETY OF HORRIFYING SHAPES AND TERRIFYING FORMS! THEY HAVE ATTEMPTED TO TAKE CONTROL OF OUR THOUGHTS AND POSSESS OUR SOULS AND BODIES!

Here are authentic accounts from the "Twilight Zone" of UFOlogy! Stories of encounters with the supposedly friendly "all-too-cute" ETs are NOT always the norm and represent only one side of the coin. Little Elliot may have befriended Steven Spielberg's cozy, cuddly alien, but all too often our almond-eyed visitors have been known to abduct, dice and slice and put us through a universe of utter torment.

Not only can the Ultra-Terrestrials be damned ornery but they have the power to interfere with both our physical and mental states and put dread into our hearts. Thus the term "UFO Fear Factor."

They can often wreak havoc on an entire household following what might seem like a benign close encounter but which ends up going well beyond a cosmic one-night stand. The Ultra-Terrestrials possess various characteristics in common with spirits from the dark corridors of demonology and have been known to produce the same sort of phenomena at UFO landing sites as you would find in a haunted house or at a séance.

* Witness grows 5 inches following close encounter! Hair of observer changes color overnight! * West Virginia man abducted by weird "vegetable"-like Ultra-Terrestrials. * Valuable objects vanish upon arrival of strange shadow beings in New Jersey home. * The mystery of the "Crawling Stumps" in Oregon. * Giants bully youngsters in Brazilian UFO terror attack. * "Fireballs" cause massive blackout. * A man named "Fred" (a pseudonym) recalls under hypnosis a horrifying sexual experience involving a half human/half animal creature. * Dr. Karla Turner, who passed away from breast cancer after she started reporting on the negative aspects of the UFO abduction phenomenon, noted: "A surprising number of abductees suffer from serious illnesses they didn't have before their encounters. These have led to surgery, debilitation, and even death from causes the doctors can't identify."

Some abductees experience a degeneration of their mental, social and spiritual well-being. Obsessive behavior frequently erupts, such as drug abuse, alcoholism, overeating and promiscuity. Strange obsessions develop and cause the disruption of normal life and the destruction of personal relationships. * Noted author/researcher Brad Steiger offers evidence that many individuals hear the guttural voices of Ultra-terrestrials commanding them to perform demonic deeds. Such was the case of a self-declared prophet of a new religion linked to the slain bodies of a family of five—all victims of human sacrifice thought to be necessary to persuade the "forces" to present the Ohio-based cult with a magical golden sword. * Some of the human implications of what the Ultra-terrestrial "invasion" represents are so potentially disturbing and disruptive that well-known talk show personality/investigator Peter Robbins declares that he has no doubt that there are "those" who are capable of just about anything in their efforts to keep the subject from us, including possibly being involved in the untimely deaths of certain truth seekers whose lives have been decidedly "glamorously" entangled with the Unknown.

UFOS - THE DARK SIDE • SUGGESTED READING

( ) **ROUND TRIP TO HELL IN A FLYING SAUCER**
UFO Parasites - Alien Soul Suckers - Invaders From Demonic Realms by Cecil Michael, Tim Beckley, Nick Redfern—Does Satan drive a flying saucer? Are demons abducting humans and performing sadistic rituals?
306 pages—Large format—ISBN-13: 978-1606110911—$21.95

( ) **UFOS – WICKED THIS WAY COMES** by Tim Beckley, Peter Robbins, Tim Swartz, Scott Corrales—The Ultra/Terrestrials possess various characteristics in common with spirits from the dark corridors of demonology and have been known to produce the same sort of phenomena at UFO landing sites as you would find in a haunted house or at a seance.
268 pages—Large format—ISBN-13: 978-1606111581—$21.95

( ) **EVIL EMPIRE OF THE ETS AND ULTRA-TERRESTRIALS** by Tim Beckley, Dr Karla Turner, Brad and Sherry Steiger, Sean Casteel—Witnesses tell tales of unbelievable aggression: "The creatures were hostile and went into attack modes several times, putting up dense fogs. One time when they stopped; It was like a backwards tornado coming from the mouth of the leader of the ships. It was like a ray that he was sending down a funnel. He did it five times, then he left..."
286 pages—Large format—ISBN-13: 978-1606111154—$21.95

( ) **CURSE OF THE MEN IN BLACK: RETURN OF UFO TERRORISTS** by Timothy Green Beckley with John Stuart—One by one they have given up their research - perhaps even their lives! — forced to go underground because of threats from the shadowy beings. Are these individuals government agents gone a muck or sinister aliens?
—Large format—ISBN-13: 978-1606110867—$21.95

( ) **TRILOGY OF THE UNKNOWN by Michael X Barton, with Timothy Beckley**—A telepathic message from what were supposed to be benevolent Nordic-type aliens turned out to put the author in great jeopardy when he was shot at by "dark forces." Cat and mouse game with Nazi UFOs, underground races and aliens who want us to keep off the moon.
Large format — 172 page—ISBN-13: 978-1606111079—$19.95

SUPER SPECIAL ALL 5 BOOKS THIS PAGE— $89.95
(MAIL ORDER CUSTOMERS)
Timothy Green Beckley · Box 753 · New Brunswick, NJ 08903
PayPal: MRUFO8@hotmail.com

ADVERTISEMENTS

THREE TROUBLING TITLES

Top Researchers Proclaim:
GIANTS ONCE EXISTED!
"T-REX" IS NOT EXTINCT!

WILL THE GIANTS KNOWN AS THE NEPHILLIM RETURN TO EARTH?
ARE SOME GIANTS CONNECTED WITH BIBLICAL PROPHECY?
DO SOME COME FROM THE INNER EARTH, OR ARE THEY PART OF A "SECRET RACE?"

These large formatted volumes challenge Darwin and proclaim that a race of 10 to 15 foot giants once existed, and not so long ago in the United States, Britain, the Middle East, Australia and elsewhere. Some claim they could still roam mountain tops and live in caves.

1 ☐ - AMERICAN GOLIATH - AND OTHER FANTASTIC REPORTS OF UNKNOWN GIANTS AND MONOGAMOUS CREATURES

Here is the full report, including scientific statements that when upright the figure stands nearly 11 feet high. Because it was removed from the earth in upstate NY some confuse it with the much more controversial Cardiff Giant. Can it still be viewed or has it been whisked away by archaeological knaves who do not want it placed under the microscope? Includes added material on giants - earthly and otherwise - by Scott Corrales, Nick Redfern, Harold T. Wilkins and Tim Beckley. - 19.95

2 ☐ - GIANTS AND THE LOST LAND OF THE GODS

Travel back into the distant past with Peter Kolosumo and Nick Redfern when giants, monsters and aliens roamed the earth and learn about: — The Origins of Mankind: An intelligent, scholarly overview of the developing picture of man's evolution as anthropologists struggle to make sense of the fossils and bones left behind. — Cosmic Catastrophes: How "extraterrestrial" disasters like crashed meteors affected the ancient Earth. — The Age of Giants: How cosmic rays from outer space may have created giants and modern anthropological evidence that bears this out. — The Mark Of The Titans: Biblical and mythological references to giants, some of whom were cannibals while others were benevolent. Did they come from "extraterrestrial space?" — Nightmares In Stone: Huge Figures Circle The Planet In A Grid. — The Lost World Of Mu: A Vast Civilization Existed In The Pacific. — Legends Of The Stars: Who Were The "Strangers" Who Came Here? — Secrets Of The Pyramids: Who Built Them And Why? — The Wandering Masters. — The Mystery Of Atlantis: Where Did It Exist? — The White Gods: They Intermingled With The Natives. Were They From Earth Or The Far Fields Of Space? - $21.95

3 ☐ GIANTS ON THE EARTH

Is the Smithsonian Institute As Well As Other Academic Foundations Withholding The Biggest Archaeological News Of Our Time? Is there a single, solid, scientific reason they would NOT want you to know that giants-some as tall as 15 feet-once roamed the earth, lived amongst us and mated with human women? Why would they want to suppress the FACT that humans not only lived during the age of dinosaurs and pterosaurs, but that giants inhabited the planet right along side both beast and homosapiens? Nearly 300 large format pages to shock your sensibilities. Did giants take humans as their slaves? Are they still "in hiding" on Earth? Did they grow up right along side of us, invisible to normal sized people? Did they descend from the sky? Climb up from the underworld? And if they are from "somewhere else" will they return, as some students of prophecy predict? Here is a non-theological approach to a mystifying topic that will astound and fascinate the reader. - $24.00

☐ GIGANTIC SPECIAL - ORDER ALL 3 BOOKS AND OBTAIN A FREE DVD ON HOW DINOSAURS MAY NOT BE EXTINCT - $57.00 + $8 S/H (Approx 600 large format pages, a virtual "encyclopaedic set/")

TIMOTHY G BECKLEY, BOX 753, NEW BRUNSWICK, NJ 08903

Credit cards 646 331-6777   PayPal mrufo8@hotmail.com (we will send invoice to pay). Just ordering one or two items? - Be sure to add $5.00 S/H

ADVERTISEMENTS

PROJECT ALIEN MIND CONTROL
The New UFO Terror Tactic — A Threat To Humans Worldwide!

What do you do when the power blackouts keep occurring, and the mysterious disappearances and outright kidnappings continue to mount?

What do you do when you hear an internal buzzing, as your body begins to shake and you go into a deep trance, unable to remember what occurred when you are allowed to return to reality a changed individual?

According to a small group of astute researchers, The Ultra-Terrestrials will not be destroying our world with laser weapons like in Independence Day. Instead, evidence indicates they want to capture our souls as well as our minds in order to accomplish their astronomic "foul deeds." They have no need to blow our fastest military aircraft out of the sky. Their best weapons are not futuristic military ones. Instead, their top-grade artillery against humanity is a numbing form of "high tech alien mind control." Utilizing a series of bizarre techniques, they are able to trick us into accepting their unorthodox and utterly evil belief systems through hallucinatory effects and establishing an emotionless reaction to their far from charitable presence on earth.

Project Alien Mind Control is well under way, and thousands of individuals and entire towns are being mentally enslaved! It is important for the well being of the planet that we all join the alien resistance and learn to elude their mind control efforts at all costs.

This is one of the strangest - most dramatic - dossiers you will likely ever read - the kind that is stamped "Top Secret" by military authorities because of "national security," and because they know it will have a devastatingly negative effect on society. Many believe that as long as we are in the "Matrix," that we will be unable to avoid their sinister, self serving, mind games.

☐ Order **PROJECT ALIEN MIND CONTROL** - $15.00 + $5 S/H

WANT TO KNOW MORE? - SUGGESTED READING

☐ **EVIL EMPIRE OF THE ETS AND THE ULTRA-TERRESTRIALS** - 6 leading researchers - including a clinical psychiatrist - provide provocative clues as to the true nature of the aliens and what lies behind their shockingly bold hidden agenda. This is the only work that describes in detail how these "visitors" have affected the personal lives of those caught up in the close encounter and abduction web of treachery and distortion. $22.00

☐ **MATRIX OF THE MIND** - Are you or someone you know a victim of electronic warfare? Big Brother's covert electronic Mind Control Program operates at the speed of light and can torture, kill and enslave ANYONE — ANYWHERE! Beware of Black Ops, the satellite that goes over twice a day, effecting even your TV set! - $22.00

SPECIAL - 3 TITLES THIS AD - $48.00 + $8.00 S/H
TIMOTHY G BECKLEY, BOX 753, NEW BRUNSWICK, NJ 08903
Send for PayPal invoice - Mrufo8@hotmail.com   Order hot line 732 602-3407

ADVERTISEMENTS

ARE ANCIENT ALIENS THE CUSTODIANS OF EARTH?
HERE ARE NEW LINKS TO THE SPACE GODS

They have been with us since the dawn of civilization, an intricate part of our religious and cultural belief systems. They have guided us, prodded us and perhaps even tried to control us. Some say they are the custodians of the planet, that they are here to show us the path to enlightenment. Others see them as being more nefarious in their intentions. Here at your fingertips are insightful works that reveal the secrets of the ages.

☐ **LEGACY OF THE SKY PEOPLE** Is there an ET origin for Adam and Eve? The Garden of Eden? Noah's Ark? As early as the 1960s, Britain's 8th Earl of Clancarty, Brinsley Le Poer Trench, made an astounding revelation that life on earth had originated on the planet Mars and the first voyagers here had been the Biblical couple. Thus the roots of the various Biblical stories taught to this day. With added material by Nick Redfern, Tim Beckley and Sean Casteel, questions include: Why the CIA and the military show an unprecedented interest in the remains of what many claim to be Noah's Ark that came to rest on Mount Ararat? Is there a new race of humans being formed in these uncertain times? According to the Earl of Clancarty, some of us are rapidly reacquiring the telepathy and psychic abilities we were originally created with. $20.00 + $5 S/H

☐ **ALIEN SPACE GODS OF ANCIENT GREECE AND ROME** Was the Mediterranean region of our planet visited by a race of "Super Beings" in ancient times? Was the Oracle of Delphi a conduit for prophetic messages from outer space – perhaps the first telepathic channeler? Researcher W.R. Drake asks: Did giants from space establish a UFO base atop the picturesque Mount Olympus? – Were they the gods and goddesses of "Mythology" idolized and given names such as Apollo, Hades, Athena, Hermes, Zeus, Artemis and Hestia? – Did the powerful deities of Greece help save Athens from being invaded by the mighty armies of Atlantis in 10,000 BC? —Is there reason to believe that the Greeks and Trojans were inspired to fight for the beauteous Helen, surely a space queen? – 318 pages, $22.00 + $5 S/H

☐ **THE ARK OF THE COVENANT AND OTHER SECRET WEAPONS OF THE ANCIENTS** Was the Ark of the Covenant a nuclear device capable of killing large segments of the population? Did "God" give it supernatural powers? Was it responsible for the collapse of the Walls of Jericho thus allowing the Israelites to take control of the city? Was Moses able to speak directly to the Lord through the two angels positioned on the Ark's top? David Medina offers proof the ancients possessed "secret technology" that made them exceptional worriers. But how did they develop such devices on their own? Centuries ago "wonder weapons" could be found in many lands, laying waste to man and property. – $20.00 + $5 S/H

SUPER SPECIAL – ALL 3 TITLES $52.00 + $8 S/H
ORDER FROM: TIMOTHY G BECKLEY, BOX 753, NEW BRUNSWICK, NJ 08903

www.ingramcontent.com/pod-product-compliance
Lightning Source LLC
Chambersburg PA
CBHW080238170426

43192CB00014BA/2488